KABOOM

KABOOM

EMBRACING THE SUCK IN A SAVAGE LITTLE WAR

MATT GALLAGHER

BANTAM PRESS

LONDON • TORONTO • SYDNEY • AUCKLAND • JOHANNESBURG

TRANSWORLD PUBLISHERS
61–63 Uxbridge Road, London W5 5SA
A Random House Group Company
www.rbooks.co.uk

First published in the United States
in 2011 by De Capo Press
a Member of the Perseus Books Group

First published in Great Britain
in 2011 by Bantam Press
an imprint of Transworld Publishers

Author's Note: What follows is a memoir, a personal account of my time
and experiences in Iraq. It is to be read accordingly and not mistaken for a
military unit's official history. Further, some names and some physical
characteristics of persons depicted in this book have been altered,
and in many cases nicknames have been utilized in lieu of the real
names of soldiers I served with and Iraqis I encountered.

A CIP catalogue record for this book
is available from the British Library.

ISBN 9780593067109

Addresses for Random House Group Ltd companies outside the UK
can be found at: www.randomhouse.co.uk
The Random House Group Ltd Reg. No. 954009

The Random House Group Ltd supports the Forest Stewardship
Council (FSC), the leading international forest-certification organization. All our
titles that are printed on Greenpeace-approved FSC-certified paper carry the FSC logo.
Our paper procurement policy can be found at www.rbooks.co.uk/environment

Printed and bound in Great Britain by Clays Ltd, Bungay, Suffolk

2 4 6 8 10 9 7 5 3 1

Mixed Sources
Product group from well-managed
forests and other controlled sources
www.fsc.org Cert no. TT-COC-2139
© 1996 Forest Stewardship Council
FSC

For my mother,
Deborah Scott Gallagher

CONTENTS

MAPS   viii, ix
INTROLOGUE   xi

I   THE RED, THE WHITE, AND THE EMO
(or American Boy Escapes)
WINTER 2007–2008   1

II   EMBRACE THE SUCK
(or Narrative of a Counterinsurgent)
SPRING 2008   57

III   iWAR
(or The Lost Summer)
SUMMER 2008   123

IV   ACROSS THE RIVER AND FAR AWAY
(or Redemption's Grunt)
AUTUMN 2008   191

V   STEPSONS OF IRAQ
(or A Short-timer's Promenade)
WINTER 2008–2009   239

EXIT STRATEGY   289
ACKNOWLEDGMENTS   293
INDEX   295

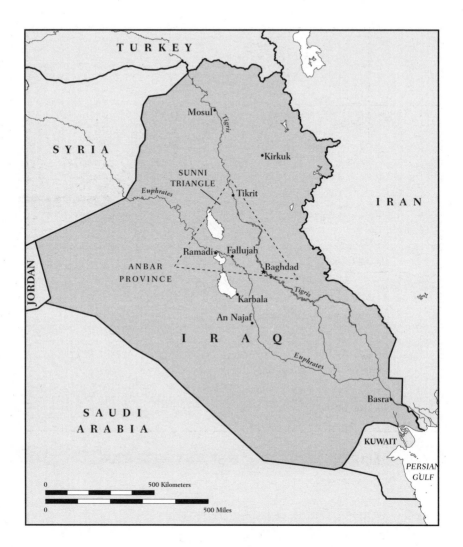

MAP OF IRAQ

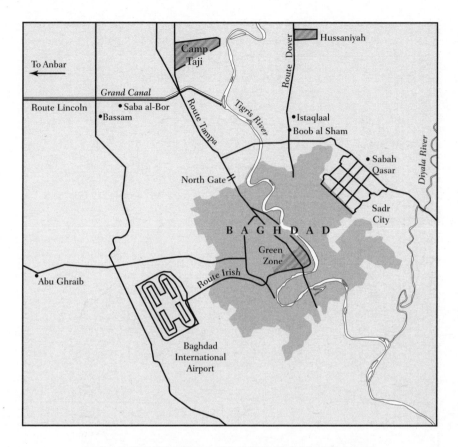

MAP OF BAGHDAD AND SURROUNDING AREA

KABOOM

INTROLOGUE

"White 1, dis, uhh, White 2." Staff Sergeant Bulldog's deep Southern drawl crackled over the platoon radio net, stirring me out of my early-morning haze. Our senior scout's distinctively dry twang was laced with undertones.

"Send it, 2," I responded.

"Dere's . . . well . . . I don't really know how to say this, so I'm just gonna say it. Dere's a dog at the car dat blew up last night. And he's licking at something, all crazylike. Prolly whatever's left."

"Huh?" I was still fighting through sleep-deprived grogginess.

"Yep. My gunner's confirmed it. Da dog be eatin' Boss Johnson. Or at least what's left of him."

Staff Sergeant Boondock's voice now boomeranged across the net, ringing with hysterics. "Holy fuck, Bulldog, this is straight mafia shit!" There was a brief pause, and then he continued. "Think I'll be able to bust Cultural Awareness out on one of the hajjis now?" he said, referring to the stun gun he carried on his ammo rack. He hadn't yet found an opportunity to unleash it on anyone but bored soldiers back at the combat outpost, and we were all waiting for the day that some Iraqi did something to warrant its electric kiss. As was often the case, Staff Sergeant Boondock's words were as accurate as they were profane: This killing belonged in a Chicago mob war, circa 1929, not here, in whatever this was, circa February 2008.

We had moved out of the combat outpost to conduct an area reconnaissance in a neighborhood where a local sheik—the aforementioned Boss Johnson, nicknamed like everyone else around here to keep the litany of individuals straight and to avoid butchering Arabic names with American tongues—had been blown up the night before. Armored military vehicles were damaged, and occasionally destroyed, by improvised explosive devices (IEDs), rockets, and mortar rounds. Human beings in shabby, fake Mercedes targeted for a hit job with such weapons got catastrophically mutilated into flesh soup.

Our principal mission for the day was to engage the local populace, attempt to prevent acts of reprisal between the Sunnis and the Shias, and learn if anyone would let us taciturn Americans in on who or what was responsible for this murder. Had it been a cell of foreign al-Qaeda terrorists? A renegade band of insurgents aligned with the Jaish al-Mahdi (JAM) paramilitary? Another prayer bead on the death string of tribal warfare? Or had it been just another act of personal retribution, free of any grandiose political or social statements? Questions, always more questions, I thought. Never enough answers. The real problem was that in the eight hours since the explosion— so loud that our security elements at the outpost miles away had heard it— not one local individual had dared venture onto the street. This, coupled with a morning wind racing in from the south and a pale desert glow shaping the village, sparked in my mind cinematic imagery of the strutting cowboy posse, unaware of how much red needed to run before the movie could end.

After all, I thought, every good story has a climax. Even the true ones.

With the local population either unable or unwilling to help us complete our primary task and purpose, I decided to turn to our secondary mission for this patrol: information operations. We dismounted from our vehicles and poured into the trash-ridden streets and alleys of our provisional home, a village fractured by the sectarian divide in the northern limits of Baghdad Province. The locals called it Saba al-Bor. My men facetiously referred to it as Paradise. We put up posters and leaflets that stressed peace and cooperation and urged the local population to avoid the temptations of religious violence. That was Higher's great fear: Boss Johnson's death could possibly augment the rift between Sunnis and Shias that already sometimes degenerated into late-night shoot-outs between rival Sons of Iraq checkpoint groups, also known by their Arabic name of Sahwa and more accurately described as security gangs paid by Coalition forces. The propensity of the Iraqi police (IP) and the Iraqi army (IA) to do the same only exacerbated the incessant effort for one quiet night without violence, an objective that would likely become more unobtainable come spring when the fair-weather fighters returned.

The threat of civil war still loomed over Iraq like the ghost of an heiress bride killed on her honeymoon, haunting the lover who murdered her. And although all of the words on the handouts were written in Arabic, it was fairly simple to decipher the messages being put out. The one with a very alive and very happy Boss Johnson standing next to the Iraqi flag, with his arm around other Sahwa leaders, proved to be my soldiers' favorite.

"This one says, 'Figure out which one of these bastards killed me, and you can have the billions of dinar buried underneath my house!'" Specialist Flashback cracked, as he plastered a poster onto the side of a falafel shop.

"That's pretty funny," Sergeant Axel said. "Mine says, 'At least the guy from *Scarface* got to die with a mountain of cocaine on his desk. All I got was this lousy tee shirt.'"

The platoon roared in approval. "Stay on task!" Sergeant First Class (SFC) Big Country yelled, but by the inflection in his voice, I knew that the soldiers' imitations had amused our platoon sergeant. He was just too professional to let them know that.

As we finished up the operation and prepped for a loudspeaker broadcast to be transmitted from the back of one of our armored Stryker vehicles, Private First Class (PFC) Cold-Cuts strolled up next to me.

"LT [lieutenant] G . . . I feel kind of weird."

"What's up?" This was nothing out of the ordinary; PFC Cold-Cuts wore his emotions on both sleeves and had looked sheepish ever since we rolled out into sector.

"I don't know, sir, he's . . . dead, you know?"

I nodded my head, conscious of where he was heading with this. I, myself, had been surprised that I felt no horror when I saw the remnants of the car and of Boss Johnson, even if his larger pieces had already been scooped up into locals' pots and pans for burial in the immediate aftermath of the car

The remnants of Sahwa leader Boss Johnson and his vehicle, the morning after a car bomb planted underneath the driver's seat detonated. The Sahwa, also known as the Sons of Iraq, proved a valuable — if tenuous — ally for American forces fighting against insurgents.

bombing. I doubted anyone ever got used to the sight of intestine bits hanging like Christmas ornaments from tree branches, but I hadn't felt compelled to express an emotion of any kind, really. There was just a nothingness, an acknowledgment of fact, an observation that my immediate environment had been altered slightly and had the potential to spiral into something more complex.

PFC Cold-Cuts continued. "Heck, we just had lunch at his place last week."

I nodded again.

He slumped his shoulders in resignation. "I guess I just thought it'd be different, that's all," he said.

So did I, I thought to myself. So did I. As we mounted back up on our Strykers, I tried to remember the person who had come to Iraq, eager to shed himself in the name of something as amorphous as an "authentic experience." Is this what he wanted to find—a local guerilla lord blown into a potpourri of blood and guts because he did business with us, the much-vaunted and ever-present U.S. Army? I wasn't sure how he . . . how I . . . would have reacted to this situation.

I knew one thing for sure, though. He would have cared more than I did.

I spoke my platoon leader words and issued my platoon leader orders on the radio, just as I had for three months past and just as I would for many more months to come. The Strykers began to roll out. We had a mission to continue. Might as well start at the beginning of all of this, I thought, continuing my daydream to mental salvation. Fuck it, all I have is time.

Might as well.

I: THE RED, THE WHITE, AND THE EMO
(OR AMERICAN BOY ESCAPES)

WINTER 2007–2008

Alright then, I'll go to hell.
— HUCKLEBERRY FINN

AMERICAN UNTITLED

I slept through 9/11. Both towers burned to the ground while I drooled on my pillow in my college dorm. I had decided to skip class that day, after a late-night video game marathon. Nine days later, I yawned along with most of my peers as the president asked for our continued participation and confidence in the American economy. He wanted us to keep shopping. So much for a generational calling for the Millennials.

At that very moment, most of my noncommissioned officers (NCOs)—young privates and specialists at the time—were busy mobilizing for war with an enemy yet to be determined.

I was drunk when we invaded Iraq, safe and secure and carefree in my frat castle. I was even drunker two months later, when President Bush declared, "Mission Accomplished." True, I was in the Army Reserve Officers' Training Corps (ROTC) by then and probably should have been more interested, but the war—and by war, I mean the invasion, liberation, and occupation parts—was only supposed to last a few months. The United States didn't do protracted conflict anymore, not after Vietnam. Shock and awe and the Powell Doctrine and all that.

So while I did keg stands and waged war on sobriety, American tanks were screaming north across the sands of Iraq, destroying everything that moved, with a harrowing expertise the Four Horsemen of the Apocalypse would envy.

The first free elections in Afghanistan? Yeah, I don't even remember those occurring. I was gallivanting across Europe, hooking up with wild French girls and waking up in strange, ancient cities. My Puritan forebears probably wouldn't have approved.

Despite my own temporary, youthful irreverence, the conflicts in both Afghanistan and Iraq continued. America's brushfire wars of the early twenty-first century did not require an engaged populace, and as a result a weary but rugged warrior caste evolved. This caste represented less than 1 percent of the total population it fought, bled, and died for—deploying to combat for months, or a year, or a year plus at a time—multiple times. Soldiers died, or they didn't; their families crumbled under the strains of deployments, or

---

3

they didn't. Such proved to be the burden of the all-volunteer force. Meanwhile, the greater society followed our president's battle cry and continued to shop, squander, and flaunt. A nation at peace, a military at war—a military I joined, through a series of haphazard and bizarre events viciously under-quantified and oversimplified by the word "life," as a young armored cavalry officer in the spring of 2005. Two and a half years later, I departed for an Iraq War preparing to enter its fifth year of blood bursts.

I wouldn't have wanted it any other way. History was happening.

I was born into a class, in a time, to a people, in a place where someone else's sons and daughters served in the armed forces. While I wasn't a politician's boy or a spurner of old money like in the fables, a child of two lawyers still qualified as a Fortunate Son in most parts of the world. I was raised in that curious subculture of Americana enslaved to emo music, new friend requests on Facebook, and lots and lots of Internet porn—part of the generation that the "An Army of One" slogan supposedly appealed to, due to our obsession with all things self. I didn't come from the breadbasket of rural America or the urban ghettos like most of my men, and I didn't seek out the military for glory or for country. I came from the West Coast suburbs, modern white-collar contentment at its most gnarled and escapist, and happened to read too many damn books about soldiers.

But we all have our own stories of how and why we ended up in Iraq. And those stories don't matter nearly as much as the simple truth that we did end up there.

What we didn't know, even though all the old soldier stories say it clear as day, is that we would always be there, even long after we left.

BACK TO THE BEGINNING

In the hours before we departed for Iraq, I sat on a couch on my back porch overlooking the sprawling Pacific blue, feet up, Guinness in hand. A bleeding orange sun cut a casual retreat across the sky, while the shadows and lights of dusk danced together in a fading embrace. If war was both hell and my immediate future, Hawaii had served as a tropical purgatory—a twenty-month stopgap wedged neatly between my youth and whatever it was that came after.

My immediate surroundings symbolized this stark juxtaposition between past and future rather pointedly. Sure, there were five or six empty kegs, pretty much guaranteeing that my housemates and I wouldn't get the deposit back—but there was also a too-full army-green duffel bag, stuffed with equipment and supplies, rigidly posting guard in the near corner. My baby blue 1974 Volkswagen hippie van—known as Rufus the Love Bus—was still parked in the driveway, but in the passenger seat lay seventy pounds of state-of-the-art body armor, augmented with a weapons rack holding seven rifle magazines, a Kevlar helmet, and a pack of rock-hard Skittles.

I should have been contemplating various mounted and dismounted warfare maneuvers or dissecting the tactical mission details of the coming counterinsurgency fight. Those were the things good army officers were supposed to brood over on the eve of battle. My mind, however, was clogged up with all kinds of civilian pollution—typical, prosaic, and beautifully, beautifully mundane. Like the kegs. And my family. And how I still sucked at surfing.

Like how I knew I couldn't deal with all the bullshit and still be there for my girlfriend, if she disappeared halfway across the globe for fifteen months and for reasons unknown, waiting for the plane to land and our lives to resume. Like how that was exactly the situation I was leaving her in.

Like God.

Like how cocaine always seemed to systematically destroy young Hollywood starlets' assets, which was totally selfish, because some of us were going to be relying on mental images of said assets for a while.

Like how the weekend before, getting drunk in Honolulu with the other lieutenants, I thought I was excited about all of this. "For God!" we laughed. "For country!" we cried, stumbling over one another. "For the Red, the White, and the Blue!" we howled, between the bars. We were nothing special; nor were our antics. This was the normal Friday night ritual for junior officers trapped in the tropical purgatory. Wild and free for the sake of being wild and free. I already missed it.

Like how I didn't want to die, but if I did, I hoped I could do it as a martyr, to appease the raging Celtic ghosts of my bloodline. Or as a swashbuckler, to satiate my cavalier tendencies and fantasies. Best yet, as a swash-martyr, to meet all of the above criteria.

My inner ravings continued, as I thought about pretty much anything that allowed me to escape the possibility that, give or take a metaphorical carcass or two, I'd bitten off more than I could chew with the whole Iraq thing. This temporary distraction eventually proved to be just that.

"Hey, dude, you almost ready?" I looked up at the screen door where Lieutenant Demolition, one of my housemates and a fellow platoon leader deploying for the first time, stood. "I just finished loading all my stuff into Rufus."

"Yeah," I said. "Give me ten minutes."

He nodded and shrugged his shoulders, yelling, "Bring on the Suck!" to no one in particular while he walked back inside. At least someone had freed himself from the quicksands of doubt.

I reached into my front pocket, pulled out a journal, and wrote a short passage. "Today is December 7, 2007. The anniversary of Pearl Harbor. I keep looking to the skies over Kolekole Pass, but the Japanese planes haven't come. I guess when you're bringing the fight to the enemy, the twisted romance in it all changes somewhat. Preemptive conflict may make sense, but it sure feels hollow."

I closed my journal and drank the last of my Guinness. Dusk had already blinked away into the dark, and if the sea was still out there, it now bled black. I stood up and grabbed my duffel bag from the corner.

Then we left for war.

THE GRAVEDIGGERS

"Sir, over here. We saved you a seat."

SFC Big Country stood up, waving me over to the table that he and the rest of the Gravediggers platoon had already secured. It was Christmas Eve, and I had raced down to the chow hall after yet another meeting of the squadron officers. At the meeting, I learned that after days and days of weapons ranges and packing and unpacking and repacking shipping containers, we were finally going to leave Kuwait the next day—on Christmas—but telling my men could wait. It was time for family dinner with the soldiers.

It had been unnecessary for SFC Big Country to stand up to get my attention; I'd recognize the pride of Iowa anywhere. A corn-fed giant brimming with competence, military bearing, and a no-nonsense brand of Midwestern keenness, he had taken great care in training and shaping this cavalry scout platoon in anticipation of our deployment. He was a veteran of Afghanistan, and we were polar opposites both physically and temperamentally—something that allowed us to play off each other's personalities and leadership styles with ease.

"How was the meeting with the brass?" he asked, using a blanket term for anyone above the rank of major. "Any motivating speeches, or was it just another PowerPoint presentation?" We shared a deep-seated resentment for grandiose mandates and regulations that failed to pass the logic test at the ground level, a requirement in most of history's armies. Too often, as a platoon leader and a platoon sergeant, we found ourselves playing *dance, monkey, dance* for the grand camo circus, and we attempted to shield our men from this bureaucratic part of the army. We weren't always successful. Militaries need parades even more than they need wars.

I set my tray down and looked back at him, shaking my head. "The standards for the fleece cap have changed again. What constitutes 'cold' is no longer up to the individual; it can now only get cold when the sun is all the way down and the moon is all the way up, weather be damned. And yes, that somehow took forty minutes to explain."

My platoon sergeant didn't bat an eye. "Good to know they're worried about the important things the day before we go into Iraq."

Closest to the entrance and exit doors, we were at the near end of the table, and as I glanced down, howls of laughter erupted from the far side of our gathering. Staff Sergeant Bulldog, the platoon's senior scout, shook his head in mock disgust at the antics of Staff Sergeant Boondock, our other section sergeant. Sergeant Boondock was doing a not-so-flattering impression of a fobbit bitching about the perceived hardships of life in the rear. A fobbit was another comprehensive label that lumped together all noncombat-arms soldiers who tended rarely, if ever, to leave the safety of the FOB, or forward operating base. Other, older wars knew them as rear-echelon mother fuckers (REMFs), and POGs, people other than grunts (pronounced like "pogue"), terms that still found their way into soldier speak. As line guys, my platoon roared in approval as Staff Sergeant Boondock clowned his way through the parody. Even Staff Sergeant Bulldog broke down when his counterpart began to wail on about the horrors of a three-day laundry turnaround.

These two NCOs led through sheer power of persona, something they may have learned while serving together in Afghanistan as team leaders. A battering ram of raw power, Staff Sergeant Bulldog was revered by his soldiers for his straightforwardness. He legitimately scared soldiers—and officers—

who didn't know him, but we all knew there was a teddy bear underneath the gruff exterior. A very wild and very burly teddy bear, but still a teddy bear.

"These goddamn, mother-fucking fobbits." Staff Sergeant Boondock had finished his impersonation and moved on to the commentary portion of his routine. "Leaf-eating REMFs, the lot of 'em. I hate them more than I hate hajjis. And that's saying something." George Orwell's walking embodiment of the rough man ready to do violence on behalf of the softer and weaker, my junior section sergeant issued instructions with the deadpan earnestness of the American everyman. In addition to his time in Afghanistan, he had served as a gunner on a Bradley armored vehicle during the initial push into Iraq in 2003. Given some of the stories we had dragged out of him about the invasion, his jagged edges were more than understandable—and completely necessary given our vocation. Soldiers are trained to kill and kill well, and they tend to remember those that have tried to kill them.

"You're always so full of hate, Sergeant," said Sergeant Axel, a stocky Oklahoman and another Iraq veteran. "Let the hate out! You know you're just jealous because we don't work with females." The combat branches of the army—like cavalry, infantry, and artillery—did not allow women soldiers. There were various reasons for this, such as the physical demands of being on the line, but most of my single soldiers seemed to believe it was because if the female soldiers were sent down to the cav, there'd be too much sex for any war to continue.

While Staff Sergeant Boondock and Sergeant Axel continued to crow back and forth—they routinely bantered like a married couple, on only the most trivial of matters—the platoon's other two buck sergeants observed the exchange in amused silence. Sergeant Spade's eyes darted back and forth like a wolf's, always scanning, always prowling. Sergeant Cheech bit down on his lip, seemingly always on the cusp of interjecting, and pushed up his outdated army-issue glasses—affectionately referred to BCGs, short for birth control goggles due to their unsuccessful track record with the womenfolk, be they in the military or otherwise. Sergeant Spade was headed back to Iraq for his second tour, Sergeant Cheech, for his third. Like all of my NCOs—with the notable exception of the recently engaged Staff Sergeant Boondock—they all had left wives and children in Hawaii, most of whom had wept hysterically when we left the base for the airfield some two weeks before.

Straddling the line between the sergeants and the soldiers was Corporal Spot, a baby-faced stoic from the Ohio countryside. He was so quiet it was sometimes easy to forget he was there—until you were reminded by a penetrating set of steely blue eyes, eyes trained expertly to execute the enemy from long-range distances with a sniper rifle.

Stuck between their leadership were the junior soldiers, better known as the Joes, ecstatic to escape the rigors and demands of daily military life if only for the extent of this meal. Making an enterprise as freakishly ginormous as the military go is no simple task, and no one understands that more than the junior enlisted soldiers who bear the brunt of it all.

"LT, I gotta question for ya."

Between bites of glazed ham, I looked over at a grinning Specialist Haitian Sensation, a young foot soldier originally from Haiti who also served as the platoon's resident weight-lifting expert.

"Send it, Sensation!" I responded, with so much fake zeal that it sent him into a fit of giggles.

Eventually, Specialist Haitian Sensation recovered and asked his question. "Smitty here says he's more gangsta' than me. What do you think?" Private Smitty's claiming to be gangsta' was almost as absurd as me being an authority on the subject; this native Arkansan loved huntin', dippin', and boozin'—in that order. Then again, Specialist Haitian Sensation read poetry by Maya Angelou in his spare time, so despite his love of hip-hop music and tough upbringing on the streets of Trenton, New Jersey, I wasn't sure his claim to the label was exactly legitimate either. All the same, this unlikely duo were inseparable and fought like blood brothers. Private Smitty just smirked, shrugged his shoulders, and spat a wad of dip into a coffee cup.

"Don't be askin' da LT stupid questions over dere," Staff Sergeant Bulldog said from across the table. "He ain't got time for you alls' bullshit." Both Specialist Haitian Sensation and Private Smitty deferred, hiding their grins between bites of food. Like all of our men, these two soldiers worshiped the NCOs—sometimes out of fear, sometimes out of respect, sometimes because they didn't know or couldn't remember how to worship anything else. The army was, and has always been, built on this unique brand of instantaneous compliance—after all, it is the NCOs who teach soldiers how to listen to the instincts that lead to survival and to ignore the other instincts, the ones that lead to a small hole in the dirt of Arlington.

I looked across the table. "Does that mean I got time for your bullshit?" I asked, directing my question at Staff Sergeant Bulldog. Smiles spread across the table like a goodwill plague.

He laughed. "Shit, sir . . . you bettah."

9

Specialist Haitian Sensation and Private Smitty were certainly not the only odd couple in the platoon. Sitting right next to me was Doc, the Grave-diggers' medic, and across from him, Private Das Boot. Doc, a quick-witted and slightly round college graduate from Seattle and of Asian descent, and Private Das Boot, a gangly, ever-serious German American hell-bent on prov-ing his mettle in battle, would soon be nicknamed "10" by members of the IP—Private Das Boot being the 1, Doc being the 0, so often were they found standing next to each other, planning their postwar trip around the world.

Then there were everyone's favorite hetero-lifemates, Specialist Big Ern and Private Van Wilder. Snippets of their reciprocating madness drifted to our end of the table, causing even SFC Big Country to grin openly. As always, Private Van Wilder's Texan twang paced the conversation, while Specialist Big Ern's understated Carolinian accent was far more precise in its delivery.

"Why don't you love me anymore, Big Ern?"

"You are such a homo. That's why I don't love you."

"You're my gunner, Big Ern! I got to know that you love me for me, no matter what! I don't care how old and crusty and heartless you are, I love you. Tell me again what going to basic training with Moses was like."

"Shut the fuck up, or I ain't gonna let you sleep in the tent tonight. You'll have to sleep in your (driver's) hole, down in the Stryker, with all the other dumbfuck drivers who don't listen to their gunners."

"Can I take those fobbits with me?" Private Van Wilder asked, pointing to some overweight female soldiers sitting at another table, luckily out of earshot. "I love me some fat chicks . . . I'm going hoggin' tonight, boys!"

This exchange caused the table of Gravediggers to explode into laughter and applause. Eight years of college may not have yielded Private Van Wilder a degree, but it had helped perfect his ability to spin yarns of ex-cessive debauchery.

Sitting on the far side of this verbal smackdown, near the aforementioned section sergeants, were the final four members of the Gravediggers: Spe-cialist Flashback, Specialist Prime, PFC Cold-Cuts, and Private Romeo. Specialist Prime, a well-traveled former trucker who knew more about the American continent than Lewis and Clark combined, was going into painfully specific detail about the machinery of a Stryker's engine with Specialist Flash-back, my vehicle's driver and another product of Main Street USA.

"Hooah," he automatically responded to Specialist Prime's prompts, using that ultimate army crutch word and unofficial motto: "Hooah" meant "yes," "no", "maybe so," "fuck yeah," "fuck no," and "FUCK," depending on the situation, the tone, and the user. In this case, I was pretty certain my driver was employing some subtle Iowan sarcasm, but Specialist Prime either disagreed or didn't care. Their technical conversation continued.

Private Romeo, a smooth-talking Puerto Rican who had adventured as a professional dirt biker in a past life, was teaching a very interested Staff Sergeant Boondock and Private Van Wilder how to cuss in Spanish. Or how to admire a passing female's backside. I was too far away to tell for sure. Private Romeo had come to us just before we left Hawaii, and just like PFC Cold-Cuts, he had become a devoted family man very early in life. The Gravediggers' resident joker, PFC Cold-Cuts had taken years off of my NCOs' life spans, and the reason was simple: He was smart and capable and wanted to know the *why* of things. Not that that was a bad thing, but sometimes in the military there is no why, or there's no time for why. There's only time for mission execution. As a result, Staff Sergeant Bulldog had taken PFC Cold-Cuts underneath his very firm wing and tended to explain why as only he could: "Shut the fuck up and do what I tell ya to do. Dat's why." Even PFC Cold-Cuts couldn't find any holes in that explanation.

As I watched the platoon joke, clown, and ramble their way through the holiday dinner, I couldn't help but think about the country that had produced them. These were the men in the flesh that society only celebrates in the abstract. The NCOs had served in the army long enough to stop caring about the whims of the American culture they protected so effectively; the Joes were just removed enough to not fully recognize how the same society that reared us had detached itself from us the day we signed our enlistment papers. In a volunteer military, we fought for the nation, not with it.

SFC Big Country issued guidance for the evening's preparations to the junior NCOs, and then we stood up and exited the chow hall. Spirits were high, I thought. So was morale. It was a good day to be alive.

Such would not always be the case.

OUT OF THE WIRE

The first time I rolled out of the wire, I wasn't as nervous as I probably should have been. I'd woken up with a strange sense of calm that morning, something I attributed to the fact that I was going on a leader's recon and thus would be attached at the hip to the platoon leader whose unit we were replacing. It was still his show, and with the Gravediggers staying back at Camp Taji for the day under the supervision of SFC Big Country, the burden of leadership melted away like a renegade iceberg finding itself alone in the Caribbean. I was there to listen and absorb—a welcome break from my normal occupational hazards and duties. It was New Years' Day 2008, and my unit—the Twenty-fifth Infantry Division's Second Squadron, Fourteenth Cavalry Regiment—had arrived on the coattails of the surge.

"Most depressing New Years' ever," Staff Sergeant Boondock announced in the shower stalls that morning. "I should be recovering from a vicious hangover right now, swearing to God that I'll never fucking drink again. This fucking blows donkey dick." I was inclined to agree.

Rolling out of the wire was what we called going outside the relative safety of the FOB for missions—where those mysterious, ambiguous terms like *the enemy* were found and where daily updates became bar tales. I had my nose in a map, studying our area of operations (AO), while my counterpart lieutenant—of the First Cavalry Division—briskly answered my elementary questions with master's-level responses.

Captain Whiteback, the Bravo Troop commander, sat across from me in the back of the Humvee, smiling wickedly. He had gotten his nickname for being the only non-Hispanic on his Stryker, which included Specialist Fuego, a former and future Gravedigger originally from Cuba. Like most officers, myself included, Captain Whiteback was just another gangly Caucasian. He didn't have to say anything; I knew I looked the part of the cherry lieutenant with my bright eyes, skinny frame, and general life awkwardness. I locked and loaded my M4 Carbine by sticking a rifle magazine filled with thirty golden rounds of kill into it and pulling back on the weapon's charging handle. The Humvee moved out of Little America and into the other Iraq—the one that was there before American soldiers arrived and that will still be there when we leave.

"You ever been to Mexico?" Captain Whiteback asked me over the mild roar of the vehicle's engine.

I nodded.

"Iraq is kinda like that, but with bombs." He paused momentarily and then smirked to himself. "And Arabs too. I guess there aren't too many Arabs in Mexico."

The scenery I glimpsed for the first time from the up-armored window was nothing new; it was the same Iraq I had seen on television for the past four years. With the stark atmosphere of a northeastern industrial city and the transient wandering of a mostly jobless population, our AO was everything I'd expected—desolate and deprived, too tired to hope, but too human not to. Knowing what to expect didn't keep my internal alarm system from blaring, however, whenever I made the mistake of remembering where I was.

The other lieutenant continued talking as we drove, pointing out schools, mosques, and various huts, tossing out many, many Arabic names, which I wrote down in my notebook with questions marks next to them. I asked him about the sheiks, and he delved into the never-ending layers of grey involved in working with these men and the tribes and families they led, as well as the insanely complicated dynamic between the Sunni and Shia Muslims. There were capable leaders he told me, but there were corrupt ones, too. Some cared about securing peace; others didn't. Some were motivated by money; others were obsessed with it. Much of the local violence occurred between the various groups with different interests vying for power.

"It sounds like the Montagues and the Capulets," I said.

He laughed. "It'd be easy if things were simple enough to boil down to just two families."

Rather than go all the way into our sector to the combat outpost, we stopped off at one of the outlying eastern villages for a meeting with one of the local sheiks. We dismounted, handed out some Beanie Babies to a swarm of overly friendly and undernourished children, and began to move into the sheik's house. The terp (soldier slang for interpreter) explained to us the source of the children's excitement—the accompanying Strykers, which locals referred to as ghost tanks due to how quietly the engines ran. Strykers aren't tanks, technically speaking, but no one felt compelled to correct the Arab children.

Inside the house, I met a group of Iraqi leaders, did a lot of listening and nodding, and drank my first glass of chai—nothing more than a hot shot of sugar. The other lieutenant received a call on his radio shortly thereafter, though, which cut the meeting short. We were needed for something a bit more kinetic in nature—a raid on a purported sleeping spot for a known insurgent.

He slapped his radio antenna. "I fucking hate fragos," he said, bitterness dripping off his words like hot icing. Over the ensuing weeks and months, the Gravediggers would become very familiar with this reactionary and fluid operational tempo. Change was the norm, and this norm was called a frago, short for fragmentary order. Trying to understand the whims and reasons behind the frago was like drinking from a fire hose: Fighting it only made things worse.

The raid turned up nothing but an empty room, a pack of wild dogs, and an old man holding his piss bag, but later that evening, only a few blocks away from where we handed out Beanie Babies, one of our brother platoons received some bursts of AK-47 fire from a rooftop during their initial patrol. No one had been hurt, and the squadron's operations staff determined it was nothing more than harassment fire meant to test the new sheriffs in town. I bumped into Sergeant D-Wizzle, one of the men on said patrol and another former Gravedigger who had left us when the other platoon came up short a team leader. It was sometime after midnight. I strolled out of our troop's headquarters with a mug of coffee in one hand and a near-beer in the other (alcohol of all types, along with most other enjoyable vices, was banned in theater by General Order No. 1), while he smoked a cigarette on the sidewalk, still looking a little flush in the cheeks.

He just snickered when I told him the staff officers said it had been harassment fire and not a planned, direct attack on their patrol. "This is my third time over here," he said. "You don't ever get used to getting shot at. Doesn't matter what kind of fire it was."

"Fair enough," I responded. I didn't know what else to say.

As I walked into the darkness back to the platoon's lodgings, machine guns crackled in the distance, which only disturbed me when I thought about how it should be disturbing me. The steady crooning of Black Hawk and Chinook helicopters arriving at and departing from the nearby airstrip soon drowned out the gunfire. Under a midnight blanket, the distant countryside of Iraq offered an odd sense of tranquility. With the scattered lights of various townships all dotting a high desert landscape, it reminded me slightly of rural Nevada. Shortly thereafter, though, the subdued lights from Camp Taji's Burger King and Pizza Hut restaurants came into my vision. The FOB is a very strange place, I thought. This sure ain't Bastogne. Five minutes later, I fell asleep on a mattress in an air-conditioned room.

The first day of my new life was over.

THE REAL WORLD: SABA AL-BOR

Anyone looking at a map of Iraq, pretty much any map made after T. E. Lawrence and the British came at least, would find a tiny dot just northwest of the Baghdad Gates. This dot was nestled close to the southern

The combat outpost in Saba al-Bor, located in the northwestern fringe of Baghdad Province. Home to over seventy American soldiers, it also served as an Iraqi police station and as a local governance center.

shore of the Grand Canal, which poured into the dirty, timeless waters of the Tigris only a few miles to the east. If the map was very old or very detailed, there would be a name next to the dot: Saba al-Bor, a town of 60,000 or so, gilded in sandstone and bathed in sectarian wars, too barren for even the scorpions and the camel spiders, a convenient crossroads for travelers and the displaced alike, with the Anbar madness in the deserts to the west, the war machine hub Camp Taji situated to the northeast along Route Tampa, and the infamous Abu Ghraib prison due south. This dot was impoverished. It was brutal. It was modern Iraq, permanently soaked in a blood-red-sea past it would never be able to part, let alone escape.

Although my unit didn't know it when we arrived, this place was to become our very own reality show, just without the camera crews. Or the adoring public. MTV probably wouldn't have been interested. Not enough inanity.

Back in Kuwait, I had begun writing an online journal—a blog, really, although I detested that description—about the platoon's experiences. For operational security (OPSEC) reasons, I came up with the pseudonym "Anu al-Verona" to describe Saba al-Bor, purloining a bit from Shakespeare and sprinkling on some local spice. Our new home was no Anu al-Verona though, and I'd learn such in time. There were ancient grudges and new mutinies to be found, sure, but civil blood and civil hands were severely lacking in this forgotten slice of the crescent moon. Perhaps most obviously, there was nothing fair about Saba al-Bor, no matter what literary nickname I gave it. No romanticism abided here. Reality endured.

In the village center lay the imposing American castle known as the combat outpost. As part of the refined focus on counterinsurgency operations, the Gravediggers and their brother platoons in Bravo Troop resided there permanently, living with the war rather than commuting to it. This vast two-story complex, originally built as a retirement mansion for one of Saddam Hussein's favored generals, stood in stark contrast to the slums surrounding it. On the first floor of the outpost dwelled the remnants of Saba al-Bor's governance center, where one lone mayor worked tirelessly to install a civil government in a tribal society; dirty, hungry, and tired soldiers lived on the second floor and prowled the roof above that, waiting, some hoping, for an attack on the premises. Even here, in the flat Arab desert and attempting to blend in, the American outpost couldn't help but be the City on the Hill. Too much electricity. Too much security. Too much activity.

Next to this compound stood proof that, at least four years after the statement was first uttered, the Coalition of the Willing was more than just an uncomfortably titled punch line. A platoon of Estonians, a battalion of IA, and a company of IP operated out of their own rustic structures, and all, albeit in very different ways, displayed a dark cynicism and fearlessness that sprouted from growing up in the Third World—the Stones having been trapped behind the Iron Curtain, and the Iraqis, locked in Saddam's Baathist basement. Coordinating all of these assets for the betterment of the Republic of Iraq proved a challenging task, one that too often degenerated into a walking monster of mental anguish for me and my men. Breaking up drunken fistfights between the armed IP and equally armed IA only amused the first time.

Helping bridge the gap between languages and cultures were the terps, who lived side by side with us upstairs. Referenced more by their American nicknames than their given Arabic names, these men simultaneously provided a vital asset for communicating with the local populace and served as instant comedy. Between Suge (pronounced "Shoog," like the hip-hop entrepreneur) Knight, Super Mario, Phoenix, and Snoop Dogg, our terps went out with us on every mission and gave us the occasional reminder of home, due to the pop-culture-related origin of their nicknames. Although the money they made was surely a primary reason for their chosen vocation and their English could at best be described as rudimentary, it was easy to forget how many of our enemies would've gladly killed our terps for working with us.

Swarming the combat outpost from the town and various outlying villages were the community leaders and sheiks. Between tribal rivalries and the always-tense association between Sunnis and Shias, the township's relationships—from the leaders all the way down to their pipe swingers—were complicated and forever morphing, with most of the details getting lost in translation. Geographically speaking, Saba al-Bor was a Sunni donut, with a jelly Shia center—all of the town hubs and markets were located in the Shia ghettos near the combat outpost, while the slightly less poor and better educated Sunni population enveloped the village itself and the rural outskirts in all four cardinal directions.

To borrow a failed strategy from a previous war in the American history books, the neo-counterinsurgency taught us that we may never win the local populace's hearts and minds, but securing their pocketbooks could be enough. Money—the type of money that this Saba al-Bor had never seen before—flowed in from our side as well as from our enemies', and it was up to the local leaders to figure out which offer(s) best suited their purposes. By the time our unit arrived, most of them had already decided we presented the better means to an end. What that end was, exactly, varied from tribe to tribe, neighborhood to neighborhood, and person to person.

The sheiks' men—referred to by us as the Sons of Iraq and by the locals as the Sahwa—enforced the whims and desires of their leadership, while proving that employment is the bedrock of any nation's stability. Most of the Sons of Iraq manned checkpoints at various intersections throughout Saba al-Bor and throughout Iraq; the American taxpayer had bought these men's loyalties for a stipend of $300 per month each and probably didn't even know it. The Sahwa's elite became bodyguards, moving like the arms of an octopus, protectively shielding their respective sheiks with tentacles bearing the ultimate peasant weapon, the AK-47, while never straying too far from their secure coral reef of up-armored SUVs. We were new to their protracted guerilla war, but they were not. A litany of hard stares, prison tattoos, and deep scars were the corporeal representations of such. I doubt still that there was a man we worked with who didn't have blood of some sort on his hands, and some of that was undoubtedly American blood. If the mass media was to be believed—a notion very few military officers subscribed to in this post-Vietnam era, as distrust for journalism was rampant and practically institutionalized in the culture—over 100,000 Sahwa members had now manacled themselves to the reconciliation process across the nation of Iraq.

The Sunni reconciliation with the Iraqi republic and Coalition forces was in full throttle in Saba al-Bor, and the Shias had decided to hop on the bandwagon while there was still room. Muqtadah al-Sadr's proclamation in the summer of 2007 that JAM elements would cease attacks on Coalition forces certainly helped, too. The Sons of Iraq program, more so than the surge, had changed the direction of this war and this country in general, and both the Sunni and the Shia leaders understood the importance of participating in the power shift. While being an American soldier in Iraq in early 2008 often meant playing the role of beat cop and counterguerilla in a land of roving gangs, our mission hinged on fostering working relationships with men who may have shot at us during the invasion in 2003 or emplaced IEDs during the throes of the insurgency in 2005 and 2006. Some of my NCOs struggled with this reality, and I probably would have too, had this not been my first deployment.

No description of Saba al-Bor would be complete without mention of Mojo, the son of a local official. He claimed to be fifteen years old, although he didn't look a day over eight. While the lack of a proper nutritional diet probably contributed to his runtlike stature, he likely didn't know how old he was, as I seriously doubted a birth certificate existed anywhere in the village. A pair of striking green eyes, a rarity for Iraqis, offset his jet-black hair. He tailed our movements around town every day, out of both curiosity and a sense of security. His parents had removed him from school two years prior due to kidnapping threats brought on by his father's cooperation with American forces. Mojo spoke excellent English, which should be enough to keep him employed for many years, be it in the backwaters of the Arab world or beyond, in the metropolises. His understanding of soldierisms, from our off-color jokes to our acronym jargon, was a bit unsettling at first. He referred to me as LT G whenever he saw me and did a spot-on impression of Staff Sergeant Bulldog strutting around with a scowl on his face.

In addition to being a streetwise urchin, Mojo was also a budding entrepreneur, and he'd let it be known that he could provide Joe with whatever Joe desired—legal or otherwise. I never read Mojo General Order No. 1, although I probably should have when it was discovered that he pimped out whores to the IP's and was interested in expanding his enterprise to our compound. We put a stop to that before it got started by threatening to turn him over to his father. At least, I think we did.

This incessant obsession with money, from the sheiks to the terps all the way down to little Mojo, cannot be overstated. It was absolutely vital to the continued development of Iraq and the American military's success in the Iraq War. While it often seemed blatantly crude, who was I, a suburbanite who had always lived in comfort, to question it? I had never known poverty or the desperation it brings. Daily, we had local-nationals come to our gates looking for jobs, and daily we turned them away, sending them back to whatever Mesopotamian hellhole they'd crawled out of. It only took a few weeks for me to grow numb to this recurrence.

Democratic birth and the quest for financial independence seem to be intrinsically linked—freedom's dirty little not-so-secret. I'm sure Sam Adams and his Sons of Liberty would agree. And while the idealist in me—back then, I guess I still thought of myself as one of those—looked upon greed as the ultimate of vices and viewed people who talked about their finances publicly as boors and covetous tools, I couldn't help but sympathize with the locals' fixation. Theirs was a penury only dreams could escape. And for a while, that dream ran through the lean, tall men in body armor from across the sea who arrived in ghost tanks and smiled too much.

They didn't all feel that way though—about us or our money. There were just enough of them out there who wanted us gone or dead, or dead and gone, that battles and skirmishes continued; thus, so did the war.

Reality endured.

SNOW PATROL

I staggered toward the latrine, delirious with too much caffeine in my system and not enough sleep, weaving like an indolent zombie. PFC Cold-Cuts bounced into me with a large smile plastered across his face, and the sound his throat emitted would be considered a giggle in most circles outside of the U.S. Army.

"It's snowing, sir!" he said.

"Cold-Cuts," I said, "it's too early for that shit." I brushed my teeth, put on deodorant more out of habit than concern for what I smelled like at the combat outpost, and checked up on the status of my novice attempt at a war moustache—still pathetic, wispy, and a general affront to facial hair everywhere. I walked back into the main hallway and spied Staff Sergeant Boondock across the way, hard rock music blaring out of the headphones wedged into his ears.

"We still leaving in an hour?" he yelled, speaking over the lyrics of the band Rage Against the Machine's "Calm Like a Bomb."

I checked my watch and nodded.

"Still dismounted?"

I nodded again and bit down on my lip, remembering the details of the early-morning mission laid out to me the night before by Captain Whiteback. Maybe a glass of chai at the local market would wake me up, I thought. There's only so much black coffee and Rip It energy drink a body can take, and I still tried to avoid nicotine this early in the deployment. I smelled bacon from a nearby breakfast plate and began to head for the chow line, when I heard Staff Sergeant Boondock's voice sound off yet again from behind me.

"You might wanna rock the long sleeves, sir. It's penguin weather out there."

He was right. And so had been PFC Cold-Cuts. For the first time in any Saba al-Bor local's memory, the penetrating, white precipitation falling from the sky wasn't metal shrapnel or a downpour of civil-affairs pamphlets. It was a gift straight from Mother Nature herself, with a possible assist from her redheaded stepchild, global warming: snow. And the kind that stuck. I was too preoccupied with mission preparations, though, to give this anomaly much attention.

One hour later, we moved out of the wire on foot. All the joking stopped as soon as the first foot hit native ground, as did any talking above a whisper. I gave the hand-and-arm signal to stagger our columns, but a quick glance around me proved that my reminder was unnecessary: The soldiers had already moved into their dismounted positions with an expertise and confidence that only excessively meticulous military training can produce. Specialist Fuego, loaned to us for the day, automatically assumed the point position, and the rest of the platoon followed his lead. They moved fluidly, calm and crisp despite the foreignness of our environment, heads rotating like they were on a swivel. Even Private Das Boot, who loped behind me with a radio on the back of his long frame, had managed to manufacture some level of comfort.

Our terp, Suge Knight, bundled up like a small child learning how to ski, walked in the middle of our formation, unsure as to why his American employers always insisted on working during the most miserable of times. He looked at me, pointed at the grey sky, and asked, "Why?" from behind the crooked cotton mask that covered everything but his eyes. He usually only wore the mask when we were in areas he didn't like or wasn't familiar with, but he wore it today because of the cold. I shrugged my shoulders and said that I'd been asking that question for twenty-four years but hadn't received a satisfactory answer yet. I wasn't sure if he understood, but he laughed along with me anyway.

A middle-aged mammoth of a man originally from Sudan, Suge had earned the trust of my soldiers by admitting that he sometimes missed the Saddam era because there had been discos back then. Anyone willing to admit that to American soldiers, they reasoned, couldn't be dishonest. Everyone in Saba al-Bor knew Suge, and Suge knew everyone. We didn't know it quite yet, but he was to become an unlikely, yet vital, asset in the counterinsurgency fight. Even a war zone appreciated a big belly, a deep rolling chuckle, and a deviant sense of humor. He wasn't all jokes though. As with many comedians, his humor hid a deep sadness. He had lost three young children during the bombings of the first Gulf war, and he still visited their graves every time he returned home. Further, many of us suspected he suffered from mild posttraumatic stress disorder, as he had survived multiple IED strikes in the three years he had worked for Coalition forces. He had seen far more war over the course of his life than any one man ever should.

Pools of brown sludge swirled at our boots with our every step. With seemingly the first drop of snow, the dirt roads and walkways of Saba al-Bor had transformed into a skating rink of earth slime, the landscape of brown contrasting with the falling white all too poetically. Unlike the photos of the Baghdad Green Zone I later saw on the Internet, snow in Saba al-Bor unleashed little curiosity among the local populace. There were no snowball fights or gasps of wonderment. The few families we ran into at the marketplace simply complained that the slush the snow melted into would cause havoc in their neighborhoods; paved roads were the exception in this part of Iraq, and huts made out of dirt were not holding up well in the face of this environmental obscurity. They asked us if we were going to do anything to help them.

"Yes," I said, "we're going to pay a local contractor to pave many of the roads in the area."

"No," they responded, "what are you going to do for us today? We need you to fix the weather."

Suge laughed in disbelief when he translated the Iraqis' hopes and demands.

"Why do they think we can fix the weather?" I asked him. Suge's African stereotypes rattled through his response: "Because Arabs are crazy in the head, Lieutenant, that is why."

We were now on Route Maples, Saba al-Bor's main thoroughfare and most prominent marketplace. A series of dead baby trees dotted the trajectory of the street from beginning to end, an ill-timed city project leftover from the unit we replaced—a stillborn symbol if there ever was one. One of the other platoons in Bravo Troop had been struck by an explosively formed penetrator (EFP)—a state-of-the-art IED whose technology supposedly came from Iran—on this very road only the week before, luckily taking no casualties from the blast. Many of my soldiers were convinced a matching EFP would be found in the remnants of the trees and were taking great care in clearing these areas as they walked past.

"It would definitely suck to die," PFC Cold-Cuts philosophized ahead of me, presumably to Staff Sergeant Bulldog, who was nearest to him and scanning around the corner of a building. "And it would suck even harder to die in Iraq. But to die from an exploding tree? Please, just lie to my wife if that happens."

Groups of locals were huddling around smoldering fires, most of which had been constructed from burning tires. According to the intel (intelligence) fobbits, insurgents often used burning tires—along with black kites and homing pigeons—as a means to relay the whereabouts of Coalition forces. I glanced over at Sergeant Spade, who simply shrugged. The groups consisted mainly of old men and children and couldn't have cared less that we were in the market. They looked more like homeless people too tired to pander for change than like terrorists. I decided the odds were in our favor that they weren't planning the next great catastrophic attack with their tires, and we kept moving.

As we headed out of the market area, Sergeant Axel bought some pieces of flat bread from a local vendor. He gave the guy $5 and told him to keep the change, which caused the Iraqi to lean over the counter and, as is their custom, hug and kiss Sergeant Axel on the cheek. Sergeant Axel backpedaled sheepishly, his face turning crimson as the rest of the Gravediggers laughed at the vendor's antics. He refused to share the flatbread with anyone who he determined had laughed too hard at his expense.

"Who's the fag now," he said, munching down on a large piece of flatbread, while Specialist Haitian Sensation and Private Smitty sulked, breadless and no longer joking.

"How come they get some?" Private Smitty asked, pointing to me and SFC Big Country. "I saw them laughing at 'cha, too."

Now SFC Big Country laughed openly. "Smitty," he said, "you got a lot to learn about how the army works." He took a big bite out of his share. "Hang around Sergeant Axel some more. He has a good handle on it."

Once we completed our stated mission—conduct an area reconnaissance of the local schools and assess their needs for future public works projects—we turned around and headed back to the American outpost. The snowflakes had degenerated into flurries over the course of our five-hour jaunt. Only Private Van Wilder still sported any cold-weather gear, a result of his claiming to be some sort of cold-blooded reptile ever since a mild case of pneumonia in Kuwait. The streets were now empty, save us, an old cripple hobbling down an alleyway oozing with raw sewage, and an Iraqi army T-72 tank parked at one of the major intersections.

My patrol brief would essentially read as it had for the past two weeks: There had been no contact with the enemy; there was dissatisfaction among the local populace with all kinds of political, social, and civil issues; and the schools still needed more supplies and more renovations. My latest arbitrary snapshot of Iraq could wait a few more minutes though, so I stopped caring about the details of the report I would write and began to count my paces. We traipsed along the mud paths of Saba al-Bor, anxious to shed our heavy gear and take our boots off for a few hours until the next patrol started. The snow flurries continued.

SHEIKAPALOOZA

Checkered headdresses of red and white and black and white dotted the gathering below, colors flamboyantly marking allegiances in the same manner they did for streets gangs back home. The Gravediggers and I were overwatching nearly one hundred local civic leaders and sheiks from the roof of the Taji Provincial Community Center, working next to and with the local security already provided—roving bands of mean-mugging teenage boys armed with AK-47s, all inevitably blood relatives to one of the power brokers yelling and gesticulating below. I looked over at SFC Big Country, who shook his head and took another drag from his cigarette, while his other hand cradled the underside of his rifle. Despite our black sunglasses, which tended to give even the most personable of soldiers a look of omniscient stoicism, I could tell he thought the same thing I did. What. The. Fuck. Question mark.

The short answer was that we were providing security for Coalition forces at Sheikapalooza—an unofficial, though fitting, term coined by Captain

The view of Sheikapalooza, at the Taji Provincial Community Center in January 2008, from a rooftop security position.

Whiteback. The meeting had been called to have an election for a sheik council that was to supervise the various Sons of Iraq groups, but it had digressed into a shouting match the British parliament would envy. All of the terps were down on the ground level with the commanders, so we weren't privy to the details of the various disagreements. That didn't stop some of my soldiers from filling in the gaps, though. Corporal Spot and Private Van Wilder had each selected a sheik he would translate for, and they were reliving their counterparts' arguments up on the roof while scanning the surrounding countryside in the prone position for dangerous knowns and unknowns.

"You ate all me Lucky Charms!" Private Van Wilder cracked, while his sheik shook his finger in anger. "You are fat enough already, Sheik Marshmallow, and you did not even leave me the rainbows! You know how much I love the rainbows!"

"I have daughters who are more intimidating than you are," Corporal Spot responded, just as his sheik rose to defend himself against the wagging finger. "I stole your Lucky Charms because I could and you couldn't stop me. Just wait until you find out what I did to your Pop-Tarts!"

Private Van Wilder grinned at the softball tossed his way. "I am familiar with your daughters," he said, pausing just long enough on the word "familiar" to cause Corporal Spot to break character and laugh. "I friended them on MySpace and later blessed them with my super sheik sperm."

I looked down again while my soldiers continued to banter. Whatever keeps them alert, I thought. Below, Captain Whiteback looked frazzled, as his hair rose wildly out of place and dark circles sagged underneath his eyes. I thought about asking him over the radio if he wanted his posse to escort him out of this clusterfuck, Death Row–style, but thought better of it. He was surrounded by colonels, and colonels did not generally appreciate my sarcasm or ill-timed quips. Especially ones based on 1990s gangta' rap.

I walked over to a group of the Iraqis on the roof with us. They numbered six in total. Nearly all of them were younger than me, and even at a very average 5 feet 10 inches I stood four to five inches above the tallest of them. I nodded and smiled, which spurred a reaction in turn by the paramilitary security guards.

"Salaam aleichem," I said, doing my best not to butcher the most basic of Arabic statements.

"Hello, mistah," they said together, and then one of them continued, "Hello, Lieutenant." One of the others pointed at my gloves. I smiled again, took them off, and handed them over. Young Iraqis were always fascinated by the hard plastic that lined the knuckles of our combat gloves, and the inevitable occurred when the teenager put them on.

"Eeeehhhhh!" Plastic had met skull. The guard punched in the head by his friend exclaimed in pain, while the rest of them roared in delight. This process went on for a couple minutes until I asked for the gloves back. They were returned, and then one of the Sahwa pointed at my M4, and then pointed at his AK-47. He wanted to make a trade.

I shook my head and said, "Sorry. No trade." I was no gun connoisseur, but I knew enough to understand that an M4 armed to the teeth with sights and accessories outclassed a bare AK-47—not to mention the bureaucratic uproar such a deal would cause. As this teenager lifted up his AK, attempting to display its killing prowess, his uniform—really just a plain long-sleeve brown shirt—raised up, revealing the dull pink shade of dead scar tissue. I grabbed his arm and pulled up the sleeve, causing him to bring his weapon back down. The dull pink encircled his entire arm and extended to the elbow; it was smooth like a layer of cream cheese. A faint scar ran up the arm, parallel to the bone.

"Big bomb," said another Son of Iraq, pointing to his peer's arm. He said something in Arabic to the boy with the scarred arm, who responded in kind.

"He say American sky bomb do this when war start. It kill abu [father]."

Per Iraqi tradition, I lifted my hand to my heart and began to express my sympathies, both for his father's death and the permanent shrapnel wound, when both teens broke out into wide grins. "No, no, very good," the makeshift interpreter said. "He and family get lots of fuluus after!"

I smirked. *Fuluus* meant money. Our condolence funds program was well known in this country and had incurred many a recipient since 2003. Despite the morbid nature of the program, at least these Sons of Iraq appeared to be happy and satisfied customers. We had that going for us—which was nice, especially when the alternative tended to take the form of deep-buried IEDs or rocket propelled grenades (RPGs).

I shook the hands of the Sahwa members—two of them insisted on a fist-pound instead—and strolled back over to my soldiers. Sergeants Axel and Spade were kneeling together in the corner. I heard Sergeant Axel say, "The sir might know," and they waved me over.

"What's up?"

"What the fuck are these guys arguing about? I thought they already voted." Security for the election had been the only task and purpose about which I had briefed the platoon, as these fire-team leaders were subtly pointing out. I made a mental note to include "and maintain security for subsequent bitching session" the next time we drew this mission set.

"Do you know who any of these guys are?"

I nodded. "A couple of 'em. That fat guy in the white man-dress? The one who looks like Jabba the Hut?" I pointed at a rotund man with a thick black moustache sitting at the head table, dead center, between our brigade commander and a civilian from the State Department. He yawned openly and pawed at his nutsack while one of the lesser sheiks ranted in front of him. Our brigade commander blinked his eyes in surprise and leaned away while this Iraqi scratched, focusing intently on the other Arab who spoke. "That's Sheik Nour, head of the Tamimi tribe in this area." The Tamimis, in addition to being the richest and most powerful of the local tribes, also, apparently, bred like jackrabbits. They were everywhere and seemed to control everything.

The two NCOs shook their heads in disbelief. "That fat fuck is the one we have to guard?" Sergeant Spade asked incredulously. The line platoons in our squadron rotated security duties daily and nightly at Sheik Nour's house because he got it into his head that everyone but Americans wanted him dead—everyone, according to him, included the not-to-be-trusted Iraqi army, the even-more-not-to-be-trusted IP, foreign Sunni extremist groups like al-Qaeda in Iraq (AQI), local Sunni extremist groups like Jaish al-Rashiden (JAR), the 1920s Revolutionary Brigade, local Shia extremist groups like al-Sadr's Mahdi Army and the Badr Corps, al-Sadr himself, foreign Shia extremist groups like the Iranian-influenced Asaib Ahl Haq, and the local retarded bum who slept at the underpass down the road and masturbated constantly. Because Nour was a rising political star in Iraqi nationalist circles, our squadron commander had complied with his request for American support, despite the fact that the sheik employed his own 150-man personal militia. Of course, our squadron commander and his security detail wouldn't be the ones staying up for twenty-four plus hours guarding pavement, eyes dripping like stale glue. Funny how that worked.

"That's him," I said. We looked down again. Another man had stood up to speak, and even Sheik Nour now paid attention. I recognized this man immediately as well—it was Sheik Haydar from one of Saba al-Bor's eastern villages and of a rival tribe to the Tamimis. Although his village was small, poor, and comparatively rural, Haydar commanded an audience here with presence; a good fifteen years younger than most of the other sheiks, he was stocky and compact with a back as straight as an ironing board, and his voice carried throughout the courtyard.

I had already met Haydar five days before. Upon our introduction, I distinctly remembered thinking, This man has killed before. There was a dark hardness about him that men cannot replicate, no matter how talented they are at feigning to be something they are not. Shortly thereafter, Haydar told me he intended to feed me a whole goat, just to see if any weight would stick to my bones. Although we both laughed, his eyes never left mine, and I could feel him probing my face, testing me for something unseen. Resisting the impulse to pull my eyes away, I responded that I'd love to share a meal with him, but that I didn't mind being lean and hungry, as it kept me from growing too comfortable. I could tell that my answer had pleased him.

Sheik Nour attempted to interrupt Haydar in Arabic, but Haydar pressed on. The past and future of Iraq was symbolized rather starkly, if a bit rudimentarily, by these two men. Nour was the by-product of a large petroleum inheritance and looked the part; his white dishdasha hid the rolls of fat underneath as well as a bathtub would hold an ocean. Haydar, meanwhile, sported a modern camel-skin coat, designer collared shirt, blue jeans, and a well-trimmed goatee. This chic ensemble, however, could not hide his obvious military posture and mannerisms, as he had previously served with the army for many years—both in Saddam's Baathist military and then in the initial free Iraqi army—only returning home to take control of his people after his father fell gravely ill. Even their headdresses conflicted, Haydar with the Sunni's red-and-white pattern, Nour with a black-and-white headdress to signify Shia. If the various power struggles currently being waged in this country and the Middle East as a whole could ever be simplified into one lucid microcosm, this was it.

"That's Haydar, right?" Staff Sergeant Axel asked. "We were just at his house the other day."

I nodded again. "Yep." I paused. "His tribe hates the Tamimis."

"Right. I remember. He said that the Tamimis get all of the contracts from the Americans because they own the gas stations on Route Tampa."

"Think that's true?" Sergeant Spade asked.

I shrugged my shoulders. I had no clue, and whether it was true or not probably wouldn't change anything in the greater Taji area. What mattered was that Haydar and his people—and pretty much every other sheik and tribe who wasn't a Tamimi—believed it to be true.

I felt a large shadow behind me. I looked up, finding that SFC Big Country had joined us. Men that big shouldn't be so good at sneaking up on people, I thought, no matter how many years they've been a scout.

"Think this will ever end?" he asked.

"Inshallah," I replied, using an Arabic term Suge had taught us. It translated as "God willing," and Iraqis utilized it early and often in conversations, especially when making plans for the future—even if that future was only a few hours away. As a result, we had quickly picked up on the secondary meaning of this term, which translated roughly to "Probably MaybeUhhIAmNotSureQuiteYetProbablyNotYeahDefinitelyNotCanWeTalk AboutThisLaterQuestionMark."

As if on cue, though, the gathering below started to dissipate, and the stream for the exits marked the conclusion to Sheikapalooza. We moved out of our security positions, loaded back up on our Strykers, and returned to Saba al-Bor.

Once we got back, I walked to the terp room and found Phoenix, Captain Whiteback's interpreter for the meeting. He was playing a World Cup soccer video game with our other young terp, Super Mario, and paused the game when I came into the room. I asked him what the sheiks had been discussing after the election for so long.

"Nothing," he said. "They have election, and then they just argue to argue about election. Then they ask about the Sahwa moneys. Always about the moneys. Then they argue some more about contracts and projects until they are tired and then they go home."

"Is that what Haydar was talking about?"

Phoenix nodded. He shared Suge's midnight-black skin and North African heritage, but our youngest terp was rail thin and wanted nothing more in the world than to become an American soldier. "Yes. He say that it is not fair same tribes and same businesses always get big contracts with Americans. He say that his village need water-plant contract."

Haydar's village fell in some of the most arable terrain in the greater Taji region, but it was also some of the most unfunded. Haydar and his Sahwa had done an excellent job at chasing three AQI cells out of their area—supposedly by means that would give the Geneva Convention some more grey hair—and deserved the massive contract the water treatment plant would provide, in my definitely biased and narrow opinion.

"Well, what did they say to that?"

"The American man in the sweater"—I assumed Phoenix referred to the State Department representative—"tell him that he need to make good bid, and if he make good bid, he will get contract."

That sounded fair, I thought. Very capitalistic. Very democratic. Very American. I slapped Phoenix on the back and stood up to leave the terp room. "Was Haydar cool with that?" I asked at the doorway.

Phoenix laughed. "No. He pretend to be, just because it was big meeting. But how can he make better bid than Tamimis? That man with the sweater sound crazy saying that."

"Awesome," I said, feeling a rant come on. "I love it when humanitarian missions reinforce the rich-get-richer notion." Phoenix and Super Mario nodded in agreement, eager to return to their soccer match.

I shook my head and walked back toward my platoon's rooms. I wished the business deals over here didn't always seem as crooked as a corkscrew.

Then I hoped another delivery of mail had come into the combat outpost, as I expected a large batch of cookies from my mom. That package wouldn't arrive until the next day.

PHANTOM EMBERS

I yawned. Sometimes, after I finished yawning, I was surprised at where I found myself. Like I knew I was supposed to be there, but not then, not yet, not again. Then I yawned again. I don't know why. I just did.

I found myself on a roof staring at a smiling ball of bright, and I was tired.

When it happened, I didn't know my platoon was a part of Operation Phantom Phoenix. The only reason I knew such an offensive had occurred was because I read about it on the Internet later. Things like that didn't always make it down the chain to our level; layers upon layers of brass, taskings, and PowerPoint presentations separated me from General Petraeus. All I knew at the time was that my platoon had perched itself up on the roof of an Iraqi household on an early January morning, scanning into a neighborhood with binoculars and optics. We were watching the Iraqi army clear through a neighborhood house by house, providing outer cordon, while Lieutenant Virginia Slim and his platoon overwatched them directly as the inner cordon.

"This sucks," Specialist Haitian Sensation said, while holding up a pair of binos. "Why can't we be the ones clearing the houses today, yo?" I arched an eyebrow his way, which caused him to laugh. "I mean, Yo, sir. Sir, yo. Sir."

Staff Sergeant Bulldog yelled from behind us, ensuring that I didn't have to quote Higher's party line about the purpose of joint operations yet again. "Don't ask da LT stupid questions," he said. "He got LT stuff to do. Just do your damn job."

I smirked, but I could tell Specialist Haitian Sensation had been hurt by the rebuke—like all of my Alpha section, he had learned that invoking Staff Sergeant Bulldog's wrath in the morning was like poking a grizzly with a stick. I patted Specialist Haitian Sensation on the back and leaned over. "Don't worry, dude, we'll get some more of that. In fifteen months, you won't even want to hear the word 'raid' anymore."

I glanced over the side of the roof to the ground. SFC Big Country directed security positions from there, ensuring that the section on the roof with me was free and able to complete our mission of looking for squirters without fear of being attacked from behind. Truthfully, I was amazed that the guys were operating as well as they were. We had been up all night on an observation post (OP) at a historical IED site, and I knew I wasn't the only one running on fumes. I took a knee and pulled a notebook out of my front right cargo pocket to recheck the mission notes. Instead, I found the journal entry I had penned hours before while on OP:

Ripped out on Rip Its and Wild Tigers and Boom-Booms of energy crack in a can flavored power citrus and arctic thunder pouring through the veins of a pseudo sugar sumo junkie completely and utterly and definitely and defiantly
ESSENTIAL
because chocolate pudding and peanut butter cracker peddling can only sustain a platoon leader high on brash and potential and circumstance and the new so long as he pings from mission to mission and from brushfire to frago and from frago to brushfire and from patrol to patrol like a manic-eyed transient hooked on the wild and fearing the banal remedy and all that comes in a powder cane of repetition operating in or around and bring it on down three hours of stolen doze in the past freakin' twoPointfive days comma that's sixty hours if you're counting at home comma which doesn't make cents already down a belt loop 'twoud appear that only the fobbits gain weight in the iraqistan and as he rights this to wrong this he can taste the blue whaling of the sleep siesta luring him to his pillow of urban camouflage boots still being on be damned face-first even down he goes like a lone proud sand castle swallowed by the night tide under a blood red moon that smiles as it cuts itself hot drops splashing like stars cue the comatose drooling see you next siesta fiesta yearesta. Period.

One month and pocket change into the Suck. I figured I'd be splattered across hajji pavement or surrounded by fat German nurses by now. Not that kind of war. Not anymore. Too many stories and too many books and too many movies scrambled into one omelet mind, I guess. I smoke cigarettes occasionally now to keep the headaches at Guantánamo Bay, since trials and tribulations don't exist there. An average second lieutenant only lives seven seconds in the 'Nam before falling down face-first into the jungle mud never to stand again, you savvy?

Ohhhh. Streaming consciousness consciously streaming.

They say if you die with your eyes open, you probably deserved it. Can't argue with that. Negative enemy contact, continue mission.

Find the fight you can't win and fight it. That's the Irish jihad. Join the ghosts.

Only the dumb and the poor, eager to make a name for themselves, are up to hassling Team America right now. No holy war for them, only the war to survive, and that's as cerebral as it gets. Nothing to lose and everything to gain. Kind of like the Gila monster flushed away into a crescent cloud of legalized liquid uppers.

White 1. Out. Lights. Out. Now that's
SAVAGE

Good Lord, I thought. Either I needed sleep even more than I realized or some junior varsity Beat had returned from the dead to turn my brain into his very own poetry bar. Well, there was some salvageable imagery in there; it just needed a sane, well-rested, hatchet-style edit. If only—

"Tired, LT?"

Fuck. I had yawned again.

I looked over at the kneeling Specialist Big Ern, who grinned knowingly at me. "Yeah man," I said. "I am. Just like all of us, I guess."

"Grab a Rip It, then!" Specialist Big Ern had quickly become the platoon's biggest advocate for the aforementioned crack in a can. "Stay away from that hajji stuff though." He referred to the Boom-Booms and Wild Tigers, the energy drinks hawked on the local market. "Drink too many of those, you're reckoning to fail a piss test. If you need a Rip It, me and Van Wilder swiped a few cases for the platoon and hid 'em in our Stryker."

I laughed. "That's one of those things I'm better off not knowing. Plausible deniability." I paused. "Good to know that Staff Sergeant Boondock's liberal borrowing policies have been passed down to his crew though."

Specialist Big Ern nodded. "Yeah, he'll be pretty proud of this get."

The next two hours ticked by slowly. We passed the time by calling out distances and directions to potential hot chicks sighted. The propensity of Saba al-Bor women to dress in all-black and everything-covered garb left a lot to the imagination, but a few targets were spotted. It was kind of hard to tell. Suge wandered up to the roof and overheard the soldiers talking about the possibilities.

"You want Iraqi woman?" he announced to no one in particular.

"Hell yeah!" Private Van Wilder replied. "You know any, Suge Daddy?"

"Oh, I know many Iraqi women," Suge giggled. "I have two wives, and they have many friends who want American husband and—"

"Wait, hold up, Suge." I glanced around to ensure that the others had heard the same thing and it wasn't the exhaustion playing tricks. They all wore the same raised-antenna look I knew I had, so I continued. "Did you just say you have two wives?"

"Yes!" The tone in his voice mixed giddiness and fake surprise that we found this factoid strange; he clearly had discussed this with Americans before. "Muslims, we can marry more than one wife, if we have money to care for them. I keep one house, with younger wife on the upstairs and older wife on the downstairs."

Suge Knight instantly became a rock star, and my soldiers were his adoring fan base. Even Staff Sergeant Bulldog, who had walked over with the intent to break up this impromptu gathering, got lured into the absurdity of the conversation.

"You can fuck both of them?"

"Oh, yes. Many times."

"You can fuck both of them at once?"

"No, no. That is very bad in Islam. One at a time is good."

"So, you're like a black Mormon?"

"Eh?"

"What's your record, Suge?"

"Record?"

"What's the most you have had sex in one day?"

Suge stroked his chin, contemplatively. "In youth, twelve times. Now, six times a day is good." He flexed. "It keep me strong!"

"Do they fight?"

"Sometimes. Then I yell at them to stop, and they stop. If they do not, I hit at them, and they stop because I am king of house. They respect me very much and must listen to me."

"You have kids with both of your wives?"

"Oh, yes. Kids are very good! They make life happy."

"How many kids do you have?"

"Ten kids. Six boys, four girls. I make the two babies when this war start. I see smoke from American tanks and American heli-choppers and American bombs so I go inside and be with wives."

"Suge, you'ze the pimp mackdaddy!"

More giggling. "I know, I know. I have very good wives and very good family. I loves them very much."

Intrigued, I asked the terp how his large family felt about his current occupation.

"I am worry that my family would be hurt if people know I work with Americans," he said grimly. "So I do not tell them."

"They don't know you work with us? Not even your wives?"

"Women cannot keep from the talk!" Suge exclaimed. "They be too proud of me and do the chatter when I am away. Then they will die!"

Captain Whiteback called over the radio at this point and told us to pack up and meet him back at the outpost. Our conversation ended. The mission was over. At least, this one was. Sleep awaited.

A few days later, I read about the details of Operation Phantom Phoenix and the major portions of the offensive taking place in Diyala Province, which lay to our east. More than ten American soldiers died there while clearing houses rigged with bombs.

One of them was a staff sergeant from Reno named Sean Gaul. I didn't know him, but I wish I had.

THE GREAT DRAGUNOV JIGSAW PUZZLE

"Hey, LT." Staff Sergeant Boondock's brusque tone cut through the incessant prattle of four Iraqi women, who were upset at being shepherded out of their house in the desert orange dawn. "You'll want to check this out."

I left Suge with the locals and followed Staff Sergeant Boondock's lead around the corner of the house—a mud hut, really, consisting only of two small rooms that supposedly housed two military-aged males, one of the men's mother, three younger women, and four children. We were operating in the farmland outskirts of Saba al-Bor, acting on a tip one of the local sheiks had provided us about a new family in his area housing insurgents affiliated with JAR. The information relayed to us had been flimsy at best, and that, combined with the unabated fatigue that came after an all-night OP transitioned, without interruption, into a predawn raid, had left the majority of the Gravediggers impatient, annoyed, and eager to get back to the combat outpost. All we had found thus far had been a plethora of poorly threaded blankets, some homemade herb the grandmother claimed helped the children with their many illnesses, and a torn Van Halen tee shirt that Specialist Big Ern thought he had owned in 1987 when he sported a mullet and drove a pesticide truck for a living.

Sergeant Axel and Private Das Boot awaited our arrival on the backside of the mud hut. They stood next to a well from which a water pipe emerged,

SFC Big Country (left) and Specialist Haitian Sensation patrol through a Saba al-Bor marketplace, in early 2008.

connecting to the residence in question. Through the eyes of a green lieutenant, everything looked about as normal as a Middle Eastern abyss could look. They didn't exactly cover what happened next in the ROTC leadership labs.

"Watch this, sir," Staff Sergeant Boondock said, not breaking a stride. He raised his arms to grasp the center of the water pipe, stood up on his tip toes, and tilted the pipe toward Private Das Boot. "Reach in there," he instructed the young private.

The soldier did as he was told. "There's hay in here, Sergeant," he said.

"Reach deeper."

A look of confusion crossed Private Das Boot's face as he strained his reach further into the pipe—confusion that subsequently turned into shock. He pulled out an piece of metal, approximately eight inches long and three inches in diameter, that glinted in the arriving daylight. It shined with polish and showed no signs of rust or neglect.

Staff Sergeant Boondock and I spoke concurrently. "Mother fuckers," I said, while he said, perhaps just as eloquently but definitely more accurately, "A mother-fucking bolt."

"How'd you know sómething was in there?" I asked Staff Sergeant Boondock.

"Fuck, sir," he replied, barely able to contain his satisfaction with himself, "you know I wake up in the morning and piss excellence."

The next half hour passed in a blur. With the discovery of the rifle bolt, I unleashed my platoon's rejuvenated energies and instinctive hunting skills upon the mud hut. The two men, who had already been separated, simply hung their heads in resignation when I showed them the metal piece, asking if they knew anything about it. Suge laughed in their faces and told me that they knew better than to claim ignorance at this point. The rest of the family stood quietly off to the side and gathered around a homemade fire in a barrel as we ransacked—as gently as possible—through their personal belongings, unearthing a trigger assembly, five ammo magazines, and at least one hundred 7.62-mm rounds in a carefully dug cubbyhole found underneath a rug. Corporal Spot unwrapped the mother load, found even deeper in the water pipe: a Russian-made Dragunov sniper rifle carefully swathed in dishtowels and very recently cleaned. SFC Big Country still furrowed his brow, though, when I suggested that we were nearing the end of the search. "We're still missing the stock," he said, racking his mind for potential hiding spots we had overlooked.

"Damn it," he continued, stalking over to the barrel where the family huddled around the fire for warmth. He shooed them away and doused the flames with water from his CamelBak hydration system. Smirking, he reached a burly Midwestern hand into the barrel, pulling out a very charred, but still recognizable, homemade wooden rifle stock. I shook my head in disbelief as Suge started grilling the grandmother. She smiled and shrugged her shoulders.

"A mother protecting her son?" I asked the terp.

"Yes," he answered. "Crazy female."

I instructed the Gravediggers to start policing up the hut and blindfold the two detainees while I inventoried our bounty; SFC Big Country walked back to his Stryker to update Bravo Troop headquarters. As Staff Sergeant Boondock and Sergeant Axel led the two men away, I snuck a glance toward the family left behind. The grandmother stared stonily into the distance, seemingly oblivious of her departing son, his friend, and the strange Americans. Two of the younger women fought back tears, while the third walked back inside, nursing the youngest of the children. The other three children wept openly, and one of them tried to run after our detainees before the women collectively scooped him off of the ground.

As we walked back to my Stryker, the sniper rifle and accessory parts in hand, I looked over at Suge. "I feel kind of bad, you know? These guys are probably just stooges, trying to make some money." I nodded back at the women and the children. "I mean, it's not like this is their fault. How are they going to support themselves now?"

He looked back at me in a blizzard of skepticism. "Do not feel bad, LT. They should not have bred with stupid mother fuckers."

One didn't always have to use big words or utilize profound analogies to articulate a philosophical known.

A DIFFERENT WORLD

The army divides its officers into three categories: company-grade officers (lieutenants and captains), field-grade officers (majors, lieutenant colonels, and colonels), and general officers (the top dogs with stars on their collars). Concurrently, there are three levels of warfare: tactical, operational, and strategic. As a junior officer who spent his entire time of service in the tactical function, my dealings with general officers were minimal, but I often interacted with—and took orders from—field grades.

I respected many of the field-grade officers I served under or encountered and found them to be men of honor, strength, and great wisdom. Men like our brigade commander, whose strict adherence to the counterinsurgency principle of precision targeting set the tone for our brigade for the entire deployment. Men like my first ROTC instructor, a devout 101st Airborne loyalist and pupil of General Petraeus, who back in 2002 convinced me I had the swagger required to be a combat-arms officer. Men like our unit's first squadron commander, who had established the cavalry in the middle of the historical infantry land of Hawaii with as much Stetson-wearing, spur-sporting pizzazz as the ghosts of Teddy Roosevelt and Jeb Stuart and George Patton demanded.

And then there were the other field grades.

For whatever reason, these other field grades always seemed to outnumber the quality ones. And they were seemingly everywhere in Iraq, intent on riding the bureaucratic beast in all its protectionist glory. As with any professional organization, the army taught me to respect the rank, if not the person. And so I did. Unlike other professional organizations though, the army mandated that I carry out these men's orders successfully and without complaint, even when they directly assaulted all known logic and experience.

And so I did, hiding my concerns from my subordinates as much as possible in a combat environment, because I was just a lieutenant and just a platoon leader and probably didn't understand the bigger picture. While I was often frustrated, I was never defiant.

None of that changed the truth, though, that inept careerists were as much a part of the military fabric as the camouflage pattern and liquid eggs for breakfast, and my experiences in Iraq in this regard were certainly nothing new in the annals of war. The players never changed, only their names.

Major Moe was the most prevalent type of other field grade. Major Moe wasn't so much a person as he was a trend; nicknamed after the character in the classic *Three Stooges* films, Major Moe could be found, in multitude, on any FOB in Iraq. If a field grade didn't grasp the nuances of counterinsurgency doctrine, didn't subscribe to the application of decentralized warfare, believed that all of the war's issues could be quantified into a PowerPoint presentation, spoke vaguely of concepts like standards and discipline but never applied those same banalities personally, and consistently displayed a clueless obtuseness about day-to-day operations, he qualified as a Major Moe. In short, Major Moe made the war for line soldiers more difficult—the exact opposite of what qualified as purpose for a deployed army officer—by focusing on irrelevant regulations and out-of-date procedures. Did it really matter that some soldiers wore fleece caps during the day when they were cold, when the Iraqi police still weren't hiring Sunnis in Saba al-Bor or anywhere else in the Taji region? It did to Major Moe and his noncommissioned officer (NCO) equivalent, Sergeant Major Curly. They didn't know any better, though, because they rarely left the FOB. And when they did . . . it got ugly.

One brisk winter afternoon, a certified Major Moe from our squadron visited Saba al-Bor. It was his first trip to our outpost, and our troop's artillery lieutenant, Skerk, gave him the tour. Major Moe picked up a bundle of *Baghdad Now* newspapers stacked at the top of the staircase and asked what they were.

"Those are copies of one of the Iraqi national papers, sir," Skerk responded.

Major Moe was confused and let it be known. "Why are they here? Why aren't they being distributed?"

"We do distribute them, sir. Every patrol that goes out picks up a stack and distributes them to the locals and to the Iraqi security checkpoints."

"That's excellent to hear." Major Moe responded in classic Major Moe fashion, lips puckered, chin protruded, arms crossed, nodding the all-knowing nod that was supposed to convey male dominance. He continued speaking. "I assume you're gathering the atmospherics of this distribution?"

Skerk replied like most well-informed individuals would in such a circumstance. "Huh?"

Staff Sergeant Boondock and I were sitting nearby, at the computers, and could not help but openly eavesdrop at this point.

"Why, yes, of course," Major Moe continued. "Atmospherics. We need to check on the local-nationals and ensure that they are all reading the newspaper."

Staff Sergeant Boondock arched his eyebrows and turned to me. "Can most of these Iraqis read?" he whispered.

"Fuck no," I whispered back. "Not here." There were many hot, dusty towns between the two rivers of the Euphrates and Tigris, and none of them contained a very educated populace anymore; most of the learned had escaped to the cities or fled the country entirely. The global media called it the Iraqi diaspora. Saba al-Bor was no exception. Unfortunately, the newspapers we distributed were intended for a very distinct minority.

Skerk eventually sputtered out a reply. "Why would we . . . may I ask why, sir?"

"Because it's important to find out if they are reading them, that's why. Like this article here—" Major Moe's fingers slammed down onto the newspaper and pointed at Arabic words—"what is this article about? If we read it, then we can talk to the local-nationals about it when we're on patrol. Then we can gather those atmospherics and send them up to brigade."

Skerk leaned over and looked at the newspaper. "Sir, that article is about dinosaurs evolving into birds." An awkward pause followed. "And, sir, truthfully, I'm not sure that the papers we give out are really being read right now. I think most of the people use them to stay warm at night."

"What?" Major Moe was outraged. "That's absurd! Like for blankets?"

An even longer awkward pause followed, as Staff Sergeant Boondock tried in vain to stifle his laughter.

"Uhh, no, sir. For their fires."

This caused Staff Sergeant Boondock's snickering to turn into an all-out howl, while I slowly attempted to slide down my chair and out of Major Moe's view from the top of the staircase.

Our interactions with Major Moe weren't always so harmless. As the months of our deployment passed, these incidents became less hilarious and more and more maddening.

Just because a field grade wasn't a Major Moe, though, didn't mean he automatically qualified as the quintessential leader of men we all wanted to follow. As a generation of men raised by single women and without fathers—as most of the junior officers and enlisted soldiers were—we didn't give our senior leaders much beyond the basic military courtesies demanded of us. Anything else they had to—and we wanted them to—earn. And we hoped they would, although it didn't always turn out that way. Like with Lieutenant Colonel Larry.

In all fairness, Lieutenant Colonel Larry was usually a hard worker and tactically competent. Though not as common as Major Moe, he still derived from an ideology and, thus, was embodied by multiple persons. All Lieutenant Colonel Larrys were bona fide Cold Warriors though—a derisive term used by junior officers of the global war on terrorism (GWOT) era to describe the senior officers and senior NCOs still hopelessly devoted to Cold War–era doctrine and techniques. Iraq, like most nonconventional counterinsurgencies that aimed for success, was fought on the ground level by small units, like squads and sections and platoons. Company and troop commanders became local gods who controlled civil works contracts and the electricity for entire townships; platoon leaders and squad leaders became their apostles, wandering the desert, spreading the good word, fighting battles for public perception one person at a time.

Field grades and senior NCOs had grown up not in this environment but in a far more rigid, structured army whose mission was simply to act on and destroy the enemy. Some thrived on this change and embraced the fluidity of a counterinsurgency, others had spent their careers on the strategic level planning for just this sort of war, but still others on the operational level seemed to have a very difficult time adapting and struggled to find purpose in our current operating environment. In these situations, friction tended to arise between the respective layers of leadership.

An incessant micromanager, our squadron's Lieutenant Colonel Larry often led through intimidation. It seemed like there wasn't a leader in his unit whose job he didn't threaten over the course of our fifteen months in theater. He claimed throughout the summer and the fall that Bravo Troop was the most undisciplined outfit he'd ever seen, which might have had an effect if he hadn't already said the same thing about the other reconnaissance troops in the squadron before and after that.

Clinical misery ran rampant through our squadron commander's staff, and some of his troop commanders had to take antianxiety medication in order to deal with his constant tirades. He routinely arrived unannounced at the squadron's combat outposts—usually during banking hours, in the middle of the day, staying just long enough to chastise us on uniform standards and a loose piece of trash, but arriving back on the FOB in time for dinner. The outpost was our home, where we lived twenty-four hours a day, seven days a week. It was more than natural for us to relax there when we weren't on patrol or on security, it was a necessity.

Behind his back, the Joes often whispered, "Do you always walk around in your full uniform back at your comfortable commander's pod on Taji, *sir*?" But due to NCO intervention, any thoughts of mutiny were instantly crushed. Most of the enlisted soldiers never spoke to Lieutenant Colonel Larry, on a personal level or otherwise, unless they had gotten into trouble for something like negligently discharging a round into a clearing barrel. Needless to say, those conversations were not conducted as teaching points, no matter how young the soldier was or how extenuating the circumstances were.

I swore to myself every day that if I stayed in the army, I would never lead like this. I also swore to myself every day that if I decided to get out of the army when my tour of duty was up, I would never treat people like this.

A military unit is structured to mirror its commander and his leadership style and priorities. During my time as their platoon leader, the Gravediggers had a reputation for being tactically skilled and mission oriented, if a bit rough around the edges and (sometimes too) opinionated—certainly a reflection on both myself and SFC Big Country, for better and for worse. Concurrently, 2–14 Cavalry ultimately degenerated into a one-party fascist state. My eventually standing up to Lieutenant Colonel Larry after I was threatened, and then writing about it, would change nothing. Through words and actions, he made it clear that he viewed me as a rebellious punk lieutenant easily discarded for my unruliness—as I would eventually be, traded within the brigade to 1–27 Infantry Battalion and away from the platoon ten months into the deployment.

But that was still many months and many passages through the wilds away.

GRAVEYARD SHIFT

I couldn't see the makeshift dip cup Private Van Wilder spat into, but I heard his deposit splash into the pool of tobacco brown before he answered my question.

"No worries, sir, we're doing fine."

In the limp, ambiguous darkness of the hours between midnight and dawn, I could only discern the outline of my soldier's shape three feet away. We were on the roof of the combat outpost, overwatching the slums of Saba al-Bor, making small talk to distract from the chill of the night. Due to his contagious good nature and quick wit, Private Van Wilder had become a leader for the Joes from the day he showed up at our unit onward. I had hurled the awkwardly vague blanket question of "How are things going in the platoon, from your perspective?" at him. His quick reply had been what I should've expected—brief and upbeat.

"Would you tell me if it wasn't?" I asked with a scoff, hoping to recover from my initial statement's idiocy. Like most junior officers who didn't drip with careerist aspirations, I always liked to project myself as a platoon leader who kept it real, and I was more than aware that my first question betrayed far too much self-awareness for an army man. Being a platoon leader was sometimes a very lonely position, as I was stuck between an immovable force (common sense) and an unstoppable power (Higher). Luckily, my soldiers laughed along with me as I learned to navigate this murky divide, rather than resenting their platoon leadership, as I saw happen in other line platoons.

"Ehh, probably not, sir," Private Van Wilder replied, in his terse Texan drawl. "It ain't your fault though—I just think Staff Sergeant Boondock would kill us if we didn't go through him first, you know?" I thought over his response and came to terms with the honest nature of it. After all, the bone marrow of the military was a rigid and clear chain of command that was only to be violated under the most extreme conditions. If my soldiers understood this, then I guessed I had found the answer to my initial question, however indirectly.

The same conclusion was found on the other side of the roof with PFC Cold-Cuts, albeit in a much different and more forthcoming manner. This young Gravedigger motormouthed his way through a multitude of subjects in only thirty or so minutes, including, but not limited to, why he believed America was in Iraq; why he didn't like being in his wife's doghouse; which members of the platoon he thought missed their families the most; what he remembered from the Iraq history classes I had conducted for the platoon in the months leading up to our deployment; what he did not remember from those classes; how good his unborn son would be at high school football; how funny it was when Staff Sergeant Bulldog told him, "Damn it, Cold-Cuts, you ain't allowed to call hajjis 'hajjis' no mor'"; why the Iraqi men were so interested in his blonde hair and blue eyes; how much he wanted to take Suge back to Hawaii with us when we redeployed; and why he could tell which Iraqi police were crooked just by looking at them. All the while he patted his crew-serve machine gun, which sat behind a drooping camo net, something that masked all the weapons' positions on the four corners of the roof.

I wasn't sure whether I needed to hug him or drop him to the ground to do push-ups when, after I announced my intention to move elsewhere in our security posture, he patted me on the back and said, "You're doing great, sir. Thanks for checking on us, but don't worry so much. We're all fine." I managed a laugh and told PFC Cold-Cuts that I appreciated his endorsement, as I would now be able to sleep soundly at night. This unleashed a fresh set of giggles from him. I continued on with my rounds.

Judging from the snapping of his body when I put my hand on his shoulder, I could tell I had startled Private Romeo when I walked up on him. He and Specialist Flashback stood together in a comfortable silence, one that I joined them in. They were providing security to the west, over the IP station that had been overrun by Sadrist militiamen in 2004, during the Mahdi Army's initial rebellion, and again in 2006, during Saba al-Bor's sectarian wars. The only activity in front of the police station on this night was a pair of humping dogs that three Iraqi policemen kept throwing rocks at.

I thought about quizzing my soldiers on their sectors of fire but decided not to insult their intelligence—they had already pulled this shift enough times and been asked that same exact questions enough times to have their sectors memorized. Few things kill morale the way the Jerry's Kids treatment does. Specialist Flashback eventually looked over at me and asked, "The TOC [tactical operations center] driving you crazy again, sir?"

I nodded and uttered a simple, "Uh huh." The TOC was technically my designated place of duty for the graveyard shift—a place where the telephone rang incessantly, the radios spouted like a broken water-sprinkler system, and the madness never ended. I had slipped out while three Headquarters platoon NCOs—one Puerto Rican, one Panamanian, and one Mexican—argued heatedly in Spanish about whose respective nation's females deserved the title of "Hottest Latinas." While certainly an appealing subject, it had lost its appeal when I couldn't follow the various points and counterpoints being made. I had subsequently sought refuge up on the roof.

"I hate going in there," Private Romeo said. "SFC Big Country sent me in there last week to get a fresh battery for a walkie-talkie, and I almost ran over the sergeant major. He yelled at me for not shaving. I told him that we had just got back from an all-night OP and that I was going straight onto security, and then he told me, 'Excuses are like assholes,' and that a good soldier would bring a razor on his mission. What does that even mean?"

"I think he meant, 'Excuses are like assholes: Everyone has one,'" Specialist Flashback explained.

"Oh." If possible, Private Romeo was even more irritated with the sergeant major's comment now. "I guess that makes sense."

"That's the one good thing about night around here," Specialist Flashback said. "At least it's just us Bravo Troopers at night." He turned to me and smiled. "Wouldn't you agree, sir?"

I bit my lip and smirked. It probably wasn't too hard to discern how I felt about these matters, and with Specialist Flashback being my driver, thus privy to my more unplugged moments, he already knew the answer to his question. Now, though, I had a moment to collect my thoughts, and in the name of professionalism, I resisted the urge to be too honest with my guys. "I don't know what you mean," I eventually replied. "The best part about nighttime is talking to Staff Sergeant Bulldog when he's trying to sleep."

A burst of automatic weapons fire rippled through the night in the distance, toward the northeast, somewhere in the Sunni sector. We all shifted instinctively toward that direction, waiting for a succeeding burst. None came. Private Van Wilder called across the update on the radio, boredom saturating every word of the report. This was Iraq. Gunfire happened at night. Gunfire happened every night.

"And that," I continued, "that's the other best thing about nighttime."

Shortly thereafter, I ambled over to Sergeant Spade's sergeant-of-the-guard position at the base of the entryway to the roof. Sergeant Spade demonstrated all the traits of a model scout—an aloof and serene temperament, a set of stabbing eyes, a casual naturalness with the rifle that hung at the low-ready like a third arm, and a big wad of dip tucked deeply into one of his cheek pouches.

"You in charge of this circus?" I asked, approaching the crouching shadow.

"You know it," came the reply, slightly slurred, due to the dip. He spat into the darkness before continuing, nodding down at Saba al-Bor. "Nothing doing, tonight, except for that shit five minutes ago. Too cold."

"Yeah, well, it's too cold for me too, but somehow I'm still wandering around on a rooftop in Iraq in the middle of the night."

He nodded. "This place isn't like it was the first time I was here," he said matter-of-factly.

"Is that a good thing or a bad thing?"

"I'm not sure yet." He shrugged his shoulders. "Ask me again in a few months."

"Everything good with the guys?" I asked. "I tried asking a couple of them, but all I got was the rehearsed 'Yes, sir! Absolutely, sir!' that you NCOs teach them to say to officers."

Sergeant Spade chuckled. "Yeah, LT, they're good. There have been some squabbles and shit, but that's normal." His words proved prophetic. Over the course of fifteen months, there were some arguments and even a few fistfights within the platoon, but nothing too serious. Things like that were bound to happen with nineteen- and twenty-year-old kids cooped up to-gether constantly, under the stresses of combat, for well over a year. It was usually kept in-house, with punishments doled out by NCOs who kept their understanding—and amusement—to themselves.

After leaving my gunner at his post, I walked downstairs and back outside to the front gate, where Sergeant Axel, Specialist Big Ern, and Private Das Boot were manning the main entry control point (ECP). A maze of criss-crossing razor concertina wire led up to the gate, with imposing T-wall barriers stacked on both sides of the entryway. Sergeant Axel and Specialist Big Ern leaned against a Humvee parked at the gate, while Private Das Boot sat up in the vehicle's gunner's cupola, diligently manning a long-barreled 50-caliber machine gun. His long legs forced the tops of his knees out of the hatch, and he compensated by bending his back forward, hunching over the weapon. This had not gone unnoticed by the other two Gravediggers.

"He looks like a crawdad in a tree up there, doesn't he, sir?" Specialist Big Ern said, using an Appalachian analogy I was unfamiliar with.

"Uhh, sure, absolutely," I said. "How's it going down here?"

Sergeant Axel, still laughing about Specialist Big Ern's Carolina slang, said, "We're good, LT. No visitors since Colonel Mohammed, Boss Johnson, and all of the other sheiks left a few hours ago."

"Right on. How much longer until the next shift comes on?"

Sergeant Axel checked his watch. "One more hour," he said. "One more glorious hour with Big Ern and the Big Soviet here!"

Private Das Boot snorted from above us, offended, as he always was when called a Russian. "I am German and American," he said. "Both sides of me hate the Russians."

"Not as much as you hate the Turks, though. Right, Das Boot?" asked Specialist Big Ern. "Remember what Staff Sergeant Boondock taught us about embracing the hate!" He then threw the revolution fist—recently rechristened in Staff Sergeant Boondock's section as the hate fist—straight into the air. It was common to see said hate fist during fragos, early mornings, and long, unending nights.

Private Das Boot gave this some serious thought. "Hmm. I do not know," he said. "That's tough. I guess they are the same?"

"What about the Estonians?" I asked. It was an honest question, as I was genuinely unfamiliar with Germany's relationship with its Baltic neighbor. Unfortunately, my history question would have to be answered another day, as bringing up the Stones led to another hot topic for my soldiers.

"I know I love that female Stone," Private Das Boot said, a grin spreading lustfully across his face. "There is nothing hotter than a beautiful woman with a gun."

"Get it!" Sergeant Axel yelled, encouraging our young soldier's fantasy. "Get after it, Das Boot, like the dirty Kraut you are!" Despite his front, Private Das Boot had still been too shy even to talk to the female Estonian soldier who occasionally dropped by our combat outpost. Everyone in the platoon figured he had an in being a fellow Euro and all, but none of us had any experience with Estonian women, either, so no one was too confident with that scheme. He kept saying he would give her his MySpace profile link, but such a prolific step in relationship development had yet to occur.

I checked my watch and realized I'd been gone from the TOC for more than two hours; consequently, I told Sergeant Axel to radio me if they needed anything and headed back into the combat outpost away from the pale moon and into a bastion of artificial heat. In the TOC, the three Headquarters platoon NCOs sat around playing cards, their Hottest Latinas debate apparently settled. "Everything okay out there, sir?" one of them asked. "No need to sound the alarms for the Alamo Drill?"

I shook my head and reached for the coffee pot. "Just another quiet night," I said. "Nothing doing."

MOHAMMED THE GHOST

It was the day after the great red dust storms ended, a little more than a week after our squadron lost its first soldier to a deep buried IED in the farmlands west of Saba al-Bor. I lay in bed, staring at the wall from the top bunk, basking in the rarest of days—one in which I could sleep in. I thought about nothing and how awesome it was to think about nothing and how if life went well, nothing wouldn't be so rare anymore. The gears of my mind were just beginning to grind toward muscle movement, mainly a product of memory rather than a conscious decision, when SFC Big Country barreled through the door.

"The IA got Mohammed Shaba!" he said, staying just long enough to drop off his now empty mug of coffee. Just like that, he was gone, I was back in Iraq, and my nothingness had burst like a star cluster, illuminating all kinds of gut-wrenching, hidden somethings back into plain sight. I cursed to myself, slapped myself in the face, and hopped off the top bunk. The nothingness was now gone. Maybe next lifetime, I thought to myself.

So, they got the Ghost. Saba al-Bor's native son, a known terrorist and wanted murderer, had been a general thorn in the side of Coalition forces for the better portion of the past year. Much of his celebrity status was overblown, mainly due to his self-designated nickname, which translated to either Mohammed the Ghost or Mohammed the Shadow, depending which terp had been asked. Nevertheless, Higher had longed after this JAM insurgent in a manner that bordered on Brokeback. Capturing him was a public relations dream, if not a key strategic blow for Shia extremism in our area. The Gravediggers had already been on a few boondoggles going after him, but we were always a room away, ten minutes late, or finding his grandfather with a full piss bag but without a grandson. When Mohammed Shaba missions came down, it usually felt like we were hunting a black dog in the night. These experiences weren't isolated to just our platoon; they encapsulated all of Bravo Troop's bouts with the Ghost. And now the Iraqi army had him. Sure, I was shocked, but good for the IA, I thought. That was what we were aiming for, after all—a self-sustaining Iraqi security force.

Yawning noisily, I strolled out of our room and into the main foyer of the combat outpost. Captain Whiteback and a few of the soldiers from Headquarters platoon were heading out the front door, en route to the IA compound to tactically question the Ghost and his fellow detainees. I bumped

(from left to right) Specialist Big Ern, Corporal Spot, Staff Sergeant Boondock, PFC Van Wilder, and Specialist Prime show off their respective moustaches and sneers. Scout platoons were smaller than most other combat units, and the relationship between NCOs and soldiers tended to be less rigid and more instruction-oriented as a result.

into Lieutenant Virginia Slim, who was coming up the stairs and taking off his helmet; he had just been over with the IAs.

"Dude," he said, "you should head over and check these guys out."

"Why?" I didn't really feel compelled to put on my gear. I was more interested in grabbing a few banana nut muffins and seeing if there were any pieces of bacon left. "Did the CO [commanding officer] say he needed me?"

"Naw, I just thought you'd appreciate the scene. They're just a couple of scared, punk teenagers. We probably could've had them months ago if we had set up a trap with XBoxes, a few porn mags, and some pounds of weed."

We laughed, and I sauntered toward the pantry. I rubbed the stubble of my face. I should probably shave too, I thought. It had been a few days.

After breakfast and a quick dry shave, curiosity got a hold of me, and I walked across the street to the IA compound. I poked my head around the fence line and spotted a crowd of IA soldiers—commonly referred to by their Arabic name, jundis—interlaced with a group of American soldiers sent over to ensure the detention process stayed peaceful. There was a post–prize fight feeling in the air. The soldiers of both countries were joking with one another incessantly, crowing like young bantams at a cockfight. They crowded around three grubby, emaciated shapes in handcuffs and wrapped in blankets that were stacked against the building. The three shapes were separated along the wall so they could not communicate; they were crouched in the traditional Arab squat, and only nervous darting glances from downcast heads confirmed them to be human beings and not teenage scarecrows made of dirt.

As I walked closer, I recognized Mohammed Shaba from the mug shots we'd used for countless previous missions: same scar across the right cheek, same long chin, same mop of black hair jetting out. In the photograph, he snarled toward the camera, menacingly challenging the viewer to dare to venture into Saba al-Bor's alleys to hunt him. Here, at the IA compound, though, he did not snarl, or challenge, or dare. He sniffled like a bullied child, trying desperately to hold back tears, cradling his swollen nose, which dripped with blood. It had been broken by the IA when he bit one of them and tried to escape. The teenager handcuffed next to him—who I later learned was another top target of ours known as Ali the Prince—wept far more openly and reeked of feces. Wait a minute. Had he really—

"Yes, sir, he actually shit himself," one of our Headquarters platoon NCOs said to me, apparently provoked by my sniffing of the air and subsequent grimace. "Gives new meaning to the term *scared shitless*, don't it?"

I nodded, hoping I appeared aloof and knowing to my enemies, who now had faces. Why I cared in the first place, I still don't know. "How'd the IA find them?" I asked.

The Headquarters platoon NCO chuckled. "They got set up by Sheik Banana-Hands," he said. Sheik Achmed, better known as Banana-Hands to Coalition forces for his obnoxiously long fingers, had JAM connections in Saba al-Bor longer than the Tigris, but he had recently warmed to the concept of reconciliation—and the financial benefits it wrought. "I'll give you the details later. We gotta bring 'em inside now. Captain Whiteback and the IA colonel have some questions to ask before these guys get hauled back to Taji."

Some of the jundis snatched the Ghost up by his elbows. He began to shake uncontrollably and dragged his feet in an attempt to stall his pending interview. He had no idea what awaited him inside the IA headquarters, and I was certain his imagination had created a far worse and far more graphic fate than was actually going to occur. As they lugged him through the front door, fear of the unknown struck again, this time in liquid form. A trickle of urine quickly swelled into a pool at the base of Mohammed the

Ghost's frayed pants. Both the Iraqi jundis and the American soldiers pointed and laughed.

There were no heroes of battle or delusions of war this day. Mohammed Shaba, a local legend prone to baiting Coalition forces with written taunts and verbal proclamations, a ghost brutal enough to kill people with point-blank AK-47 shots to the skull, a shadow guerilla who blew up American soldiers with crescent bombs (local terminology for EFPs) and then bragged about it, had literally pissed his pants at the prospect of consequences. He did not have my sympathies; nor did he deserve them.

His next stop was Camp Bucca, the national prison that had replaced Abu Ghraib. He would not be there as long as he should be.

When I walked back to the Gravediggers' corner of the combat outpost, SFC Big Country had already torn the Ghost's mug shot off the target wall. It lay crumpled up in the trash can. I thought about pulling it out and saving it for posterity. If nothing else, it was one more thug off the streets, and I knew the locals would be relieved to hear the news of his detainment. I decided to leave the mug shot in the trash though. I already had my lasting snapshot of Mohammed the Ghost, and it certainly wasn't the snarling menace captured in that photograph.

MOVEMENT TO CONTACT

I was literally boots up in the back of my Stryker when Lieutenant Virginia Slim's breezy accent sizzled over the net.

"X-ray [the radio call sign for the TOC], this is Steel 1! We got contact with enemy rifle fire on Route Swords, to the north, from dismounted personnel. We're developing the situation! Steel 1 out!"

Located on the complete opposite side of town from Lieutenant Virginia Slim and his platoon, the Gravediggers had spent a quiet day in OP overwatch. Half of my platoon was on duty with the Iraqi police; the other half were racked out in the vehicles, trying not to drool on one another. After Steel platoon's radio call, though, I loaded everyone up in anticipation of the radio call I knew would follow, as we were the only other maneuver element in sector: "White 1"—it was Captain Whiteback using our platoon's official color designation for radio traffic purposes—"move to far end of Route Swords to support Steel. Cordon off the northern section of the route."

Briefing the Gravediggers scout platoon on their tasks and purposes for an upcoming patrol. Either the platoon leader or the platoon sergeant gave such a brief before every platoon operation, no matter how commonplace or routine.

I responded just as rapidly. "This is White 1. Will comply." I switched over to the platoon net and, trying not to sound too anxious, gave the order to move out. "Gravediggers, let's roll. Route Swords. Time now." Three minutes after the contact call had stirred me from my day-dozing, my platoon screamed through the streets of Saba al-Bor, riding toward the sound of the guns.

Planning while on the move was not something recommended in any army leadership manual or officers' guidebook I had ever read, but it was something we all learned to do early and often in Iraq. SFC Big Country and I identified cordon locations for each of our Strykers, and I told the platoon to kick out all of the dismounts we had to provide local security.

"Make sure you dismount to your right and take cover behind our vehicles," I said. "The contact Steel is reporting will be to our south. Let them flush the shooters out to our positions, and do not engage unless you positively identify your target." I didn't necessarily need to repeat the rules of engagement (ROE) that had been hammered into us in the previous weeks, usually by fobbit brass, but it felt like the sort of thing a lieutenant was supposed to say in these kinds of situations.

I double-checked to ensure my rifle was locked and loaded, told Suge Knight to follow me onto the ground, and prepared to dismount with my platoon. Then I felt my vehicle come to a screeching halt, heard Sergeant Spade give the order from his gunner's cupola to drop ramp over the humming engine, and began to move out of the back. As my first boot hit the Stryker's ramp though, while Suge pushed up behind me, I heard SFC Big Country's voice roar over the radio speakers: "Contact to the north! I repeat, to the north!"

To the north? What the fuck? I knew that I had heard Steel's radio transmissions correctly, so how was the contact coming from the north? I didn't have much time to analyze the situation though, as directly in front of me an Iraqi army T-72 rolled by—heading north—machine gun blazing away, while rounds steadily ricocheted off of it. I couldn't help but gawk at how empty the streets were. I still stood on the Stryker's back ramp when SFC Big Country's vehicle launched a smoke grenade directly to my front, masking the movement of our dismounts team with a wispy grey cloud. It hissed like a snake.

Whistle. Whistle. Crack.

Close. Close. Very close.

Only now, when the rounds fired from the north began to ricochet off of my Stryker, did some fusion of training and survival instinct kick in. I grabbed Suge, who was more disoriented than I was, and we ran to our right, stacking up on a building behind Staff Sergeant Boondock's dismount team.

I took a deep breath, bit down on my lip, and tried to assess the situation. Staff Sergeant Boondock and his team—consisting of Sergeant Cheech, Private Van Wilder, and Private Das Boot—were directly in front of me, trying to communicate through hand-and-arm signals with dismounted IA personnel across the way, stacked up on another building. Sergeant Axel's dismount team—consisting of Corporal Spot, Specialist Haitian Sensation, and Private Smitty—was across from that building, also stacked up. There were IA tanks operating to our front and to our rear, both rattling with automatic fire. I grabbed my radio and asked SFC Big Country, who was now in charge of our mounted personnel, if any of our gunners could positively identify what the IA's were shooting at.

"That's a negative, White 1! Cannot positively identify!"

Just as my platoon sergeant finished his radio transmission, two bullets whistled by the dismounted IA soldiers across from us, thudding into the building some seven feet from our position. The IAs responded by spraying their AK-47s wildly over their shoulders, not bothering to look where they were shooting.

Shit had hit the proverbial fan. I desperately tried to recall the book answer to this situation, but all I could come up with was using our Stryker as a shield while we actioned on the objective, like I had seen paratroopers do with tanks in an episode of *Band of Brothers*. I looked back up to see Staff Sergeant Boondock already directing my vehicle to do just that.

"You read my mind," I yelled, relieved that I'd thought of a tactically sound maneuver, albeit about five seconds late.

"I got you, sir," he responded, giving me the Aloha shaka'. I could have sworn he had winked at me from behind his black sunglasses too. This was his third deployment, and having experienced more than one man's fair share of combat, he adopted a relaxed posture in an attempt to settle down his young lieutenant and the three soldiers he had stacked up with him, most of whom were experiencing two-way live rounds for the first time.

I radioed back to SFC Big Country to relay to Captain Whiteback that we were maneuvering half the platoon north and keeping the other half in cordon because, if arbitrary gunfire was any clue, it sounded like Steel was still in contact to the south, too. While the IA dismounts refused to budge from the safety and cover of the building, Sergeant Axel and his team bounded over to our position without incident. That brought our dismounted total on the ground to ten, including Suge. Behind my Stryker, driven by Specialist Flashback and gunned by Sergeant Spade, we gradually plunged north into the unknown, like a needle in search of a vein. The T-72s to our left and right continued to exchange machine gun and rifle fire with *something* that was about three hundred meters directly to our front, rounds pinging off of the tanks' armor and the surrounding buildings. Corporal Spot and Sergeant Axel assumed the wings of our impromptu staggered column, scanning every window and peering down every corner. The area we moved into offered little concealment and even less cover; we had trampled straight into hell's garden, where fountains flowed with raw sewage and a soil-bed of refuse and broken glass gnawed on itself below our feet.

As we pressed forward, the rounds fired in our direction tapered off considerably, until the only fire I could identify came from the T-72s. My men showed considerable restraint throughout our movement, ignoring the temptation to begin firing rounds under the guise of harassment fire, waiting to positively identify not only a target but an enemy target. I was sure I hadn't been the only one, though, who had been stroking his safety trigger as we walked, hunched over, attempting to minimize our own target silhouettes.

The Stryker stopped at some residual miscellany of concrete in the center of this no-man's-land. I took this opportunity to radio back to my mounted elements and exchange situation reports with them, while the soldiers spread out, finding cover, rifles and machine guns oriented in a half-moon shape bowing north. The T-72s now turned around and headed south, out of our view.

"White 4, this is White 1," I said.

No answer.

"White 4, this is White 1," I repeated.

No fucking answer. Nothing but radio static.

I broke into a profanity-laced tirade, which culminated in my beating my hand mic against my helmet. Despite the tenseness of our situation, my rambling antics cracked a few of the guys up. Still nothing more than a very serious mind doomed with a clown's soul, I thought. Then I remembered Sergeant Spade still had radio communications from the Stryker, and I had him relay our update. Deep breath. We still had commo with the outside world.

"4 copies," Sergeant Spade yelled down from his hatch. "The section in cordon is still in position and reports that the IA are the only ones shooting now. Also, Steel still reports receiving contact in the south."

I looked over at Staff Sergeant Boondock, who just shrugged his shoulders. "Keep moving?" he suggested.

"Roger," I said, signaling to the soldiers to resume their column positions behind my Stryker. No more than twenty meters after we continued our movement, though, my Stryker came to a halt. I heard Sergeant Spade's voice rise in pieces above the engine and other extraneous noise.

"LT . . . a bunch of guys . . . waving . . . civilian clothes . . . they might be Sahwa . . . armed."

While I didn't have the sights Sergeant Spade did in his hatch, a quick glance around my Stryker confirmed his report. There were definitely Iraqi men to our front who were definitely waving at us and definitely armed to the fangs with foreign rifles. The problem was, we couldn't walk behind the Stryker all the way north until we could confirm that these men were indeed Sons of Iraq. A series of shabby huts canalized the maneuverable terrain ten meters in front of our current position. The civilian world referred to this as a stalemate. The French called it an impasse. American soldiers knew it as a clusterfuck.

I felt compelled to instigate some course of action and remembered the first thing they taught us at the armor officer basic course: It was better to execute a shitty plan quickly than to wait around for the perfect plan. Well, I could do that. To hell with it, I thought, these bastards can't hit anything they shoot at anyway. Stepping around the side of the Stryker, I started walking toward the group of armed, faceless Arab men and told my guys to stay put. I took three steps, then felt a firm hand grab me from behind, at the neck collar, yanking me backward.

"No way, sir. Let me go first," Specialist Haitian Sensation said. He was nice enough to say it like I had a choice in the matter, as he had flung me back with the chiseled ease of someone who regularly benched twice my body weight. I regained my footing, smirked to myself, and followed, waving and loudly yelling all the friendly Arabic I could think of. The rest of the dismounts wedged out behind us.

The group in question turned out to be Sahwa, as we had hoped. Actually, they were Colonel Mohammed's Sahwa and had somehow ended up in a massive gunfight with the IA in a bizarre turf war instigated by a routine traffic checkpoint. I talked to Colonel Mohammed—as a retired Iraqi air force helicopter pilot, he still felt entitled to such a title, an assessment all of his people readily agreed with—and he was clearly rattled by the exchange, livid with the IA, and shocked by our being there. He also quickly claimed that groups of armed, masked men, unknown to him and unaffiliated with his Sons of Iraq, had joined the firefight soon after it began. They had been located near the Sahwa headquarters and had also been firing south, both at the IA and at us. He stressed that any bullets sent our way came from these men—not from the Sons of Iraq. No one knew where these armed, masked men had dematerialized to now.

Had the Sahwa intentionally been firing at us, hoping to kill an American in the midst of the chaos? Did the unknown masked men armed with AK-47s actually exist? Had the IA used a sledgehammer to swat a fly? Questions, questions, questions, and no amount of talking would yield anything resembling a coherent answer in the hours and days and weeks to come. To be blunt, though, my platoon didn't really give a fuck about the whos, the whys, or the hows of what had just happened. They were content with being able to go back to the combat outpost to squeeze in a few hours of sleep before our night patrol.

Personally, I had a hard time sleeping. My left leg kept twitching like it used to do the night before a big test. So I bought some cigarettes from Mojo and went out to the back porch. Staff Sergeant Bulldog was already there smoking. We nodded at one another but didn't say anything. Then I took a long drag, listened to the austere Islam prayer chants being broadcast over loudspeakers from a nearby mosque, and waited for the next frago.

II: EMBRACE THE SUCK
(OR NARRATIVE OF A COUNTERINSURGENT)

SPRING 2008

COIN [the military acronym for counterinsurgency] presents a complex and
often unfamiliar set of missions and considerations. In many ways,
the conduct of COIN is counterintuitive to the traditional U.S. view of war—
although COIN operations have actually formed a substantial
part of the U.S. military experience.
— *U.S. Army Field Manual No. 3-24* (2007),
Counterinsurgency Field Manual, 1–148

A COLD SPRING

The pale curtains of the desert sun opened softly every dawn. Spring arrived, bringing with it a heat eager to oppress.

Everywhere we went, it was always the same. The same tired mixture of anger, sadness, and hope. The same matching black pools of the browbeaten. The same bottled mistrust of a foreign people to whom the concept of trust was foreign. A people caged by their prisons of origin but hell-bent on survival, nonetheless. It wasn't like back home, where the homeless glared at shadows and backs and ideas. Over here, the poor cast their antipathy openly, in the light and at faces and ideals. I found it less jaded but more vacant and more hostile in intent—more like a junkie just realizing he already has injected his last life-fix.

With nothing to lose, it was easy for them to be honest with us. The eyes told all.

The stare: history's chronic shame. To the victor goes this eternal barb, the unblinking eye of the masses.

Telling them we knew what was best and that they needed to start relying on their own government and police so we could leave, that everyone would win that way and any help we could and did provide in the meantime at least offered a new spring in a land of endless, destitute winters, often didn't have the effect I thought it would. Or should.

Whether I thought we were there for something other than oil didn't matter when they thought we were. Open up the freedom present and treasure it, Iraqis! That's a bow of independence. . . . Pretty, isn't it? Give us back the wrapping paper; we're trying to recycle our democracy exports.

Thanks for the . . . gift? mistah. Leave a blank check and go home and try to eat us away or drink us away or life us away.

If looks killed, there would be far more than 4,000 American ghosts trapped in Babylon's sand spunk.

I had heard it before—the Hawaiians have a term for this visual hate. Da stinkeye, bruddah-man, bettah stay in Waikiki, haole, ya dig? I had seen it before—drunk college-boys in pastel Polo shirts with fat wallets should be more careful where they venture in the slums of the dirty South. And I had felt it before—scarecrow tourists with cameras and smiles and perfect white teeth didn't penetrate into the seedy backwaters of Dublin unless they wanted trouble. Have you ever knifed another man just to feel his very essence pour out of him in pools of running red and guts of unidentifiable slop onto the sidewalk?

Umm. Yes, we did. And no, no I have not.

Still, though. This was different. The flowers and hugs and cheers from the liberation only lasted for a few months before one stare became ten stares became one hundred stares. Suddenly the stare was the norm, house by house, block by block, and town by town, and all of the flower petals dried up, and we suddenly recognized that those cheers of gratitude were actually pleas for salvation. There were thousands of them, and they were everywhere. This pattern of starbursting degeneration, roughly translated from Arabic, meant occupation.

They told me, Lieutenant, you can't change a culture overnight. I knew that. I wasn't trying to change a culture. I was trying to defy the laws of existence.

I hated being hated. Strength and hardness didn't necessarily have to intertwine. But it sure was simpler that way.

The Iraqis might no longer have believed our black-as-the-abyss sunglasses could see through walls, like they did back in 2003, but I still felt better when I put them on. It made it a lot fucking easier to keep walking past the hollow stares of people when I thought that they thought I wasn't looking into their eyes. They wanted me to escape their pain without effect or a spare thought. They needed to believe I was that callous, and that was the reason I walked past them.

I later wondered if such was ever even an option. We tucked away what hopes we could, tried to ignore the moment, and hardened our souls for the strong duration. We knew that no flowers or hugs or cheers awaited us on the far end. All we had was this spring, searing in climate but cold in nature. At least it was ours and ours alone.

JUST ANOTHER FRONT

This today was just like any other except for the todays that were different.

A giant alarm clock rang with acrimony, bringing in the day far more brusquely than God intended when He designed the sluggish rising of the sun. I yawned loudly, slapped myself in the face, hopped off of the top bunk, and sauntered toward the TOC for intel updates, while SFC Big Country turned on the coffeemaker and went to the soldiers' rooms to wake them up. When I returned from the TOC, SFC Big Country handed me a fresh cup of coffee, Staff Sergeant Boondock was staring at the wall cursing to himself, and Staff Sergeant Bulldog—a notoriously slow mover in the morning—grunted from somewhere deep underneath his blankets.

"Time to get up, sheik," I told him. "Your doting followers await."

Some mixture of profanity-laced grogginess and Southern slurring usually let me know that he was awake. Then I joined my men at the gear racks just outside of our rooms, where we donned layers and layers of cumbersome body armor, swelling in mass and bulk like the knights of yore. The three newest Gravediggers—Specialist Tunnel, Private Hot Wheels, and Private Stove Top, fresh arrivals from Hawaii—watched in confusion as Private Van Wilder emerged from his room dressed only in his underwear, rubbing his rather sizable belly.

"Don't act like you're not impressed," he cracked. And then, to a laughing Private Smitty, he said, "The FNGs [fucking new guys] keep staring at my balls. . . . They must want me. Can you really blame them?"

All of our new soldiers qualified as certified good ole boys from the American South, and all were proud infantrymen. Specialist Tunnel, from Arkansas, arrived eager to match his twin brother, who had already earned his combat patch in theater and survived an IED-strike. Private Stove Top, a native of the North Carolinian coast, and Private Hot Wheels, from the Georgian swamps, came to us straight out of basic training, but it hadn't taken much prodding for them to come out of their shock-shells. When Private Smitty accused Private Hot Wheels of being a redneck because of his accent, Private Hot Wheels snapped back with, "I ain't a redneck. I'm just country. Rednecks aren't smart enough to go armadillo huntin.'"

Some thirty minutes later, after a quick breakfast, twenty black sunglasses bowed toward my map, listening to a plan they knew would change on the move. A background of pounding bass, coming from Staff Sergeant Boondock's Stryker and courtesy of the rock band Metallica, provided a steady backdrop for my words about rules of engagement, the same words I said the day before and the same ones I said the day after. After I finished, I asked if there were any questions, and there weren't. I told the platoon to mount

Staff Sergeant Boondock (right) and Private Das Boot stand in front of a pair of armored Stryker vehicles in the farmlands outside of Saba al-Bor. Providing overwatch security for the local community, while usually tedious, became a necessity in the Iraq counterinsurgency.

up, and SFC Big Country barked out last-minute priorities of work to the junior NCOs.

"Let's rock and roll, you stupid bastards," Private Van Wilder crowed, as he rolled into his driver's seat. "I got a hot date tonight with a fat Iraqi chick, and I don't want to be late. Fat chicks love my molest-ache!"

I climbed into the back of my Stryker, which had already been prepped immaculately by Sergeant Spade, Specialist Flashback, and Private Smitty. All I needed to do was plug in and start conducting radio calls. In the beginning, I had tried to help my guys ready the vehicle, but this had only horrified Sergeant Spade, who thought it reflected poorly on them; now I just stayed out of their way and let them do their jobs. Phoenix was already loaded up in a seat and bantered back and forth with Private Smitty, arguing about some video game fallout from the previous evening. I gave the platoon three minutes, then asked them if they were ready to begin our patrol.

"White, this is White 1," I said. "Report your redcon [readiness condition] status in sequence."

"This, uhh, White 2," Staff Sergeant Bulldog drawled. "We redcon-1."

"White 1, this is White 3. We're redcon-1!" Staff Sergeant Boondock burst.

"This is 4," SFC Big Country thundered. "Let's roll."

"On your move, 2," I said, watching the wheels of my senior scout's vehicle churn forward. I let X-ray know we were departing, and then, just like every day, our Strykers moved past the gate, out of the wire, and into the enduring reality of Saba al-Bor.

Our stated mission for the day was to conduct an electricity assessment of one of the local Shia blocks. We weren't supposed to use the term *presence patrol* anymore—some doctrinal debate fought at levels way above me had resulted in this change in policy—but pretty much anytime an American convoy of combat vehicles maneuvered in Iraq, it acted as such. At every corner and sidewalk in every neighborhood of our AO, the reactions were exactly the same—the children waved giddily, hoping for chocolate; the women dressed head to toe in black robes stared rigidly at the ground; the old men nodded with hard, empty eyes; and the young men stared back at us callously. All cleared a path for our Strykers. Somewhere over the course of this war, they'd learned not to get in the way of the armored vehicles and their machine guns.

We turned onto Route New York, a side street off of Maples, and stopped at an empty lot across the street from a long-abandoned school. Staff Sergeant Bulldog found an open area for us to coil our vehicles. "This work, 1?" he asked.

"Sure does," I responded. "Let's get on the ground."

Tired, dirty boots met Mesopotamian soil for the umpteenth time. SFC Big Country, ever the perfectionist, adjusted the vehicles slightly, optimizing security scans for our gunners. Like locusts descending on ancient Egypt, Iraqi children surrounded us immediately, clamoring for our attention and clawing at our pockets. "Mistah, mistah, gimme chocolata!" they screamed. "Gimme football! Gimme, gimme, gimme!" My men reacted differently to the horde, depending on their general patience disposition and the amount of sleep they got the night prior.

"You gimme chocolata!" Private Smitty replied, picking up one of the kids, twirling him around.

"Gotta love the effects of the welfare state. Go play in some traffic," Specialist Flashback said, reaching for a cigarette and ignoring the children gathering around him.

"Nothing like enabling future terrorists," Staff Sergeant Boondock shouted, all the while handing out candy. He noticed me arching an eyebrow his way and started chuckling. "Don't judge me, LT, and don't you dare think

I've gone soft. It's all a part of my master plan."

I turned to a small child with doubting eyes, ruffled the hair on his head, and pointed at him. "Ali Baba?" I asked, using the Arabic term for thief and general villain. The group of kids around him giggled hysterically and chanted, "Ali Baba! Ali Baba!" while the victim of my slandering protested his new label. I put my hands out and let the kids play with the hard plastic that lined the knuckles on my gloves.

The children ran away from Private Das Boot, petrified that the American giant would accidentally step on them. They pointed and whispered from afar though, and Phoenix translated their murmurings: "A man that tall must be able to see the whole world." Private Das Boot just snorted and shook his head, bumming a cigarette from Specialist Flashback.

"Don't these little bastards ever go to school?" Sergeant Cheech asked. I didn't think it was a serious question, although it was a legitimate one.

I looked across the coil and saw Corporal Spot turn to Sergeant Axel. "Think it's cool if I give them dip and tell them it's chocolate?" he asked.

"No," SFC Big Country said, walking up behind them. He had a large trash bag filled with toys sent to us from family members back home. He attempted to organize the gaggle of children into a single-file line of disciplined order, a concept so foreign to them that they simply laughed at his directions and encircled him. Most of the children barely came up to his waist, and while towering over them, my platoon sergeant began to pass out small plastic cars. Pandemonium ensued.

"Stay in line! Goddamn it, stay in line!" he yelled without effect. He ignored the temptation just to throw the bag into the middle of their youthful jubilee, though, and handed the toys out to the snatching hands one at a time.

"Now the fireworks start," Doc said to Specialist Tunnel, watching as the kids began to steal the cars from one another, often using the toys themselves as synthetic weapons of mass destruction against each other. This phenomenon inevitably led to hysterical cries and tears. Staff Sergeant Bulldog strutted over to one of the head-cracking bullies, grabbed a toy away from him in a huff, and brought it over to a well-mannered runt standing away from the mass, watching quietly.

"Staff Sergeant Bulldog, you're the biggest bully there is!" Specialist Haitian Sensation yelled, smiling. "You bullied the bully!"

Staff Sergeant Bulldog nodded, satisfied. "You know it."

"Time to go," I said, moving away from the vehicles with one dismount team, while the other one stayed with the Strykers for local security. Half the children followed our movements into their neighborhood, something I didn't mind. Being encased by a bubble of Iraqi street urchins probably contributed to our security element in ways I barely comprehended. The enemy had to fight the public relations battle as well, and shooting at Americans surrounded by local kids wouldn't go over well with the Arab soccer moms.

The Iraqi children spiraled around our wedge formation, collecting rocks out of sewage dunes the way their Western counterparts picked out seashells on beaches of white sand. I sporadically selected local citizens to engage in discussion, sometimes seeking out the welcoming faces, sometimes seeking out the hostile ones. This day was like any other day spent asking the populace to explain the details of their daily existences: Life in Iraq sucked and had always sucked and continued to suck. The specific neighborhood didn't matter; the citizens of Saba al-Bor all had the same complaints. "We don't have clean water." "We don't have jobs." "We only have fifteen minutes of electricity per day because the Sunnis take it all." But the Sunnis say the Shias take all the electricity, I remembered. "They Ali Babas. We think America very good. Gimme water, mistah. Gimme job, mistah. Gimme power, America." Gimme, gimme, gimme.

"We're trying," I told them, "but shit like this takes time." I felt momentarily obliged to instruct the locals to turn to their own government for these civic matters, as a way of empowering themselves, but quickly discarded such thoughts. I'd already learned that lesson. Mere mention of the Iraqi government just led to another stratosphere of bitching from the Saba al-Bor citizenry. I also internally debated whether I should discuss the history of America's evolving democracy and explain that civil services took time to establish themselves, especially in Third World countries. Ever heard of the Articles of Confederation, Mister Unkempt Iraqi Man addicted to the handout? That era made the Paul Bremer years look like pure genius. I smiled to myself, thinking about this lunacy. I had tried that approach once too, some weeks ago. It hadn't spawned the intended effect.

I sometimes felt my compassion for fellow human beings leaking out of me like oil leaving an engine, so slow it was barely evident and yet dripping with enough regularity that I knew the problem was severe in nature. I had only been deployed for three months; twelve more months of seepage waited. I hoped being cognizant of this leak would help me plug it back up when the time came to do so. Not that such a time awaited on any near horizon.

I took another sip of chai. I now conversed with a group of local men who claimed the Sunnis didn't let them use the fuel station on the other end of town. They also insinuated that the Sunni Sons of Iraq were housing a sniper somewhere near this fuel station, knowing full well that the word "sniper" ensured we would check out the validity of the tip—even if "sniper" for Arabs usually just meant an unknown person firing a gun somewhere within audible distance. This qualified 90 percent of Iraqi men for sniper status.

As the conversation continued, I caught a fleeting glimpse of two pairs of alluring dark eyes peeking out at us from behind a cracked front door across the street, alluring dark eyes that belonged to young female faces and flowing black robes that failed to cover every curve the way they were designed to.

I wasn't the only one who took notice. Phoenix left me alone to discuss business in broken sign language with the men, while he walked across the street, waving the young women out. Usually this direct tactic failed to work, but today it somehow managed to succeed; I assumed the girls' parents were not home. Without my terp, my conversation with the locals quickly dissipated, but Phoenix's exchange had just begun. We spent the next ten minutes pulling security around a house in a small alleyway of Saba al-Bor so that our twenty-one-year-old terp could flirt with two giggling Iraqi teenagers in Arabic. I finally yelled, "Phoenix! Wrap it up!" He smiled, embarrassed on finally realizing an entire section of scouts was watching him, but he still pulled out a piece of paper to write down his cell phone number. He gave one of the girls the paper and waltzed back over to me.

"I big pimp," he said.

"You big liar," I responded. "Those chicks think you're an American, don't they?" His black skin and dummy rifle often confused the locals.

He shrugged his shoulders and repeated one of his favorite sayings, picked up from watching Staff Sergeant Bulldog play poker. "If you ain't bull-shittin', you don't deserve to be playin'."

When we returned to our Strykers, a frago message from Captain White-back awaited us. Due to an extemporaneous meeting at Camp Taji regarding squadron uniform standards, he wasn't going to be able to make a planned engagement with Sheik Banana-Hands, so he needed me to go in his stead.

And. Roger.

Time passed differently on missions; seconds, minutes, and hours disappeared into an abyss of repetition and flickering echoes, sometimes slowing things down, sometimes speeding things up. Sometimes time stopped so that the mind could take a mental snapshot of an unchecked shadow, a dead dog, a lonely child, a desert sun fading into the abstract possibilities of to-morrow. A stranger in a strange land issued habitual orders on the radio with-out any real thought. And then we were on the south end of Saba al-Bor, traveling on Route Swords, to Sheik Banana-Hands.

Goddamn it. Remember why you're here, I thought to myself. It isn't for your dreams. It's for theirs. Stay sharp.

"Chai hunting again, sir?" My platoon sergeant asked on the radio.

"It is absolutely instrumental to the continued development of Iraqi se-curity that as much chai as possible be consumed by Coalition forces," I replied. "It's somewhere in the counterinsurgency manual."

My Strykers automatically moved to the intersections, gunners scanning alleyways and rooftops, waiting, hoping really, for a heat signature to be identified as a terrorist's skull. Ten Iraqis in body armor and carrying AK-47s were clustered around a small gate in front of Sheik Banana-Hands's warlord manor—a sizable two-story house by Western standards but ab-solutely Gomorrah-esque for Saba al-Bor. As soon as Specialist Flashback dropped the back ramp, I stalked over to the Iraqis position with Phoenix. Private Smitty scurried by me, assuming the point position. He took his un-official role as my guardian very seriously, and I'd still been unable to figure out which NCO tasked him with that mission. It wasn't like I wandered off by myself. Not anymore, at least.

Sheik Banana-Hands greeted us at the gate, hand outstretched, smile open and welcoming—just a bit too open and welcoming for Staff Sergeant Boondock. "I'll take charge of the dismounts out here, sir," he said, chuckling at my offer to join us inside. "Let me know when I can use my weapon again."

We walked into Sheik Banana-Hands's office, Private Smitty in front, Sergeant Cheech and Corporal Spot filing in behind me. They posted security inside the room with one of the local Sons of Iraq, with whom Private Smitty exchanged cigarettes. I joined the sheik at the back end of the room, away from the doorway and all of the windows. We sat down across from one an-other on hard wooden chairs, and Phoenix grabbed a plastic chair from a corner and sat next to me.

"Captain Whiteback is very sorry he could not make it today. He only missed this because an emergency popped up at the last minute."

The sheik covered his heart with his long fingers. "I hope no one is hurt," he said.

I thought about the meeting Captain Whiteback had been forced to attend and the circumstances leading up to it; Lieutenant Colonel Larry and Sergeant Major Curly believed the line commanders and first sergeants weren't listening to their demands for strict adherence to the published uniform standard. "Me too," I replied. "How are you, though?"

He sighed heavily and stroked his recently trimmed grey beard. "I am very tired," he said. "I have been awakened in the night many times due to Mahdi Army attacking my checkpoints."

"I know. We've been sent out three times in the past week to help."

He nodded. "Yes, thank you, thank you, from the bottom of my heart. Coalition force support is very important to us, and it gives my men strength. But it is not just no sleep that makes me tired."

I arched an eyebrow Phoenix's way, thinking something hadn't been communicated correctly, which caused the sheik to continue talking.

"You will see it is harder to sleep when you get old," he said. "You are still young. Your mind stays with you with the years that come."

Phoenix's translation wasn't the greatest, but it got the point across. The sheik had explained a concept I already understood and was slowly beginning to experience more and more: The weightier the decisions of the day, the longer they lingered in the night. Enough of my soldiers had accused me of being an insomniac that I had started to believe them.

We continued to talk, three very different men of very different cultural backgrounds and motivations and experiences, stuck in this moment of time like a bug caught in a spiderweb. This particular web stuck with bureaucratic inanity and slowness: What the sheik's people needed and craved, we couldn't provide or wouldn't, in the name of legitimizing the Iraqi government; what I needed and craved, he couldn't provide or wouldn't, due to the potential future of his nation and his neighborhood, his family and himself. We both knew America's time and interest in Iraq was fleeting.

Some forty-five minutes later, after a second round of chai, I realized that I was yawning and we were no longer talking about security or electricity or medical clinics but about Clint Eastwood movies. I thanked Sheik Banana-Hands for his hospitality and began to stand up, but he leaned over and squeezed my shoulder, speaking in his native tongue.

"He say that he has gift for you, LT," Phoenix said.

Sheik Banana-Hands yelled something in Arabic at his Sahwa bodyguard and clapped, which caused the bodyguard to bounce up from his chair like a jack-in-the-box and disappear into a side room. Phoenix whispered into my ear. "He say something about tube of mortar."

Fifteen seconds later, the younger Iraqi walked back in, holding a Russian military mortar tube and tripod. Both were immaculately clean. The sheik spoke again.

"He say that his men find this in neighborhood behind house, position facing to the market," Phoenix translated.

I tried not to sigh audibly. It was all a part of the counterinsurgency game. Like we didn't know they all had their own personal caches leftover from the sectarian wars. Whatever, I thought. It was one more weapon off the street.

I thanked him, cupping my right hand over my heart. "It pleases me that you and your men care so deeply for your people," I said. "Security brings peace, and peace is what we all seek."

Sheik Banana-Hands also placed his right hand over his heart. "Peace is wonderful," he said. "Both in here"—he tapped at his chest—"and around us."

I stared at the wall behind the sheik and fought through the arriving space-out. Phoenix nodded in agreement, moved by the profundity of Banana-Hands's words. I used to have both, I thought. Now I just hope for either.

I didn't say that though. I just stood up and shook hands with the sheik. "Let's move," I told my soldiers, as Private Smitty scooped up the mortar tube and tripod.

We walked back outside, and I told Staff Sergeant Boondock to load up the local security. I thought about getting back to the combat outpost. The Joes would flock to the phones and to the computers, of course, still connected with the old world, while the NCOs would head to their makeshift poker table, content and comfortable in our new one. I had a patrol debrief to write, but after that, a nap was more than in order.

When I got back to my Stryker and got on the radio, however, SFC Big Country relayed a message from the TOC. They needed us to meet up with a local woman who worried her son had fallen in with a bad crowd—the insurgent, IED-emplacing kind. She wanted us to talk to him and hopefully scare him out of a future that would lead to American 50-caliber rounds riddling his body. Fuck it, I thought. Anything for a mom.

"White," I said. "Throw up the hate fist, and let me know when you're redcon-1. We got another follow-on mission."

"This, uhh, White 2," Staff Sergeant Bulldog drawled. "We redcon-1."

"This is White 3," Staff Sergeant Boondock boomed. "Hate fists are up, and we're redcon-1!"

"This is 4," SFC Big Country thundered. "Let's move."

"On your move, 2," I said, watching the wheels of my senior scout's vehicle churn forward.

This today was just like any other except for the todays that were different.

OLIVER TWISTED

Just another day in the Suck. Just another day of counterinsurgency tedium, solving a nonconventional, nation-building, political problem with a conventional military used to nation destroying that sometimes forgot it was trying to be nonconventional. Just another day of our dismount teams walking with me between creeping Strykers, winding through the back alleys and alley backs of Saba al-Bor. Just another day of talking to the locals and listening to their multitude of gripes, bitches, and complaints. Just another day of "mistah, mistah, gimme—"

"Please, sir, I want some more."

Last calling station . . . say again? You're coming in lucid and earthshattering.

I looked down at the originator of the voice. Three Iraqi girls, all with shining black eyes and long black hair, had crowded around me and Suge Knight. They had their hands outstretched, hoping. All three were dressed in pink Barbie sweats caked in months' worth of mud.

"What did you just say?" I asked.

I doubt any of them understood me, as they repeated their original request: "Mistah, mistah, gimme chocolata!"

I shook my head. The sun must be getting to me, I thought. I yelled at one of the gunners to toss down three bottles of water and turned back to the three children. I handed one of the girls a bottle of water, then I handed Suge one, and I kept the third.

"He has chocolata," I said to the girls, pointing at an oblivious Sergeant Cheech, located twenty feet to our front, peering down an alley. The girls bounded off in the direction of my finger, moving like hunters zeroing in on wounded prey.

"You okay, LT?" Suge asked me. "You do not seem happy."

Staff Sergeant Bulldog takes a local Iraqi child for a spin on a commandeered bicycle.

I smirked and patted him on the back. "I'm good, man. Drink up, and we'll keep moving. But no Coke!"

Suge giggled and spoke. "You are good leader of me, LT!" A few days before, I had learned that Suge suffered from diabetes, something he had known about for ten years or so. Such knowledge hadn't stopped his sugar cravings and soda abuse, though, something we were all trying to wean him off of now, for his own good.

I took a swig of cool water, and as it dribbled down my throat, my dismount radio crackled. "White 1, this is White 3."

I snatched up the hand mic, eager to find out if Staff Sergeant Boondock had discovered something beyond the status quo of disgruntled locals. "Send it, 3."

"Yeah . . . we have a situation back here. I think you may wanna check it out yourself."

I glanced over at Suge, who had wandered over to Specialist Tunnel's position to yell at some surly teenagers for failing to produce their ID cards in a timely manner. Artful dodgers, the lot of 'em. Staff Sergeant Boondock was a block over, near a house I had purposely chosen to bypass; some weeks earlier, after putting out a small house fire, we smelled burning fur and went inside the house to investigate. We found the smoldering carcasses of dead dogs scattered across the main room, as lifeless as the Arabian Desert itself. After questioning the neighborhood, we learned that after the fire started, the locals had hauled the already-deceased wild dogs into the house, hoping to create some sort of roasted meat for food. That was the type of poverty found here—and why something as simple as a candy bar sent throngs of children into mass hysteria. I didn't want to head back down that street, but if Staff Sergeant Boondock—he of the "The way out is through" mantra— had discovered a situation that required the lieutenant's attention, duty beckoned, sensibilities be damned.

"We're en route," I said.

In the distance, I spotted yet another mob of Iraqi children serving as brush to the redwoods of American soldiers. Staff Sergeant Boondock's transmission had brought over SFC Big Country as well, but as Suge and I strolled up to their position, they both started to wave us away.

"My bad, sir," Staff Sergeant Boondock said. "I think I misunderstood the little fucker. His house got blown up last year, but at first I thought he said they still had bombs there. False alarm."

"Well, we got Suge here now," SFC Big Country said. "We might as well make sure." My platoon sergeant had his hand on the shoulder of a young boy with squinty eyes, dirty black locks of hair, and a lackadaisical strut, whom he guided up to our terp.

"You got the condolence funds paperwork in your vehicle?" I asked SFC Big Country. Only Allah knew how this kid's house had really blown up, but we had learned very painfully that the best way to defuse angry Iraqis was to hand them a stack of confusing paperwork that potentially led to financial reimbursement, if filled out correctly. It was like the Victorian-era British Poor Laws or, in more modern terms, what the lady at the DMV did to keep the line moving.

"He say that Ali Baba blow up his house ten months ago," Suge translated. "It kill his whole family except for him and little brother. He ask for mulasim [lieutenant]."

Corporal Spot, who pulled security away from the Stryker, turned around and shook his head in troubled dismay. Suge continued.

"He say that his brother is at house now. They still live there, and neighbors watch over them."

"What about the bomb, Suge?" I asked. "Get to the bomb." I wanted to sympathize with the kid, and I would—just as soon as I got back to the combat outpost and didn't have to worry about snipers turning my head into a passive verb.

Suge nodded at me and switched back to Arabic. The boy responded, and Suge translated again. "He say that there is still bomb in his front yard. He say that his brother stays there to guard it."

"I knew it!" Staff Sergeant Boondock erupted in passion. "I fucking knew the kid said there was something still there."

"Where's his house?" SFC Big Country asked.

Suge pointed across the street. "He say his house is right there." It wasn't near the roasted-dog house, luckily.

I walked up to the boy, putting out my gloved fist so he could pound it. He proved wary of the plastic lining, though, and instead seized my hand and tugged.

"What your name?" he demanded in broken English.

I looked down at the child, amused at his impudence. The cocky Iraqi kids were few and far between, but they tended to be the ones that stuck with you. "Schlonic," I began, using an Iraqi slang greeting. I pointed at my chest. "My name is Matt." I pointed back at him. "What is your name?"

He stuck a thumb into my leg, which caused everyone else to laugh, including Suge.

"Maaaahhhhhtttt," he said, struggling with the terseness of the English vowel. "My name Yusef."

"Well, Yusef, lead the way," I told the boy, tousling his hair. As he dashed across his neighborhood, four American soldiers and one terp in tow, his tiny body literally shook with excitement. We followed, wedging out into formation, rifles at the low-ready.

Yusef's house—or more accurately, what was left of it—had certainly seen better days. Building rubble and concrete bits of foundation were dispersed around the area the boy led us to, and holes the size of bowling balls perforated the roof. A front stoop led to an entry room that simply wasn't there anymore, leaving a large hole between the last step and the beginning of the house. A small boy with curly black hair, presumably Yusef's younger brother, sat on the stoop to nowhere. His shorts on the right side hung inconclusively off of his right leg; he was missing the foot entirely, and the leg itself was permanently twisted around at a 90-degree angle just below the knee. The right side of his face was covered in dark pink scars, starting at his hairline and jutting downward, across his cheeks, to the top of his chin.

We waved at him, but he continued to stare vacantly at the ground directly in front of him, indifferent to our mission.

We had approached from the side, and Yusef stopped ten feet short of his house to point to a noticeable depression underneath a tree to our right. A quick burst of Arabic followed.

"He say bomb in that hole," Suge translated.

I told Suge to stay back with the child, and I skulked up to the pit in question, moving as circumspectly as a beaten wife, while the other Grave-diggers clover-leafed around. A 40-mm Russian mortar, rusty but still impos-ing, lay right in the middle of the depression.

"Well . . . there it is," SFC Big Country said. "Hey, Suge, ask the kid if this is the only one."

Suge exchanged a series of words with Yusef and yelled back. "Yes! Only one bomb!"

"Can we move it?" Staff Sergeant Boondock asked.

The answer to this question was obviously no, but no one felt like calling Explosive Ordinance Disposal (EOD) for just one corroded 40-mm mortar, no matter how potentially explosive. The very real possibility of self-removal existed, but honestly, we would have rather blown up and died an embar-rassing death than overreact and live as a punch line. We all simultaneously turned to Corporal Spot, remembering that he had received some mortar training before he became an active duty scout. "I'll check it out," he said.

Corporal Spot moved down into the hole and peered at the mortar round. "I don't see why we can't move it," he said matter-of-factly. "It looks like the filling's all gone."

Great. The filling was gone. Unfortunately, at the Scout Leader's Course, they taught me about screen lines, actions on contact, and how to call for fire. Nothing about mortars or mortar fillings. All I knew about mortars was that, much like dynamite and angry women, they went Boom! when tampered with. SFC Big Country and Staff Sergeant Boondock didn't seem any more at ease either.

Corporal Spot seemed relaxed, though, and looked at me. "I can pick it up, sir. It ain't a big deal."

I felt a familiar buzzing at the back of my brain, laced with faint traces of fear. Just in time, I thought. The lieutenant in me kicked back in and stated that you should never have a soldier do something you yourself wouldn't do. I hopped into the hole and sidled up next to Corporal Spot.

"I got it, man," I said.

"Just move it slowly," he said. "It's nothing as long as it ain't attached to anything."

I picked the mortar up, doing so with my nondominant hand, and tried to ignore the impulse to close my eyes. Nothing happened. I smiled in relief, broadly and easily and purely, probably for the first time since we had left Kuwait. Staff Sergeant Boondock took a picture of me clowning around with the mortar. We exchanged some relieved chatter; SFC Big Country was especially thankful that he didn't have to make the call back to the TOC letting them know he had let his lieutenant blow himself up.

We began walking back to our Strykers, Suge falling in beside us. I turned to Yusef. "Shakrin," I stuttered, thanking him for his help. He nodded. There was nothing else to say. The crippled and disfigured boy continued to stare at the ground. I doubted this Oliver Twist would ever find a patron. I just hoped that someday he would see something other than dirt and concrete on that piece of ground.

SFC Big Country and I sat on the front stoop of the combat outpost that afternoon, watching our soldiers file in, dirty and tired after yet another long mission, eager for a few hours of downtime. As Suge and Sergeant Axel walked by, they debated whether or not the first sergeant would stop Suge from getting two plates of dinner again. Suge maintained that because he had two wives to satisfy, and because Allah forbade him from eating the sausage that smelled oh so good, he needed two dinners, but the first sergeant didn't buy it.

"You alright, sir?" my platoon sergeant asked me. "You've looked pretty tore up all day. You got the Iraqi ass-piss?" referring to the mysterious sickness we all came down with in the initial months of our deployment, one time or another. No amount of good hygiene, soap, and classes led by the medics totally cleansed the combat outposts of the Iraqi ass-piss.

I did my best to smile. "No ass-piss, and I'm good," I said. "I just need a Guinness." As I finished my sentence, Specialist Haitian Sensation walked up, after clearing his weapon at the clearing barrel.

"Hey, sir, Sergeant," he said, "can I ask you guys a question?"

Our missions through the ghettos always affected him; it didn't take a very insightful platoon leader to recognize this was due to his own upbringing around poverty in Haiti. Still, the gravity of his follow-up question managed to rattle me out of my own introspection.

"What do you think I'd need to do to adopt one of those kids? One of the orphans? For when we go home, I mean."

SFC Big Country took a drag from his cigarette. "I have no clue," he said. "But we'll look into it, if you're serious about it."

I scratched my head, searching for a light-hearted witticism to mellow out the immensity of the situation. I couldn't think of one, so I told Specialist Haitian Sensation it would be a lengthy process, but hell, all we had was time in Iraq, after all. He smiled contently and walked into the combat outpost. We followed shortly thereafter.

PAYDAY

As I walked down the north hallway of the combat outpost, fresh from a long discussion with Suge about the British missionaries who originally taught him English, I heard a faint humming from the main foyer of the building. When I rounded the corner into the foyer, that faint hum became a low roar. What the fuck is going on? I thought. A quick glance down the stairs provided an answer.

It looked like every Son of Iraq in Saba al-Bor and its surrounding villages was crammed into our ground-floor room. Dozens upon dozens of young military-aged Iraqis snaked around the room, resembling a coiling line, which extended all the way out of the front door, where dozens more young men awaited. The Iraqis were separated by clothing and grouped accordingly; some wore khaki brown shirts with matching baseball caps, others sported navy-blue armbands emblazoned with Iraqi flags, and still others wore non-descript black vests and blue jeans. All were chattering excitedly. Most of the sheiks had rounded up their men into various gaggles, but that hadn't stopped a few outliers from cutting the line, leading to continuous, animated protesting from the other Sahwa. Our troop's artillery officer, Skerk, who doubled as the contracts officer, sat at a table at the far end of the room, handing out stacks of crisp American dollars. Even from afar, I saw the stress on his face and the veins in his thick Slovakian neck throbbing. He and the terp Snoop Dogg kept trying to get the sheiks to organize their men better, but any improved arrangement only lasted through the next payment. It was a never-ending cycle of chaos.

I didn't have another mission for a few hours, so I decided to wander downstairs and see if my fellow lieutenant needed some help. As I reached the ground floor and became immersed in the sea of Sahwa, I saw that two soldiers from Headquarters platoon were posted behind the payment table as armed guards, and one of them was Specialist Fuego. I nodded at him and smirked; he responded by cocking a fake pistol with his hand, aiming it toward his mouth, and pulling the trigger. Sweat and body heat saturated the room, despite all of the wide-open doors and windows. As the Sahwa members were not allowed to carry their AK-47s into the combat outpost, the presence of the armed guards provided me some peace of mind.

"Salaam, Haydar," I said, patting the sheik on the back. I exchanged a quick handshake with him, then kept moving to the front table. After grabbing an exuberant teenage Sahwa by the shoulders and putting him back in line, I finally got there.

"I thought this shit wasn't happening until Friday," I said to Skerk, taking a seat to his left.

"We had to push it up," he replied, still counting out fifteen twenty-dollar bills per man. "Fridays are their holy day."

"Oh, yeah," I said, a bit embarrassed to have forgotten such a basic bit of cultural information.

"These cocksuckers," he continued, taking a quick break from his count to spit a big wad of dip into an empty bottle, "I staggered the groups timewise to avoid this clusterfuck. And what do they do? They all show up at nine in the morning, all together, all claiming that this was the time their group was supposed to fucking be here."

"Who's manning their checkpoints right now?"

"Good fucking question. I told Captain Whiteback I wasn't going to pay any of them, except for Haydar's guys, who were slated for this timeslot. He told me I still had to do this, and we'd fix it next month. Probably the right call—we don't need a riot breaking out here—but still . . . fucking Christ!" He went back to counting out twenty-dollar bills and verifying names on his checklist, while Snoop Dogg, who stood on Skerk's other side, yelled at the Son of Iraq at the front of the line to keep his hands at his sides.

So. It seemed that the American efficiency in schedule making hadn't rubbed off on our Mesopotamian comrades quite yet. In Saba al-Bor, where jobs were as scarce as a happy Hemingway ending and stable, legal finances were even rarer, the promise of a monthly stipend at the American castle meant one showed up early and eager, timelines be damned.

"Hey, man, I'm gonna go try and get these guys to calm down for you," I said, realizing that I contributed nothing staying seated.

"Thanks." He spat into the bottle again. "And good luck. It's a war out there!"

I stood up and bumped back into Sheik Haydar, whose men were just now beginning to cycle through the payment station. Dressed in his standard camel-skin coat, blue jeans, and red-and-white headdress, Haydar waited in line with his men behind Sheik Banana-Hands's Sahwa. Behind them were Colonel Mohammed and his Sons of Iraq, and behind them waited Boss Johnson II's group. Other than the already occupied Snoop Dogg, I didn't see any terps, so, with the grace of a donkey, I attempted a conversation with Haydar.

"Shakrin," I started. "Shakrin for keeping your men in line." I then clarified my statement by pointing at his men and using the hand-and-arm signal for a file.

Haydar laughed deeply and opened his eyes wide. "Crazy, this place! I tell that we all get the money, we just . . ." He began to gesture with his hands, searching for a way to describe patience.

"Daheftihim, daheftihim" (I understand, I understand). "It looks like your men all have their armbands now, yes?" I grabbed a piece of cloth on my uniform at the shoulder, then pointed at his men lined up behind him, who all wore navy-blue armbands with Iraqi flags.

"Yes," Haydar said, nodding. "We got last ones six days ago."

Impulsively, I flashed an obnoxiously American thumbs-up and smiled openly, both of which were met in kind by the sheik. I then heard some louder-than-normal yelling from behind us and, after shaking Haydar's hand one more time, walked that way to check it out.

I soon found the source of the clamor: Boss Johnson II stood between two men, both of whom were still shouting at each other. One of them wore the khaki brown shirt of Sheik Banana-Hands's group, while the other was decked out in the black vest and blue jeans that signified Boss Johnson II's men.

Boss Johnson II had assumed his brother's leadership role post–car bombing and with the exception of spotting the dead Johnson a few inches and having a thicker beard, he was the spitting image of his sibling. If he mourned his predecessor's demise, he did so in the private confines of his own home. The day after locals scooped his brother's remains into a kitchen pot, he had shown up at the combat outpost, contracts in hand, eager to talk to Captain Whiteback about finances.

I eventually got the two rival Sahwa to stop yelling by repeatedly shouting, "Shut the fuck up. Just shut the fuck up!" over them, but I was unable to figure out how the argument had started, as neither of these Sons of Iraq nor Boss Johnson II spoke even the basic English that Haydar did. My rudimentary Arabic certainly wasn't any help, either. Boss Johnson II just kept shaking his head and mumbling, "Ali Baba! Ali Baba!" which did not ease the palpable tension of the moment.

Luckily, I saw Specialist Haitian Sensation and an IP known as the Bulldozer outside of the front door, near a broom closet Mojo had recently turned into a shop. I waved both over, knowing that the Bulldozer's English and Specialist Haitian Sensation's Arabic would improve our current station.

"This place is wild'n' out!" Specialist Haitian Sensation grinned ear to ear, as usual, flashing his pearly white teeth. "It's worse than the Superdome during Hurricane Katrina." I froze, unsure how to respond, while my soldier continued, giggling. "It's okay, sir. I'm black—I can say that!"

I blinked my eyes now, even more unsure of how to respond, and changed the subject. "Think you and Bulldozer could help me out here? These guys are arguing, and I have no idea why."

The Bulldozer, suitably named for his dense build and even denser approach to searching houses, and Specialist Haitian Sensation quickly went to work, coaching one another through words and phrases in the different languages. My soldier, who already spoke fluent Spanish, French, English, and Haitian Creole, had proven a quick study, and his grasp of the Arabic language expanded daily.

"Well, sir, this guy"—Specialist Haitian Sensation pointed at the Sahwa member in khaki—"says that his group already went through, and he was late, so he just tried to get his paycheck. These other guys"—he now pointed at Boss Johnson II's crew—"they stopped him from cutting and told him they'd slice open his mother's throat or something if he got paid before they did. That's the juice of it, ya feel me?"

I sighed. "Yeah, I got you," I said. "Thanks. He's right. Banana-Hands finished up already. You"—I pointed at the Sahwa in khaki—"you stay here." I pointed at the ground and then at Boss Johnson II. Turning to Boss Johnson II, I continued, "Tell Boss Johnson II here that I'm considering him responsible for this man's getting paid now." I grabbed the hands of the two men who had been arguing and raised them in triumph, like a boxing referee. "Today, you get paid together, or you don't get paid at all! Sunni and Shias, unite!"

The Bulldozer laughed with delight at my solution but assured me it would work. "They be friends for money," he said. "For now." He and Specialist Haitian Sensation stayed with Boss Johnson II and the men, ensuring such.

I took a deep breath and assessed the progress of the line. It wrapped itself all of the way out of the entryway and into the concrete courtyard that led to the main ECP. As I debated whether to sneak back upstairs quietly and let this debacle sort itself out, I spotted the terp Super Mario, Mojo, Mojo's father, Rahdi, and Abu Adnan in the open courtyard. Abu Adnan, dressed in a mud-stained grey dishdasha, yelled passionately at Rahdi, who kept trying to speak in rebuttal to no avail. Figuring Saba al-Bor's mayor could use some assistance, I walked up to their circle.

Abu Adnan was a sheik and Sahwa leader of one of Saba al-Bor's eastern villages, just northeast and over a ravine from Haydar's village. Unlike Haydar, though, Abu Adnan had facilitated AQI movement and operations in his village throughout the Iraq War, and many Shia leaders still held blood grudges against him for unknown sins committed in years past. Several of his brothers were locked away at Camp Bucca for extortion, kidnapping, murder, and an RPG attack on an American tank, respectively. Like a mutating cockroach, though, Abu Adnan simply refused to go away, somehow managing to avoid his own detainment by continually promising Coalition forces valuable intelligence and his personal loyalty. Although he was a weak leader prone to blaming others for his own failures, his tribe was large, well connected, and absolutely vital to the reconciliation—an inconvenient truth that undoubtedly played a role in Higher's decision to keep him around.

"What's up?" I asked Super Mario.

"Abu Adnan, he says that Saba al-Bor Nahia [the local council] fuck him out of trash-trucks contract. Mayor Rahdi, he says that trash-trucks contract decided by Taji Qada [the provincial council]. But Abu Adnan, he's no good at listening. He just keeps yelling and saying Rahdi fuck him out of contract."

The two Arabs suddenly noticed my presence, and I shook both of their hands. Taking advantage of Super Mario's presence, I interjected into their conversation.

"Why are you giving Rahdi a hard time, Abu Adnan? You know if he says something is at the Qada, that's where it is at. You gotta trust your mayor."

"Yes, yes, but of course," the young sheik said, smiling guardedly. Abu Adnan was one of the youngest sheiks in our area, along with Haydar. "But, Lieutenant, where is Captain Whiteback? I must speak with him."

Secrets don't make friends, Sheik, I thought to myself. But instead of vocalizing this sarcasm, I said, "He's busy right now, Abu Adnan. I know he wants to talk to you though. We've been hearing a lot of rumors."

"They are rumors, untrue rumors!" Maybe I shouldn't have hinted at his untoward liaisons in front of Rahdi and Mojo, but Abu Adnan's reputation did not qualify as shocking news to anyone. "My men are good men. The Shias are trying to discredit me!"

I could sense both Rahdi's and Mojo's discomfort, as they were both Shias. "Don't worry about that now, just show up to Captain Whiteback's security meeting next week, and you can talk to him then. For now, concentrate on keeping your men in line, and tell them to wait their turn to get paid."

I turned to leave, but the sheik grabbed my shoulder. "Yes, well, some of my men are not on your lists."

Jesus, I thought. We'd been over this how many times already with the Sahwa leaders? If I let this go unchecked, Skerk might strangle Abu Adnan by the time he and his men made it to the front of the line. I had to make the correction.

"Then they won't get paid," I said. "You know the rules. All of the lists are approved at the beginning of the month by you and the security council, and that's the list we use at the end of the month for payment."

The sheik spoke again, and I saw Super Mario straighten his back in surprise and bite down on his lip. "Translate what he said," I instructed the terp. "Word for word."

"He say that you are liar because Americans always have more money and that you won't give it to him because of his brothers at Bucca."

I felt the red rise instantly. "Dude, do not ever claim I'm lying," I shouted at the sheik, purposefully getting as uncomfortably close to his face as possible. My Irish temper had caught fire, but I still managed to resist the urge to strike him with a left cross. Already, he had broken eye contact and was skulking away from me. I continued yelling. "Take it up with Skerk if you don't believe me. But they aren't getting paid if they aren't on that fucking list." I paused, took a deep breath, and continued speaking. I hated these petty Arab alpha-male games. Really, I did. They offended my idealistic liberal sensibilities.

"That's the way it works, Sheik. If you don't like it, I'm sure we can find someone else willing to run the Sahwa contract for your village."

Super Mario translated my rant, and Abu Adnan quickly sputtered out an apology, bowing his head toward me respectfully. He also left shortly thereafter, under the pretense of checking on his men in line. Rahdi patted me on the shoulder and thanked me for my help. Mojo poked me in the stomach.

"Want some cigarettes?" he asked. His green eyes sparkled with eagerness.

"I'm good," I said. "I still have some left from the last pack I bought from you."

"What about some Boom-Booms? Wild Tigers? Some Iraqi porn?"

I closed my eyes, smirking, and tried to ignore the headache coming on. My temples pounded, and I was dehydrated. "No, thanks, Mojo. I'll let you know when I do, though."

I walked into the Internet room five minutes later. Across from me, Private Smitty showed Phoenix how to set up an e-mail account on Google and patiently explained the purpose of a password hint. I sat down, plugged my headphones in to listen to music, and logged on to my blog. I thought about where all of the men downstairs, currently employed by the Iraqi government and the U.S. Army, had been one year ago, before the reconciliation. Before the Sahwa. I was fairly certain they had been caked in gunpowder and dripping with American blood. I trusted that some of the sheiks truly believed in freedom, if not for their country then at least for their neighborhoods and their people. Did their pipe swingers? Did these paramilitants believe in anything beyond the promise of a monthly stipend, and should they even have to? Could someone with a full stomach and a warm bed ever rightfully doubt the intentions and ideals of those without, who sought the same thing through whatever means presented themselves?

I didn't know the answers to these questions. So I began to type what I did know.

DEAR JOHN

The first came in a MySpace message. The second came during a phone call, initiated after some postmission e-mail hackings. The third arrived in a care package in the form of divorce papers, tucked carefully between a jumbo can of Slim Jim beef snacks and ten logs of smokeless tobacco. The fourth was indirectly expressed, when the recipient wasn't picked up at the airport for leave.

Those were just the Dear John letters we knew about while in Iraq. Things got worse once we redeployed back to Hawaii.

Dear Johns were as old as war itself. In them, wives and girlfriends explained to their deployed soldier why they no longer loved them, and why Jody—the nonmilitary guy back in America who led a simple, soft life—made her happy. Some were filled with excuses, others with guilt, but all conveyed the message plain as day that their sender wasn't willing to wait. Human beings have always been fickle, needy creatures, and all the gravities of war and the dependence on loved ones it spawned for the soldiers fighting them did not change that.

Before we left, it all sounded so simple, so banal—like a relic of past wars, ones that didn't have instant communication tools like the Internet. No one believed it could happen to him. At least, not at first. Not until it kept happening. Not until we realized that it really was that simple, and that when we departed the civilized world to fight a war no one cared about, let alone understood, emotional vacuums ripped open, and, now, things weren't just uncivilized where we were. We became slaves to circumstance.

Upon returning home from a previous deployment, one of my NCOs discovered his young bride had run off with Jody. Shortly thereafter, he put Jody in the hospital for six weeks, permanently crushing the guy's nasal cavity in the process. He consequently spent some time in jail for assault, but law and justice have never been the same thing.

That was the warrior's fantasy and, conversely, also his nightmare. Give us something to love, and we'd kill for it. Give us something to hate, and we had no choice.

This NCO's forearms were covered in tattoos that read "Trust No Bitch" in Latin. He explained that the phrase wasn't just referring to women. His horror story was not rare—certainly not rare enough. Every military base across the world was saturated with Dear John tales, gnawing at the underbelly of our continental consciousness. Not that anyone cared. After all, these things happened. It was the military. It was war. It was life.

Our soldiers were not saints, and in many cases, they weren't the greatest husbands or boyfriends either. But that was beside the point. Soldiers were trained to be loyal, and the type of loyalty we learned in Iraq could not be conveyed to those back home, whether they stayed true or not. We relied on one another to survive, trusting each other with our very lives, under the most trying of circumstances. That was not something even the most eloquent of us could explain to civilians, no matter how hard we tried.

Dear Johns crushed men of otherwise unquestionable strength and total resoluteness. In the time they most needed something right and theirs, it was taken away from them. It wasn't like getting dumped—it had a far more resounding impact on the soldier. He became rougher, harsher, crueler. With his ties to home cut, he more fully embraced the Iraq environment, as he had no choice but to do so. Truthfully, it usually made him a better soldier, but he lost some vital slivers of his humanity in the process. The lost pieces were scattered in the desert of a far away land and would not be coming home with the rest of his body when the tour ended. Every man deserved to hide away his own hopes in his cave before the big hunt. Not every man returned to his cave to find them still there.

As the physical manifestation of every soldier's worst fears, Dear Johns didn't just impact the recipient. They affected the psyches of teams, sections, platoons, and troops, bringing home to everyone the recognition that the same thing could happen to them and forcing them to wonder if it was going to. Or if it already had and they just didn't know about it yet. This mind fuck was the worst part for many. Fifteen months was a long time to be left alone with our own thoughts, and all of this only compounded the normal stresses on relationships trying to survive a fifteen-month combat deployment.

In the mean time, we waged a counterinsurgency.

My Dear Johned soldiers said they got over things. It took time, of course, and a lot of talking and venting and even some crying, but they all said they were better off because of the experience.

That was what they said.

DOMINOES

"Days like this, I think to myself, Self, Iraq ain't so bad!"

Staff Sergeant Bulldog laughed uproariously at his own statement, which caused Staff Sergeant Boondock and Doc to join in, caught up in the good cheer. The Sons of Iraq gathered around the table with us gazed on in confusion. Suge, seated directly to my left, yelled at a small boy, who ran off toward a nearby hut. I wiped some beads of sweat from my hair with my hand as my Kevlar helmet lay at my side. We had all taken our helmets off.

"More chai is coming!" Suge yelled. "Time for a new game!"

After a grueling burst of patrolling, when we had been out on Route Tampa for sixteen to eighteen hours a day for a solid week hunting vehicle-borne IEDs (VBIEDs), which was really just a fancy way of saying car bomb, I directed our platoon's area reconnaissance mission on this lazy March morning to the southwestern outreaches of Saba al-Bor. The solace of spring permeated the countryside, complete with idle greenery, plenty of shade, and

The sight of American Strykers and the presence of razor concertina wire were norms for locals in this pocket of Iraq.

slow, meandering streams. We needed a break, and our troubles, resentments, and angers blew away here, like leaves in the wind. A few soldiers and I had dismounted to talk with the local Sahwa at their shed and subsequently struck up a game of dominoes, or as Staff Sergeant Bulldog called it, bones. Our four Strykers were parked in a tight coil twenty feet to our north, where the gunners provided security overwatch and the rest of the platoon slept. We had been out in sector for three hours, and I had no intention of bringing us back to the combat outpost for at least a few more. We needed this. More importantly, we deserved this.

"Suge, how'd you get so good at bones?" Doc asked, as he lit our terp's cigarette.

"Oh, I have played the dominoes very much," Suge said, pleased that his victories had not gone unnoticed. "I remember this one game, in youth, when a Syrian tried to knife at me for beating him so good!" He blew smoke from his mouth, retrospectively cursing in Arabic about the stabbing Syrian, and stroked his grey moustache. "Syrians, they are crazy, you know," he finally said. "Craziest of the Arabs, those fucking Syrians."

My two section sergeants just stared at Suge, waiting for his rambling to stop, before they interjected. Staff Sergeant Boondock arched an eyebrow my way, as if I were somehow responsible for our interpreter's lunacy.

"I don't know nuthin' about no Syrians, but I do know me and my Iraqi partner here, we's gonna smoke this round of bones for sure," Staff Sergeant Bulldog said, adding a grunt at the end for emphasis. The teams were me and Staff Sergeant Boondock, Suge and Doc, Staff Sergeant Bulldog and a teenage Sahwa who kept staring at him wide-eyed in wonder, and a duo of thirty-something Sons of Iraq. So far, Suge's team and Staff Sergeant Bulldog's team had alternated winning, mainly due to the domino prowess of those two.

Just as a small Iraqi boy returned to our table with a tray full of chai, my dismounted radio buzzed, coming in as clear as God on Judgment Day. "White 1, this is Bounty Hunter 6." It was Captain Whiteback.

"Nooooo!" Staff Sergeant Boondock bellowed. "Don't answer it, sir! For the love of God, don't answer it!" He grabbed Staff Sergeant Bulldog's partner by the shoulders and pressed his face next to his own. "Think of the children!"

We all knew what this meant—it meant a frago; more importantly, it meant an abrupt end to our separate peace. I sighed and responded, ignoring Staff Sergeant Boondock's plea. "This is White 1."

"White 1, Bounty Hunter 6. Frago follows." Our commander paused. "It's Task Force Cobra related."

This caused Staff Sergeant Boondock to break into an inaudible wail. Task Force Cobra* consisted of special operations personnel and Ranger Regiment soldiers whose sole mission was to conduct raids on high-level enemy targets. Although based in Baghdad proper, they occasionally came up our way, following their targets. They were clearly the best of the best, and their successes were well known and well documented; as a result, most regular army soldiers were awestruck when they saw Task Force Cobra soldiers operating. Like us, Task Force Cobra wore the American urban camouflage uniform. Unlike us, however, they weren't beholden to counterinsurgency doctrine and were infamous across our brigade for destroying houses and terrifying locals, then leaving the mess for the landowning unit to clean up. Back in the winter, they destroyed a house in eastern Saba al-Bor with 105-mm artillery shells dropped from an AC-130 Spectre Gunship. They believed the house was wired to blow up, but it turned out to be abandoned. The Iraqi neighborhood was understandably irate. Task Force Cobra consisted

---

* Note: not their official name or unofficial call sign.

of professionals and experts certainly, but they only had to focus on the raid itself. Nothing else mattered in their line of work.

"Two brothers got detained last night," Captain Whiteback continued. "IED makers for AQI. They rigged up a suicide vest for their cousin last year that blew up in Ramadi, killing ten people in a market. I need you guys to go check out the damage Task Force Cobra did to the neighborhood during the detainment process." Anticipating my reaction, or perhaps arguing with himself out loud, he continued, "Their job isn't to worry about second- and third-order effects. As the landowners that's our responsibility."

"Roger, sir."

"They're at a farm east of your current location. Oh, and take pictures. Lots. Squadron needs them for the PowerPoint slides. You know how it is, something didn't happen unless there's a PowerPoint slide to prove it."

"Roger, sir."

"Sorry to end the game, but duty calls."

I stared at the radio in disbelief. Everyone else was already heading back to the vehicles. Had he really hinted about knowing about the dominoes game?

"Say again, sir?" I asked.

"Nothing." I thought I heard a faint trace of amusement in his voice. "Get the grid for the farm from the TOC when you guys are ready. Whiteback out."

I put my helmet back on, gave the Sons of Iraq fist pounds, and gave my mounted soldiers the "we're rolling out of here, time now" hand-and-arm signal. Specialist Flashback dropped my vehicle's ramp.

"How was dominoes, sir?" asked my driver, sleep still hanging off his question like an apostrophe.

"Dominoes?" I responded, indignantly. "I was off fighting the fight. Building trust with local leadership, boys, building trust. Heading off the insurgents' offensive before they even got a chance to initiate their charge. Hell, think of the medals we earned today! And it's not even lunchtime yet."

Private First Class Smitty (recently promoted) and Private Hot Wheels giggled appreciatively from the back, but Sergeant Spade was unimpressed. "Lose again?"

"Sure did. Staff Sergeant Bulldog and Suge smoked us all."

I felt my gunner smirking above me. "We're redcon-1, sir."

I put on my headset and conducted a radio check. "Embrace the frago," SFC Big Country said from his vehicle. "Or it will embrace you."

"Roger that," I said.

"Get this, sir," said SFC Big Country. "I heard muffled excitement coming from my driver's hole, so I asked Specialist Prime, 'What the hell are you reading up there, *Playboy*?' He responded with, 'No, Sergeant, *Popular Mechanics*.'"

"What can I say," Specialist Prime said. "I like *Popular Mechanics*."

My other Strykers reported their redcon status, and we started moving east. Back into sector and back to the mission and back to Iraq.

Approximately two kilometers later—a distance we covered in under five minutes—Boss Johnson II waited for us as our Strykers pulled up to the main entrance of his farmlands. He greeted me as I dismounted.

"The other Americans came last night," he said through Suge. "In helicopters."

"That is what I understand," I responded. "Why would they have done that if your area is secure, as you claim?"

Even through Suge's paraphrased Arabic, Boss Johnson II understood my not-so-subtle insinuations, and he stared back at me protractedly. Then he shrugged. "One of the men they took was one of my captains. The other was his brother. He was also Sahwa."

Of course, I thought. He already knew what they were doing. No wonder he wasn't more disturbed but still felt compelled to make a show of walking us in to assess the damage. I ignored the temptation to remind Boss Johnson II that he now had two openings on his security contract and matched his pace. Suge walked a half step behind us, and a section of Gravediggers, under the strict guidance of Staff Sergeant Boondock and Sergeant Cheech, fanned out around us in a diamond formation. Three minutes later, we reached the crest of a small hill and found the farm in question.

The first thing we noticed was the car. A modest station wagon was parked in the driveway, sharp pieces of glass glinting in the surrounding dirt. Every one of the windows was smashed in. One elderly Iraqi man, four women, and eight young children huddled in a group squat nearby, at the base of the farm's main lodging. I took a few photos of the car, and at Boss Johnson II's urging, the old man stood up and walked over to us.

"Salaam aleichem," I said, taking off my gloves and sunglasses, remembering the basic lesson of some COIN class conducted long ago.

"Salaam." The man was quite short, but unlike most Iraqis his age, he did not hunch his back. A red-and-white checkered turban and closely trimmed grey beard framed a rather unnerving face: With one chasm-black eye and one twitching blue eye the shade of a robin's egg, he looked more like a classic jihadist than the affable old farmer with bad bloodlines Boss Johnson II had described.

"What happened last night?"

"It would be easier for me to show you," he said, gesturing for us to follow him into his house. We did.

As expected, the house was trashed. Furniture lay overturned. Cabinets were unhinged. Clothes had been left in heaps on the ground. A poster of Mecca was torn off the wall, and three pieces of it sat on the ground. No rug was left unturned, no hiding place untouched. There was even the carcass of a small dog left in the backyard that, with the continual advance of the sun, was now completely infested with flies. The dog's frozen scowl from the other side of eternity was still trying to alert the AQI brothers. When I asked the old man if he knew why the other Americans had done this to the house, he claimed he knew nothing of his brothers' extracurricular activities.

"They treat us like sheep," he said. "They put numbers on our backs and embarrass us in front of our wives and children."

I felt for the guy; really, I did. He seemed harmless enough—and certainly clueless enough. But even though I hadn't heard the full story—yet—I trusted that my countrymen didn't tornado random houses without justification. Not now. Not five years into the war. Not after Abu Ghraib. Even they had to abide by certain rules. I asked the twitching blue eye if he was familiar with our repercussion funds program.

"I do not want money," he replied matter-of-factly. "I want to know what my brothers did wrong, and I want my respect back."

To color me shocked would have done a disservice to the power of crayons everywhere. I had never met an Iraqi who didn't want to talk about money or the potential for financial imbursement. I certainly empathized with his hints about lost pride and internalized anger. That probably didn't matter to him, though, and he had already made his needs and wants very clear. There was nothing left to do. I spoke a few more pretty, hollow words, took a few more notes, and snapped a few more photographs. Then I told the Gravediggers we were leaving. Private Das Boot still stared at the dead dog in the backyard. Corporal Spot's bright blue eyes blinked continuously in bafflement, and even Staff Sergeant Boondock walked like a man eager to return to a part of the war zone that made sense.

As we came out of the house, the women and children remained squatting to our immediate left. Most of the women stared at the ground, but the youngest of them followed my soldiers' brisk movements with the stare—

something the children massed around her soon mimicked. I wasn't the only one in our group who noticed this development.

"This is very bad situation, LT," Suge said. "The kids do not know their fathers were Ali Babas. They do not know that Americans bring peace to their country. They only know that their dog is dead and their fathers are gone."

I groaned. "I know, Suge," I said. "I know."

The elderly man, noticing the glares of his brothers' wives and his nephews and nieces, began clucking and yelling at them in Arabic. They scattered behind us, disappearing to various corners of the farm. Boss Johnson II shook my hand, saying he'd come to the combat outpost later in the day to see us, and walked the other way to where he had parked his car.

Suge's mind was still with the children as we moved to our Strykers. "They will grow up hating America!" he said, restating his point more clearly. "And they will be wrong, but that will not change anything."

"Yeah." I needed a Rip-It and some of Doc's little white pills. "We call it the domino effect back home. This probably will be the defining moment of every one of those kid's lives, and they don't even know the facts. What a fucking travesty."

My anticipatory musings didn't impact my terp the way I hoped. "Dominoes, Lieutenant? What do dominoes have to do with this?"

To my front, Staff Sergeant Boondock heard his cue. "Did I hear our crazy-ass terp mention something about . . . bones?" I started laughing while he pressed the issue. "I sincerely recommend you make that happen, LT. Das Boot needs something to cheer him up after seeing that dead dog. That goofy German still looks like he's going to cry. And it's not like we got anything else going on. Let's chai it up."

We went back to the Sahwa checkpoint for another game of dominoes and another round of chai. Soon, the events of this day were just another page of chicken scratch in my notepad. There they rested, festooned permanently with the smudged dirt of the desert, earmarked in case I ever needed to care again about that farm and those people and this day.

Into the notepad. It wasn't like there was any other place for it to go.

RULES OF ENGAGEMENT

Over the course of our deployment, only a few events continually stuck with me, keeping me up at night, weighing me down as mental anchors. The Sahwa firefight was one; almost losing Private Hot Wheels in June was another. Most everything else felt too surreal in memory, and those I buried away to be dealt with at a later date, at a time when I could afford to get lost in reflection and deliberation. The events of this night, though, I couldn't bury, or even pretend to, temporarily or otherwise. They were that fucked up.

We spent the day pulling security on Route Maples for General Petraeus and his entourage so that the Pegasus himself could buy a falafel at the Saba al-Bor market. Immediately after the general left, flying by helicopter back to Baghdad, we moved straight into a night escort for an engineer unit tasked to fill the potholes on Route Lincoln, a key highway that led to Anbar to the west and Camp Taji to the east. The mission was straightforward enough—we would surround the engineers in a Stryker diamond and chill out while the concrete dried. The initial set of potholes was at the intersection of Routes Lincoln and Islanders, just south of the Grand Canal, on the northwestern corner of Saba al-Bor. We established our outer cordon security positions, the engineers went to work, and I prepared for a long, quiet night of waiting.

Five minutes later, Staff Sergeant Boondock's voice ripped across the radio net.

"White 1, this is White 3. We got some real shady mother fuckers low-crawling onto the road, coming down from the canal. It looks like two . . . yeah, two personnel."

I had been lying down in the back of my vehicle, reading T. E. Lawrence's war memoir. I bolted straight up when I heard Staff Sergeant Boondock's report and started studying my map. The White 3 vehicle was on the complete other side of the Stryker diamond, oriented due south, overwatching Route Islanders.

"Keep watching them," I said, stating the obvious while I sorted through my conflicting thoughts.

Were they sure they'd seen two guys low-crawling? It was night. They still hadn't done anything wrong yet. Technically. Not yet. Were they sure? Why were they low-crawling? A few units in the brigade had been shot at, ourselves included, but no one had shot back yet. There was a reason for that. After all the briefings and lectures about previous units' war crimes, cover-ups, scandals, and prison sentences, everyone was trigger shy. No one would say it, but everyone felt it. Had I left my rules-of-engagement card in the laundry? Why were they low-crawling? Why couldn't we just shoot, again? They hadn't displayed any hostile purpose. Yet. It wasn't just night, it was midnight. Farmers wandered around that road all the time. So did kids. But it was midnight. I used to sneak out at midnight as a kid. Staff Sergeant Boondock said they were shady. Were he and his men sure? Could they be sure with night vision? Could they ever be sure with night vision? Were they fucking sure?

"Any heat signatures?" I sputtered out.

Five or so seconds passed before Staff Sergeant Boondock responded. "Roger! Roger! My golf [gunner] reports that they have set down a boxlike object 250 meters from our position."

Three simple words hung on my tongue like a swing: Light them up. A quick burst or two of 50-caliber machine gun rounds would suffice. Although I had come to Iraq prepared to kill, I hadn't come needing to. But now—kill or be killed. Never had this war been so clear, so pure, so obvious, so clean. Light. Them. Up.

But I didn't give that order. I couldn't. Or maybe I wouldn't. Not yet. They hadn't dug anything yet and thus hadn't emplaced anything. I couldn't stop thinking about the investigation a shooting would inevitably initiate, a truth that mortified me later in hindsight. I understood that such retrospective studies were usually healthy for a military unit, and I was more than familiar with the COIN principles of precision and restraint. Part of what made an American soldier an American soldier was that he fought with rules that sometimes hindered him in an attempt to keep sight of the ideals and principles that led him to fight in the first place. But I also understood that events that started out just like this became war crimes. I knew that events that started out just like this led to soldiers going to jail. The blunt truth of it all was that we had no idea who was actually down on Route Islanders, and because of that, we couldn't open fire. Everything was too grey, and we currently lived in a black-and-white world and served in a black-and-white army. It was still just too damn grey.

I kicked out my Bravo section's dismounts, one team led by SFC Big Country, the other by Staff Sergeant Boondock. They stood behind the cover of their Strykers and were on order to move south to the two personnel's location. I told Sergeant Axel, the 3 vehicle's gunner, to beam the targets with a bright naked-eye laser in order to let them know we were watching. Then I told him, "If they start digging, or don't stop whatever it is they're doing, or do anything other than totally freeze, open fire and engage the targets." There.

Staff Sergeant Boondock (near) and Private Das Boot scan for enemy movement after hearing gunfire in the distance. As the Iraq War evolved into a counterinsurgency fight, the leadership of Coalition forces stressed to its troops on the ground to only fire their weapons after the target had been positively identified as an active combatant.

I had satiated the gods of "what if" and found a way for my soldiers to still do their job. It was the best I could come up with under the circumstances.

"Roger. Will comply!" Sergeant Axel responded.

I had given the order to kill. Haughty enough to condemn two individuals to The End because they had been dumb enough to be seen in a war of shadows. Somewhere in the time-space continuum, the boy who had cried after his first fistfight—not because he was hurt but because he thought he had done something to upset the instigator and didn't yet understand the concept of bullying—hung himself with a calendar rope.

"X-ray, this is White 1." It had been a few minutes since I had sent up a situation report to troop headquarters. Remembering to do so at this precise moment became my biggest regret of the whole ordeal. I still don't know why I did it.

"This is X-ray." It was one of the TOC NCOs.

"X-ray, we have a possible IED emplacement happening time now, at our location. Grid to follow. We're employing ROE and will engage with fire if detainment is no longer a viable option."

"Negative, White 1, you will not engage!" Captain Whiteback now spoke on the other end of the radio call. What the hell was he still doing up? I wondered. I wouldn't have called this up if I'd thought he was still awake. "Attempt to detain the individuals. Do not open fire unless the individuals attempt to directly engage you."

"This is White 1 . . . I copy the only way we can open fire, even after positive identification, is if these guys open fire at us with rifles or try to detonate the IED on us?"

"Roger," came the reply. "You have to be absolutely sure."

I sighed, disbelievingly, and switched back to the platoon net. "You monitor the commander's traffic, 3-Golf?"

Sergeant Axel's voice was so sharp, it could have cut through steel. "This is 3-Golf. Roger."

I howled and ripped the hand mic out of our radio, throwing it into the back of the Stryker, waking up a very confused Suge. Truthfully, I was angrier at myself for calling up a situation report than I was with the commander for making a commander's call. Sergeant Axel did as he was told and lasered the two shapes. They stood up and darted back into the canal. I instructed the two dismount teams to pursue them. After forty-five minutes of searching, nothing had been found but two sets of muddy footprints behind some broken reeds.

"What the fuck?" Staff Sergeant Boondock raged over the radio. "It's not like these goddamn mother fuckers are the fucking Vietcong and tunneled the fuck out of here. Where the fuck did they fucking go?" He was frustrated. We were all frustrated.

I instructed the dismount teams to move back north, sweeping the road, to investigate the boxlike object Sergeant Axel had initially spotted. Specialist Tunnel and Private First Class Das Boot (recently promoted) stumbled over a compact, bricklike object covered in tumbleweeds on the east side of the road.

"What's that?" Specialist Tunnel asked.

"I don't know," PFC Das Boot said. He leaned down, pulled aside the tumbleweeds, scratched, and sniffed.

Staff Sergeant Boondock walked up behind the soldiers. "What the fuck are you guys doing? Das Boot, are you high? Back the fuck away from that thing!"

After marking the object with Chem-Lights, the army term for glowsticks, we called EOD and waited. In the mean time, the engineer unit had finished up their pothole fillings, so they waited with us. EOD arrived an hour later, and it turned out the brick was a medium-sized pressure-plate EFP designed specifically to penetrate Coalition force armored vehicles. EOD detonated it without incident, and we continued our escort mission deep into the night. We didn't finish up until four in the morning, and we all went straight to bed. No one said anything to anyone about what had happened. There wasn't really anything to say.

The next day, the platoon played enough of the Guitar Hero video game that they didn't care about the rules of engagement incident anymore. I still did. While talking on the back porch, Staff Sergeant Boondock told me that he wouldn't have given the order to engage like I had. I didn't believe him. He also said that the rules now were too constrained, too political, totally different from his last tour in Iraq, and that no Joe's life was worth one lousy dead hajji.

"Shit's always clear in hindsight, sir," he said. "Nothing made sense last night, and that's a fucking fact. All that matters is that we're all still here. If this is the most fucked up thing we deal with on this deployment, we've had it easy."

Later that week, an individual detained by a unit to our south admitted to attempting to emplace an IED at the exact spot and on the exact date we had observed him. Like most emplacers, he was just a poor teenager who had been paid $20 for his act, which he used to feed his family for a week. Other than identifying his emplacing partner, he knew nothing of intelligence value and was later sentenced to six months at Camp Bucca. His partner's dead body was found some four months later in Baghdad, next to a prematurely detonated IED he had been putting into the ground. Sometimes I wondered how he spent those four months of borrowed time.

SADR'S SPRING JAM

March 25, 2008, day: The Gravediggers and I were out in sector conducting security sweeps in the eastern villages. A radio call from Captain Whiteback informed us that Muqtadah al-Sadr had lifted the freeze on attacks against Coalition forces by his militia, Jaish al-Mahdi. Half of my men said, "Fuck." The other half said, "Fuck yeah." We spent the rest of the day patrolling the Shia havens of Saba al-Bor, but all appeared normal.

March 25, 2008, night: The steady purring of distant automatic fire stirred me out of sleep an hour after I collapsed into it. A second passed, and then my entire room shook with inevitability while a M240B machine gun on the roof of the combat outpost returned fire directly above us. I rolled out of my bed, getting my legs wrapped up in my poncho liner, breaking the fall to the ground with my face. Staff Sergeant Bulldog barreled through our door like a runaway freight train. "It on now! Oh yeah, it be on now!" he boomed. We all started throwing on our gear in great haste, with the notable exception of SFC Big Country, who yawned loudly from his bed and scratched his head. "You probably have time to put on pants, sir," he advised, causing me to look down at a pair of boxer shorts contrasting sharply with the combat boots, body armor, and helmet I had managed to get on my body. I peeked my head out of the doorway and didn't see any terrorist hordes coming up the stairs, so I silently agreed with my platoon sergeant's assessment. The gunfire above us continued while I found my pants.

Five minutes later, my platoon and I sprinted out of the combat outpost to the dark shadows in the motor pool we believed were still our Strykers. We locked and loaded on the run. The gunfire that originated at our location had spread across the city almost instantaneously.

The reports came rushing in. "Tracer rounds to the west, Lieutenant." "Flares to our east." "Audible contact with shots to our south, sir." There was a bright flash and then a resounding BOOM. "Umm. You probably heard it LT, and saw it, but that was an explosion to our north."

The firing from the roof had stopped altogether by this point, until we heard a burst of rounds strike the outside wall of the outpost directly to our front. The hissing of M4 bullets spraying above us reminded us that other soldiers were still on the roof, and they were firing at something on the other side of the wall.

"Get into the fucking vehicles and get redcon-1!" we yelled to one another.

March 26, 2008, day: I stood in the street, looking at a building with a sloping roof and two cannonball-sized holes in the middle of it. We had spent many hours zigzagging through the various Shia neighborhood cores, chasing a lot of ghosts and a lot of gunfire but finding nothing. Only now, in the light of the morning, did we comprehend the full scope of JAM's resurgence. The aforementioned holes were the gift from the main gun of an Iraqi army BMP (armored personnel carrier), and the aforementioned building was the local Sahwa headquarters.

The one Son of Iraq who showed up for work this day expressed his displeasure with the situation. I thanked him for his devotion to duty and asked him where his coworkers were. He looked at me like I had a dick growing out of my forehead and said, "At home, of course. It is not safe here." I asked him why he wasn't at home then. "Because my father kicked me out and told me to go to work, and I have nowhere else to go."

Phoenix laughed at the Sahwa member and asked if we could go visit one of his girlfriends. "It depends," I said. "Can her mom make chai?"

March 26, night: We spent the night conducting a counter-IED OP on the southern end of Route Islanders. Many hours in my vehicle were spent discussing the finer intricacies of deer hunting, a pastime at which both PFC Smitty and Private Hot Wheels considered themselves expert. I couldn't tell if they were more horrified or shocked to find out that the first time I had fired a gun of any sort was in a military uniform. I, in turn, explained to them that Suge Knight was an interpreter, not an interpolator.

The next hot topic had to do with which one of Staff Sergeant Boondock's designated call signs for our soldiers was the most offensive. Ironically, the troop's equal-opportunity representative, he chortled with pride when PFC Das Boot identified himself as White 3-Kraut. I pointed out that Doc's nickname of "Twinkie"—yellow on the outside, white on the inside—would probably offend an outsider the most. As we rolled back into the combat outpost, Captain Whiteback relayed the latest frago concerning the next morning's mission. We slept in our vehicles for two and a half hours.

March 27, day: Somehow analogous of the Gravediggers' current mission, Iraq, and life in general, a scrawny, dirty rooster started to crow an hour after sunrise but quit with a coughing cackle halfway through the attempt. My Stryker lay parked in the driveway of Sheik Nour's sprawling compound. For reasons obvious to everyone, Sheik Nour pushed up the dates for his vacation to Jordan, and we were tasked to ensure that he made it to Baghdad Airport without exploding into bloody bits of Mahdi Army propaganda.

While we waited for the sheik to finish packing, Specialist Flashback and Sergeant Cheech pontificated about deployment cycles.

"Three deployments. Wow. Just think Sergeant Cheech, you've spent a tenth of your life in Iraq," Specialist Flashback observed.

"Gee, thanks for pointing that out," Sergeant Cheech replied. "Next time, do me an actual favor and shoot me in the foot, okay?"

Sheik Nour shortly waddled up to the back of my vehicle's ramp, while his servants followed with three pieces of vintage leather luggage. Nour stared expectantly at Sergeant Cheech, who gave him a wild-eyed "you-must-be-fucking-crazy-this-is-my-third-deployment-to-this-hellhole-of-a-country-and-I've-missed-the-birth-of-two-of-my-children-for-you-and-your-people-I-came-here-to-seek-out-and-destroy-I-am-not-fucking-carrying-your-damn-luggage" look. PFC Smitty and I quickly loaded up the suitcases instead; I had done far more embarrassing things in life than that, albeit usually under the influence of alcohol. Higher diverted our route before we departed due to multiple IED attacks on Route Tampa in the previous hours. The ride passed uneventfully, and the sheik spent the majority of it perusing Specialist Flashback's College Girls edition of *Playboy*.

March 27, night: We conducted another counter-IED mission. Specialist Big Ern sang twenty minutes of soul music, punctuated with a Tina Turner song, while Sergeant Axel and Specialist Prime competed in an infrared Chem-Light match. In the back of my vehicle, PFC Smitty got bored.

"Weeeh!" Private Hot Wheels exclaimed from his position in the rear hatch.

"What the fuck was that?" I said, startled by the pitch in my soldier's voice.

"Sorry, sir . . . uhh . . . Smitty poked me in the ass with an antenna pole. I didn't like it."

Fifteen minutes before the scheduled end of mission, an IED exploded four hundred meters to our south, on a convoy of supply vehicles, just outside of our AO. My Bravo section raced down there to find a broken rearview mirror and a few rattled souls, but no casualties.

Despite the facts that this IED exploded out of our sector, had obviously been emplaced before our OP started, and was out of our OP's scan due to a series of canal rises, we still saw the irony of the situation. "I'd keep this one out of the blog, LT," Staff Sergeant Boondock told me. "Nothing like a counter-IED mission that has an IED explode during it. People are going to start getting the wrong idea about our heroics, you know?"

March 28, day: We drove up to the main checkpoint in Saba al-Bor and found the IAs and the IPs not searching any of the entering or departing vehicles, although they immediately started searching them once they spotted our Strykers. They told me, to a man, that they always searched the vehicles. I was told later that I lost it on them and yelled in ways my soldiers had never seen before. I didn't remember much of it.

I walked back to my Stryker, yawning noisily, trying to ignore the body soreness underneath my armor and the buzzing in my mind that demanded rest.

"Tired, sir?" Sergeant Spade asked.

"Nope," I lied. "You?"

"Hell, no. I'll sleep when I'm dead."

After six hours of joint checkpoint operations with the Iraqi security forces, we left and paused for fifteen minutes to observe them from a distance. They continued to search all the vehicles, which shocked us all. An hour later, another platoon passed through the checkpoint and reported that the Iraqis were no longer searching any vehicles moving into or out of town. They stopped to remedy the situation.

March 28, night: Finally. A combat mission. We were tasked with a raid deep into the countryside, far beyond even the dimmest of Saba al-Bor's checkpoint lights. The target was a key leader of a renegade JAM golden group, who had trained substantially in Iran. We owned the night; he owned a wanted poster. We were motivated. He was fucked.

I briefed my men that this would be a snatch-and-grab mission, quicker than most romantic comedies. "We should be home before breakfast," I told them, because that was what I had been told. In the mean time, PFC Smitty handed me another Rip-It, and adrenaline pumped through my body, raping the fatigue into submission.

An hour or so later, we set the cordon. "Time to move in, dismounts," I ordered. Staff Sergeant Boondock and his team took the lead, followed by me and Phoenix, then Staff Sergeant Bulldog and his section. We hadn't even stacked up on the first building yet when a burst of AK-47 fire roared through the dark stillness from somewhere close. To the east, I gauged. The radio soon provided an answer. Two individuals had been spotted and had their hands up. Scared farmers, maybe. Maybe not. They were both detained without further incident. No one had been hit. We continued our movement.

We crept up to the target house, using hand-and-arm signals the entire way. "No need for flashbangs," I whispered to Staff Sergeant Boondock and his team, referring to our stun grenades. "The teams will leapfrog through the house. Separate the males. Don't let them talk to each other." Then the radio spoke again. Two individuals had hopped out of a window in a house to our north and were running straight into the cordon like quails in the brush, rustled right into the hunter's sights. One of the runners was our target, the gunner reported, as the mug shot was a perfect match.

We moved through the house anyway, as nonlethally as lethal soldiers could. It wasn't just grandma; there was dad, and mom, wives one and two, and the kids. All kinds of kids. We hit the mental switch, calmed down from the raid hype, and became counterinsurgents again, clearing the house and searched for bomb-making materials and fake IDs. We brought the family some bottles of water, and I had a chat with the man of the house about his just-detained eldest son.

March 29, day: "Why are we still here, LT?" I couldn't tell anymore if one of my soldiers had asked that question or if I had asked it of myself yet again. "Because Higher says so." Why? "Because Higher says so.

"And no, it doesn't matter that they said so from an air-conditioned TOC ten kilometers away on an eight-hour shift while we sweat through hour sixteen of this clusterfuck."

Lieutenant Colonel Larry wanted more intel and to prove a point to the villagers that they shouldn't harbor insurgents. I thought this violated the COIN principle of precision targeting, but what did I know? I was just a lieutenant. We had already detained ten more military-aged males in the area to be brought in for tactical questioning. Sergeant Spade escorted an Iraqi woman and her grandchild from the other side of the village. The man detained with the original target needed positive identification; we may have inadvertently rounded up another top target but lacked confirmation. During the area sweeps, though, we had run into a family whose names matched our records.

The detainee sat in the shade on a small patch of grass, blindfolded, with a bottle of water next to him. Three of my soldiers pulled security around him. Phoenix talked to the woman, who sighed, shook her head, and turned to me. "Ali Baba?" she asked. I nodded my head in the affirmative. She clucked to herself and told the terp that the detained man was in fact her son and her grandson's father. The little boy ran over to the detainee. "Abu?" Phoenix asked him, using the Arabic word for father. The boy nodded and began to cry. His grandmother yelled coldly at him, which caused him to snap up and run back her way. He stopped halfway, turned around, and ran back to his father to kiss him on the forehead.

A month before, this scene would have caused me some sort of internal anguish. Now, it just brought me that much closer to getting out of my gear and out of the fucking sun.

"Hey, LT. They need you on the radio." It was Sergeant Spade.

"Of course they do." I grunted. "Sergeant Spade, take PFC Cold-Cuts and walk the woman and the kid home." I reached into my Stryker and pulled out a plastic bag full of Beanie Babies that my mother had sent me to distribute. I held it down to the child, who smiled and picked out a giraffe.

March 29, night: Somehow, we had made it off the raid objective. We now patrolled the streets of Saba al-Bor dismounted, with the stony silence of men too exhausted to care anymore about being exhausted. I remembered the adage, "Don't worry about the soldiers who bitch; worry about the ones who don't," so I worried about all of them.

We searched an ambulance to see if it was running weapons out of town. It wasn't. We distributed some pro-Iraqi security fliers to various Sahwa checkpoints. We identified ten armed men on a rooftop and yelled at them to come down to the street or die violently. They turned out to be a very skittish group of Sons of Iraq petrified that the Mahdi Army would attack them.

March 30, day: We spent another day at the main checkpoint in town, handing out pamphlets and overwatching the IAs and IPs. Taking the pamphlet that showed masked men with RPG launchers and read, "Violent men die violent deaths," the kids began to arrest one another. "Ali Baba!" they screamed. "Bucca!" they cried, referring to the national prison. It was funny the first few times. Not so much the 820,973th time. I told Staff Sergeant Bulldog that my eyeballs hurt. He laughed, which caused me to laugh, which caused the entire platoon to laugh.

"It wasn't even that funny," I said between wheezes.

"Nope, sure wasn't!" he said, still laughing uncontrollably.

March 30, night: The Internet told me that Sadr had called for a ceasefire on attacks against Coalition forces and the Iraqi government. It also used the term *Mahdi Army Revolt.* I looked this up on Wikipedia, and there was already an entry. Huh, I thought. I guess the last six days actually did happen. So that was what they were calling it. After all, history didn't count unless it had a snazzy name reference.

I checked in with Captain Whiteback. He was talking on the radio to squadron headquarters with his crazy eyes, and he looked frustrated. I decided to come back later. Back in my room, the NCOs played poker, bullshitting. As I walked in, Sergeant Axel wailed in pain. "Gah! I got dip in my skeeter bite! It burns!" I thought he referred to a mosquito bite, but I wasn't sure.

Meanwhile, Staff Sergeant Boondock munched on milk bones, dog treats my mother had sent me in the same care package as the Beanie Babies. The milk bones were intended for bomb-sniffing dogs.

"These are delicious, LT!" he cackled, much to the acclaim of the others. "I wish I was a dog, 'cause then I'd eat milk bones all the damn time!"

I shook my head, completely speechless and yet not really surprised at these antics, and crawled into bed. As I closed my eyes, I tried to think of how to describe the past week of my life. It'll have to end with the milk bones, I thought. Nothing else would make sense.

WISDOM FROM THE HOME FRONT

A lot of shipped items made their way to the sands of Iraq over the course of our deployment by way of the U.S. Postal Service. Most of the appropriately named care packages, sent by family members and friends, contained allotments of boxed foods, magazines, and random notes of encouragement for the soldiers. Mail call usually meant snack time, and the spoils of such were usually shared among the group. Other care packages consisted of health foods, toothpastes, blankets, books, and small toys, sent for us to pass out to the Iraqi populace. Although these weren't met with the same sort of celebration, they certainly meant more to those on the receiving end—and there was no surer way to snap out of a bad day or a brooding mood than to hand out Beanie Babies to local children while on patrol.

Between the care packages though, other boxes arrived; the motivations for shipping these packages were at best odd and at worse perverse. Like the ones that included a photograph of a rather buxom—and obviously available—three-time divorcee not so subtly looking for military health care coverage. Or the ones with a corporate return address carefully stamped in the upper left-hand corner and a collection of tightly wrapped golf shirts emblazoned with the corporate logo in question. I never claimed that Saba al-Bor was Gallipoli or the La Drang Valley, but we still didn't get to slip away to Baghdad Lakes Country Club for eighteen holes between missions. Even the Iraqi children were taken aback, and momentarily silenced, when they ran up to the Strykers asking for chocolate and were instead tossed a golf shirt some six sizes too big.

Besides those curiosities, my favorite stack in the combat outpost's mail room was that of letters written to soldiers by American schoolchildren. Most of them offered the same commonplace banalities sent our way from the greater American public—thank you for what you do; please return home safely; we'll pray for you. Empty words from an empty people—they wanted to show that they cared, but our experience was so unlike anything in their realm of understanding, only trodden clichés could fill their vacuum of confusion. This wasn't their fault, though—something I didn't yet understand when I was still in Iraq.

At least the children had an excuse for their simplicity—they were in elementary school—and at least they wrote us in crayon, which the nonconformist in me appreciated. Further, gems could be mined out of these letters with stunning regularity; in a postmodern world addicted to irony and understatement, nothing could have been a more authentic reminder of home. Real American children wrote these real American letters with real American crayons, and the Gravediggers collectively gathered them up in the winter and spring of 2008:

> *I hope you don't die, soldier. That would be bad.*
> *I feel sorry for you.*
> *I think war is worse than math.*
> *My daddy doesn't want me to be in the soldiers, 'cause he says that the Irack will last forever. Maybe if he changes his mind I'll see you in the Irack.*
> *My cousin was in war but he got hurt. Now he has a big beard and drinks beer all day long. My mom says he should get a job.*
> *Can you send me back a bad guy's head? That would be cool.*
> *I'm going to study real hard, so I don't have to go to Iraq. Do you wish you had done better at school?*
> *I hate cursive. Do you have to write in cursive for war?*
> *Is it like the movies? Do our letters make you feel better?*

The letters did make me feel better. I always meant to write that kid back and tell him so. I never got around to it. I still don't know why.

UNDER THE CRESCENT MOON

We slipped out under the crescent moon, carefully treading through the midnight blackness, and adjusted to our night-vision devices while locking and loading our M4s. Shades of green ebbed and flowed before our eyes, in a hallucination of amorphous haze. I uttered a quick message to our headquarters over the radio, letting them know that we were departing, and followed the shape in front of me disappearing into the dark horizon.

A group of Bravo Troop NCOs unwind over a game of poker at the Saba al-Bor combat outpost. Due to an intense operation tempo, soldiers at combat outposts rarely made it back to the large forward operating bases, where comforts like hot showers and fast food were found.

"Sir?" PFC Das Boot said from behind me, as I moved away from both him and the radio on his back.

"What's up?"

The young private's German accent crackled. "Staff Sergeant Boondock told me to stay ten steps behind you. Is that okay for you for when you need me to bring up the radio?"

"That's fine, man. That's fine. I'll let you know when I need you."

I turned back around. Sergeant Cheech took the point position for that night's patrol, and the platoon fell into a staggered column behind him without a pause. Staff Sergeant Bulldog's Alpha section moved in front of me, while Staff Sergeant Boondock's Bravo section moved behind me.

Better keep up, the doubting part of me thought.

Don't worry about that, responded my cocky side.

Few experiences in my life were as eerie as a late-night dismounted patrol through Saba al-Bor. Fear played a part of it, admittedly. Nerves, too. There were bits of excitement as well. Sensual overload ensued every time—every sense churned away on the fumes of our remaining wits to keep us alert, with every turbo button in our brains being mashed over and over again to keep us moving.

I saw the smoke from burning tires smoldering away all over the town. I smelled the raw sewage toxins so prevalent in the southern sector. I heard the insurgency of barking wild dogs chronicle every explicit detail of our winding movements. I touched Suge Knight's shoulder next to me to guide him through the dark as he leaned over to whisper about the historical significance of the Prophet Muhammad's grandson, Husayn, while we passed a Shia mosque towering alone in no-man's-land. I tasted cool, bracing water from my CamelBak as it rushed into my dry throat—and I walked, and then I walked some more. Throughout, I exchanged various hand-and-arm signals with my men to my front and to my rear. *Stop. Take a knee. 360-degree security here. Linear danger area ahead. Bring up the lieutenant. Send an update back to SFC Big Country and Bravo section. Keep moving.*

While we were impressed with our stealth—as were the various groups of locals we snuck up on, shocking them into quiet conciliation while they huddled around burning tires and newspapers for warmth—we were certainly no Delta Force, and missteps occurred during the opening minutes of our patrol. Some of the younger soldiers in front of me began to bunch up the formation, seeking out subliminal comfort with closer proximity to another human being. Staff Sergeant Bulldog quickly remedied this, however, maneuvering through his section with a hammer's grace, physically moving the Joes back to their proper place and distance. A few minutes later, I saw a body—I registered the stocky cut and hasty strut as PFC Smitty's—fall over a curb some ten feet in front of me, stagger up, and follow that with some muffled expletives. I smiled, something that inevitably brought on the god of karma, and I immediately fell myself.

"Mother fucker," I hissed, as I stood back up, holding my rolled ankle, cursing at the terrorist hole that had seized my leg, instantly more sentient to the additional weight compressed around my chest in armored plates and various gear additions. "Stupid-ass country and its stupid-ass bullshit."

"What?" Suge asked. "Are you okay, Lieutenant?"

"I'm fine," I growled, temporarily livid that a near-blind terp with a slight hobble and without the benefit of night-vision goggles somehow managed never to fall.

The hand-and-arm signals continued. *Keep moving. Stop. Take a knee. Crossing a linear danger area. Bring up the LT.*

I sauntered up to a Sons of Iraq checkpoint, while my soldiers fanned out around me, posting far-side security. A group of Iraqi men gathered around a small fire, AK-47s hanging loosely from their backs, all sporting matching khaki hats and khaki jackets.

"We got four of 'em, sir," Private Romeo said back to me, as he moved to his far-side position.

"Schlonic," I said, hand raised.

"Hello, mistah!" they responded, trying to act as awake and as alert as possible, scrambling up to shake my hand. We'd snuck up on them by emerging silently out of the shadows of the night, surprising them by not rolling past in our monstrous Strykers first. They knew that they should be closer to the street in order to stop any late-night traffic that came by. They also knew that there should have been six Sahwa working at this hour at this checkpoint.

"Where are the other two?" I didn't feel like dealing with the normal bullshit and glad-handing. Suge's voice matched mine in both pace and tenacity; this was his fourth year of interpreting, and I was his seventh lieutenant. His English may have been shoddy at times, but his understanding of American standard operating procedures and platoon leader moods was not.

A rapid flurry of Arabic words emerged posttranslation. "Don't bullshit me," I warned, not bothering to wait for Suge. I'd had this discussion and heard these excuses before.

After a pregnant pause, one of the Sons spoke to Suge. "He say that the other two are sick, and they were unable to find new guys," Suge translated, voice dripping with disgust.

I smiled to myself. This bothered him more than it did me. I pulled out my notebook and red lens flashlight and wrote with great demonstrative flair. "Tell them we'll be letting their sheik know about this and that Captain Whiteback will be docking their pay. Again."

Keep moving. Stop. Take a knee. 360-degree security here. Linear danger area ahead. Bring up the LT. Talk to the Sons of Iraq. Keep moving. Send an update back to SFC Big Country and Bravo section. Keep moving. Stop. Take a knee. Keep moving.

We now walked Route Swords, south to north, staggered column intact, silence assured. The mental tracker I kept in my mind placed our positions just short of Sheik Banana-Hands's palace. I impulsively checked my watch; it'd been three hours since we left the combat outpost. I chided myself for letting my mind wander over the course of the patrol, thinking about things and people and dreams that were left in the old world instead of concentrating solely on the mission at hand. It wasn't going to be like it had been, anyway, I reminded myself. Or how I wanted it to be. Or how it should have been. Why bother.

I heard shouts in Arabic to my front, and the sound of an AK-47 cocking reverberated in the still of the night. My men immediately dropped to the ground and sought out whatever cover they could find. I spied PFC Cold-Cuts just ahead of me huddling behind a generator, and Specialist Flashback across from me rolled into a ditch on the side of the road. I'd moved to my left, found myself kneeling in the door frame of a store, and felt Suge behind me, crunched over in the same position. Twenty M4 Carbine rifles were wedged tightly into shoulder pockets, oriented systematically to our north, night-vision lasers dancing around multiple shadows and shapes that resembled human silhouettes.

"Hey, mutha fucka!" Staff Sergeant Bulldog yelled somewhere to my front right. "We Americans, who's you is?" Positive identification of the enemy. That was all that any of us wanted.

It must be Banana-Hands's bodyguards, I thought, wandering on their own dismounted patrol. It's got to be. No one else would be down here at this time of night. If they weren't his bodyguards, they would have shot already. Unless they hadn't seen us yet. I refocused my night vision. Three green blobs, all standing up and holding rifles, paced frenziedly, heads scanning for our movements.

I heard Staff Sergeant Bulldog yell again in the direction of the green blobs, and I figured he thought the same thing about their being Sahwa bodyguards. I remembered that Arabs—be they Sahwa, terps, terrorists, or bums—struggled with Staff Sergeant Bulldog's Southern accent and didn't think he was speaking English. I needed to execute a shitty plan quickly rather than wait for the perfect one to develop.

"Let's go, Suge," I said, walking into the middle of the street.

"Salaam aleichem!" I yelled. "Americans!" I injected as much nasal white-bread suburbanite as I could into my voice for clarity's sake. I also swung my rifle back down into the low-ready and began to stroke the safety trigger. If they started shooting at me, I figured at least my soldiers would finally have the positive identification they'd been aching for.

On my fourth step forward, I saw the green light of God, a powerful naked-eye laser, shine by me and center directly on an Iraqi's forehead—Sergeant Spade's own way of telling the mystery men that we were Americans ready and willing to turn their lives Jurassic. That'll work too, I thought.

I continued walking and came up on three frozen members of Sheik Banana-Hands's bodyguard posse. They stuttered their way through a conversation, filling it with apologies, explanations, and offers of chai. I made them clear their weapons, and we kept moving.

I looked over at Suge, who shook his head. "Stupid men do stupid things," he said.

"Are you talking about me or them?" I asked.

He laughed. "Them, of course! You are the lieutenant. You are smart. Sometimes crazy, yes, and you don't always listen to me, Suge Knight, when you should, but you are very smart."

I wasn't sure if he had complimented me or not, so I kept my mouth shut.

We walked around a corner and started moving back west. The bright lights of the combat outpost shined in the distance, washing out my night vision. Like a proud citadel rising out of medieval lowlands, our home contrasted starkly with the dirty paucity we now trudged through. I felt my pace quicken slightly, with the visual promise of our mission's end and the simple pleasures that came with it.

Ten minutes later, I counted my soldiers in through the T-wall barriers. Twenty out, twenty in. End of mission. SFC Big Country brought up the rear of our patrol, ensuring that no one strayed from the pack.

"Another productive mission," I said, my words laced with undertones.

He looked down at me, grabbed my shoulder for leverage, and began to stretch his legs. "Hell, sir," he said, "we all made it back. That's the most important thing."

When he finished stretching, we took a seat on the front stoop. I accepted his offer of a cigarette and took a quick drag. I coughed but did my best to muffle it. I still didn't get a buzz from tobacco, but it usually made the headaches go away.

"You're right, of course," I told my platoon sergeant after a few minutes of silence. "That is the most important thing. Mission accomplished." I paused melodramatically. "Think we'll get a banner?"

He laughed and said no, probably no banner. I looked up at the moon, which still grinned madly. We would sleep before it did. I took another drag from my cigarette and watched smoky embers rage into nothingness on the concrete. Then I walked inside, eager to shed my body armor, hoping that our patrol had tired me out enough that I would be able to sleep instead of think about things beyond my control.

I fell asleep eventually, despite myself.

ROCKETS AT THE SOCCER FIELD

"*LT G!*"

Captain Whiteback's bellow echoed through the combat outpost. I was in my room sometime around midnight and, in perfect army asymmetry, had just finished briefing my platoon sergeant and section sergeants on the tentative schedule for the next three days. The key word was tentative, of course. I slumped my shoulders and shook my head. "Why does Allah hate the Irish man?" I asked Staff Sergeant Bulldog, who just snorted in response.

"Better go see what he wants," SFC Big Country advised, while Staff Sergeant Boondock sneered wickedly. "It's fragolicious!"

It certainly was. Twenty minutes later, we Gravediggers sat in our Strykers at redcon-1, waiting for our terp. The night-blind Suge stumbled down for the mission, helmet in hand, and staggered face-first into the side of the Stryker, falling over. He bounced up, rubbing his head, and yelled at the driver "to turn on Stryker lights, crazy man! It is night out here!" Then our platoon peeled out of the motor pool, set to investigate a reported cache of Katyusha rockets spotted by a group of Iraqi children playing soccer.

When we drove up onto the objective, however, my senior scout reported that a group of IP vehicles was already on the scene. I dismounted with Sergeant Cheech, Corporal Spot, PFC Smitty, Private Hot Wheels, and Suge and told the rest of the platoon to stay mounted and stand by. As I dismounted, Specialist Big Ern played the "Jack Sparrow Anthem" from the *Pirates of the Caribbean* movie soundtrack over his Stryker's external loudspeakers.

"I know you love this song, sir," he shouted down to me.

I laughed and gave him a thumbs-up. He was right. I did love that song.

I strode up to the cluster of Iraqi police standing next to their trucks, while my soldiers established a security perimeter. I started rattling off questions at the IPs, but they just gazed back at me quizzically. A few more seconds of vulgar silence passed until Suge, being the old African lion that he was, lumbered up to our position, all smiles and apologies, and began to translate.

"What are you guys doing here?" I asked.

The first IP spoke. "Yes, we arrested a drunk tonight!"

I turned to Suge. "No, man, ask them why they are here." I pointed at the ground below me. "Right here."

Suge clucked at himself and nodded in understanding. He translated again.

"Because there are rockets over there!" the second IP said, pointing directly to our north.

I shook my head in frustration. I don't get paid enough for this, I thought. "Yes . . . yes, I know that." I decided that asking how they found out about the rockets was a fruitless endeavor and settled on a less Machiavellian approach to tonight's matters. "Have you guys found the rocket cache yet?"

Suge looked at me, confused. He was having a tough time tonight. I pointed to the north. "Where exactly are the rockets?" I said, trying to contain my grimace.

The second IP spoke again. "Over there!" pointing directly to our north.

I rubbed my temples and said, "Fuck it. Follow us. Sergeant Cheech, Spot, let's bust out the metal detector and—"

A third IP came running up out of the darkness. "Mistah, come, come. We find rockets!"

We followed, and sure enough, we found a small cache of Katyusha rockets in the middle of the field north of the road, buried snugly in a small, manmade cavity at midfield. One of the Iraqi police had marked the position by sticking one of the aforementioned rockets straight into the ground, angling it vertically out of the mud. I turned to Suge, bamboozled at this incredibly foolish marking method.

"Fucking Arabs," mustered my terp.

My soldiers, who wisely refused to go within ten feet of the cache upon seeing the obviously toyed-with rocket, asked if they could return to their Stryker before an IP accidentally killed everyone.

I pursed my lips thoughtfully. "I'll race you there," I responded.

For the next twenty minutes until EOD arrived, we overwatched the IPs from the safety of our Strykers, ensuring that they didn't snatch a rocket for their own personal stashes—something I was aware may have occurred before our arrival.

In the meantime, the men in our 3 vehicle roared in hysterics as PFC Das Boot attempted to piss into a bottle to avoid dismounting to relieve himself.

"But Sergeant . . . I do not mean to brag, but my dick, it will not fit into the hole."

"Das Boot," Specialist Big Ern asked from the gunner's cupola, "did you use an air pocket or did ya try and stick the whole thing into the bottle?"

Private First Class Van Wilder (recently promoted) did not stop laughing for ten minutes. Staff Sergeant Boondock pulled out his whiteboard and drew a sketch for PFC Das Boot, explaining the importance of leaving a small pocket of air at the rim to improve flow when urinating in a bottle. I was told later that PFC Das Boot eventually achieved mission success in this endeavor.

EOD pulled up, and I briefed their lieutenant on the situation. Fifteen minutes later, all of the Gravediggers had buttoned up in their respective Strykers and listened on the radio as SFC Big Country and the EOD platoon sergeant ensured that everyone was safe before the controlled detonation.

"White, this is White 4. Report when all personnel are secure in vehicles."

I looked over at PFC Smitty, whose face peeked out of the other rear hatch, and winked. I had ensured that Specialist Flashback parked our Stryker parallel with the detonation area, so we had an ideal view for the detonation. Fuck it, I thought. This is war. Everything we do is a combat risk. What's a little fireworks show?

"This is 1. We're good!" I exclaimed with just enough fervor that an awkward silence followed on the radio.

"Hah, hah, this is gonna be so awesome, sir," PFC Smitty said.

"I hope so. Remember, I'm only allowing this because I conducted a thorough risk assessment," I said with just enough dry inflection in my voice to let my guys know I was kidding. "You got the camera on record, Sergeant Spade?"

"You know it," my gunner said.

"You set, Specialist Flashback?" I asked my driver.

Silence followed.

"You set, Flashback?" I repeated.

More silence.

"Yo, Flashback."

Snore. Snore. Followed by a deep exhale. And then more snoring. I decided to let the detonation wake him up. He could watch the whole event later on the recording.

The EOD platoon sergeant's voice came back on the net. "Ten seconds until detonation."

"Five . . . four . . . three . . . two . . . one . . ." I bit down on my lip and braced for the explosion.

"Fire in the hole! Fire in the hole! Fire in the hole!"

KABOOOOOOOOOOOOOOOOOOOOOOOOOOOOOOOOOOOOMMM.

A small mushroom cloud composed of bright orange smolders and fireball bits pierced the darkness in a flash. Sergeant Spade said later he had seen larger explosions during his first deployment, and was thus a bit underwhelmed, but given that my explosion experience up to this point had been limited to Fourth of July picnics, I certainly was not. A moment of panic had nipped at my brain when I felt a wave of transitory heat brush past my face.

Bits of metallic shrapnel did not arrive with it though, thus ensuring that my oral risk assessment conducted earlier could remain a punch line and not a talking point in front of endless field-grade officers' desks.

I looked across from me. I knew my visage matched PFC Smitty's, which glowed through the moonlight—hanging jaw, arched eyebrows deep-fried in wow, and a slight tightness around the temple area that served as visible evidence that men sometimes did recognize the evaded consequences of their stupidity, if only after the fact.

EOD collected their equipment, thanked us for our patience, and moved out. There was now a large hole in the middle of the soccer field, but at least there weren't any rockets. I woke up Specialist Flashback, and after the other vehicles had woken up their drivers, we rolled back to the combat outpost. We were all asleep within the hour. Another day of missions and patrolling and fragos and counterinsurgency tedium awaited.

THE BROTHEL

"We got nothing, LT." Staff Sergeant Boondock's voice ricocheted off the thin walls of the Iraqi hut we had raided in the dead of the night. "No males, military age or otherwise. Our guys must've bounced already. Nothing here but the mom, the teenage daughter, a younger kid, a baby, and a crazy-ass grandma who won't stop giving me the evil eye. Easy, lady! Put down the broom and come outside."

I stood with the terp Super Mario in the main room of the house, explaining to the mother why we were there. Yes, of course, you can pick up the crying baby. No, we are not here to talk about your eldest daughter being so sick that she's in the hospital, although that is awful. Yes, I want everyone in the house outside. Now. No, you cannot talk to each other. I want to talk to each of you separately. Yeah, including the grandmother.

An hour before, I had been sitting in Sheik Banana-Hands's living room, drinking chai and watching Suzanne Somers's workout videos on very expensive and very golden Arabic couches. My soldiers pulling inner security—Sergeant Cheech and PFC Smitty—were slightly confused by the sight, but I had keyed in on the fact that all my soldiers thought he was a dirty-old-man months ago. Finding him in his pajamas at night learning about the wonders of the Thighmaster only confirmed my suspicions. To his credit

SFC Big Country, the platoon sergeant of the Gravediggers. An Iowa native, he stressed cavalry scout skills for all of his men, and enforced discipline when necessary. He also advised me on mission planning, and his insights were always both perceptive and precise.

though, he hadn't appeared the least bit embarrassed when he found us on his front porch, checking up on him due to a recent assassination threat put out by a JAM cell. He simply invited us in and lectured me about the benefits of "a woman with experience who still exercise. Heh heh heh. You must become habibi [lover] to an older woman as a young man. It is very important."

Sheik Banana-Hands was in the process of bestowing upon me a brand-new chai set when my dismount radio buzzed with want. "White 1, this is White 4." SFC Big Country had the unmistakable "I-am-relaying-a-frago-from-Higher-would-a-plan-every-now-and-then-seriously-kill-these-bastards?" crispness to his voice.

"This is 1."

"Frago."

"But I'm getting my chai set! Can't it wait?"

"Not for a raid, unfortunately."

"Raid? Fine. At least it's not another market assessment. I'll be right there."

Two minutes and a chai set bequeathal later, I received the full rundown from Bounty Hunter X-ray. Fadl, a local thug for a Mahdi Army splinter group, had been spotted at a local female shop owner's house in the northern Shia portion of town with another unknown man. Our source said that Fadl routinely came to this house at night to pay the mother money to freaky-freaky with her teenage daughter.

A family without a man of the house and unable to sustain themselves financially was not a rarity in Saba al-Bor. Unfortunately, neither was the solution utilized by this particular family. After a quick radio rehearsal and confirmation of the house's location, our ghost tanks raced off into the darkness, grateful for this unscheduled variation in the nightly patrol grind.

The vehicle cordon called set. The dismount teams were stacked. I gave Staff Sergeant Boondock the Aloha shaka', and in they swooped, a silent, efficient testament to hours spent training under the rigid specificity of my NCOs. The raid itself lasted no more than two minutes, yielding no Fadl and no unknown man either.

"Time to tactically question," I said, mouth racing after one too many Rip-Its. "One at a time on the patio with me, everyone else in the main room, where you can watch and verify that I am not committing horrible infidel acts to your family members. No talking though. My men are going to search your house. Don't worry, they won't break anything. You don't have any weapons? Not even an AK? No banana-clip magazines? Okay. You first, grandma."

I found two chairs in the main room and pulled them out to the patio. I took off my helmet, set my rifle to the side, and instructed the elderly woman to sit down next to me.

"Hello, ma'am," I said, completely certain that the manners so carefully ingrained into me by my Southern mother would be lost in translation. "My name is Lieutenant Matt, and I need your help."

"I know nothing," she responded to Super Mario's translation automatically. "I am an old woman. I am tired. Let me go back to bed."

"I will," I promised. "Just help me first. We're trying to find bad men we know are causing harm to your family."

"I know nothing."

"We'll see. Maybe you know something important that you do not know is important."

Five minutes and many rebuffs later, I felt stonewalled.

"Fine," I said. "You win. Bring me the little girl. Damn it, I said no talking in there! Translate that as soothingly as possible, Super Mario."

"What's soothingly?"

"Nevermind. They got the point."

A young girl walked up to me shyly, taking Super Mario's hand, which guided her to the seat next to mine. She had big black eyes and wore her hair in pigtails. Her mouth hadn't closed since she had first seen the American giant, PFC Das Boot himself, some minutes earlier.

"Hi," I said. "My name is Matt. What's yours?"

She gazed at Super Mario for many seconds before answering. "Asma."

"What's her deal?" I asked the terp.

"She is surprised I speak Arabic," he said, "because I wear American uniform."

"Ah. Okay, Asma. I was hoping you could help me out."

"With what?" she whispered, avoiding any and all eye contact. Her eyes kept swinging back behind me, to the doorway where her mother and her older sister still were.

"Do any men live here?" I asked.

"Not since my father died."

"When was that?"

"One year ago, I think."

"Do any men come here now? Men who aren't in your family?"

Her eyes betrayed her once more. She tried glancing behind me again, and when I moved my body so as to block her vantage point, she suddenly became very interested in a piece of concrete below her.

"No," she said. "The only men that ever come here come during the day to our shop."

"Please, don't lie to me. I thought we were friends. Aren't we friends?"

There was a slight pause before she answered. "No."

I couldn't believe it. My friendship request had been rejected by an eight-year-old. "No? Why not?"

"Because you are American," she replied matter-of-factly.

Well, at least I got one honest answer out of her, I thought. Super Mario laughed, in spite of himself, and gave it a shot. "What about me?" he asked. "I am Iraqi. Can we be friends?"

She didn't even bother to hesitate this time. "No, you are Iraqi, but you are American now. We cannot be friends. I'm sorry."

I tried to ask her who had said we couldn't be friends, but one could only ask an eight-year-old so many questions before the kid oystered up. There were pearls of wisdom tucked away in there, but I certainly wasn't going to uncover them.

"Hey, sir." Staff Sergeant Boondock loomed in the doorway. "House is clear. No weapons, no propaganda, not even an expensive TV. Nothing."

"Any sign of a man being here recently? Clothes or something?"

He shook his head. "Nope. The only thing is . . . well . . . I think the story we got is right. There's only one mattress in the entire house, and it's in the older daughter's room. Queen size. That doesn't make any sense."

"Okay." I hadn't been looking forward to this questioning. I was awkward enough with girls, even when I wasn't accusing them of being terrorist whores selling their body to Mahdi Army insurgents hell-bent on my bloody destruction. "Might as well bring her out here, then."

Out came an Iraqi girl so homely it was striking. She was built like a rectangle, seemingly hadn't washed her hair for weeks, and wore way too much bright red blush. She claimed she was twenty-three, but I wouldn't have placed her a day over sixteen. The dynamics of this questioning had changed considerably from the last one. Now, my interviewee kept trying to stare at me, while I avoided any and all eye contact.

"I was hoping you could help us out by answering a few questions."

"Sure. I'd love to help out the Americans."

"Right. We know you know a man named Fadl. Tell us where he is now."

"Fadl? I do not know a Fadl." I looked back up at her face, searching for signs of a wry grin but found nothing except dreary eyes probing me like I was an alien freshly arrived from Mars. Just like the slutty girls back in high school, I thought, an empty face with an empty gaze. She had seen too much of the primal desires of man already to have any sense of awe anymore. There was no intrigue left in human relationships for her.

"There is no reason to lie to me. We know what is going on here. I don't care about that. We need to talk with Fadl."

"I do not know anyone by that name," she said. I couldn't decide if I had picked up a tinge of smugness in her voice, or if that had been my imagination. I asked her about her bed and was told that the whole family slept on the mattress with her. That was as far as I was willing to go with that subject. We couldn't help people who didn't want to be helped.

I now asked the mother to come out to the patio. I could hear the frustration seeping into my own voice. My men paced anxiously, waiting for me to finish. I went with the expedited version of tactical questioning.

"Do you know a man named Fadl?"

"No."

"Do bad men come here at night?"

"No."

"Are you lying to me?"

"No."

The mother stared back at me, just as aloofly as her teenage daughter had minutes before, and then smiled. I had lived with a single mother long enough to know that this woman was feigning deference. Behind this masquerade of feminine submission was a tartness as sharp as razor blades and a will as staunch as steel. Boyish charm or no, this woman wanted me out of her house as soon as possible—and that meant perpetuating the lies of her family members. I decided that she was thinking that the known horrors of Fadl were still better than the unknown horrors that could occur if it was learned she'd helped the Americans.

I tilted my head and looked back at her. "I understand why you're lying to me. You are scared. I would be scared too." I pulled out my notepad, tore out a piece of blank paper, and handed that and a pen to Super Mario. "Write down the number to the combat outpost," I told him, before continuing my talk with the mother. "Call us if you get scared again. We can help you." I took the paper from Super Mario and pressed it in the mother's hands. "We want to help you."

She bit her lip and whispered back at me. "I will." She looked around her, absorbing the tall, broad-shouldered, straight-backed, clean-shaven, stoic profiles of SFC Big Country, Staff Sergeant Boondock, Sergeant Spade, and PFC Das Boot. For the briefest of moments, I thought she was going to collapse into one of their arms and begin weeping. Instead, she simply bit her lip again and stared down at the ground. It was the final, and surest, sign for us to depart.

On our way out though, I waved the teenage girl out of the house and to the front walkway. She brushed past her still motionless mother and strolled up to us.

"Tell Fadl," I said as soon as she came within earshot, "that we're going to capture him or kill him. It's only a matter of time." I turned around and walked on to our Strykers, not bothering to listen to a fresh set of protests of ignorance.

A few days later—after receiving intel that Fadl had left town—we conducted a patrol in the same neighborhood as the house in question and decided to pay a visit. The dismounts hadn't even knocked on the front door yet when the gunners radioed us, saying that they had stopped a car with two military-aged males trying to break the cordon and make an escape.

Neither of them was Fadl. They were just two nobody punks, drunk on something and high on something else. They eventually admitted, though, that they had visited with the dreary eyes on the queen-size mattress. For a price, of course.

Fadl's fleeing Saba al-Bor hadn't solved all of the family's problems—certainly not the financial ones. We called the IPs, who detained the two for being under the influence, and then we remounted our Strykers. Perhaps there was something kinetic in nature out there for us to deal with.

If there was, we intended to find it.

THE MOSQUE RAID

I saw the stun grenade before I heard it. The flash washed out my night vision, blinding me momentarily. Then I heard the blast break the early-morning silence, crashing like a ceramic plate dropped to the ground. Harsh, rigid shouts in the distance followed, some one hundred meters to my front. This is not good, I thought. I need to do something.

I squatted on the side of the road and switched knees to relieve the pressure. I was currently just one small part of a great camo odyssey, along with five members of my platoon—Sergeant Spade, Specialist Tunnel, Specialist Haitian Sensation, PFC Cold-Cuts, and PFC Smitty—a squad of American military police (MP), a squad of Iraqi police, and approximately forty members of Task Force Cobra. The reason for such a miscellany of Coalition forces boiled down to one thing: Task Force Cobra's heavy-handed reputation. When they told us that they had a target in Saba al-Bor, in the vicinity of the Sunni mosque on Route Gold, our Higher begged them to allow a unit from Bravo Troop to accompany them. Shockingly, Task Force Cobra's leadership acquiesced. However, because of the raid's proximity to the mosque, Task Force Cobra's patrol leader—presumably a special ops captain or major, although he wore no rank and told me to call him Steve, so I didn't know for sure—asked for Iraqi police support so that they could use the Iraqis to clear the mosque if necessary. This, in turn, meant a squad of MPs joined the mission, as they were under orders to go everywhere the IPs went. All of this baggage frustrated the Task Force Cobra supersoldiers to no end, as they normally operated as an independent entity. Concurrently, my role in all of this was crystal clear.

"Dude," Captain Whiteback said to me before we left the combat outpost on foot, "you're the ranking normal army guy out there. Just make sure they don't break too much, okay? We'll still be here tomorrow; they won't."

Easier said than done. My radio gurgled with a report from Task Force Cobra's assault force. "We got two men on the ground! They've been temporarily disabled by the flashbangs, and we're searching them now. We're on the roof of the mosque."

Goddamn it. They were supposed to come no closer to the mosque than the building directly east of it. If one golden rule existed in our modern counterinsurgency, it was that Americans did not enter anything Muslims considered holy. To do so constituted a public relations disaster and always seemed to have second- and third-order effects that crippled the greater COIN effort. All of the Iraqi police were across the road from me, gazing into the darkness with confused expressions.

"These guys say they're security guards for the mosque," the assault force reported. "Both have AK-47s. One of them matches the target's description, but the name on his ID card doesn't match."

Steve's voice responded. "Roger. Clear the building and continue tactical questioning."

This, I thought again, is definitely not good. I stood up, turned around, and found Sergeant Spade. "I'm going up there," I said. "Watch the guys and the MPs. I'm taking the IP squad with me."

I jogged across the road and told the MP NCO he and the IPs were coming with me, after which we strode up Route Gold toward the mosque.

Task Force Cobra's support force kneeled on both sides of the road in a staggered column. As we neared the front gate of the mosque, a Task Force Cobra soldier materialized out of the night and put his hand up. Like seemingly every member of his unit, this soldier was as tall as SFC Big Country and as muscled as Staff Sergeant Bulldog. He towered over me, the MP NCO, and the Iraqis.

"Whoa, Lieutenant, no one goes past here except TF Cobra," he said.

"Bullshit," I responded. "That's a fucking mosque. You guys aren't supposed to be in there, and you know it. You need the Iraqi police in there now."

The giant tilted his head and smirked down at me. This bastard is amused, I thought, fuming. Nevertheless, he turned around and whispered into his radio. Ten seconds later, presumably after receiving a response, he turned back around and nodded.

"Alright. Go ahead. The APL [assistant patrol leader] will meet you at the back entrance."

I nodded back and started walking. The back entrance? Good Christ, that meant they were already in the building. I prayed they weren't executing their normal clearing procedures.

When we walked around the side of the mosque, the APL stood at the back entrance. Unlike Steve, the APL wasn't special operations but rather a new member of the Ranger Regiment. He had served in a standard army unit on his first deployment. Only a year older than me and a junior captain in rank, he and I had discussed mutual friends and traded junior-officer gripes back at the combat outpost before the mission ensued.

I pointed at the door, and the IPs and the MP NCO understood, moving inside. I saw Task Force Cobra soldiers already inside. "Dude," I said to the APL, "what the fuck?"

"I know, I know," he said. "We're not supposed to be in here. But they found a second ID card in the guy's shoes that matches the name we have, and he said he's a guard here. He killed soldiers and marines in Fallujah as a sniper, you know? Steve said to go ahead and clear it. . . . You know how it is. The IPs live here. They won't be looking too hard for fear of actually finding something."

He had a point. The Iraqi police weren't exactly known for their trust-worthiness or their dedication to duty. And I hadn't known exactly what the target had been wanted for before the APL told me; learning certainly sparked the vengeful part of my being. Still, though, this all felt wrong.

"Shouldn't we call the imam?" I asked, referring to the clerical head of the mosque.

"I think it's too late for that," he replied. "We're almost done."

I followed his steps into the main room of the mosque. My infidel boots met a hallowed floor made of solid grey concrete. Bookshelves lined the walls, filled with holy texts. Scattered pages and a few books lay on the floor beneath the shelves, left there by hasty Task Force Cobra soldiers. Rugs, mats, and blankets were heaped together all around the room, and I somehow doubted that was how the imam kept them organized.

I arched an eyebrow the APL's way, and he blustered out a response. "We're trying to be as respectful as possible," he said. "Really."

The APL's radio buzzed. It was Steve requesting his presence in an adjacent room. As I started to follow, however, I heard the oh-so-distinctive sound of glass shattering outside. Please, tell me that is a drunk Iraqi dropping a bottle, I thought. I knew it wasn't.

I walked out of the mosque to a side street located on the far end of the building, next to the initial target house. I found four Task Force Cobra soldiers standing around a white car underneath a streetlight. The driver's side window was smashed in, the glass scattered in the car and on the ground below it. One of the soldiers was sizing up the butt of his rifle against the rear window on the driver's side, while another one of the soldiers showed him the best place to strike the glass. I guessed this was a Ranger NCO conducting an impromptu window-breaking session with a Ranger Joe.

"What the hell are you doing?" I asked.

Four massive, thick shapes turned toward me simultaneously. I suddenly felt very alone, very small, and very cognizant of being an officer. I realized it would be far too easy for these giants to stuff a strange, lecturing, 140-pound lieutenant into the car through the broken window.

"Just conducting a class," the Ranger NCO said matter-of-factly.

"Right. I'm not trying to be gay or anything, but we'll have to deal with this tomorrow; you won't. So don't break anymore locals' car windows just because you're bored, okay?"

Five seconds passed, and three of the soldiers turned toward the Ranger NCO who originally spoke.

"Roger," he said.

"Roger what?" I responded sharply. I'd never been one to abide rigidly by proper military decorum, but these guys were out of control.

"Roger, sir."

"Thank you, Sergeant." I turned around, started walking, and took a deep breath. What did they feed these guys, I thought, horse tranquilizers? I was glad they were on my side.

I walked back to the mosque and met Steve and the APL on the front steps. I told them about the car incident, and while the APL was contrite, Steve just barked a laugh and said, "They did? Those fuckers!" Having found nothing of significance in the mosque, we walked back to the combat outpost, two detainees in tow. Ten minutes later, the detainees and Task Force Cobra flew away to Baghdad in their helicopters.

Captain Whiteback called the imam that night and apologized profusely. Nevertheless, there was a protest at the front gates of the combat outpost the next morning by local Sunnis outraged that infidels had violated their mosque. It threatened to turn into a full-blown riot until Captain Whiteback called in the Sunni sheiks and threatened to take away their Sahwa pay if they didn't disperse their people. The protest ended shortly thereafter.

III: iWAR

(OR THE LOST SUMMER)

SUMMER 2008

Rumble, young man, rumble.
— Muhammad Ali

IN A LITTLE PLASTIC BIN

I sat alone in a Porta-John mumbling to myself. I held a flashlight in one hand, and my rifle stood upright in the corner, muzzle down. I had locked the door already, something I kept checking repeatedly.

It had been a long day. A really long fucking day. So I fled to my sanity box and decided to work through things:

ShootMoveAndCommunicateBOOMBOOM.

Scouts Out.

ShootMoveAndCommunicateBOOMBOOM.

Scouts Out.

ShootMoveAndCommunicateBOOMBOOM.

Scouts Out.

The days bleed into nights, and the nights bleed into days, and there's really no point in acknowledging the difference anymore. The sun just means we drink more water; the night just means we live in the green world of night vision rather than the grey world of day vision. Patrol. Eat. Sleep. Patrol. Go to meeting. Patrol. Eat. Make phone calls home and ignore the strain in their voices since they're doing the same. Patrol. Sleep. Get woken up in a panic; it's time for a new and fragolicious patrol.

Emotional burnouts. All of us. Life is nothing more than a Frogger game with IEDs. Mesopotamian sand rests at the bottom of my lungs like spare change in a swimming pool. I'm still removing bits of Boss Johnson flesh grunge from my memory with a spatula.

Chew tobacco.

Chew tobacco.

Chew tobacco.

Spit.

If you ain't cav,

you ain't shit.

Born after the 'Nam. No illusions about what war is and what war does to the human condition exist or ever existed. Sure, it still shocks the senses into nothingness, but I can't claim ignorance to this inevitability. Going here was almost like finding a validation for being so disillusioned in the first place. Yeah,

---

I did it backward, but at least I did it. At least my children and grandchildren might be tricked into thinking that the iWar destroyed my generation's wits and yielded our indulgences, not knowing the real culprit had been cartoon overdose some twenty years previous. How embarrassing would that revelation be? Ruined before puberty; truly, a historic achievement worthy of posterity.

iWar?

Yeah. iWar. iWar. Fitting, in that succinct, catchy pop-culture kind of way. Perfect for this era of irony and commercialization and technology. Just like iPod, iTunes, iPhone, and iRack. They can learn all about the iWar on the e-world, just by sitting down at a computer. They just choose not to.

I War. Subject. Verb. Where's the object? We're still looking for it, some five years later. How's that for iRony?

A generation has to be involved and interested for a generational calling to occur. Something beyond stretching the limits of the small warrior caste has to transpire in that wet dream of slogan speak and Orwellian doublethink.

I'd never do it for real, of course.

Still, though. It's there. And enticing during those select moments when I honestly don't care anymore. I don't care about you, I don't care about me, and I certainly don't give a fuck about things. Anythings. Everythings. Things.

I just want all the hurt to go away.

My officer basic course class just sent our second member to Fiddler's Green, the cavalry equivalent of the afterlife. Well, we didn't send him. A mortar attack did, just as a catastrophic IED blast sent the first. Did any of us think we could actually die back then? Like really die? For real die? They almost got Lieutenant Demolition with an EFP last week. His Stryker engine ate it. Would my Stryker engine do that for me?

Close only counts in horseshoes and hand grenades.

And in atomic bombs.

Life makes sense in this little plastic bin.

The black dogs of self-doubt can turn into ravenous monsters, especially late at night. Especially here. Especially when I'm alone. Especially when I can't sleep. Especially happens too much.

Talk to the people.

Okay.

I know people care about the iWar. But not enough, given the circumstances. Not even close. Agree or disagree with the war, I don't care—just give a fuck. Be able to find Basra on a map, know that the Tigris isn't some sort of unholy crossbreed found at the San Diego Zoo, try to figure out the difference between a Sunni and a Shia even if it conplexes and perfuses the mind beyond repair. I wish I could issue some loud, righteous proclamation here about the repercussions of such continued resounding American apathy, but who are we kidding? The warrior caste is simply too small nowadays and too proud. There will be no reckoning for all of this. We'll fight the fights not because we necessarily want to but because no one else will. We were bred to protect. Even if we're protecting nothing more than an isolationistic yawn prefacing the continental slumber history demands occur after protracted warfare.

Stop talking to the people. They aren't listening.

Okay.

They never were.

I used to dream of a life without consequences. Like that defiant sand castle though, it got swallowed up by a crashing surf of memories, washed away, lost in the swirl of bleeding blue.

iWar. Mine, not yours. This war. My War. Our War. We War. I War.

You peace. Out.

Savage wars of peace. Kipling's phrase about insurgencies and counter-insurgencies. Savage phrase, that war of peace.

Lord, give me the strength not to attack with a baseball bat every fool and every chickenhawk and every child of apathy and every soft elitist and every intellectual hack and every Jody scumbag and every yuppie and every thirty-something fraud still finding himself when I get home. It's not worth my time. Do give me the strength to convince them to stop breeding and to kill themselves, in the name of bettering humanity. It's the only chance we have.

And, yes, I am that self-righteous. And kidding.

One of the above statements is true.

Nothing is when it is still today and I already don't remember tomorrow.

There are many horrors found in Iraq, but I doubt any are as deliberate as monotony, sucking away at inner Hooah-beats like a parasitical terrorist bug.

Long stretches of boredom interrupted by brief moments of sheer terror. Does this moment count? I am terrified. And it doesn't feel so brief. I've been in here for more than a few minutes. I'd check my watch, but clocks stopped corresponding to time a few months ago.

I'd never do it for real, of course.

Things. Hurt. War. People. Pain. Hunger. Hopeless. Pointless. All of it. We are born crying, maybe live long enough to really cry again, and then die unable to cry anymore. Does it matter what happens in between?

Yes.

It's white in here. As white as the future, blank as an albino. Like the foam of the ocean. Like mom's pristine carpet. Like what the stars look like winking behind illumination rounds.

Like escape.

I'd never do it for real, of course.

Hurt. There's just so much of it. Especially here. It's an abyss. I can't help these people. No one can. They can't help themselves, and neither can the great American sympathy.

There it is again. The siren's song of gone. A freedom bird that doesn't land anywhere at all. It just hovers there, waiting. The ultimate escape. Enticingly empty and hollow and spotless and smooth. Oh, so smooth.

The eternal scream versus the fleeting smile.

My men need me. They have real problems. Real concerns. Real issues. This life is temporary for me; I'll be able to get out. They don't have that luxury. This mad Celtic depression brought on by self-aggrandizement and shattered hopes and broken ideals is beyond cliché. I don't see them cowering in a Porta-John, rocking themselves through a mental crisis in a deluded trance, do I?

Well, no. But that's kind of the point of doing it here. To be alone, away from prying eyes and judgmental minds.

Good point.

Shut up and drive on.

Worry about the things I can control. Just do that and I'll be fine.

I want to control it all. Then I'd be fine.

Just don't be soft. Just don't be soft.

That has always been man's greatest tragedy, hasn't it? It's not the doubting of God's intentions, or even of His existence, that really tears apart our souls. It's that we honestly believe we'd do a better job than Him if granted the opportunity.

I may not be as hard as I want to be, but I ain't fucking soft.

Red splashed across white makes pink. I learned that in art class, during summer camp. We had art class after lunch and before tennis lessons, which was before swimming lessons. I didn't like art class or tennis lessons because I hated waiting for swimming lessons.

It'd be pink. A pink mist.

Too messy. Too banal. Too cowardly.

That one dead Sahwa's jawbone still had falafel in it, even after the flashlight bomb blew his face off. Finding that was a bad day. Worse than today. And that day ended. Falafels taste like hajji and hell heat and body armor and alone.

I don't eat falafels anymore, even when Suge buys them for me.

Exhale and tug on the lip. It feels. Funny. It feels funny. Nothing to see here. Move along. Just a wolf crying boy. Still, though. I can hear my heart. Something, anything, to get the brainberry juices flowing again. There it is. Nice. I'm good.

There are some poor-ass Iraqis out there who need this platoon leader to attempt to actually give a fuck and to pretend like he knows what the fuck he is doing in the first place. They need me. And they aren't the only ones. The men need me, and they need my smirk. So pull up my pants, grab my rifle, and smirk. Like spitting in the devil's eye, that smirk. Especially here.

I'm back. To the Anythings. The Everythings. Things.

My men need me.

I opened up the only door from the sanity box to Iraq. I took a deep breath and smirked to myself. I needed to write a patrol debrief upstairs. I started walking that way.

"I'm good," I remembered out loud. "I'm good."

THE BON JOVI IED

As part of our recurring duties as night watchmen at Sheik Nour's compound, we patrolled Route Tampa, the highway stretch that served as the logistical spinal column for the massive American body draped across Iraq. During this mission set, I always put out the same radio call every four hours to the gunners pulling security:

"White, this is White 1. Wake your vehicle up and get redcon-1. It's Tampa time."

On Memorial Day weekend, Specialist Cold-Cuts (recently promoted) sat perched in the gunner's cupola of my vehicle. After my radio call, I realized I hadn't heard him speak over the internal net recently. Given his proclivity for talking, I found this odd.

"Hey, Cold-Cuts, you ready, dude?"

Silence followed.

"Yo, Cold-Cuts?"

"I think he's asleep, sir," PFC Smitty said matter-of-factly from the driver's hole.

I leaned across my seat and tugged at Specialist Cold-Cuts leg and yelled into my headset. "Hey, Cold-Cuts, you redcon-1?"

The platoon walks through northwestern Saba al-Bor on a dismounted patrol near a mosque. Groups of Iraqi children routinely joined the patrols, eager for conversation and candy.

"Wha . . . huh?" The unmistakable smacking of lips confirmed PFC Smitty's assessment.

"Dude, wake up and get redcon-1. We need to patrol Tampa again."

Specialist Cold-Cuts started to stammer out an excuse, thought better of it, and then giggled. "Sorry, LT. Really. Last thing I remember I was awake. I promise. I thought my eyes were still open."

I shook my head. "I'm sure. Just rotate out next time, okay? There are four of us down here, including myself. Suge's the only one on this vehicle who doesn't pull security. The gunner is pretty much the only person who can't fall asleep when we're stationary."

"Roger, sir, it won't happen again. I'm redcon-1." He paused. "Hey, I drooled all over myself! There's a huge puddle of it up here!"

I looked back at Sergeant Axel, who wore a headset in the back of the vehicle, and we shook our heads at one another. It wasn't really Specialist Cold-Cuts's fault; someone should have been up with him. And we'd all fallen asleep on security before, I sheepishly admitted, including myself. After you'd pulled this mission for the 3,000th time, things like this happened.

"Want me to play the Spice Girls?" PFC Smitty asked me. "I know how that song always cheers you up."

I laughed. "Maybe later, man. We can't overplay our go-to song."

Minutes after midnight, our four Strykers rolled out of the alleyways surrounding Nour's estate and turned south onto Route Tampa. "Still no sight of Nour's niece," Staff Sergeant Boondock reported from his vehicle. "Where is that little hottie? She's the whole fucking reason I park my vehicle close to the swimming pool."

"How old is she again?" I asked. No American knew for sure, and most didn't want to ask the question, for fear of getting an answer they didn't want to hear.

"Fuck that statutory shit, she's old enough," PFC Van Wilder replied. "If she's old enough to be prancing in front of American soldiers like she does, she's definitely old enough for us to watch her."

Fair enough, I thought. PFC Van Wilder's statement reminded me and my Stryker crew of his conversation with Specialist Big Ern a few weeks back, when the former returned to the combat outpost from leave and greeted the latter: "Admit it, you missed me," PFC Van Wilder had said, grinning ear to ear.

"Naw, I didn't," Specialist Big Ern replied.

"Really?"

"Oh, alright. Come here and give me a hug. How was leave?"

"Wild. A crazy chick asked me to choke her out during sex. It was awesome."

"That sounds awesome. Can we stop hugging now?"

My vehicle howled in delight recalling that story. The radio soon disrupted our joviality.

"White 1, this is Strykehorse X-ray."

I groaned. Radio calls at this time of night from the squadron TOC rarely brought good news. When they had radioed us some four hours before, they told us to look out for a man named Ali driving a white pickup truck. Finding that description slightly vague, I asked for more details. Like whether or not he was Arab. They told me they weren't sure.

"This is White 1."

"Roger, move south to Checkpoint 55. There's a convoy there that has come to a halt on the far side of that checkpoint. They're reporting there's a box there with some wires coming out of it. They need someone to check it out."

"They can't check it out themselves?" I responded, stating the obvious. "If it's bad enough for them to stop, why haven't they called EOD?"

The radio man on the other end of our transmission just snickered. "It's a large convoy of fobbits, making their once-a-year run between FOBs. So no, they can't check it out themselves."

I just shook my head and relayed the frago to my platoon. Flabbergasted, Staff Sergeant Boondock spat out, "Good Christ, this is disgusting. You know it's bad when a TOC roach is making fun of these ass-clowns."

As we drove up to the near side of Checkpoint 55, our senior scout spotted the convoy. "Those mutha fuckas, they on the other side of the checkpoint," Staff Sergeant Bulldog reported. "They keep beaming us and shit with their lights, but none of 'em are on the ground. How the fuck can they even see anything from where they're at? They're too far away!"

"That's why we're here," I said. "We'll check it out for them."

As PFC Smitty dropped the Stryker's back ramp, Sergeant Axel asked if we should wake up Suge. Our terp slept in his seat, sprawled out like a rape victim. He hated the long missions at Nour's but refused to allow any of the younger terps go with us on them, insisting that we were his platoon and our missions were his missions.

"It's cool," I said. "We won't need him for this. Let the old man sleep."

I met our dismount teams on the ground, and we strode south in a wedge formation on the other side of the road from the convoy. One of the convoy soldiers laser-beamed the area of concern. SFC Big Country took out his flashlight, turned it on, and surveyed the spot.

"Broken banana crates," he said calmly, picking up a large piece and tossing it off the road. "They stopped all the traffic on Tampa for broken banana crates."

Some of the Gravediggers laughed. Others cursed. I stayed silent. I felt numb to these types of moments by now. They happened often enough.

While SFC Big Country took a fire team to inform the convoy that all was clear, Staff Sergeant Boondock picked up the remaining pieces of the crate and started pelting Specialist Tunnel, using every colorful epithet for "pogue" imaginable. We still hadn't found the reported wires though, and I knew that we would inevitably be asked whether anything had blown up or not. I retraced our steps to the north and, through the darkness, spotted a long, dangling cord connected to a small, squarish piece of plastic.

Instinctively, I reached for my radio, but before I keyed the hand mic, I caught an odd glint in the moonlight. I walked up to the long cord and kneeled down. Instead of finding wire, I stared at five inches of spool. I yanked on the spool, and a cassette tape flew into my hands.

I flipped the tape over to find it was Bon Jovi's *Slippery When Wet*, a classic relic from the 1980s. After asking the soldiers if any of them wanted a vintage tape of 1980s glam rock, I tossed it to the side of the road. I told everyone to mount back up and found my platoon sergeant returning from the far side of the checkpoint.

"They have anything to say?" I asked.

SFC Big Country laughed. "Yeah. They said, 'Thanks.'"

"What, those mutha fuckas' don't own no flashlights?" Staff Sergeant Bulldog asked. "What the fuck?"

"It could be worse," Staff Sergeant Boondock offered as we traipsed back to our vehicles. "We could've called in EOD for a banana crate and a cassette tape. That would have been pretty fucking embarrassing."

As we walked back north in our wedge, Private Hot Wheels busted out the chorus to Bon Jovi's "Wanted Dead or Alive," and the rest of the platoon either joined in or started booing. We got back on our respective Strykers, and I called for redcon statuses.

"This, uhh, White 2," Staff Sergeant Bulldog drawled. "We redcon-1."

"White 1, this is White 3. We're redcon-1!" Staff Sergeant Boondock burst. "Hate fists are up!"

"This is 4," SFC Big Country thundered. "Let's roll."

"On your move, 2," I said, watching the wheels of my senior scout's vehicle begin to churn forward.

The patrol continued.

A STAR-CROSSED RECONCILIATION

Evenings spent at Sheik Banana-Hands's manor rarely failed to entertain. The old sheik brimmed with melodrama and fatalism, traits that made it easy for me to overlook his JAM ties and questionable loyalties. In addition to his Thighmaster fetish, he loved all things caramel, regaled us with old soldier tales from the Iran-Iraq War, and blamed all violence in the history of civilization on feminine wiles. Even Staff Sergeant Boondock eventually warmed up to our impromptu discussions with the sheik, under the pretense of providing lethal muscle to balance out my baby face on the local counterinsurgency approach.

With the purpose of discussing rumored weapons traffickers working in the sheik's Sahwa, we stopped by his place on a dry summer evening. Staff Sergeant Boondock, PFC Smitty, Private Hot Wheels, and Suge Knight joined me and the sheik inside, while the rest of the platoon established a security perimeter. Usually, we bantered for a few minutes, easing into the uncomfortable specifics that spawned the meeting in the first place. Tonight though, the sheik skipped over such niceties.

"I just receive a call from my men!" he said as soon as we sat down on his immaculate gold couches. "They say they capture someone trying to run over here from Sunni side of town in the dark. Maybe they trying to plant IED!" He pointed at his map of Saba al-Bor, prominently displayed underneath a hilariously austere portrait of himself floating in a background of orange clouds. He pointed at the road that bisected the Sunni and Shia areas of our little Iraq microcosm—known as Route Flames by Coalition forces. "They are bringing the person here so I can question him."

"Interrogate away!" I told him with a sly smile. "We'll be here drinking chai if you decide he's worth keeping."

Staff Sergeant Boondock radioed the rest of the platoon, updating them on the situation, and after five more minutes of Suzanne Somers exercise videos, we heard a car pull up outside. Sheik Banana-Hands sprang up from his chair, and we followed him out the front door.

Two Sons of Iraq exited the front of a sedan, and while one pulled security with his AK-47, the other opened the rear door to bring out their captive. I half expected the reincarnation of Saddam Hussein to appear. Instead, a small girl with darting black eyes and tears streaming down her face skulked out of the back of the car. I estimated her age to be thirteen, and she couldn't have weighed more than ninety pounds.

"What the fuck?" Staff Sergeant Boondock asked behind me. "This night is getting fucking bizarre."

Sheik Banana-Hands's men frisked the young girl and, having determined she was weapons-of-mass-destruction free, turned her over to their leader. He grabbed her by the shoulder and led her back inside. I looked at my men, shrugged my shoulders, and followed. It wasn't like we had anything better to do.

The girl's rags contrasted sharply with the sheik's material prosperity, and she quickly became fascinated with an encased jewel collection in the back corner of the room. After being instructed to sit down on the golden couches—something she clearly found uncomfortable—Sheik Banana-Hands spoke to her in Arabic. She stared at the ground in shame and occasionally whispered back in response. Suge leaned over and translated for me.

"He ask her what she is doing running from Sunni side. She say she live near here and was going home. She say she is Shia. She say please don't tell my father. She is crying again."

"I can see that, Suge."

"Oh, of course! He ask her if she put the IED in the ground. She says no, no, nothing like that. He say then why do you violate curfew? Only Ali Babas violate curfew. She say that she is no Ali Baba, but she is scared to tell him why because he is powerful sheik. He say that he will take her to jail now and her father can get her there if she does not tell truth. She say she will tell truth, but not in front of Americans. They scare her."

I looked around the room. I knew that how she saw us differed from how I saw us, but still, we were hardly in our most intimidating form. Staff Sergeant Boondock had his helmet cocked back, grinning widely, and PFC Smitty and Private Hot Wheels leaned against the back wall, pulling security casually with big wads of dip in their mouths. I myself was more interested at the moment in a mosquito I couldn't seem to swat than channeling raw American fury; coming to terms with my own boogeyman status proved a didactic experience. Subsequently, the sheik led the girl into a side room, returning some forty seconds later. His deep belly laugh filled the room like a balloon filled with hot air.

"She has Sunni boyfriend she visits at night!" he said between wheezes. "She say her father would beat her if he knew she had a boyfriend, especially a Sunni boyfriend!" The girl reemerged behind him, still petrified and unsure how to react to the old man's hysterics. I bit my lip to suppress a smile in light of the girl's embarrassment. "You understand why I laugh?" he asked.

"Yeah," I said. "My grandma was horrified when my mom told her she was marrying a Catholic. Same concept, right?"

My own family tale sent the sheik into a new fit of laughter. "Hah! Yes, yes! Catholics are like Sunnis! Ha ha!"

"Kind of like that Romeo and Juliet story, ain't it, sir?" PFC Smitty shook his head from the other side of the room. "Her daddy prolly *would* kill her if he found out."

Suge stood up, patted the girl on the shoulder, and barked orders at the sheik's men. He turned back to me. "I tell them to take her home and not to tell father. She has suffered enough tonight. I do not think she will try to sneak over to Sunni side for long time. That is okay with you, LT? I thought it is what you would want."

I nodded.

Sheik Banana-Hands clapped his hands, ensuring his men followed Suge's instructions. After the sedan pulled away, girl in tow, he couldn't stop chuckling to himself. He turned back over to me and Suge, intertwining his long, long fingers into the Arab hand-and-arm signal for working together. "Maybe there is hope for future," he quipped. "The younger generation have their own reconciliation!"

"This guy," Staff Sergeant Boondock muttered under his breath, "is seriously fucking demented."

SHOOT-OUT ON MAIN STREET

I walked in an old-world dream when the gunfire started. I sat straight up in the back of my Stryker and, according to my vehicle crew, yelled into the internal radio, "Burn it all down, you fuckers. Burn it all down!" I didn't remember that part.

While manning a late-night OP on Route Islanders, the platoon pulled security, slept, or discussed Captain Whiteback's upcoming change-of-command ceremony with Captain Ten Bears. Having worked with the affable Captain Ten Bears on the squadron staff in my pre–platoon leader days, I knew the troop would be in capable hands—hands that claimed to contain the strength of ten bears, always with a sly laugh.

In the meantime, a single gunshot echoed to the east, toward the town center of Saba al-Bor. A few seconds passed, and then a small burst of rounds erupted. Silence followed.

"1, this is 3," Staff Sergeant Boondock reported through a bored yawn. "Gunplay in town again. One shot followed by a burst."

"Roger," I said, fully awake by this point. What we had heard was a nightly occurrence, and nothing to get too excited about. What we heard next was different.

A barrage of AK-47 output erupted just to the north of the original volley of gunfire, succeeded by the unrestrained chattering of automatic weapons.

Sporadic bursts of both continued, and the black swirl of the sky lit up with tracer rounds. By the time Captain Whiteback told us to head that way over the radio, our Strykers were already barreling in that direction.

The firefight continued as we got closer. "Be ready to dismount," I said. "If you haven't already locked and loaded, do so now. Gunners, let us know what you see. Ensure your night-vision devices are on, and for Christ's sake, listen to the NCOs."

As soon as our Strykers came within sight of the entrance into town—Route Maples, home of Saba al-Bor's largest market and its main artery—all of the gunfire so prevalent moments before crashed off with the alacrity of a cliff-jumping lemming.

"White 2, does your gunner have contact with anything? Either audio or visual?"

"Negative. Neither."

"What about the dismounts in the rear air-guard hatches?"

"Negative. Neither do dey."

"Roger. Same here. 3, 4, you all see anything different?"

"Nope," and, "That's a negative."

"What. The. Fuck. Over."

Our Strykers crept forward, machine guns scanning for any sign of movement, until we came to the northern reach of Route Maples. In theory, a Sons of Iraq checkpoint existed here, although none currently manned their posts. Specialist Cold-Cuts spotted a group of crouching silhouettes off the street and in the adjacent field, all oriented southward. With the arrival of our ghost tanks, the Sahwa scurried over to us, and we met them on the ground. Super Mario provided the translation, although most of it wasn't necessary. Frantic, panicked pointing transcended the language barrier.

"Ali Baba shoot us! From down there!"

"Yes! Yes! Ali Baba! Shoot! We shoot back!"

"We shoot back lots!"

"Okay," I said. My temples began to throb; I already knew it was going to be one of those nights. "Did you actually see who was firing at you?"

"Ehh . . . no."

"Okay . . . did any of their bullets actually hit anything around here? Like damage something?"

"Ehh . . . no."

"Okay . . . did any of you do anything but fire indiscriminately in the general vicinity that you heard the gun shots come from?"

"Ehh . . ."

I told the Sons of Iraq to resume their posts on the street, while we pressed south on Route Maples. I issued a silent prayer to God asking that somewhere in this hellhole, someone stupid would present himself as a known enemy and a viable target.

Not a soul stirred as we pressed south—not surprising considering the time of night and the minutes-old violence. We eventually made our way to the very southern intersection of Route Maples, finding a near-identical reflection of the scene we had just left in the north. Here though, a group of Iraqi police and Sahwa huddled in doorways instead of lying in a field. They ran up to us, and frantic, panicked pointing followed.

"Ali Baba shoot us! From up there!"

"Yes! Yes! Ali Baba! Shoot! We shoot back!"

"We shoot back lots!"

I sighed and rubbed my temples.

Before I could ask for a damage assessment of the area, the unmistakable tread churning of T-72 tanks rolled in from the west. The Iraqi army had responded to the scene too and, as per their standard operating procedure, busted out their metaphorical sledgehammer. They cleared every house within a three-block radius, filling the streets with irritated families and producing zero insurgents.

Ten minutes later—after the arrival of the IP command—damn near every security element in Saba al-Bor perched itself somewhere along Route Maples. After a rather heated discussion with the IA lieutenant and Sahwa commanders, the IP colonel and I convinced them that the majority of rounds exchanged had been friendly fire. While I was initially open to the possibility of an enemy combatant firing a few rounds at the southern checkpoint, the piles of brass collected at the two checkpoints and the lack of any positive identification persuaded me that failure to adhere to trigger discipline had been the biggest threat during the skirmish. Amazingly, no one had been hurt, despite the number of rounds expended. The IPs consequently returned to their normal patrolling schedule, and I instructed the Sons of Iraq to return to their checkpoints. Then I asked the Iraqi army lieutenant, a chubby man with an immaculately trimmed moustache named Zuhayr, about his plan for the duration of the night.

"I . . . I cannot say in front of my men." Having worked with Lieutenant Zuhayr before, I knew that choosing between paper and plastic at the grocery store overwhelmed him. Still, though, I expected at least a half-hearted lie on his part. Staff Sergeant Spade (recently promoted) and PFC Smitty turned around from their security positions, as confused as I was by this secret plan of no plan.

"What do you mean, you can't say? If you have actionable intelligence, action on it. Do you need our help? I doubt clearing every house is going to do anything but piss off the locals. Why don't we go back to the combat outpost, make some calls to our informants, and—"

Lieutenant Zuhayr turned around and walked away from me. The red clarity seized me, and I exploded in rage.

"HEY!" My voice echoed across the side street we had huddled on, startling everyone. Standing my ground and calling the IA officer back to me with my index finger, I tried to make my lecture as constructive as possible. "If I'm gonna risk the lives of my men by coming here tonight, we're going to work fucking together or I will fucking skull-drag you back to the unemployment line myself." I paused, letting Super Mario translate my words while he attempted to match my anger. The IA lieutenant stared dully off to my right.

I hated these petty Arab alpha-male games. Really, I did.

"I know your major insists that we work together, so you better drop the bullshit attitude and realize that smashing things isn't always the correct course of action." I then decided to use one of the locals' favorite analogies. "After all, even the most ferocious tiger needs a tail. Now," I said, taking a deep breath—"this is your mission, your town, and your country. We are willing to help. Do you need it? Yes or no. Either way, brief me on your plan."

He looked back at me with his eyes bouncing back and forth. "I . . . I do not know who shot at the checkpoint. Perhaps it was a ghost."

I felt my anger break, and I relaxed my posture. "That's cool, man. I don't know who shot at the checkpoint either. It wasn't a ghost though."

I looked at my IA counterpart and tried to relate to him. Men who couldn't admit that they didn't know something or refused to admit that they were wrong about something always failed as leaders, be they American or Iraqi. I was no Dick Winters, but I knew enough to understand that people responded to authenticity, and soldiers did not differ in this regard. This poor bastard never stood a chance. He worried too much about people's opinion of what he was doing rather than just doing it in the first place.

Lieutenant Zuhayr finally said that he'd meet me back at the combat outpost, and we'd plan from there. He left some of his men at the Sahwa checkpoints, beefing up their security temporarily. We exchanged forced pleasantries and a too-hearty handshake. As we walked back to our Strykers, Staff Sergeant Spade and PFC Smitty laughed about their normally goofy lieutenant temporarily turning into the Incredible Hulk.

"You should've knocked his ass out," Staff Sergeant Spade said. "We had your back."

"You know what you should've said, sir?" PFC Smitty offered.

"What's that?"

"You should've said, 'Fuck you and your street. We're going home to America to drink some beers. Handle your own problems.'"

I laughed. We all could've used some beers.

After we got back into our vehicles, I briefed the rest of the platoon on what had happened. Then we returned to the combat outpost and made some telephone calls to our JAM and AQI informants. No one knew anything about the incident.

ON MARTYRDOM, SUICIDE, AND PRESS COVERAGE

In late May, word disseminated through 2–14 Cavalry that Lieutenant Colonel Larry would only promote junior officers to developmental positions if they planned to make the army a career. This positional power play seemed to me to be an overt reaction to the long list of junior officers in our squadron getting out of the military once our tour ended, a list that included my name. While I enjoyed the army, valued my service, appreciated the experience, and certainly had nothing against the institution, I'd already decided that I held other ambitions for my life. As I was happy to stay a scout platoon leader, Lieutenant Colonel Larry's edict originally sounded like good news to me. This reaction didn't last very long.

The next day, Captain Whiteback called me into his office and informed me that the squadron field-grade officers had decided to move me to the position of executive officer (XO) in another troop. This switch, while technically a promotion to a job of greater authority if not higher rank, would take me off the line and away from my soldiers. Although not pleased with this reality, I grudgingly acknowledged that such was the nature of the position. Further, as no new lieutenants were in country, Captain Whiteback said SFC Big

Staff Sergeant Boondock (left) and I join a group of local teenagers and their donkey for a much-deserved break. Though many citizens of Saba al-Bor owned motor vehicles, farm animals being used for manual labor was not an uncommon sight.

Country would assume platoon-leading duties for the Gravediggers. I became especially aggravated by this, not because my platoon sergeant wasn't up to the task, but because it showed an egregious lack of planning and foresight on the part of my superiors. Surplus officers crawled around every staff office on Camp Taji, and the thought of a line platoon going short in such an environment lit my already short fuse.

I told Captain Whiteback that I'd be the best damn XO I could be—if it came to that—but that I still planned on leaving the army, and thus I would be denying another lieutenant who planned on staying in an important opportunity. I also told him how I felt about this reactionary method to filling officer slots, describing it as "self-important chimpanzees making a square peg go into a round hole, logic be damned." He said that he understood but also knew I was really only saying those things because I wanted to stay with my platoon. This was true, I admitted, although it didn't detract from the validity of my other points. I asked if I could speak with the field grades to elucidate my position. Captain Whiteback sighed and agreed, but he warned me that they wouldn't be as sympathetic as he had been. His words proved both understated and prophetic.

Over the ensuing days, I talked with Major Moe and with Lieutenant Colonel Larry. I explained my points succinctly, then patiently listened to recruiting pitches for re-upping. I thanked them but restated that my future lay elsewhere. Then I patiently listened to speeches about times for questions and times for shutting up and executing and how this moment fell into the latter category. I nodded and said I understood their point but respectfully disagreed as it applied to my current station, and I kept my thoughts about the fatalistic subordination of a professional officer to myself. Major Moe left it at that. Lieutenant Colonel Larry did not. In Captain Whiteback's office at the combat outpost, he first told me that he wouldn't move me or anyone else leaving the army to the XO position. He also informed me, in the vintage nasal whine that served as his ass-chewing voice, "You're not going to stay a platoon leader either. The next bullshit tasking that comes down the pipeline has your fucking name on it."

Rage quickly replaced Rip-It juice as the primary sustenance of life in my body, but I bit my tongue, said "Yes, sir," and waited to be dismissed from the office. Then I went to my computer and banged out a short piece about the experience in an attempt to calm down. It didn't help very much. I posted it to my blog that night, without sleeping on the matter and without consulting Captain Whiteback, as per the army's published blogging policy, which stated pieces needed to be vetted by the writer's chain of command. I simply didn't care anymore. I was tired, I was angry, and I had just been threatened for doing nothing more than telling the truth about my plans and wanting to stay with my men. I felt constrained by what I believed to be institutional middle management more interested in career progression than leading soldiers and who wanted yes-men in their ranks more than they did independent thinkers. Perhaps irrationally, I believed that a small act of defiance, like posting an unvetted blog piece, would help me regain control of the situation. I also still believed in truth. Looking back on it, it was really all I had anymore.

Were my actions recklessly immature? Yes, I figured out later that they were, but only after I returned home and regained some safety and perspective. I had neither of those comforts at the time. These actions were also undeniably genuine. And after six soul-draining months in Iraq, authenticity meant far more to me at the time than maturity did.

The original blog piece, titled "The Only Difference Between Martyrdom and Suicide Is Press Coverage," significantly changed the course of the remainder of my deployment and, for at least a day or two, caused quite a ripple around the army. It follows in italics. It is, and was, a rambling collection of my thoughts during this process juxtaposed with the various conversations I'd had with Captain Whiteback and the field-grade officers about the potential promotion to XO. The title came from a line in a Chuck Palahniuk novel, and it was also the name of a popular song by the rock band Panic! At the Disco.

I'd brushed aside the informal inquiries for months now. No, not me. Not interested. Keep me on the line. I want nothing to do with a lateral promotion to XO that involves becoming a logistical whipping boy and terminal scapegoat for all things NOTGOODENOUGH. I've been out here in the wilds too long, dealing with matters of life and death, to go back to Little America for PowerPoint pissing matches. Not me. I'm that too-skinny, crazy-eyed mustang who drives a hippie van with a McGovern bumper sticker and keeps his hair long and actually read the counterinsurgency manual rather than pretending he did, even quoting it during meetings and out in sector in this era of recentralized warfare, remember? You aren't gonna break me, no matter how enticing the fires of the FOB are.

Semper Gumby. Always flexible.

I guess they forgot, and instead focused on matters of competency. Cue outright offer.

Cue Lieutenant G "thanks but no thanks" response.

Cue illogical backlash from Higher, acting like a spurned teenage blonde whose dreamboat crush tells her point-blank that he prefers brunettes.

Cue finding myself on the literal and metaphorical carpet of multiple field grades, sometimes explaining, sometimes listening.

Mostly listening.

Yes, sir. I'm getting out. No, I'm sure. Definitely sure. Surer than sure. What am I going to do? Don't tell him Option A; he'll scoff at Option A. He believes dreams are only for children. Option B will suffice. Well, sir, I'm going to go back to school, somewhere on the East Coast. Haven't decided if I'll focus on the Spanish Civil War or Irish history yet, though. I think I'd be a pretty good wacky professor. I already like to ramble, and I look good in banana-yellow clip-on ties. Sir.

No, sir. I'm not saying that at all. I would absolutely bust my ass as an XO and perform the job to the best of my ability. I'm just saying I'd be screwing a peer of mine, who is staying in and could use this professional development, ben-

efiting both him and the big army in the long run. Uncle Sam agrees with me.

No, sir, I don't think I'm selling myself short. Recognizing one's own weaknesses isn't a weakness in and of itself. Crushing balls is only my thing with people who aren't wearing an American uniform.

If I throw enough clutter in the way, something will stick.

This is the army, son. Your opinion doesn't matter.

Roger. Acknowledged. I'd figure I'd proffer it, just in case.

You need to start thinking big picture, Lieutenant. That's what officers do.

I roll out of the wire everyday to bask in a Third-World cesspool craving my attention for nothing more than the most basic human need—hope. Is there a bigger picture than that, or just different vantage points from safer distances?

Yes, sir, I will remember to think things out more rationally next time. (Pause long enough to make the point that this was already a well-thought out decision.) Of course. Sir.

No, sir, this isn't just because I want to stay with my platoon. (Maintain eye contact so he doesn't think you're lying, for the love of God, maintain eye contact!) I won't lie though, sir—it was a factor. Just not my motivation.

Nice work, liar.

Another reason? Well, sir, two of my best friends in the world are Lieutenant Virginia Slim and Lieutenant Demolition. [Note: Both of their platoons fell under the operational control of the other troop at this point in the deployment.] *If I were to become their XO, I would be extremely uncomfortable with possibly having to order them and their men to their deaths. As their peer, I should be right there next to them. Hell, I probably would insist on it.*

Yes, I know that was a good point. Don't say that out loud. Don't say that out loud. Phew. That was a close one. I almost out-louded rather than in-loaded.

Yes, sir, I have full confidence in my platoon to be able to succeed without me. SFC Big Country would be more than capable of performing the job of a platoon leader. But he's an NCO. He shouldn't have to deal with lieutenant bullshit. That's my bullshit to deal with. I'm the soldier's buffer. (Cough. From you. Cough.) If a butterbar [new lieutenant] *were here, I'd understand. That's the natural order of things. But since an opening occurred without a backlog, I really strongly really definitely really definitively believe that it should go to a lieutenant who wants it. Hell, there are some of them out there who NEED it. Aren't I being a team player here?*

The ballad of a thin man walking a thin rope. Moonwalking a thinly veiled rejection of his superiors' life decisions. Wondering why they are taking it per-

sonally. People are different. They want different things out of existence. Let's not act like I'm a ring of Saturn stating the case that Pluto's planet status should be reconfirmed.

Don't fall on your sword, Lieutenant. No one likes a martyr.

Can't help it, I'm Irish. And. Yes. They do.

Fine, I'm not going to make you do it. (Even though I spent three days trying to do so.) But you are now on my shit list, and I want to fuck you over for daring to defy and defying to dare. A bullshit tasking will eventually come down the pipeline, and I got a rubber stamp with your name on it. And, yes, I know your performance has been outstanding, and we have consistently rated you above your peers, at the top echelon. Doesn't matter now.

You're right. It doesn't. Doesn't matter at all. Even if I've only haggled a few more months with the Gravediggers, it was worth it; I came here to fight a war, not to build a resume. My men need me. And. I need them. It would have been worth it for a few more days.

Victory.

Mustangs don't blink.

You know where we learned how not to?

It wasn't behind a desk.

Every day of free roaming makes it worth it.

I initially gave no second thought to posting the piece. I had a vague understanding that my blog had become relatively popular in certain e-circles, but I still didn't fully appreciate the power of the Internet. Two days later, I left for leave and for Europe, where I gallivanted across the continent with Lieutenant Demolition, my girlfriend, and her roommate on a much-needed break. By the time I returned to Iraq and to the Suck eighteen days later, the details of "The Only Difference Between Martyrdom and Suicide Is Press Coverage" were a distant memory. Well, for me, at least. Not so much for the rest of the squadron.

Captain Whiteback later explained to me the series of events that led to that posting's gaining a readership following on Camp Taji. Arnon Grunberg, a writer who'd been embedded in Saba al-Bor for three days the month before with one of our troop's other platoons, linked to my blog on his blog site. I spoke with Grunberg briefly during his time in Saba al-Bor, mainly about the organizational structure of the army, but a bit about my blog site as well. When he wrote an article about the state of the Iraq War for the online political magazine *Salon*, a link to his blog site was included in the byline, which in turn contained a positive blurb about my site and me. Unbeknownst to me, *Salon* published Grunberg's article only a couple days after I posted "The Only Difference Between Martyrdom and Suicide Is Press Coverage." According to Captain Whiteback, Lieutenant Colonel Larry read the article, subsequently referring to Grunberg's blog and then to mine. Even though I had registered my blog with my unit prior to the deployment, and Captain Whiteback had mentioned the website to the field-grade officers on multiple occasions in a positive fashion, only with Grunberg's mention did my writings become worthy of interest to my chain of command. And in a twist of fate far too poetic to be coincidence, the first piece they read centered on their attempted professional bullying of me in the past week.

Back from leave, I walked into a tempest of fury.

According to the staff officers, Lieutenant Colonel Larry forced some of them to comb through my blog—all six months' worth—to search for any hint of an OPSEC violation. They were unable to find any because I had taken great care with this matter, although not for this purpose. However, because I posted the piece in question without showing it to Captain Whiteback first, my squadron commander ordered me to shut down my blog, effective immediately, under the pretext of "conduct counter to good order and discipline." My grandfather, a career navy officer and retired two-star admiral, later told me that citing this regulation was a commander's ultimate cop out in lieu of actual substance.

I did as ordered and posted one final piece explaining the situation, taking full responsibility for my actions. Other than getting yelled at for having "an authority problem" and "a persecution complex," I received no punishment. I wasn't counseled on paper or removed from my platoon leader position, mainly because there wasn't anyone they were willing to replace me with. They even promoted me to captain the next month, right on time with my peer group, because my blog drama had nothing to do with job performance. As he put on my captain's bars, Lieutenant Colonel Larry muttered snidely about wanting to punch me through the wall. I smirked and saluted.

The passing of time did not yield bygones. I had committed heresy against the church of the officer corps by airing my grievances publicly. Some careerists gave me a very open and a very personal cold shoulder, although most of my friends and fellow junior officers found the whole thing hilarious, as it reinforced our contempt for the Cold Warrior mentality of fraudulent pseudostoicism. Lieutenant Colonel Larry told me I had discredited the unit. After much internal deliberation and self-examination, I eventually interpreted that to mean that I had discredited him, as all he ever seemed to care about was how many people had read the piece and who they were. At no point was I ever asked, "Why did you write this?" Higher seemed interested only in treating the symptom, me, not the problem itself, the state of the unit. Perhaps the unit's leaders didn't want to hear the response. They must have known how unhealthy our squadron was.

I received widespread and fervent support in the aftermath of my blog's death from a variety of active military, retired military, and civilians. A Judge Advocate General (JAG) lawyer called me at the combat outpost, saying he wanted to help resurrect my website, as he believed my chain of command had no legal right to shut it down, even under the Uniform Code of Military Justice. I thanked him but said that I didn't want to distract my platoon or myself any further from the mission at hand. Hundreds of e-mails poured in from people across the globe expressing their gratitude for my dispatches and for bringing the war home to them, as well as their disdain for my command's reaction. Some came from the Pentagon, a few others, from the Department of Defense. Former military members living as expatriates wrote from Indonesia, France, and Chile. Two different people claimed that they had shared my website with General Petraeus, as an example of an ideal twenty-first-century counterinsurgent's tool, and one stated that the general "was a fan." I had no idea if this was true or not, although even the possibility of it led to some serious *holy fuck* moments. In the ensuing months, Lieutenant Colonel Larry answered multiple congressional inquiries brought on by some of my more passionate followers, who had expressed their outrage to their congressional representatives.

Personally, I thought the whole affair was much ado about nothing, with a lot of smoke and not much fire. I had been in the wrong, and while others handled the situation poorly as well, I was the lowest-ranking individual involved. That was how the army worked: Orders were orders, and I was a soldier first. I understood and accepted all of that.

Shortly thereafter, the press—the officer corps's undeclared hostile enemy—got hold of the story.

Ernesto Londono, a writer from the *Washington Post* embedded in Baghdad, penned an exposé in July chronicling the rise and fall of my blog. Concurrently, my hometown paper, the *Reno-Gazette Journal*, did the same. Two days after the *Washington Post* published Londono's article, the *Stars and Stripes*, a prominent military newspaper, reran it as their cover story. I refused to comment for the articles, again not wanting to distract myself or my men any further than necessary, but my parents were free of such burdens. They asked if I minded whether they spoke to the journalists, and I told them no, I didn't, just as long as they spoke honestly and for themselves. They did so, and as a result, thousands upon thousands of readers across the globe read my father's lambasting of Lieutenant Colonel Larry as a middle-management bureaucrat who made a mockery of the First Amendment to the U.S. Constitution.

As Lieutenant Virginia Slim said of the matter, "Wow. Don't fuck with a lawyer when constitutional rights are involved. They can and will publicly humiliate you."

The *Stars and Stripes* cover catapulted me to minor celebrity status in Iraq, and I autographed a few dozen copies for amused soldiers, NCOs, and officers. Not everyone found the articles funny. Predictably, a new set of ass chewings and lectures about professional decorum ensued, despite the fact that I had personally refused to speak with the journalists. Again, no punishment followed. Beyond the initial post, I still hadn't done anything wrong.

The questions about how many people had read my post and who they were stopped.

After a few months of correspondence with officers around the military, I pieced together the chain of events that followed the *Washington Post*'s article publication. Big Army (i.e., the Pentagon) had been caught off-guard by the article because Middle Army hadn't informed them of their decision to shut my website down. Ironically, many envoys of Big Army—what might qualify as part of Big Brother in our postmodern American republic—loved my blog for its realism, the very reason it got axed. Some of my readers wanted to portray the whole ordeal as a governmental gag order, but that simply wasn't accurate. Big Army had to back up Middle Army's decision postverdict; that was what bureaucracies did. The institutional culture demanded such, even if it didn't agree with or understand the original decision. If anything, my father's much-publicized analysis of the circumstances proved far more accurate than the Big Brother hypothesis.

The hoopla surrounding the articles eventually faded, and for a few more months at least, I finally got what I wanted in the first place—to be left alone with my platoon to continue to fight the Iraq insurgency on the ground level. The whole matter was so silly, so trivial compared to what our day-to-day lives entailed. I continued to write for myself because I needed that outlet and that therapy. The blog originated as a communication tool to stay in contact with family and friends but had somehow morphed into something else entirely. With the website's end, I let go of trying to wake up the American public to our war and finally learned to concern myself with matters I could control and impact.

Thus, my last connection to the old world was severed. Given the time and events to come, nothing could've been more necessary.

THE HOT WHEELS INCIDENT

As I traveled back to Saba al-Bor from Europe, my platoon's good fortune and luck finally ran out, with tragedy narrowly evaded. After months of chasing insurgents, dodging IEDs, and dealing with trigger-happy Iraqi security forces, something as routine as refilling a generator served as the culprit. Private Hot Wheels barely survived, and the rest of the platoon—especially some of the Joes—never really quite recovered from the experience.

Although I wasn't there—something I haven't yet forgiven myself for, be that illogical or not—I pieced together the events of the evening in question by talking to the involved soldiers and reading their sworn statements. I also watched the security camera footage that captured Private Hot Wheels being engulfed in flames, a scene permanently carved in the crevices of my mind. I only watched the footage once, but once proved enough. Things like that didn't fade with time.

While the Gravediggers pulled force-protection security at the combat outpost, Specialist Haitian Sensation and Private Hot Wheels received the task to refill the generators that powered the building. Just before midnight, they moved to the fuel point together, and Private Hot Wheels finished filling his can first. "Go ahead and start filling up the first generator," Specialist Haitian Sensation said. "I'll be right behind you."

Concurrently, Doc and PFC Smitty walked downstairs and outside the outpost, bringing out the garbage to the trash point located in the far reaches of the motor pool. As Private Hot Wheels began filling the generator, the metal fuel spout bumped into the starter cable hanging across the fuel tank, causing the positive-to-negative charge contact to ignite the fumes. The fuel can exploded, setting the young soldier and generator on fire. He immediately screamed for help. The soldiers in the TOC first thought they were hearing the death throes of a shot animal, until they saw the fire flash on the se-

Private Hot Wheels takes a knee while providing security during a dismounted patrol.

curity camera.

The explosion shook the combat outpost and immediately brought Specialist Haitian Sensation running from the fuel point to the northwest of Private Hot Wheels, and Doc and PFC Smitty came running from the northeast. Private Hot Wheels stumbled away from the generator, collapsed on the concrete next to it, and was rolling around on the ground in an attempt to douse the flames when the three other soldiers found him. Acting without hesitation, Specialist Haitian Sensation ran inside for help and a fire extinguisher, Doc ran to open up the medical aid station, and PFC Smitty started beating Private Hot Wheels's body to help put the fire out. PFC Smitty then heard sparks from the generator.

"I heard the generator making funny sounds, and Wheels was caught under some pipes," PFC Smitty recalled. "I just thought I had to get him out of there. So I grabbed him underneath his chest plate and pulled him out of the corner, like anyone would." PFC Smitty suffered minor burns on his hands and his arms for grabbing Private Hot Wheels in this manner, but his actions probably saved Private Hot Wheels's life. About five seconds later, a bigger, secondary explosion from the generator sent a new round of flames everywhere. Luckily, both privates were safely around the corner. However, all of Private Hot Wheels's rolling and PFC Smitty's beating had not extinguished the blaze on his body. Private Hot Wheels was still on fire.

Meanwhile, Specialist Haitian Sensation had burst into the combat outpost yelling and ran upstairs to grab a fire extinguisher. "I yelled, 'Help! Wheels is on fire! Wheels is on fire!' but either people couldn't understand me, or they thought I was kidding," he later said. "It took a couple seconds for them to figure out I was for real."

One of the first respondents from inside was Super Mario, a young interpreter who had spent many late evenings and early mornings learning about America from Private Hot Wheels and my other young soldiers. As Specialist Haitian Sensation picked up the fire extinguisher at the top of the stairs, Super Mario ran past him down the stairs. He found PFC Smitty struggling with a now immobile Private Hot Wheels outside.

"Quick," Super Mario told PFC Smitty, "tear open a sandbag and pour it on him." Super Mario's resourcefulness finally put out most of the inferno on Private Hot Wheels, as he and PFC Smitty dumped bags of sand on his body. Specialist Haitian Sensation, a few seconds behind, finished the job with the fire extinguisher. Some of the soldiers thought he had been on fire for fifteen seconds; others said two minutes. The time stamp on the video footage read thirty-four seconds.

By now, the rest of the troop had keyed in on what had occurred. Two Headquarters platoon soldiers arrived with more extinguishers and put out the still-raging generator fire. SFC Big Country, Staff Sergeant Bulldog, and others loaded Private Hot Wheels onto a stretcher and carried him into the aid station, where Doc immediately hooked him up to an IV and performed what medical treatment he could. Meanwhile, the TOC radioed for a medical helicopter.

"He kept asking about his face," Staff Sergeant Bulldog told me later. "He was worried that girls wouldn't like him if his face was burned. I was like, 'Your face is good!' 'cause it was." Private Hot Wheels had been wearing his full equipment kit during the refueling process, so his body armor protected much of his core. Further, his clear lens glasses saved his eyes. But the cloth on his arms, hands, and legs had burned away instantly, and that was where much of the significant damage had been done.

"We trained for a lot of events, a lot of worst-case scenarios, before we went to Iraq," SFC Big Country recalled. "But there is nothing on this earth that can prepare you for the feeling of having to carry one of your soldiers to a medical bird [helicopter]. It was the worst thing I've ever experienced in uniform."

The subsequent investigation determined that the mixture of an army-issued metal spout and a civilian generator played a role in the accident. Extinguishers were soon moved next to our brand-new generators, and safety classes were conducted across Baghdad Province for soldiers regarding re-fueling operations. Those classes were not taught to suggest that Private Hot Wheels did anything wrong; he did not. Freak accidents happened. This happened.

Private Hot Wheels flew to Baghdad, then to Germany, and then to San Antonio, Texas, home of Brooke Army Medical Center, the preeminent burn-treatment center in the world. He arrived in Texas less than forty-eight hours after the accident occurred, a testament to the might and mobility of the U.S. military. While we continued to fight the insurgency in Iraq, he fought for his life half a world away. Over 60 percent of his body suffered second- or third-degree burns in the blast. Serious complications from smoke inhala-tion and inflamed organs arose over the succeeding summer months. Multiple times, bacteria seeped into his bloodstream, causing serious infections that brought him to the brink of death. With his family praying at his bedside, though, and the burn center's subject-matter experts treating him, he powered through it, and the center discharged him in late October 2008. Private Hot Wheels's long road to recovery was, and would continue to be, riddled with battles of a different kind than the rest of us experienced or understood.

In the weeks following the generator fire, a rumor circulated among the junior soldiers that the fire hadn't been an accident but rather the result of a well-hidden sticky bomb placed behind the generator by an Iraqi contractor working for JAM or AQI. While the NCOs quickly crushed this fabrication, worried that such misinformation could further disrupt the unit's already shaky mental structure, I had more sympathy for it. It was simply the product of nineteen- and twenty-year-old kids trying to come to terms with something horrific, seeking out a logical explanation for an illogical situation. Accidents weren't supposed to happen in wars; that wasn't what Hollywood had taught us. But bad guys happened in wars. Subterfuge happened in wars. Sticky bombs happened in wars. That much they knew. That they understood. Still, though, no substance ever existed for the sticky bomb theory, and what happened to Private Hot Wheels remained a freak accident.

Though he was gone physically, Private Hot Wheels's presence stayed with the Gravediggers for the duration of the deployment. Soldiers routinely checked the website his mother established to chronicle his medical recovery. They swapped their favorite Hot Wheels's quotes and stories often, as if maintaining the mental image we had of him as a healthy young soldier would help heal the pale and skinny burn survivor in Texas. After the NCOs packed up his belongings and shipped them home, his bunk lay empty for many months, despite multiple bed shifts and comings and goings of soldiers. Private Hot Wheels hadn't died—thank God—but he loomed over the platoon like a lost ghost nonetheless. Freak accident or no, the men were now down one of their own, and they would have to finish without him. We all felt less whole, less complete, as a result.

What went unstated, of course, was that maybe something else could happen, and the next time, Fortuna might not grace us with her presence. I knew I felt it, and I saw it in the eyes of the others as well, especially after we finished talking about Private Hot Wheels or the generator fire. But we sucked it up and drove on. No other choice existed.

Specialist Haitian Sensation, in particular, had a tough time in the aftermath of the incident. "I smell the flesh burning sometimes still," he told me weeks later. "I'll be thinking about something totally different, or working out, or watching TV, or whatever, and then it just hits me. And I can't help but wonder, you know? What else could we have done? What if I had been standing there, too? I just don't know."

I didn't know either. None of us did. We just tried to remember that things could've been worse and kept moving. No other choice existed.

THE RUNDOWN

A power vacuum threatened to tear apart the Sunni community of our AO over the summer of 2008. Colonel Mohammed fled Saba al-Bor when it became clear the Iraqi security forces intended to detain and jail him for his past status as an AQI prince. Things became even further

Iraqi security forces pose behind a detainee, arrested for his alleged involvement with al-Qaeda in Iraq. Such photographs were often taken after such operations and reproduced as posters in mass form. This was done for the purpose of public relations, in the hope of instilling trust within the greater Iraqi populace for their military and their police.

muddled when AQI members dressed in IA uniforms assassinated Sheik Zaydan of Bassam in his own house with a point-blank pistol shot through the roof of his mouth into the brain. Bassam, the village to Saba al-Bor's south, rested on an invisible fault line between the Grand Canal villages of our area and the Abu Ghraib district. AQI still maintained a powerful presence in and around Abu Ghraib, and judging from the recent uptick in violent events, they seemed to be interested in expanding northward. Sahwa leaders, minor sheiks, major wannabes, and newcomers of various stripes all began jockeying for influence in light of these events.

To help quell the terrorists' offensive and to reestablish a sense of order, a meeting was called in Bassam for all the local Sunni chieftains, American officers, and Iraqi security-force leaders. Both Captain Ten Bears and Captain Whiteback, on his last day of command, attended with our squadron commander. So did the IP and IA colonels. Haydar went, as did Abu Adnan, Boss Johnson II, and Colonel Mohammed's former deputy, Osama. From all accounts, a productive meeting ensued; however, when a 57-mm rocket flew over them as they exited the house after the meeting, the details of such were scattered to the winds of evermore. The rocket men missed their target, significantly overshooting the meetinghouse. Instead they decapitated a seven-year-old girl playing in her house with her family.

Retribution was in order, and Coalition forces were the obvious choice to enact it. Identifying the villains served as the first point of order. Two days later, Captain Ten Bears, now in command, sent my platoon with an intel geek to Haydar's house, knowing that this sheik maintained his own extensive intelligence network. Although our unit maintained a strong relationship with Haydar, it had deteriorated slightly in the preceding months, as he felt we didn't give him and his village enough attention or funds. Whenever we tried to explain that we were simply trying to empower the various echelons of Iraqi government and weren't playing favorites, he would laugh scoffingly, "Government? This is Iraq, not America. We are tribal society, not democracy. Don't you Americans read any history books? The sheiks *are* government in Arab culture!"

Another event factoring into Haydar's dissatisfaction was the state of the water-plant contract. Predictably, it had been awarded to a cousin of Sheik Nour, and thus to the Tamimi tribe. As a result, the areas to the north and east of Haydar's village benefited, but Haydar and his people did not. And although he knew that such decisions weren't made at our level, he still gave us hell about the situation because we were there and we had to listen.

"I will never listen to fancy American in suit again!" he said, smiling bitterly. "We make very good bid, and I explain how it is fair to give us just this one contract instead of Tamimis. Just this one! And fancy American say yes, yes, he understands. And what happens?" Haydar slapped his head in anger and left the answer to his rhetorical question adrift.

We all sat on the ground in his rectangular meeting room, waiting for the feast always provided for dinner at this residence. Haydar and two of his advisers intermixed with me and five members of the Gravediggers—Staff Sergeant Boondock, Sergeant Fuego (recently promoted and permanently back with the platoon), Doc, Specialist Tunnel, and PFC Smitty—with Suge attempting to provide translation for us all. The rest of the platoon pulled security and would rotate in for food over the next hour. As per the Arab custom, we sat without chairs, facing one another in conversation. On the far wall of the room hung portraits of Haydar's grandfather and father, both dressed in the traditional dishdasha and turban and both the spitting image of their successor. The current sheik often reminded us that his grandfather worked with the Turks of the Ottoman Empire, his father with the British. It was a subtle way to point out that while the American presence in Iraq was temporary, his family's was not.

In an attempt to change the topic of discussion, I asked him about the rocket attack. He looked back at me knowingly. "Yes," he said. "I have my eyes looking into it."

"Will you share that information with us if you find anything out?"

He nodded. "Of course. As long as my American friends promise to support me over Abu Adnan, if it comes to that."

Confused, I looked over at Staff Sergeant Boondock, who shrugged his shoulders in response. "Support you in what, Haydar? I'm not following."

He stroked his chin and smiled. "Nothing particular. Not yet, at least. I speak in . . . hypo . . . hypo . . . hypo . . . ."

Suge struggled with the translation of the last word. "Hypotheticals?" I proffered.

"Yes! That is it! Hypotentacles! That means maybes, yes?"

I tried not to laugh at Suge's crossbred word and considered Haydar's statement carefully. "You're a smart man, Haydar," I said. "You know how we feel about Abu Adnan. We wouldn't ever support an act of violence between villages or Sahwa leaders, but in terms of having our respect and our ears, you have nothing to worry about from him. Captain Whiteback felt that way, and I know Captain Ten Bears feels that way, too."

He nodded again. "As much I believed," he said. "My head needed to hear it to agree with my heart." He clapped his hands and barked orders in Arabic to the kitchen, where some of his junior Sahwa temporarily served as cooks and waiters. "Now we eat!"

That we did. Dishes and dishes of roast chicken, masgouf (a grilled fish mixed with spices), kafta (lamb meatballs), flatbread, and eggplant salad appeared, with dips of amba (a pickle condiment) and hummus providing additional flavor. Dates dipped in sugar served as our dessert. Halfway through the meal, Haydar's three-year-old son, Ghazi, ran into the meeting room to give his father a hug and a kiss.

"This is why we fight," Haydar said as he picked up his giggling son and twirled him in the air. "So that they might have peace in a land that has never known it."

I immediately pulled out my notebook and wrote that quote down, as Suge mumbled his agreement in broken English and celebrated with a cigarette. That, I thought to myself, is the most profound fucking thing I've heard in a long time. True dust of the desert. I wondered how much better it sounded in Arabic.

The next day, Haydar called Suge at the combat outpost and gave us the names of the three men responsible for the rocket attack. He said that his sources would be willing to write out sworn statements against the men, contingent on our detaining them first.

The names didn't surprise anyone. Two of them belonged to the Daraji family, an inbred Sunni clan whose members all lived together in a small village southeast of Bassam. The patriarch had been arrested the prior year for a lethal IED attack on an American convoy and still called Camp Bucca home. Various sons, cousins, and nephews had been jailed or were wanted for arrest or questioning. These men didn't necessarily qualify as straight AQI; they were more like poor rural labor contracted for acts of terror. Ironically, all three of the rocket men worked as Sons of Iraq in the Bassam area, albeit at different checkpoints. Not that any of that mattered. They had brutally murdered an innocent young girl, and we got the green light for a raid. Our clarity of purpose returned.

The day after that, in the tranquil silence of the predawn, we raided the Darajis' small village.

Captain Ten Bears's plan had the three line platoons of Bravo Troop striking three target houses in the greater Bassam area simultaneously, while the Estonians pulled outer-perimeter security as the cordon. Acting in accordance with Higher's desire for more joint patrols, a three-man fire team of Iraqi army jundis augmented all of our units. One of the other platoons detained their man immediately, and the other one found no one home. At our objective house, we sorted through a multitude of women, children, and young men without finding our specific target, Ali, the reported rocket trigger puller. "He is at his Sahwa checkpoint now," his younger half-brother and second cousin eventually told us. "Why do you seek him?"

"Uhh, we just want to talk," I responded. "He said he had information on some Ali Babas."

"Ah, very good," responded the Iraqi. "There are many Ali Babas in this area, especially in the Sahwa."

As my platoon walked out of the house and back to the vehicles, I gave them the hand-and-arm signal for "Let's hurry the fuck up" and shook the young Daraji's hand. "Just tell him we'll come back next week," I said, ignoring the urge to wink behind my sunglasses. "We're not in a rush to talk with him or anything."

"Of course. Thank you for coming."

"No problem! Take care!"

Making a liar out of me almost immediately, our Strykers screamed out of the village as though with the wrath of God. We moved to the Sons of Iraq checkpoint on the southern end of Route Islanders as quickly as the tight turns of the canal roads allowed.

By the time we arrived at the checkpoint, however, Ali Daraji was nowhere to be found. His fellow guards said that he hadn't shown up to work that morning and they didn't know why. While searching the surrounding area though, Staff Sergeant Spade discovered a grey sedan parked behind a dirt mound that matched the description of Ali's vehicle given by Haydar's sources.

"Yes, that is Ali's car!" piped in one of the Sons of Iraq, eyes shifting nervously, when he realized what Staff Sergeant Spade had found. "I switch with him last night. He take my car."

Suge now seized the moment. Our terp used his imposing size and backed the smaller Sahwa guard against a wall, roaring menacingly at him in Arabic. Two minutes later, he turned back to me, slapped his helmet and sighed, and said, "Fucking Iraqis." The guard now wore the look of a plane-crash survivor, mainly because, I learned later, Suge had threatened to have us drop the Son of Iraq off alone in a Shia neighborhood if he did not cooperate.

"What's the deal with the cars?"

"He say that Ali Daraji make him trade cars last night at his house. He say that Ali Daraji tell him he needed to borrow his truck to move things. I think he tell truth. I put the fear of Allah in him."

I smirked. "Looks like it. What kind of truck does this guy own then?"

Suge barked in Arabic at the Sahwa, received his answer, and nodded. "Old white truck with flat bed in back."

The TOC kept radioing for updates, and with SFC Big Country on leave, the acting platoon sergeant—Staff Sergeant Bulldog—and I talked over the situation.

"This guy could be anywhere," I said. "He has to know we're looking for him by now. We may have to call it a day."

"Maybe we should swing back da house one more time, make sure that white truck ain't there," Staff Sergeant Bulldog recommended. "Just to make sure."

"Sounds good to me." We loaded back into our Strykers and moved east from whence we came, with Staff Sergeant Boondock's vehicle in the lead.

After months of pleading, we had switched Staff Sergeant Boondock to the senior scout position with Staff Sergeant Bulldog's blessing. This helped both men's careers as Staff Sergeant Bulldog was more than ready for a platoon of his own, and such a move freed him up in the event that one became available.

About halfway back to the Daraji village, our front Stryker slammed on its brakes, just past a small turn to our left that snaked north into more farmlands. This brought the entire patrol to a halt. A few seconds passed, and I keyed the hand mic.

"3, this is 1. What's up? Why'd you stop?"

"We're staring at a vehicle that matches the new description," he said. "It was traveling west until it stopped when we came up on it."

Before I could respond, Staff Sergeant Boondock spoke again. "He's moving! He's fucking gunning it north! We're past the turn though!"

"Take the lead!" I yelled to PFC Smitty, who slammed on the accelerator and took the north turn in pursuit of the fleeing truck. From the gunner's cupola, Sergeant Prime reported that we were about seventy-five meters behind the truck but closing. The Stryker engine hummed with glee as we winded through backcountry dirt roads on a high-speed canal chase.

My heart pumped with excitement, but I attempted to maintain calm on the radio. "2, 3, follow us. We got a bead on this fucker." And then on the internal net: "Prime, when we get close, point the 240 [M240B machine gun] straight at him to let him know we mean business. Smitty, how fast are we going?"

"Heh, sir, you don't wanna know. We're good. Don't worry." I found out later the answer to my question was forty-nine miles per hour—in a nineteen-ton armored vehicle.

Approximately thirty seconds later, with the truck's speed fading and us within twenty meters, Sergeant Prime aimed his machine gun straight north. "He sees it!" he reported. "The truck's turning right, into a driveway!"

"We're dismounting!" I yelled, while PFC Smitty parked our vehicle perpendicularly to the driveway. As the ramp dropped, I jumped out of the back with Sergeant Fuego, Corporal Spot, Specialist Tunnel, and an IA jundi right with me. Suge eventually followed.

As we rounded the corner of the driveway, a lone Iraqi male tossed a metallic object into the lawn, turned around, and crouched over in a defensive position resembling that of a cornered animal. He found five rifles oriented on the tiny spot just between his eyes. He then put his hands up in the air.

No question existed as to the man's identity; in person Ali Daraji looked almost exactly as he did in his target photograph, just with a beard and longer, curlier hair. My men searched him and the white truck, finding pistol cartridges, seven fake identification cards, a large hunting knife, and a computer hard drive. Corporal Spot and Specialist Tunnel walked into the lawn and found the Glock pistol he had thrown off his person moments before.

Staff Sergeant Boondock walked up a minute or so later with his dismounted team and found me crowing in jubilation as the soldiers finished up their search. Sergeant Fuego had flex-cuffed and blindfolded Ali and sat him underneath a nearby tree.

"We got the bastard!" I exclaimed, ecstatic that we had nabbed our guy, adrenaline from the chase still coursing through my veins. This moment was why I had fought to stay with my platoon, I was sure of it. This was why I had told the Establishment to kiss my skinny Irish ass. It made all of the melodrama of the last two months worth it. "We got this stupid-ass raghead, and he won't be killing anymore little girls with his stupid-ass rockets anytime soon!"

Staff Sergeant Boondock laughed. "Easy, sir. Save the racial epithets for me. I call them ragheads and hajjis; you're supposed to call them local-nationals."

I bit my lip, chided myself, and nodded. Although amused, he was right. I needed to stay cool, no matter how excited or satisfied.

"But," the NCO continued, "my preferred slur to describe the Iraqi people is camel jockey. If nothing else does, that better make the cut for that book you're going to write. And you better not quote me saying anything *soft*!"

I laughed. "Gotcha, on both accounts." Then I grabbed Suge and started questioning Ali Daraji. Extremely unhelpful, he refused to answer anything about the rocket attack, or anything else for that matter. He just glared at me and Suge sullenly, not speaking at all. We relaxed his flex-cuffs and gave him a bottle of water anyway.

The house in whose driveway we made the arrest belonged to a family with no connection to Ali Daraji or his clan. Though initially surprised and scared to find us on their property, they became very hospitable once we explained how we had ended up there, and they brought out chai for everyone. The children of the house began chanting, "Bucca! Bucca! Ali Baba, Bucca!" (Prison, prison, the thief goes to prison) at Daraji.

We stacked all of the collected evidence in front of Daraji, took off his blindfold, and told him to smile his biggest terrorist smile. The three jundis posed behind him, backs straight, faces hard. Then, with my digital camera, I snapped the photograph affectionately known as the money shot, nicknamed after the climactic move popularized in modern porno films. The money shot would be used both at Ali Daraji's eventual trial and for Coalition forces' posters and propaganda, showing the strength and independence of the Iraqi army to their people. With the rundown over, we now went back to the combat outpost.

"Thank you," I whispered on the way back to no one in particular. "Thank you. I really needed that."

ALL BECAUSE OF A POPSICLE STICK

"What the fuck was that? Did you hear that?"

I sure had. The unmistakable sound of nearby rifle fire nipped at my eardrums over the running Stryker engine. Instinctively, Staff Sergeant Bulldog, Corporal Spot, PFC Smitty, and I dropped to one knee on the ground, using my vehicle as cover. We had just finished clearing a reported IED site on Route Tampa—nothing more than a dirt mound with a long popsicle stick stuck in the middle of it—and were walking back to our Strykers when the gunshots started.

"3, this is 1," I said into my dismount radio. "We're hearing gunfire. What do you guys see up there?"

Staff Sergeant Boondock's Stryker sat one hundred meters to our front, oriented due south, our direction of travel.

"We got six or seven dismounts spread across Tampa, walking in some kind of fucking line formation. Two of 'em just shot their rifles off to the west. Isn't there an IP station around here?"

"Roger," I said. "There's one just southwest of your position." As we remounted the Strykers, I intended to drive us down to the dismounts' location and verify whether they were IPs or not. I didn't think any type of enemy force would walk across Route Tampa in a line formation, but after seven or so months in Iraq, I'd seen stranger things.

"White, this is White 1. Let me know when you're redcon-1," I said, now back on my vehicle. "3, we're going to drive down to those dismounts and see what the fuck is up. I think those guys are probably spooked Iraqi police, but we'll see. After that, we'll continue to Nour's for security operations for the night. We'll be there for the long haul, until 0900, so remember to rotate out your gunners, and—"

"Break! Break! Break!" Staff Sergeant Boondock's voice ripped across the radio net, interrupting my verbose mission vomit. "We're taking fire! I say again, my vehicle is being shot at by those mother fuckers!"

I waited for the inevitable burst of 50-caliber from Specialist Big Ern to return the favor. When it didn't come, morbid thoughts raced through my mind. No, I thought. Not another one. Not like this.

"Sir, I saw the muzzle flashes," Sergeant Cheech said from my gunner's cupola. "They were definitely firing right at the 3 vehicle."

"If it's IPs, flash your brights!" I finally shouted over the net. "If it's not, kill them!"

Three millennium seconds passed before Staff Sergeant Boondock replied.

"Big Ern lasered them, and whoever they are, they've put their hands up in the air. Sir, that shit was damn close. A couple rounds ricocheted off of the LRAS [laser range-acquisition sight, mounted on the top off all recon-variant Strykers], and Big Ern heard the rest whistle by."

"We're driving up," I said. "They better be IPs; otherwise, I'm going to kill them myself."

"I'm going to kill them no matter what, especially if they are IPs," Staff Sergeant Boondock responded, his voice as sharp as a razor blade. "They just tried to shoot my gunner."

I had about fifteen seconds to figure out how to handle the situation. "Move up there, Smitty. Sergeant Cheech, call Squadron and tell them that we have received fire, most likely from IPs, but everyone is fine and I'm on the ground unfucking the goat rodeo. Haitian Sensation, wake up Suge and tell him what's going on." Only one real option existed, and I knew it. The Iraqi police's notorious record for friendly fire was simply inexcusable after the amount of training American forces had provided them. Further, if I didn't get hot, Staff Sergeant Boondock would, and his wick didn't burn out as quickly as mine did; nor did it tend to care about things like the Geneva Convention. Finally, and certainly most importantly, Specialist Big Ern had been about a foot or two away from getting shot by Iraqis supposedly on our side. The platoon was in no position to load a second member into a medical helicopter because of yet another "accident." By the time my fifteen seconds had ended and PFC Smitty had dropped my vehicle's back ramp, I pulsated with an old friend. I hopped out and headed straight for the first IP uniform I saw, locking and loading my rifle for effect. I heard the golden round snap into place, there if I needed it.

"I will fucking kill you myself if you ever, ever pull that fucking shit again, you stupid-ass mother fucker!" I screamed, my voice echoing up and down Route Tampa. I made a move to shake the IP by his collar, thought better of it, and instead backed the bigger man up into a circle of his comrades. There were seven of them in total. Months' worth of frustration, anger, and passion poured out of me like water from an uncoiled hose. "You are the luckiest pieces of shit on this fucking planet tonight, because my soldier should have killed every single one of your asses with his 50-cal. Do you fucking understand? You all should be fucking DEAD. Don't you understand that?"

They didn't. Suge jogged up to us at this point, wheezing apologies. He had stopped to put on his cotton mask. He distrusted the Iraqi police and claimed they were all JAM. Many terps in the Baghdad area shared his dread and paranoia of being identified and uncovered by the Iraqi police as an American interpreter. They had good reason to think such, too—according to Suge, two months before my unit arrived in Iraq, one of their fellow terps had been dragged from his bed while home on leave and executed in his front yard by JAM members. His wife later told the other interpreters that three IPs had led JAM to their house.

My soldiers circled around us, establishing a security perimeter, and Staff Sergeants Bulldog and Boondock and Sergeant Fuego walked up behind me, listening to the conversation.

"What . . . what do you want me to say?" Suge asked, still breathing heavily.

I sized up the Iraqi police. Fourteen saucer eyes and seven hanging jaws met my glare. I had them by the balls, and they knew it. I took a deep breath and continued, no longer shouting. "Tell them they just fucking shot at us. Tell them they almost killed one of us. Tell them we are on the same fucking side. Tell them if they ever shoot at my platoon again, or at any American for that matter, I will kill every single one of them myself, with my own M4, right here in the middle of Tampa."

Suge translated, struggling to match my fury, his mask drowning out most of the force of his words. I knew my language had to be very precise to make up for this. Asking him to remove his mask simply wasn't an option.

This was his country, his home. If he felt uncomfortable here, he had his reasons. Suge had risked enough already; he didn't need a punk junior officer from across the sea patronizing him by telling him his home was safe enough to walk around in sans mask.

"I want to know why they fired," I said. "Did they have positive identification of an enemy force?"

"No," Suge translated. "They say that they hear sounds and get scared."

I felt Staff Sergeant Boondock bristle behind me. "How did they not see our lights?" I asked.

"They think that we are terrorists putting in IED. They say that Stryker lights look like car lights. They are crazy, Captain! Stryker lights are much higher in air! They are very scared what you will do to them."

I looked at all seven IPs. "Who fired his weapon?" I asked.

No one spoke. They all simply looked at the ground. At least they're loyal to each other, I thought. That's something, at least.

"We can smell their rifles, sir," Sergeant Fuego said. "We'll be able to tell that way very easily."

"That's okay," I replied. "I just wanted to see if any of them would speak. Suge, tell them that since they won't own up to who fired, I'm holding them all responsible. I want all of their identification cards."

As I collected their police IDs, I glanced back and saw Staff Sergeant Boondock literally shaking with rage. His face was beat red, his eyes as dark as an abyss, and he kept pacing back and forth like a madman. Staff Sergeant Bulldog patted him on the helmet and whispered something in his ear. Sergeant Boondock nodded at Sergeant Bulldog, shook his head side to side at the IPs, and walked over to check on the soldiers on the perimeter. I knew what he thought. This had happened his last time here, too. Only last time, the perpetrators weren't wearing a police uniform, and he could fire back.

Even with all of the successes of the American counterinsurgency effort circa summer 2008, the Iraqi security forces' performance remained spotty. I had worked with multiple militarily sound and tactically competent IA officers and jundis, IP officers and police, and Sons of Iraq—and many, many more who didn't qualify as either. With the IAs and IPs, the excellent ones didn't seem to stick around very long before they moved on to other assignments. Part of the problem was cultural: After decades under Saddam's authoritative rule, all Iraqi military/pseudomilitary organizations reflected that approach to leadership and mission planning. Officers ruled with iron fists and tended to hold tightly onto any and all information; meanwhile, the NCO corps of these organizations lacked the independence, pride, and initiative of their American counterparts. Further, joint patrols were easy for Higher to order but far more difficult to execute. Beyond the language barrier, there existed cultural, social, and training blockades. Too often, finding that thin line between the counterinsurgency principle of allowing the local security forces to complete the mission their way, and still doing it in a correct way, became an exercise in imaginative rationalization. All of this compounded the very obvious trigger-discipline issue that plagued Iraqi security forces throughout the country. Yes, they got better every day and with every joint patrol. But at what increment could one measure success, especially when the definition of such constituted total autonomy and self-sufficiency in a jointly operated environment? Fair or not, America's body clock in Iraq moved faster than the sands of time. We wouldn't know for sure how successful our training of the Iraqi security forces had been until we left Iraq totally and left the Iraqis to their own wits and devices.

But I wasn't going to fix any of these grander issues on this night. I thanked God that no one had been hurt or killed, be it Specialist Big Ern or an IP choked to death by me or my NCOs. After writing down the IPs' information, I told them I'd hand over their ID cards to our military police, whose sole mission consisted of overwatching the Iraqi police. Then I said, "When every one of you goes home tonight, I want you to kiss your wife and tell her that you should be dead. And then remember that kiss the next time you feel like shooting into the darkness."

We loaded back up onto our Strykers and continued our movement to Sheik Nour's manor.

"You looked pissed out there, sir," Specialist Haitian Sensation said back on our vehicle.

"I was," I said curtly. "I still am."

"I know what you need!" he said. I saw him hit a button on the iPod hooked up to our internal radio, and a familiar beat filled my ears.

"So, tell me what you want, watch really, really want!" Specialist Haitian Sensation crooned along with the song.

"If you want my future, forget my past," PFC Smitty drawled from the driver's seat, completely off beat.

"If you want to get with me, better make it fast," Sergeant Cheech muttered from his cupola, completely embarrassed to be contributing.

"Now don't go wasting my precious time!" Sergeant Tunnel (recently promoted) boomed, while bouncing to the tune in his rear hatch.

I sighed. I had no choice but to join in. "Get your act together, we could be just fine."

Our platoon kept moving south on Tampa, while my vehicle sang along with the Spice Girls due to a clairvoyant attempt by my soldiers to calm me down from the incident with the Iraqi police. It worked.

All of the Iraqi police involved spent the next day and night in jail as our military police conducted an investigation of the shooting, and they subsequently spent a week on suspended duty. All seven returned to the job full-time the week after that. While more escalation of force and friendly fire incidents occurred in the brigade's AO over the course of our deployment, I never read or heard about one happening at that particular IP station.

HELL

The sun was a hammer.

High noon. Mid-July. A patrol that required dismounting. A new contender with an old face ascended to challenge the concept of war for peace. It reigned in flares of tyranny, punishing the masses and the elite alike. What it lacked in staying power, it made up for in promises of daily rebirth, rising from the ashes of night as a big ball of phoenix.

Down went the ramp and out went the soldiers.

97 degrees . . . 98 . . . 99 . . .

It started with baked air, enveloping us as soon as we exited the air-conditioned vehicles. A man on fire on the outside differed from a man on fire on the inside. On the inside, life burned into clarity. On the outside, life burned out. Every breath brought in a rush of too-familiar heat. Each movement, each action, felt surreal and forced, executed far too deliberately to be natural. I took a gulp of water. The dry taste remained. Walk, damn it. Walk.

100 . . . 101 . . . 102 . . .

"Stay hydrated, guys," Doc said. "Don't wait until you're thirsty to drink water."

The personal tragedy faded away on days like this. With the heat so unrepentant, so unapologetic, no alternative existed. It was, and always had been, and would continue to be, so. Iraq was all we did, all we knew, all we

An exhausted Staff Sergeant Bulldog takes a deep breath in front of the combat outpost in Saba al-Bor, while a group of Iraqi civilians wait in line for mattresses. The governance center occasionally held mass aid distributions for the Saba al-Bor population, giving away items like bottled water and clothing. Because the governance center was collocated with the American troops, the soldiers inevitably became responsible for securing the distribution effort and maintaining the peace.

remembered. Patrol, damn it. Patrol.

The lightest glide, the heaviest step. The extra gear weighed down my bones—bones that had already sacrificed so many crucial pounds to the sun gods on days just like this. How much more weight can a body lose, I wondered. I hadn't been this thin since high school, and my face showed it, no matter how much food I shoved down my throat. The skinny frame of a teenager, the sad eyes of an old man. Talk to the locals, damn it. Talk.

A man on fire dances for rain.

105 . . . 106 . . . 107 . . .

"Would you rather die in a freezer or a refrigerator?" PFC Van Wilder asked no one in particular. "At first I chose the freezer, 'cause it'd kill me faster or whatever, but now I think I'd rather die in the fridge, 'cause there's more food in there. I want to go out with a full stomach, you know?"

Sweat flowed as an exoskeleton of lacquer, underneath cloth and body armor alike. It felt like a river of lizards running free, each bead and drop a separate reptile stream. As a child of the desert, I understood and appreciated its arid, parched, barren beauty. But this defied understanding. This defied appreciation. We walked in a forsaken land. Take notes, damn it. Take notes.

111 . . . 112 . . . 113 . . .

Not a cloud in sight. Not a sandstorm in reach to cool everything down with dust and clutter. Only rays graced the horizon, subjugating rays cracking their whips of light.

"It's hotter than Africa right now!" Specialist Haitian Sensation exclaimed, somehow still smiling. "It's hot enough here to make a brotha' want to invest in an igloo, you feel me?"

Oh, no, not today, I thought. Not the kids. A throng of Iraqi kids recognized my officer bars and wrapped around me like a wire on a spool. I tried to avoid their eyes but couldn't. A little girl tugged at my sleeve. "Mistah," she asked. "Chocolata?"

I glared down at the little girl. She held out a small piece of chocolate for me. I smiled. "Shakrin," I said. Good Lord, I thought. I must look like hell when the kids are offering me chocolate instead of demanding it. Care, damn it. Care.

115 . . . 116 . . . 117 . . .

"Captain, I will teach you trick for heat in Iraq," Suge said. "You must drink lots of chai! The chai is hotter than sun, so it make your body and mind cool. So, we stop for chai soon, yes?"

As with some of its powdered cousins, it became too easy to overdose on lines of sunshine.

Time passed differently here. Back home, we were slaves to stimulation, part of a microwave society addicted to instant gratification. In the Middle East, especially over the summer, we joined the locals as slaves to existence, part of a microwaved society sustained by instinct. Not better, not worse, just different. Slower. Harsher. Grittier.

Hotter.

120 . . . 121 . . . 122 . . .

The thermometer stopped there. The mind stopped there. We kept moving.

BACK TO THE FOB

As the platoon traveled north on Route Tampa, my mind again wandered elsewhere.

In from the wilds. Provisionally. Like foxes at a farm, feigning domestication to prowl for scraps, anxious to return from whence they came, complete with their spoils. Don't make the hate for the housebroken and fire seekers too obvious, or It'll give us away before we complete mission. With all the shadiness and mis-

information of a too-smooth rogue picking up his date before the big dance, oiled up and emanating spring cologne and radiating charm and assuring her father that she'll be home by midnight, ten minutes prior even, and oh, of course sir, I only have the noblest of intentions. Right. Just don't check the glove compartment.

Of course we're going to rape and pillage the bountiful and the civilized. We'll finish up well before midnight. It's what the periphery does to the conventional. Take what you need in a mad eruption, blinded by the passion and the craving and the need, and race back to the lands of the untamed, before the regulations and parameters strike or, even worse, you getgotcaught permanently behind the bars of bureaucracy and have to work there, like any other staff mutt, comfortably numb in Little America, far from where actions reign supreme in eternal pyramids of grey, but flowcharts and spreadsheets and percentages have no meaning tangible or otherwise, but freedom is free to those willing to look for it in the daymares of suicide bombers wrapped in black mystery and nightdreams of intestines splattered across a stop sign like bleeding spaghetti noodles and function lords over form like a stoned pre-electric Dylan trapped on stage at a boy-band concert, confused as fuck, but ready to dominate anyway because nature demands it of him. That place could make you lose it, you know, if you spent too much time out there. Where? Out there. Crazy.

Hit the switch. Civilization beckons. Time to behave.

When our Strykers reached the front gates of the FOB, I heard my voice on the radio net as I repeated the timeline for the platoon. "White, this is White 1. It is now 1130. You have three hours to shower, eat at the chow hall, stock up on tobacco, and do whatever else you need to do back here. We're leaving at 1430 and rolling straight back into sector. We should be back at the combat outpost sometime after midnight." I paused, racking my mind for that other thing. "Most of us probably need haircuts too."

Three hours of quiet. Three hours of autonomy. Three hours in which I was my only responsibility. Three hours in which every slamming door and every loud noise wasn't an IED exploding in the distance or the long-prophesized great mortar strike. I wasn't all that hungry, and I didn't crave cigarettes or dip like many of my soldiers did. But I would go straight homicidal on both the joker and the thief if I didn't shower. Hot water, cold water, I didn't care—just as long as it looked clean and sprayed off the Iraqi grime.

Specialist Haitian Sensation hit the brakes on the vehicle, jarring PFC Smitty awake in the back. I heard Sergeant Cheech cursing at someone outside the vehicle from the gunner's hatch.

"What's up?" I asked him on our internal radio.

"Fucking fobbit freaked out about the 240 [machine gun]. He wants it pointed straight up in the air, and, yeah, I fucking forgot to do that when we hit the gates. But it's not like I forgot to clear it. He acted like I had the thing oriented at him and set on fucking burst."

I chuckled to myself. This same thing happened to at least one of the gunners every time we rolled back to the FOB, about once every two weeks. They were so used to scanning that they lost track of when we had moved back into the wire and into safety.

"Eh, he's just doing his job," I offered.

Sergeant Cheech's continued slurring suggested that he did not care about the details of said fobbit's job description.

The aroma of Saba al-Bor that we wore and brought with us did not match the scents of the FOB. Not that I could smell the distinction anymore, but I could still see other soldiers avoid the Gravediggers as we walked.

"Man, we must smell," SFC Big Country said, laughing. "Either that or the females found out about Van Wilder's intentions for his time off."

"They should be so lucky," PFC Van Wilder said in response. "And three hours? What am I, a fuck machine? I'd spend most of that time napping."

We split up, destinations and priorities separating as naturally as a banana from its peel. I moved with a group of my junior soldiers to the chow hall, shielding my rank insignias. I hoped to deceive a nemesis of mine—a certain fobbit warrant officer, he of the pristinely pressed uniform and dirty weapon, who waddled rather than walked and enjoyed lecturing my soldiers about their filthy uniforms while they waited in line to eat. He served as the complete antithesis of my men, who stalked even here, clearly uncomfortable with their surroundings, gaunt and pale and strung out on Rip-Its, and whose weapons were the only thing on their person to have received delicate attention in many days. My ambush, though thoroughly planned and well laid due to my boyish face and slight stature, did not lure in the transgressor, as we were left alone to eat and joke in peace.

"Maybe next time, sir," Specialist Cold-Cuts told me, noticing my obvious disappointment.

We headed to the post exchange (PX), where my soldiers bought a healthy amount of unhealthy tobacco products, and I purchased a box of Cocoa Puffs. While standing in the checkout line, my Joes basked in a favorite FOB sport: smelling the perfume and other pleasant fragrances of passing females.

The combat outpost lacked sensual reminders like this. A group of FOB soldiers, both males and females, passed us, and their conversation became a source of ire for my men.

"Can you believe it, Prime? Those fobbits are bitching about their paperwork," Sergeant Big Ern (recently promoted) drawled to Sergeant Prime (also recently promoted), his voice saturated with disgust.

Specialist Prime shook his head in disbelief. "That's pretty unbelievable."

One male's statement lingered with Doc. "Did he actually just say he'd rather be *out there*? Is he talking about outside the wire? What the fuck? He makes it sound like it's a different planet."

I interjected and said what an officer was supposed to say in these circumstances: "Easy, guys. It's the army. Everyone has something to bitch about, and someone has to be back here." When I finished the last sentence though, I realized my voice lacked any vitality whatsoever. I agreed with their sentiments—the mix of jealous resentment and repulsive aversion we had for anyone who wasn't one of us and hadn't experienced exactly what we had tended to flood the canals of rational empathy while we were back at the FOB. No one ever claimed we were fair with our castigations.

Specialist Haitian Sensation stepped in, gracefully allowing my lifeless lecture to end. "Yeah, you're probably right, sir. I wouldn't want to be back here anyway. Too much crazy bullshit."

As we left the PX, I bumped into the two squadron supply NCOs, who patted me on the back and asked if the platoon or I needed anything. They were good men and better supply sergeants—if I'd told them I needed a yellow school bus, they would've said, "Sure, no problem. Just give us a couple days to track one down." They weren't fobbits, I justified, because they actually worked and worked hard. This led me to think of all the cooks and mechanics who slaved away at the outposts to support the combat soldiers but very rarely received appreciation for such; every soldier fought his or her own battles over the course of a fifteen-month deployment. I needed to remember that.

Some time and a quick haircut later, salvation arrived in the form of splashing drops of lukewarm water. All things savage swirled away, certain to be replenished another day, but not on this one. No extra baggage or weight followed me into the shower stall; I stood starkly naked and drowned in a fairly bearable lightness of being. I was clean. I was warm. I was content. I felt like me again, and that proved enough to get me through another few weeks.

I checked my watch a few minutes after that. It read 1415. It came too fast, I thought. Maybe. But my soldiers strode right along with me, not sparing a moment back here at the FOB.

"I hate it here, sir," they said. "We always get bitched at for garrison bullshit."

"I know. Lord help me, I know."

We made the timeline and moved back into sector. Mission accomplished. Things weren't right here anymore, I thought, as we departed Little America for Iraq. Or maybe we weren't right anymore. I didn't know. Either way, it was time to go. We didn't belong here.

SUGE KNIGHT, INTERNATIONAL MAN OF MYSTERY

One lazy summer afternoon, while the Gravediggers conducted security operations for the combat outpost, Captain Ten Bears borrowed Suge, as his terp was on leave. The ever-dutiful Suge, who had been boots-up in his bed watching Turkish soap operas and smoking cigarettes, needed to translate for our commander at a large Sons of Iraq meeting taking place for the Tigris communities in the Falahat area to our east. He donned his body armor quickly, loudly proclaimed himself to be the only interpreter worth a fuck, and staggered off downstairs, presumably to the Strykers staged in the front of the outpost.

Although neither Captain Ten Bears nor Suge knew about it until they arrived at the meeting, a large faction of American and Iraqi army generals were attending as well, in an effort to learn more about the Sahwa program on the ground level. Television crews from the Baghdad news stations followed, and when one of the general's terps got sick with sunstroke, the nearest interpreter was quickly snatched up to take his place—Suge.

"It is not easy for me to hide," Suge explained to me later that night back at the combat outpost. "I try to slide down my seat when they look for terp, but I am big and black and have smart face! I also look good in U.S. Army uniform. So they pick Suge."

While Suge wasn't able to escape the general's clutches, his skin color did manage to confuse the local TV crews. On the nightly news, the local station did a report of the meeting and showed Suge in a brief clip, identifying him as an "unknown American colonel who speaks Arabic," much to the delight of our other terps, who started saluting him and calling him "sir" around the outpost. They weren't the only ones to tune in to the local Iraqi news that night. Not five minutes after his segment aired, Suge received a phone call from his wives, who wanted to know why he had dressed up in a U.S. Army uniform pretending to be a colonel when he was supposed to be away tending to his construction business.

Our terp maintained his cool despite being pushed into a corner by visual evidence. "Me, in an American army uniform?" he told his wives. "You are crazy women! Why would I do that?"

"But we saw you!" they said. "The news said you were an American colonel, but it was you, waving your finger, lecturing the people in the meeting!"

"You have been smoking the hashish!" Suge yelled, referring to the local marijuana product. "I am simple construction worker! How can I be American? I do not even know English!"

After he hung up the phone, he sighed, slapped himself in the face, and moaned about forgetting his mask at the combat outpost before the mission in question. Then he claimed to be in the clear. "They are good females," he said. "They believe me."

SFC Big Country and I weren't so sure.

"Suge," SFC Big Country said, "sometimes my wife just nods her head and says, 'Okay, whatever.' Are you sure your wives aren't just doing that? I mean, you were on the news. It's kind of hard to deny something like that. Why don't you just tell them the truth?"

Suge refused to consider this. "They are women! They will be too proud of me and do the talk. I lie to them to keep family safe." He snorted. "I did look good on news though, yes?"

I laughed and said yes, he had looked very sharp.

"You know, Captain," he continued in his British-taught English as he lit another cigarette, "this is not first time I have been on the news."

"Oh yeah?"

"I have not always been a man of family. In my youth, I was very wild. I thief, I fight, I drink the whiskey—"

"You don't drink alcohol anymore, Suge?"

He shook his head morbidly. "My wives, they make me stop three years ago. They say that we have kids to spend money on instead. I have to do the sneak now. But, in youth, I journey to Europe in search of women and whiskey. I tell my father I look for better work."

"Suge, what does this have to do with you being on the news?"

"It is coming. Be patience. I first go to Greece, then to the Hungary, and then to Italy. Ahh, Italy!" His eyes looked skyward at this point, and the wonder that seized his speech when he spoke of the free world returned. "Whiskey, tequila, beer . . . it was the excellent time for me. And best part is, even if you fail to find woman for the night, you go spend money on prostitute. Many beautiful prostitutes in Italy."

"So, you became a pimp in Italy?" Neither my platoon sergeant nor I could keep a straight face at this point. This was vintage Suge.

"Hah, no, no, nothing like that. In eight months in Italy, I spend all my money that I save from five years' work in Africa! Too many whiskey and women. Worst part, my papers [work visa] ended during those months. I could not find the work even now that I actually look for it." He shook his head again and bit his lip, recalling lost opportunities. "A friend of mine write from the Portugal. 'Come to the Portugal!' he say 'Good work and you don't need papers!' So I hop on next train to the Portugal."

A dark cloud came over the horizon of Suge's face. "But they stop me in France!" His voice changed tones here, as he mocked the French accent. "They say, 'No, Africa man, you cannot go to the Portugal. You have bad papers! You cannot go to the Portugal. You go to jail instead.' I stay there for three months, and they put my picture on the television, saying I was criminal from Africa. But I was just trying to go to work in the Portugal, and I tell them that! They finally believe me, and they put me on the boat for Africa and tell me I can never come back to France or Italy. Not ever."

I stared at our terp in confusion. "Suge, that story doesn't make any sense."

Unperturbed, Suge took a drag from his cigarette and shrugged his shoulders. "Fucking French," he mumbled to himself, the matter evidently closed.

A few months later, after he returned to the combat outpost from a brief family vacation, Suge realized he had left his diabetes medicine at his house. Unable to think of another course of action, he instructed his wives to take a taxi from their residence to Saba al-Bor, where he met them and picked up his medication. Unsurprised to find him wearing an American army uniform, they spent their time nagging him about forgetting his pills, and afterward, even Suge admitted the gig was up.

"They are very proud of me," he said contentedly.

RECENTRALIZED WARFARE

I had trained and studied for, and brooded over, a very specific type of war. The manuals called it decentralized warfare, a practice dripping with successful historical paradigms for insurgencies and counterinsurgencies alike. In it, small units like sections and platoons and troops functioned as nigh-independent entities, operating free of homogeneous rigidity and traditional military slowness. In this malleable, flexible world, creativity and ingenuity replaced firepower and overwhelming force as the central pillars of an army's output. Ideally, a decentralized army struck like a swarm of killer bees rather than a lumbering elephant; an elephant's strength and power certainly had its time and place, but since the end of World War II, an increasing number of global conflicts had called for the precision of a swarm instead. One did not simply mark time in decentralized warfare; one made it. This concept seemed a lieutenant's dream and a general's nightmare, with power dispersed and control scattered into a thousand corners. In conventional warfare, the order of war dissolved into anarchy as time yielded more and more blood. Unconventional, decentralized warfare was the exact opposite. In fluid theory and historical practice, victorious counterinsurgencies served as a shining inverse to said conventionality because, through anarchy and bloodshed, order could eventually be established. This was the war I trained for, brooded over, and studied.

Then there was the war I fought.

As the summer of 2008 progressed, we at the ground level of the American counterinsurgency lived the strategic shift away from decentralized warfare. I was sure very good reasons existed for this, and although I wasn't privy to the details, it didn't take a Clausewitz to figure out that this was the beginning of the much-ballyhooed exit from Iraq. Meanwhile, at the combat outpost, the concerted recentralization of our efforts seemed like a very odd way to thank the soldiers responsible for turning the tide of the Iraq War. We no longer fought in a neo-Vietnam black hole of Islamic extremism—the COIN era had turned the war into an isolated conflict of manageable proportions, and a lot of that was due to letting loose the initiative of junior officers and NCOs, who solved their own local problem sets. After two or three years of that, being reined back in by powers more concerned with uniform standards than electricity shortages wasn't really a cause for celebration, despite the grander vision.

An elephant could only pretend to be something else for so long before reality reestablished itself. In our case, a red, white, and blue elephant remembered it preferred trampling to stinging.

On a mid-August afternoon, the Gravediggers and I were conducting a vehicle-maintenance refit back at the FOB when Captain Ten Bears contacted me on the radio regarding a frago.

"We think we have one of our top targets isolated," he said. "Abu Mustafa, a high-ranking member of a JAM golden group. He's visiting his family in a village in a different troop's area, but he's still our priority because he operates in Saba al-Bor."

"Roger that, sir."

"Get the target packet from the squadron intel geeks at the FOB and start planning. The operations staff will let you know when it's time to execute. Also, keep the other troop up-to-date. Coordinate that through the squadron TOC."

"Roger that, sir."

My commander laughed. "You got all that, bud? It's a pain in the ass, I know."

I smirked. "When is it not?"

The mission initially excited me and my platoon. First, any change in our daily monotony felt like a breath of fresh air, as we were far too comfortable with our environment by this point in the deployment. Second, this was legitimate, actionable intelligence, not just information or flimsy hearsay. It seemed too good to be true, and I should have known better. Alas, though, the hope-dope sprung eternal.

I walked from the maintenance bay to the squadron headquarters and collected the target packet. I recognized most of the details of Abu Mustafa's packet from conversations I'd had with various sheiks, Sons of Iraq, and locals. He had worked his way up through an extreme wing of the Mahdi Army from the very bottom, rising from IED emplacer to street thug to street king to bomb maker to financier to network operator. He bounced around constantly, seemingly always on the run, rarely returning home to the village where his wife and children lived. He wielded power by evoking fear and brutally killed other JAM members who did not follow his orders quickly enough or who disagreed with him—which, through the process of elimination, also propelled his rise through the ranks. I recalled a muggy night way back in February, when a Son of Iraq informant refused to utter his name above a whisper, his words drenched in absolute terror. That memory seemed a lifetime away.

Bagging this mother fucker might make our month, I thought. And there was always the chance that he was stupid enough to try and fight back with gunfire. . . . The guys would absolutely love that.

I grabbed a map, wrote out my plan, walked over to the TOC, and briefed our new squadron operations officer on the basics. A major, he turned out to be far too grounded, sharp, and fair to deserve the Moe label. I chided myself for yet again stereotyping field-grade officers before I interacted with them.

"Sir, I plan to establish the vehicle cordon here," I said, pointing at my map. "We'll kick out the dismounts here, moving in two sections, one for clearing the house, the other for inner-perimeter security and support. If all goes well, the target will be detained here."

"Looks good," he said and then added a few constructive tweaks. "We'll let the landowners know," he continued. "Go conduct your rehearsals and stand by for confirmation of the target's location from the intelligence gurus."

My platoon met me at the staging area, we went over the plan, and we only waited for five minutes before the squadron TOC called on the radio. "White 1, this is Strykehorse X-ray. The target is green. Go ahead and move out, time now."

"Roger that," I said and then switched over to our platoon net. "Let's roll!" Our Strykers ripped toward the FOB's gates, as if the sheer act of motion could somehow prevent the inevitable monkey wrench.

I went over the plan one last time on the radio as we moved. "Remember, lock and load as soon as the ramps drop, before you get on the ground. Cordon, keep the crew serve weapons oriented out. Dismounts, slow is smooth, and smooth is fast. We've done this a thousand times. When we—"

"White 1, White 1, this is Strykehorse X-ray."

"This is White 1."

"We need you to turn around and report to the TOC, time now."

Bamboozled, I asked for clarification. "Say again, over?"

"We need you to turn around and report to the TOC, time now."

"Uhh, roger, over. I'm halfway out the front gate, heading to that raid you just told me to execute. Perhaps I can take a rain check?"

"Negative, things have . . . changed. Return to the TOC, time now."

I sighed into the hand mic. "Roger that," I said, my voice marinated in disgust.

As we pulled back into the staging area on the FOB, the platoon net buzzed.

"Ain't this mutha fucka' a time-sensitive target, sir?" Staff Sergeant Bulldog asked. "Or are we gonna meet him for dinner?"

"Maybe he's not there yet," I said, pausing. "Maybe. Just stay redcon-1 here guys. I'm sure whatever the holdup is, it won't last long. I'll be right back."

I ran into the squadron TOC. Some sixty minutes later, I returned.

As I staggered back to my Strykers, I found SFC Big Country, Staff Sergeant Bulldog, and Staff Sergeant Boondock smoking cigarettes on the front side of the lead vehicle.

"Well?" they asked simultaneously.

"Well," I sighed. "Well. There was some . . . debate between some captains and some majors as to who should execute this mission. We were originally tapped to go because we were available and on the FOB, and the squadron operations officer wanted speed."

"That makes sense," SFC Big Country said.

"That it does," I replied. I needed to be more forthcoming about what had happened with these three, I thought. They deserved it. "Not everyone agreed. To make a long story short, Lieutenant Colonel Larry got involved, and while we're still doing the raid, we're now under the landowner's command for it."

"Jesus fucking Christ, you're telling me some invisible lines on a fucking map and a bunch of territorial officers bitching at each other did this?" Staff Sergeant Boondock fumed. "This is bona fide bureaucratic bullshit, sir. This dude is high level, and like Bulldog said, it's a time-sensitive mission! What the fuck are they thinking? This isn't some goddamn cowboy movie where the bad guy waits for us at a corral."

I nodded. "I hear you. But our time is not our own to manage anymore. We anticipated rather than reacted. Lesson learned." I smirked. "Now the four of us, we have to go meet up with the landowning commander. He's going to brief us on his plan."

I found the landowning captain's plan a solid one, though more complex than mine, certainly, as it had more moving parts and involved units that had never worked together before. Whereas my plan aimed for crashing lightning, in and out just long enough to nab Abu Mustafa, this aspired for rolling thunder, a methodical cordon with a very clear step-by-step process. Admittedly, his brief was better than mine; I found it very smooth and thorough, and it lacked my infamous crutch phrases, like "fuckin'" or "you know?" Further, he had color maps, which contained all sorts of cool—if irrelevant—

demographic breakdowns in pie chart form. Even disgruntled, I still appreciated shiny things.

Some two and a half hours after we got the initial confirmation of Abu Mustafa's whereabouts, we finally kicked open the front door to his house. No one was home, although we found food in the pantry and a few other signs of recent habitation.

"Guess we was late for dinner," Staff Sergeant Bulldog said as we moved back to our Strykers after clearing the house.

Various possibilities for the mission's failure swept through my mind. Maybe the presence of so many Coalition forces tipped Abu Mustafa off; anything larger than a roving platoon stuck out as out of the ordinary for any village in this part of Iraq. Maybe he had guards posted on the outside of town and fled at the first sign of Americans. Or maybe we just took too fucking long. Whatever the case, Abu Mustafa had escaped and, as far as I knew, wouldn't be found at any point during our deployment.

The recentralization movement continued. In the ensuing months, Higher developed an obsession with quantifying every aspect of the war effort. PowerPoint slides and pie charts and information overload for the sake of information overload then became our raison d'être—the more of those things we did, the more we were left alone to conduct legitimate counterinsurgency operations the way we knew how. The mass quantifying reached a personal apex when I tracked "nose time," the number of minutes a military dog spent sniffing for explosives over the course of a mission.

We certainly were no swarm of killer bees. As I looked back on the experience though, I liked to believe that if nothing else, we made our elephant cut some of its excess lumbering weight. That was something, at least.

That was the war I fought.

MERRY MEN AND MICROGRANTS

"Why the hell are we doing this again?" Staff Sergeant Axel (recently promoted) asked.

"So our squadron's microgrant bar graph on the brigade PowerPoint slide can be the highest," Staff Sergeant Spade answered offhandedly. "Don't worry, it's all good. We're about halfway done. If we keep the same pace, we'll be done, in what, another four, five hours?"

The Gravediggers, 2nd platoon of Bravo Troop, 2–14 Cavalry, circa August 2008, at combat outpost Bassam. Front row, from left to right: Corporal Spot, Doc, PFC Stove Top, PFC Smitty, PFC Romeo. Middle row, from left to right: myself, Staff Sergeant Boondock, Sergeant Tunnel, Specialist Haitian Sensation, Sergeant Fuego, Staff Sergeant Axel, PFC Van Wilder. Back row, from left to right: PFC Das Boot, SFC Big Country, Sergeant Prime, Staff Sergeant Spade, and Staff Sergeant Bulldog.

    I didn't bother correcting my NCOs, as I silently agreed with their cynical assessment of our mission's purpose. The Gravediggers and I had spent our entire sunny morning on Route Maples, writing down local businesses' contact information, and we were bound to spend our entire sunny afternoon the same way. The microgrant program had developed in and with the American military's COIN efforts; in theory, it supplied local Iraqi-owned businesses with a small sum (generally US$300 to US$500) for specific refinements to aid their commerce. These businesses were supposed to be vetted beforehand for any shady connections, and their refinement purchases were supposed to be verified by American units after the issuing of the microgrant—again, all in theory. In practice, the microgrant program devolved into another quantifiable figure that unit commanders used to compete for officer evaluation report (OER) bullets. So, when Captain Ten Bears got the order to devote his entire troop to mass microgrant projects in Saba al-Bor over the course of three days, I knew we weren't meeting the program's intent. But other than a sarcastic comment or two to my peers, I shut up and executed. I wasn't walking the pariah road again.

My platoon's slice of this mission proved the smallest in area but held the largest number of businesses. Approximately two miles long, Route Maples served as Saba al-Bor's main strip as nearly every building, shanty, and tarp on both the east and west sides of the cluttered street contained a business of some kind. Later that night, as I organized our mission's collection efforts, I totaled 532 local businesses on Route Maples.

"Dude, I feel so dirty doing this!" Skerk yelled over to me, both of us jotting down names, type of business, and phone numbers supplied by the owners. "It's one thing to witness a scam like this, but it's a whole other thing to be the one peddling it!"

As our troop's artillery and contracts officer, Skerk oversaw the microgrant program in our AO. For the first few months of our deployment, he used its funds the way we had been taught to—precisely targeting specific businesses that supported the efforts of Coalition forces, helping them out with a new freezer or upgraded furniture, and allowing news of the benefits of working with us to spread through the populace by word of mouth. Obviously, that was before the microgrant program came onto Higher's radar. Now, Skerk served as the ringmaster in a circus of mass microgrant issuing. We often joked about which specific American taxpayer had paid for the random object deemed "vital to commerce" by an Iraqi business owner, but it was only funny because the concept of money meant nothing to us anymore.

While I listened to a young Iraqi grocery shop owner explain to me why he wanted to use his pending microgrant on a foosball table, I thought about how unenforceable all of this was. We couldn't take back a grant after the fact, whether the Iraqis bought something pragmatic or not. And while our guidance for dealing with this problem had us telling transgressors that we had added them to our terrorist watch list, we could only issue the threat so many times before it became an Arabic punch line.

I glanced across the street, spying Staff Sergeant Bulldog's team snaking its way north in parallel with us. Staff Sergeants Bulldog and Boondock, Sergeant Fuego, PFC Van Wilder, Private First Class Romeo (recently promoted), and Super Mario all had ice-cream cones and seemed to be laughing and joking with a few Iraqi police and local children. Leave it to my guys, I thought to myself. They'd be able to turn a concentration camp into a poker game.

"Hey, sir!" SFC Big Country yelled from three stalls behind me. "Suge wants to apply for a microgrant so he doesn't have to walk up this damn road with us anymore. It's Iraqi welfare!" Both my platoon sergeant and my terp chuckled openly, slapping each other on the back, while eating flatbread and sipping on juices provided them by the local vendor they had just talked to.

Despite my black mood, I smiled. I wished I could make the best of situations like this and (again) decided to make a concerted effort to be more like my men. Yes, this mission qualified as fucked up beyond all recognition (FUBAR), but none of us could do anything about it except finish it. I really needed to learn to worry only about matters within my control.

Suge walked up to me and patted me on the shoulder. "This is very good program, Captain! It make the people very happy and make them like the Americans very much. It is always good to give poor people money."

SFC Big Country followed. "Kind of like Robin Hood, huh, sir? I know how you like those old stories."

I looked up at my grinning platoon sergeant, who clearly had keyed in on my current temperament and decided to poke at it. "Gee, thanks, Little John," I said. I almost continued on to say that we weren't exactly taking from the rich to give to the poor, but I stopped myself. Rich was a relative term, and the Western middle class funding this trillion-dollar effort in Iraq, while tragically trapped—also a relative term—in American society, would be considered beyond affluent by Saba al-Bor standards.

"I fucking love your platoon," Skerk said, pointing across the street.

Staff Sergeant Bulldog had seized control of a donkey cart and was softly lashing the trotting donkey down Route Maples, much to the delight of the local Iraqis. On the back of the cart, Staff Sergeant Boondock and PFC Van Wilder attempted to surf the ride, waving to the shoppers as they passed.

"I guess that makes them the Merry Men," I said, shaking my head in wonder.

"Then who is Suge?" SFC Big Country asked. Our terp had wandered over to the nearest grocer stall and already held a glass of chai in his hand as he talked with the shop owner.

"You're wrong if you aren't thinking a very drunk and very crazy Friar Tuck," Skerk stated.

We all laughed. "Too bad your blog got axed," SFC Big Country said to me, as we continued up the street. "This would make for a good story."

I nodded. "I'll save it for that book everyone thinks I'm writing."

We finished our mass microgrant assessments three and a half hours later and headed back to the combat outpost. Later that night, after I'd finished organizing our collected information and putting it onto a PowerPoint slide so Higher could understand and quantify it, I thought about the bigger things again. One of the central tenets of our counterinsurgency operations called for us to inject funds into the lifeless Iraqi economy. Did it really matter if all of the microgrant awardees didn't actually meet the arbitrary bureaucratic standards put out? Wasn't it inevitable that we were funding some of our enemies by doing things like this? What would COIN architect General Petraeus think about how my platoon had spent our day? Would he believe it to be a grey means to a less grey end, or would he consider it part of the bastardized counterinsurgency spirit passed down through the ranks of a conventional army still struggling to adapt to nonconventional warfare?

I didn't know what he would think. I didn't even really know what I thought. So I went to bed and dreamed of a world less complex.

TRASH VILLAGE

Just before my platoon and I departed for a late-morning counter-IED patrol of Route Tampa, Captain Ten Bears called me into his office and told me that Lieutenant Colonel Larry had finally found a new platoon leader to replace me with and that he would be in Saba al-Bor the following week. I nodded and said that I had known this moment was coming—I had been operating on borrowed time ever since the blog fiasco. They still weren't sure what my next position would be, but my troop commander guessed that the squadron staff lay in my future. Captain Ten Bears patted me on the back and told me not to let the Man get me down and to get moving on our mission.

I walked down the stairs and outside to the motor pool. I promised myself that I'd make every remaining minute and moment count, in order to savor my last experiences as a scout platoon leader. I also promised myself to finish as strongly and as passionately as I had started when I assumed the position some twenty months before. The men who waited at our Strykers, who had taught me what true honor and true stoicism were, expected and deserved nothing less.

They taught me some other things along the way, too.

"I'm telling you, food tastes better out of the garbage," Doc said to the confused laughter of the rest of the platoon. Apparently, he had been found rummaging through the trash, looking for a half-full bag of potato chips.

"Ain't our medic supposed to be sanitary?" Staff Sergeant Bulldog asked. "You're the last person who should be doing that shit."

Doc shrugged his shoulders, grinned, and shared his potato chips with PFC Das Boot.

I called the platoon in, SFC Big Country and I gave the mission brief, and I told them to mount up. The other news could wait.

We moved out of Saba al-Bor and east on Route Lincoln, reaching Route Tampa in fifteen minutes. Our initial counter-IED patrol called for us to move between the Grand Canal in the north and the Baghdad Gates in the south. But as soon as I checked in on the radio with the squadron TOC, they already had a different task and purpose for us.

"Roger, White 1, we read you loud and clear. We received a report from an Apache pilot an hour ago about a big metal object and possible IED he spotted from the air. We need you guys to check it out. Grid to follow."

Fuck, I thought. Flyboy information. While helicopter pilots meant well with their reports, all too often what we found on the ground resembled nothing like what they saw from the air. Like the time we woke up a pack of wild dogs that they thought was a VBIED. Or the time we discovered a teenager peddling Jordanian porn out of the trunk of his car instead of the reported RPGs.

I relayed the frago and grid to my platoon.

"Hey, sir," SFC Big Country immediately said, "that grid is right in the middle of the city dump on the west side of Tampa. Either that grid is wrong, or that pilot is blind. There's all kinds of metal in a dump."

Jesus, he's fast, I thought. I plotted the grid on my own map, and my platoon sergeant, as usual, was spot-on. I called back to squadron and asked if they were aware where they wanted us to go. They said that, yes, they were and just to execute and let them know what we found.

"White, this is White 1," I said. "Go ahead and rock those hate fists. We're taking a field trip to the dump. Hopefully, we can confirm or deny the IED report from our vehicles."

Some thirty minutes later, it became unmistakably clear that we couldn't. With Staff Sergeant Boondock navigating in the lead vehicle, we wound our way through the dump, but there was absolutely no way to reach the grid in question without walking to it. The dismount teams met up on the ground.

As soon as I set foot in what we'd soon designate Trash Village, the pungent smell of compost blitzed my nostrils. I gagged and felt my stomach rumble. Layer upon layer of refuse, debris, and scrap besieged us. We walked on a coating of plastic wrappers, empty cans, soiled clothes, and everything in between, with blotches of runny, black mud filling the gaps. Up a small rise to our north, in our direction of travel, sat multiple stacks of metal paint cans, patterned to mimic building structures.

"You have got to be fucking kidding me," Staff Sergeant Boondock said. "Are those houses?"

They were. As our wedge formation crested the knoll, we came upon six or seven of these buildings. Frail, sallow creatures sat on tires in front of their paint-can houses. They didn't acknowledge our presence as we strolled past, nor did they even seem aware of it. I took off my sunglasses and blinked repeatedly, verifying that these grey-skinned people with eyes devoid were actually human beings. The men and the women wore rags of various sorts, clearly pulled out of the dump where they lived. Most of the children, however, walked around completely naked and completely lacked the verve and bounce of even the most destitute child in Saba al-Bor. Staff Sergeant Spade pulled a Beanie Baby out of his pocket and tossed it to a little boy we passed. The little boy just stared at the ground where the toy lay and never looked up to see who threw it there.

Makeshift pens of thin wire rested behind the paint-can houses. Various gatherings of bulls, cows, goats, and pigs all lived together there, munching away on their own waste or on the garbage around them. They proved to be the only fat farm animals I saw during my entire deployment to Iraq—obviously more a product of their diets than their health. I whispered a Hail Mary to myself, a prayer I hadn't said since high school, and tried to push the thought of these people eating these animals out of my mind.

Primal, internal sirens implored us to keep moving past this place. As we followed a narrow trail deeper into the dump to the designated grid coordinate, we progressed away from the paint-can houses and eventually came parallel with a shallow, coffee-brown lake. A small gust of wind whipped up just as we passed this body of water, bringing a scent of mummified illness with it. I gagged again, feeling nauseous, and held my breath to avoid puking.

"You alright, sir?" Corporal Spot asked from behind me. "I feel like yakking, too. This is the most disgusting place I've ever been."

I nodded and gave him a thumbs-up, refusing to speak. When we finally got to the spot and SFC Big Country picked up a large, metallic-yellow alarm clock, no one said anything. We simply turned around, filing down the trail, and broke back out into a wedge as we neared the trash shanties.

I didn't remember much of our walk back. The brain and the senses just shut down, as a means of protecting themselves. The body kept moving simply out of habit. Our four Strykers, green and powerful and humming, seized the horizon as a beaming oasis of escape. Our steps became strides. In hindsight, I'm surprised no one broke into a trot.

As we passed the last of the paint-can buildings, Staff Sergeant Spade's Beanie Baby still sat on the ground untouched. The little boy and a woman old enough to be his grandmother sat on a tire nearby. Feeling her eyes on me, I reflexively looked over at her. I stared at her grey, sagging cheekbones to avoid looking into her eyes.

"Salaam aleichem," I said, waving my right hand. I thought I saw her head nod, although the movement seemed so slight I couldn't be sure.

The Arabic greeting I uttered meant, "Peace be with you." No wonder she didn't say it back, I thought. I might as well have been speaking Greek to that woman.

We got back on our Strykers and drove back to Tampa. No one joked; no one laughed; no one said much of anything. It took a few hours to get back into our normal operational rhythm and banter.

SFC Big Country and I finally talked about Trash Village and its inhabitants the next morning, back in Saba al-Bor at the combat outpost. After making some phone calls to contacts in squadron, he had learned that the Iraqi government had offered to move those people out of the city dump, but they had refused, citing their direct access to the trash as their primary means of survival. We decided they were outcasts of some sort, possibly religious ones, as I remembered reading an article on the Internet some months before about a similar situation up north in Mosul. Then we sat around thinking to ourselves about all of that for a few minutes. I decided I was glad I hadn't been to that place in the beginning of the deployment. I doubted that the earnest youth I had been could've brushed it aside as easily as I just had.

"Doc said he's not going to eat out of the garbage anymore," my platoon sergeant eventually said.

"Probably a smart decision."

"Yeah. Probably so."

RAMADAN

On my last night in Saba al-Bor, I watched a man die.

We had spent most of the day and early evening showing the new platoon leader around the city and its outlying villages. We stopped by Sheik Banana-Hands's Sahwa headquarters, where he gave me a black-and-white Shia headdress as a thank you gift. Not to be outdone, Haydar presented me with a red-and-white Sunni headdress and a brand-new white dishdasha at his house, while we waited for the sun to set so we could begin our Ramadan meal.

The month-long Muslim religious observance known as Ramadan honored the revelation of the Qur'an to the Prophet Muhammad. Every year, practicing Muslims refused to eat or drink anything from dawn to sunset, instead spending their days praying and reflecting on how to better live as Allah intended. Once night arrived, however, the people gathered for nightly feasts, replenishing their bodies for the next day of fasting.

Suge, who also fasted for the observance, warned us that "the fucking Iraqis go crazy in the mind during the Ramadan, without food and water. Other Muslims are good at the Ramadan and keep their mind, but not Iraqis. They are loony people." He proved a visionary later that night.

Taking a break from packing, I walked down the stairs of the combat outpost to take a piss when I heard a vehicle come to a screeching halt outside at the front ECP gate. Loud shouting in Arabic followed, and some five seconds later, four IA jundis burst in, carrying a man in an Iraqi army uniform whose guts spilled wildly out of his stomach. A blood trail followed, dripping like red liquid from a smashed juicebox.

Our reaction was immediate and the product of many hours of strenuous, rigid training. I yelled into my radio, and within one minute, all of the troop's medics had opened up the aid station, carried the wounded man to the table inside, and began conducting first aid. The TOC called for a medical evacuation and reported that the helicopter would arrive in ten minutes. Staff Sergeant Spade, the sergeant of the guard for the night, ran outside and marked the landing zone for the helicopter with Chem-Lights.

Despite our swift reaction, the prognosis for Nasim Abdul Qasim, an IA sergeant, was not hopeful. Doc and the rest of the medics worked quickly and ably, trying desperately to reestablish a pulse. Sergeant First Class Bisel, the Headquarters platoon sergeant and a proud Pittsburgh native, pressed down on the man's stomach with a large gauze pad, attempting to keep his intestines inside of him. Noticing his dilemma—there seemed to be more spilling intestine than gauze pad—I grabbed a pair of gloves and my own gauze pad and pushed down on an open area. I felt a surge of blood and guts rise up from the other side.

"We're losing him!" Doc yelled. "There's no pulse!"

I kept glancing at the man's eyes. They didn't blink, but his irises kept flickering from white to pale blue, like a mood ring. I'm watching life fade out, I thought. This is fucking weird. My skin prickled.

"Don't do that, sir," SFC Bisel told me. "Trust me. Concentrate on the stomach and leave the face alone. You don't want that sticking with you."

I nodded, gulped, and reestablished firm pressure on my gauze pad.

Somehow, the medics restored the man's existence. Just as we received the report that the medical chopper would arrive in two minutes, they detected the faintest of pulses. We tightly wrapped as much of his core as we could, intestine slop covering the floor, and loaded him up on a stretcher. Four American soldiers lifted the wounded Iraqi and carried him out to the helicopter. The four IA jundis stood in the hallway, pacing back and forth.

Ten minutes later, as our soldiers mopped up the floors and cleaned up the aid station, we received the report that Sergeant Nasim Abdul Qasim had died on the helicopter en route to a Baghdad military hospital.

The jundis originally claimed that a group of insurgents had driven by and shot at them with AK-47s, hitting Nasim Abdul Qasim in the process. When SFC Bisel and the medics pointed out that three different bullets had entry points in the lower back and that the stomach served as the exit point for all three, their story changed to a negligent discharge burst going off while one of them cleaned his rifle. They blamed the fasting effects of Ramadan for the carelessness. The running theory among the American soldiers revolved around rebellious jundis disliking an order their NCO put out and shooting him from behind. The IA major I spoke with said he'd look into that possibility.

After that, I walked upstairs and finished packing. Across from me, one of my NCOs did the same.

While my shift out of the platoon was an inevitable known, Staff Sergeant Boondock's was not. We learned about it only two days before the IA sergeant died, with no explanation beyond "because Sergeant Major Curly said so." Staff Sergeant Boondock moved to another troop in our squadron, and Staff Sergeant Spade replaced him as our second section sergeant. While no one understood the purpose of Staff Sergeant Boondock's reassignment at the time, I later learned secondhand that it had occurred because Lieutenant Colonel Larry felt he and I were "too close." While this revelation filled me with guilt, it also proved to me one last time that our squadron leadership was hopelessly out of touch with what it took to be a leader on the ground in Iraq and, as far as I was concerned, demonstrated that they were more interested in soothing their own egos than helping soldiers. Platoon leaders switched out in combat routinely. Section sergeants did not. Staff Sergeant Boondock, easily one of the squadron's most tactically proficient NCOs, had developed ten months' worth of standard operating procedures and technical procedures with his section—taking him away from them after all that, and failing to anticipate a serious decrease in combat effectiveness as a result, was akin to putting an octopus on land and still expecting it to swim.

My replacement and the remaining NCOs were certainly up to the task of reshaping the platoon, but that didn't change the fact that their having to do so was completely unnecessary. Further, the fact remained that Staff Sergeant Boondock had been punished for my actions. It wasn't my fault that our leadership was so petty, but it was my fault for pointing that out to the greater e-world. Staff Sergeant Boondock became a section sergeant in his new troop, but being the new guy, he wasn't able to talk his way into the senior scout position he treasured so much and had so rightfully earned.

In the following months, thanks to the hard work of Captain Ten Bears, the Gravediggers, and the other men of Bravo Troop, Saba al-Bor cemented itself as central Iraq's preeminent COIN success story. Enemy attacks and activity plummeted, while civil projects skyrocketed. Reelected as the mayor, Rahdi oversaw these improvements; meanwhile, Mojo's business expanded to include cell phone plans. According to the brigade's numbers, over 30,000 displaced personnel returned to Saba al-Bor during Bravo Troop's time there. In February 2009, a JAM recruiter arrived from Sadr City, looking for fresh enlistees and promising young men the opportunity to kill Coalition forces. Not only were there no takers, but a bakery shop owner, tired of waiting for the slow-arriving Iraqi police, shot him dead in the street on Route Swords. A year prior, none of the people in that area would even talk to us for fear of JAM's believing them to be informants. Saba al-Bor had certainly come a long way since our arrival. A place in Iraq that assorted, though, always sat perched on the cliff edge of sectarian warfare. Only time would show the true effect of all of our efforts and whether they could last.

The morning following the Ramadan death, after I got big hugs from both Suge and Bulldozer the IP, the Gravediggers and their new platoon

Staff Sergeant Spade (near), Staff Sergeant Axel, and PFC Stove Top walk through Trash Village in the summer of 2008.

leader dropped me and Staff Sergeant Boondock off at Camp Taji. I still didn't know what my next job would be; I had orders to report to the squadron headquarters the next morning to find out. I left the platoon in my replacement's capable charge—the new platoon leader proved himself both skilled and patient in the months to come, and believing such would be the case ahead of time certainly put my mind at ease during the transition.

As we pulled up to our FOB room pods, I shook my successor's hand. "Just get them home," I told him. "Nothing else matters."

He nodded. "Don't worry, man. I will."

I said my farewells to the NCOs and soldiers, all of us promising to stay in touch and to hit up the bars together when we got back to Hawaii. Then Sergeant Tunnel, Specialist Haitian Sensation, and PFC Smitty helped me carry my bags to my room.

"Thanks, sir," PFC Smitty twanged. "For everything. You'll always be our platoon leader."

I felt myself tearing up, so I told them to stop shamming and to get back to work. I closed the door to my room, locked it, and collapsed on my bed. For the first time in a very long time, I felt completely empty and completely alone. I had no idea what to do with myself. I stared at the ceiling in total silence for many hours.

IV: ACROSS THE RIVER AND FAR AWAY

(OR REDEMPTION'S GRUNT)

AUTUMN 2008

I wanna stand up, I wanna let go
You know, you know, no you don't, you don't
I want to shine on, in the hearts of men
I want a meaning from the back of my broken hand

Another head aches, another heart breaks
I'm so much older than I can take
And my affection, well it comes and goes
I need direction to perfection, no no no no
—The Killers, "All These Things That I've Done"

⟦FOBBIT INTERLUDE⟧

Hello. My name is Matt. I'm here for that meeting thing.

(Hi, Matt.)

I had to come here. Don't think otherwise.

(Hi, Matt.)

My name is Matt, and I have secrets.

(We all have secrets.)

My name is Matt, and this secret is that I was a fobbit for ten days.

(Tell us more. That's why we're here.)

I don't want to. Leave me alone.

(Tell. Us. More.)

Will you leave me alone then?

(Yes.)

Can I leave afterward?

(Yes.)

Fine. That's all I ever wanted, anyway. To be left alone.

(Hi, Matt.)

So, like I said, I was a fobbit for ten days. And it felt good. Smooth. Simple. Safe. Nightly showers, scheduled mealtimes, a basic sense of security, all in the bubble of Little America. Not like the line. No strange, unexpected things happened on the FOB, but strange, unexpected things happened out there. Especially if you spent too much time out there. Not like the line at all.

(Where?)

Where? Out there. Crazy. Where stuff occurred. Where things happened. Where all of it felt real.

(Hi, Matt.)

Existence as a staff officer was like being a self-licking ice-cream cone. Sure, it tasted good at first, if a bit vanilla. But it quickly turned into a self-destructive pattern of melting purpose. In theory, we existed to support the squadron's main efforts, the landowning troops. In practice, we survived by satiating Higher with graphs and charts and talking points and other digital excess venerated by the corporate camo culture. Nothing could have been more obscure and fake.

(And?)

Crashed over facade.

(And?)

Well, our lives were nothing more than a PowerPoint circle jerk, with the yes-men and the careerists and the listless laze all fighting to eat the cum cookie in the middle, because eating it garnered them attention. Attention meant positive OER bullets. And OER bullets . . . well, they weren't like real bullets.

(We all have secrets.)

At some point during those ten days I forgot I was still in Iraq.

(Tell. Us. More.)

I liked it. And hated myself for liking it.

(We all have secrets.)

Jambo!

(And?)

A man could have liked it forever if he remembered to turn off the pride and passion buttons.

(And?)

I forgot.

(Forgot what?)

I forgot nothing. I became the squadron's information operations officer: Higher's little joke with itself, having the famous blogger serving as the writing pun. En vogue, in yoke. Most of the soldiers and NCOs and officers I worked with on the FOB were good guys and wanted to contribute directly to the war effort. But the flagpole had other plans for us.

(Tell. Us. More.)

After all, there was a war to forget.

(And?)

And . . . and . . . and. I wanted to patch myself back together. Really. Physically. Mentally. Emotionally. Serendipitously. Really. I did.

(We all have secrets.)

But I kept thinking about how this escape was my escape, not our escape. They were still out there, still fighting, still sucking. This made my escape cheap and empty, and so it turned out not to be an escape at all. I guess I forgot to turn off the pride and passion buttons.

(Yes.)

Unless the field grades in charge of the unit staffs held combat experience on the line—a rarity, given the generational gap within the officer corps—micromanagement reached new apexes every day, and the disconnect between what was and what should be continued to widen.

(Forgot what?)

I forgot nothing. Out of the wire, corporals made daily decisions that held strategic-level consequences. On the FOB, majors couldn't shade a PowerPoint slide a particular color without getting prior approval.

(Yes.)

Crashed under facade.

(Yes.)

Don't get me wrong—life as a fobbit wasn't easy. It wasn't hard, but it certainly wasn't easy. People worked hard. But with the flagpole so close, we couldn't work smart. Life didn't drain out here like it did outside the wire. It soul-sucked. Not from the inside either. From the outside. The way a pool cleaner sucks out the stomach of a little kid sometimes.

(Hi, Matt.)

Hi.

(Tell us more. That's why we're here.)

Jambo!

(Forgot what?)

I forgot nothing. Like this: Jambo! It's Swahili. The Ugandans, who worked as contracted security guards on the FOB, said it. They were the only happy people on all of Camp Taji, so they said, "Jambo!" It wasn't like hello. Or hola. Or salaam aleichem. It was jambo! Always with an exclamation point. I tried saying jambo! sometimes, but I wasn't very good at it. A person can't mimic joy.

(Hi, Matt.)

I saw fliers telling me to join the biweekly Camp Taji softball league or the flag-football league. The PX sold ninety-some monthly magazines, hot off the presses. The lines for the fast-food restaurants—Burger King and Pizza Hut and Taco Bell—never ended. Musicians routinely held concerts, thinking they had come to the real Iraq. They would have had better luck finding it in downtown Detroit.

(And?)

Where was I? I didn't know. I still don't know. Little America, Bizarro Iraq. That's all I knew.

(Tell us more. That's why we're here.)

This is such bullshit. Leave me alone. That's all I ever wanted anyway. To be left alone.

(*Tell us more. That's why we're here.*)

No.

(*Yes.*)

Why?

(*Because we will listen.*)

What?

(*Yes.*)

Fine. But you promise I can leave after this?

(*Yes.*)

Fine. After that, after those ten days I mean, Lieutenant Colonel Larry called me into his office and told me that they were trading an officer to 1–27 Infantry, also of the Second Brigade of the Twenty-fifth Infantry Division, for another officer. The original officer they wanted to trade wasn't mentally sound anymore because of the deployment, and so they were now trading me so 1–27 Infantry didn't think we traded crazy people. I didn't want to go, even after all of the drama. I had grown up in 2–14 Cavalry. Everything I knew about the army happened in that organization, and everyone I knew in the army served there. But I had no say in the matter and didn't want to give Lieutenant Colonel Larry the satisfaction of knowing I felt nervous. "Now," he said with a thin, leering smile, "don't think this has anything to do with the blog." I nodded, saluted, and left the office. I saved my smirk for later.

(*And?*)

Crashed through facade.

(*And?*)

They thought they had fucked me, sticking a too-skinny, crazy-eyed mustang into a foreign environment full of infantry grunts. But they hadn't. I found redemption. I got back to a combat outpost. I got back to the line. I got back to soldiers.

(*Yes.*)

It wasn't my combat outpost. It wasn't my line. They weren't my soldiers. But it would be. They would be. And I escaped Camp Taji. A right escape. A true one. A legitimate one.

(*Yes.*)

The fires of the FOB almost broke me. Almost. But almost only counts in horseshoes and hand grenades.

(*And?*)
And in atomic bombs.
(*Hi, Matt.*)
Can I go now?
(*Yes.*)
Thanks.
(*See, that wasn't so hard, was it?*)
I forgot.

WELCOME TO THE WOLFHOUNDS

If one pulled out a map of Iraq again—after ensuring that it dated from the post–Baathist Party era—a thick black dot with a jagged scar down its center would be found just northwest of the slums of Saddam (now known as Sadr) City in Baghdad, next to the Tigris River's eastern banks. Across the river and far away from the crossroads of Saba al-Bor in the remote west, this dot found attention in the same manner that monsters do in a child's closet. Locals didn't so much say its name as they spat it out: Hussaniyah, a city originally built as Republican Guard housing for the large military base to the west in Taji. Roughly 600,000 Iraqis called this place home in late 2008, a place so densely Shia in nature and population that Sunnis dared not venture across the highway that served as its western border. Due to the transient nature of much of the population, a blood-red-sea past didn't soak this dot, but the spewing sewer water of the present did. There was no point in reflecting back on better times when none existed.

The expansive badlands of north-central Iraq lay above Hussaniyah, while Diyala Province and the former terrorist capital of Baqubah were a short drive due east. West of the highway—known to Coalition forces as Route Dover—rich Sunni manors basked along the Tigris's shore all the way south to Baghdad, artifacts of Saddam Hussein's old power base and the privileges he bestowed upon his tribesmen.

While Sadr City served as Jaish al-Mahdi's foundation and Najaf remained its spiritual home, Hussaniyah represented the paramilitary group's strongest and proudest outpost; it was akin to a baseball organization's highest minor-league level, the last obstacle in the way of the big show. JAM insurgents came to H-Town to prove themselves to the Sadr City brain trust, and if tihey did so and survived, they sometimes punched their ticket to that citadel. This usually meant our enemies had everything to gain and nothing to lose—a dangerous set of circumstances for counterinsurgents intent on separating the paramilitants from the populace. The jagged scar found on the map divided Hussaniyah in two, leaving a barren one-mile stretch of no-man's-land in the center. The west side, former Republican Guard officer and NCO housing, contained neighborhoods of relative comfort, but the east side, former Republican Guard enlisted housing, held ghettoes as vile and Third World as anything else found in Iraq. Usually, JAM's financiers and cell leaders lived on the west side. Its trigger pullers and IED emplacers lived on the east side.

My new unit—the 1–27 Infantry Battalion, better known by the moniker the Wolfhounds—was headquartered at a large joint-security station (JSS) just south of Hussaniyah. One of its companies (the infantry equivalent of a cavalry troop) patrolled everything west of Route Dover; another company, the one I'd soon join, patrolled everything east of Route Dover. This neatly divided the problem sets the various companies faced into Sunni and Shia. We shared JSS Istaqlaal with a battalion of Iraqi National Police (NP) commandos, who served in this area instead of the Iraqi army. The local Iraqi police were also found in H-Town and the smaller population centers of Boob al-Sham and Sabah Qasar (both located south of JSS Istaqlaal), and they were just as shady and of questionable intent as they had been in Saba al-Bor.

On the day I reported to the Wolfhounds, my new battalion commander told me he didn't care about what had occurred in 2–14 Cavalry, he just expected me to perform as an army officer to the standards demanded and needed by American soldiers. He then asked if I preferred to stay at Taji as a staff officer or to be sent out to the JSS. There were no platoon leader slots available—not that a young captain with nearly two years of platoon leader time needed any more—but a slot for a lethal targeting officer in Alpha Company remained open. I tried not to sound too eager when I responded, "The JSS would be awesome, sir," and then thanked him profusely for the opportunity.

Although their problems were minor when compared to what I experienced with 2–14 Cavalry, the Wolfhounds organization certainly had its own internal issues and its own flaws, just like any other unit. Consequently, when I talked to the platoon leaders deep into the night, trying to calm them down about the failures of a bureaucracy designed to make their men carry the greatest burden, I referenced my own days as a know-it-all lieutenant. But these failures weren't really mine to critique or carp about. 1–27 Infantry and its leaders—the field grades and otherwise—gave me a second chance to fight the war on the ground level when, quite frankly, I wasn't owed one, and pettier leaders would have kept me from it simply out of spite for being in the newspapers. Initially, I was nothing more than "the blog guy," but with time, and after proving myself capable, I regained my identity and my swagger. The blog guy became Captain G, and Captain G contributed to the war effort, which is why I went over there in the first place. Subsequently, I settled into more of an observer role, rather than playing an active character myself, with regard to the unit's structural dynamics.

If JSS Istaqlaal were a solar system, it would have orbited around The Hammer. It seemed as if all operations revolved around his actions and goals for the area, whether they actually did on a particular day or not. As the battalion's senior company commander, The Hammer led with a prototypical blend of strength, smarts, power, humor, and grace. He led men in the most intense of environments as naturally as most of us walked. His soldiers worshipped him while concurrently fearing his every step; this led them to push themselves to new limits of competency no one else believed possible. His superiors' respect for his leadership was based more on awe than remembrance. Just as we junior officers who served under him secretly hoped to be more like him, The Hammer's superiors secretly hoped they had been more like him when they were company commanders. Our fantasy was just as impossible as theirs. Men like this were revered for a reason, and that reason was grounded in their scarcity. As an armor officer in an infantry battalion, The Hammer quickly took me under his very large and broad wing—in addition to all his other gifts, he was also built like a brick house, something that certainly didn't hinder his status as a local legend, especially in the hyper-macho world of combat arms—and schooled me in the ways of the grunt and how they differed from the ways of the scout.

A self-described bull in a china shop, Captain Frowny-Face commanded the other rifle company stationed at JSS Istaqlaal. Sporting an old-school flattop and an equally old-school mentality, Captain Frowny-Face earned his nickname for going straight through obstacles rather than around them, the personal feelings of others be damned. A yellow smiley face, with a flattop and a straight line in lieu of the actual smile, soon became his visual emblem and could be found all across JSS Istaqlaal, from Porta-John walls to the sides of storage units to the computer lab. Due to his traditional approach to commanding a company, Captain Frowny-Face never let his soldiers know what they meant to him and instead preferred to have them believe that they were responsible for his perpetual frown. During a few revealing talks in the company TOC though—usually late at night, waiting for a long mission to end—he occasionally revealed to us junior officers milling around just how much he cherished commanding Alpha Company. I worked for both The Hammer and Captain Frowny-Face at JSS Istaqlaal, and despite my very pronounced and very public decision to leave the army at the end of our tour, both men took me in as one of their own and continued to develop me professionally.

Both companies burst with talent at the platoon and squad levels. In Alpha Company, both Lieutenant Mongo and Lieutenant Dirty Jerz proved a new theory of mine correct: The more passionate a platoon leader got after a mission, the more proficient he was during said mission. Lieutenant Mongo, who played defensive tackle for West Point before he got commissioned into the infantry, liked to come off as a meathead football player, but I quickly learned there was much more to him than that. He led from the front, both literally and figuratively, and with his tireless emotional strength, he seemed intent on breaking the army before it broke him. He, like many of us junior officers, believed the army needed to be the learning organization it professed to be rather than the zero-defect institution it really was. While most of us, myself included, eventually shrugged our shoulders in apathetic acceptance of this reality, Lieutenant Mongo never could bring himself to do that. I didn't just respect his unwillingness to compromise, I envied it. Outside of the wire though, he carried himself as a sort of beardless Caucasian Santa Claus with the local-nationals, delighting children and adults alike with a deep, jolly belly laugh.

Lieutenant Dirty Jerz tended to favor a far more silent approach to the platoon leader's eternal bout with bureaucracy. Just as competent as his larger and louder peer, he had learned as a prior-service enlisted soldier to pick and choose his battles with Higher. He also happened to be the only person I'd ever met from the state of New Jersey who wasn't a scumbag, something he knew and laughed about, hence his nickname. His soldiers liked to gibe Lieutenant Dirty Jerz for going over to the "dark side" of the officer corps, but their respect for him was both transparent and unwavering. This sometimes rattled other officers in the battalion, who weren't used to seeing such open displays of loyalty from soldiers and NCOs for their lieutenant.

Lieutenant Rant served as Alpha Company's artillery officer. Like Skerk in Saba al-Bor, he handled all money issues and contracts for Hussaniyah. As a result, he quickly reached the top of the list of Iraqis' most wanted men on JSS Istaqlaal, and rightfully so—his competence and drive had no equal. Another West Pointer, Lieutenant Rant could wax poetic on any subject—and often did. The role of steroids in modern baseball, the generational gap within the officer corps, the eternal benefits of pajamas, and Chihuahua ownership were just a few of the topics of Lieutenant Rant's hour-long discourses with himself and an attentive—or otherwise—audience. Our company XO, Captain Clay, and the Headquarters platoon sergeant, Sergeant First Class Hammerhead, needled Lieutenant Rant endlessly. I shared a room with these three, and the debates' intensity was usually only matched by their absurdity.

The Great White Hope, one of The Hammer's platoon leaders and one of my old housemates from Hawaii, helped ease my transition to the Wolfhounds. An armor captain from Wisconsin, The Great White Hope loved the high life as much as he hated staff officers feigning knowledge of life out of the wire, and his will seemed as tenacious as his skin was fair. Luckily for him, we wore far too much equipment and body armor for the Iraq sun to do any real damage. He certainly provided a welcoming face for me in my first days as a stranger in a strange land. The ever-poised Captain Pistol Pete served as The Hammer's recon platoon leader, while the maniacal Lieutenant Goo served as his artillery officer. As was often the case in deployed military life, after a few weeks of getting to know these men, it seemed like we had been comrades for years. It certainly felt like years.

Once I slid over to Alpha Company to be their lethal targeting officer, Captain Frowny-Face put me in charge of their two human intelligence (HUMINT) collection teams—army speak for intelligence soldiers embedded with combat units. Staff Sergeant Sitting Bull and Staff Sergeant Jorge led these two teams, and they and members of their team—like Sergeant Secret Agent Man and Specialist Wildebeest—would soon become my soldiers. Further, given that my new position required more time behind a computer than a platoon leader's did, I also became well acquainted with Specialist Gonzo, the company's communications expert. Staff Sergeant Sitting Bull's reputation preceded him: While assigned to an assaulting company in Sadr City, he had practically single-handedly identified and deconstructed a JAM cell that emplaced EFPs en masse, a story that even reached our ears up in Saba al-Bor back in April during Sadr's spring uprising.

The differences between Saba al-Bor and Hussaniyah were many, as were the differences in the personalities that marked the experience. But from 2–14 Cavalry to 1–27 Infantry, from Suge to Specialist Gonzo, and from the struggles in the Sunni farmlands west of the Tigris to the hemorrhaging in the Shia sewer blocks east of the great river, enough similarities arose for me to realize that my microcosm wasn't the particular AO I operated in. My microcosm was Iraq. The principles of counterinsurgency remained the same, as did the basic lessons of the experiences.

Such a realization scared the fuck out of me—because it reminded me that I still had six months left. Six months left in a combat zone. Six months away from love, safety, and escape. Six months still in danger and still trapped in the too real. Six months left.

We still had six months in Iraq.

THE GOLDEN HOUSE

I spent my initial month at JSS Istaqlaal with Havoc, The Hammer's company. As the Wolfhounds' senior company commander, he was charged with orienting me to their battle space and various problem sets before I settled into my position with Alpha Company. That was the official party line, at least. Unofficially, I knew he would observe my mission-planning, decision-making, and tactical abilities as a means of gauging my competency in order to ensure the 2–14 Cavalry hadn't sent over a walking disaster in addition to a problem child. I understood the nature of this feeling-out process and did my best to meet The Hammer's high expectations and standards. As when male dogs meet one another and immediately start smelling one another's nether regions, if my new unit was going to put me in charge of soldiers, they needed to verify first that I had both my brains and balls in order.

One of my first missions in this new stead was leading a Headquarters platoon patrol back to Camp Taji, where we picked up a State Department representative and escorted him back into sector for a meeting with the local Shia chieftain, Sheik Modhir, and the 1–27 Infantry XO. While the NCOs and soldiers of the patrol provided inner and outer security, I joined the State Department man inside for the meeting. The State Department representative served as a part of our brigade's embedded provincial reconstruction team. Although these units had been in Iraq for a couple years as a means of jump-starting local and national civil services, it hadn't been until the Sunni awakening and the Sahwa movement that these reconstruction teams really began to make headway. We lived classic counterinsurgency—clear, hold, and build.

I'd never been to Sheik Modhir's residence before, but the soldiers briefed me on what to expect. "Sir," my Stryker driver said, "his place is fucking big. Like, cocaine-dealer big. Ever seen *Scarface*?"

"Of course. About thirty times."

"Well, it's just like that, but with Iraqis instead of Cubans and Sons of Iraq instead of drug dealers." A short pause followed. "And American dollar bills instead of cocaine."

Sure enough, as our patrol turned off of Route Crush and into the sheik's property—which lay just west of Hussaniyah proper, straddling the border with Route Dover and the Sunni lands—my jaw dropped in awe. The splendor of the multiple-villa compound contrasted starkly with the squalor surrounding it on all corners. Thick, green palm trees lined the driveway, shading the first—and last—real lawn I saw in Iraq. The grass sparkled with the vitality of color and the audacity of health, both of which were rare sights in the land of turbans. Already unnerved, I let my eyes leave the landscape to absorb the estate's architecture. A total of five separate buildings rested across the expansive grounds. The largest, which I guessed to be the main house based on its three stories and new paint job of white with gold trim, stood in the center of the lawn, cresting it like a new sun. Two smaller lodges lay off to the main house's southeast and appeared to be older structures, judging by their worn structures and fading paint. Two more lodges off to the main house's southwest mirrored these, but these structures also shone with white paint and gold trim. As the Stryker's ramp dropped, I hopped onto the ground. A Sahwa member gave me a thumbs-up and a toothless smile that reminded me of a meth addict and pointed at one the smaller lodges in the southwest. I assumed this was Sheik Modhir's meeting house and started walking in that direction. The State Department rep—who had earlier introduced himself to me as Kevin—and his interpreter followed, while a squad of soldiers automatically formed a security diamond around us.

I slowed my pace to match Kevin's as we approached the meeting house. "Have you ever met with this guy before?" I asked.

He nodded and smiled somnolently. "Many times. It's always . . . an experience."

The view of the Iraqi village Sabah Qasar from the rear hatch of a Stryker. Navigating the narrow dirt roads proved a great challenge in these massive armored vehicles. Tragedy occasionally occurred when a too-brave soul or darting child got too close and was subsequently crushed to death.

In his early thirties with thin brown hair, he wore the business casual attire of a young banker—sharply pressed khaki pants, a crisp collared blue shirt buttoned all the way to the neck, and an expensive silver watch that screamed with severity. The bulky set of body armor and black Kevlar helmet encompassing all of that didn't so much ruin his look as emphasize it. Whereas my dirty, sweat-stained urban camouflage blended in with my body armor, the conflicting dress combination made Kevin look even more professional.

I nodded. "I'm new to this AO, so I'm not quite sure what to expect."

"He's a smart man," Kevin said, "and very powerful on this side of the Tigris. Problems sometimes arise simply because he's so cognizant of both."

Kevin's terp snickered on the other side of him. "He's also very prideful," he said in flawless English. "And he gets more and more prideful every day."

About five steps away from the meeting house, an old Iraqi man with sagging brown skin and a stooped back stepped out of the front door, bearing both the patience and care of a turtle. He wore an elegant white dishdasha that seemed to glitter in the sunlight, despite its being made of cotton. A bushy salt-and-pepper moustache and a lazy blue eye peeked out from under his traditional Shia black-and-white checkered headdress.

"Salaam aleichem, Modhir," Kevin said, shaking the old man's hand, then cupping his heart.

"Hell-llloe," the sheik replied in broken English. "It is good to see you."

Kevin's interpreter introduced me as "Naqib (Captain) Matt," and Sheik Modhir repeated his greeting as we shook hands. "Hell-llloe. It is good to see you."

I turned around and found the staff sergeant in charge of the squad on the ground. "We already have outer security established, sir," he said. "I got three Joes to send in with you guys, if that works." I nodded in agreement, always amazed at how easily and automatically NCOs took care of these matters.

"I'll hit you up on the radio if anything comes up," I said. "And I'll get the sheik to bring out some chai."

The staff sergeant chuckled. "Sir, that's one thing you don't have to worry about. They have superchai here, and there's no end to it."

"Fair enough," I said, unsure what superchai was, and followed Sheik Modhir and Kevin into the meeting house. The interpreter and the three soldiers assigned to inner security followed.

Couches and chairs of real leather and blonde wood outlined the perimeter of the front room. Crystal vases rested on the tables, filled with exotic red flowers, while chandeliers lit the room in a sort of golden glow. Oil paintings of rivers and waterfalls and forests that resembled the old American Midwest were scattered across the walls. In the back of the room, on a large oak desk, sat two brand-new MacBook laptops. Meanwhile, as my eyes swept back across the room, I saw the battalion XO already sitting on one of the aforementioned chairs, with two members of his security detail on the nearby couch.

This is the fucking Iraqi version of Versailles, I thought to myself.

Kevin and the interpreter took seats next to Sheik Modhir, facing the battalion XO. While I sat on a far couch, facing the group, the soldiers who followed me in moved to the end of the room and found seats of their own. I quickly took off my helmet and wiped my brow, becoming aware of just how much I had sweated in the midday heat. Then I took out my notebook and prepared myself for a long bout of listening.

"It is good to see you again, Modhir," Kevin said, beginning with the normal pleasantries Arabs demanded in social situations. "How is your family?"

"Fine, fine," the old sheik replied. "Although Rassim's wife has been sick. He has been away for a week keeping for her."

No one knew exactly how many children Modhir had or, for that matter, how many wives. His eldest son, Rassim, managed the internal operations of the family and the tribe. Another of Modhir's grown children, Hamid, dealt with Coalition forces and, more specifically, with any and all contracting through Coalition forces. Hamid was one of the men who, sheerly through the amount of time they spent together, had become a close acquaintance of Lieutenant Rant.

After Sheik Modhir asked Kevin about his parents, the battalion XO pushed the conversation back into the business realm. "Modhir here was just asking me why the Provincial Council is getting more and more of the allotted budget every month," he told Kevin. "Maybe you'll have better luck explaining it to him than I did."

Kevin looked sternly over at Modhir. The sheik's one good eye met the gaze steadily, while the other one drifted over toward me. Creepy, I thought to myself. My eyes darted around the room in an effort to avoid his empty, still blue. I found a painting of loggers in a broad, powerful river and studied that while I listened to the continuing conversation.

"Sheik, we've discussed this before," Kevin said. "You know how important it is for the Nahias and the Qadas to learn how to manage the money for themselves. They are Iraq's future."

The interpreter spoke, followed by Modhir in turn. The interpreter nodded and turned to Kevin. "He says that he is the chairman of the Qada, so it is just a waste of time to give them the money instead of just giving it directly to him, like it used to be. He says no one knows where the Nahia stops and the Qada starts. He says it is much simpler just to give him and Hamid the money because they know what is best for the area."

I bit my lip and avoided the impulse to shake my head. I had argued these same points with less powerful sheiks in the Saba al-Bor area, usually to no avail. This was turning into an identical discussion, just with bigger players and broader scopes. Explaining to autocrats—autocrats whom we had empowered, and necessarily so, to curb the violence during the reconciliation—that it was now time to relinquish power in the name of democracy and free enterprise often felt like the textbook definition of insanity. Further, separating the local Nahias from the provincial Qadas never seemed as clear-cut as it should have been, mainly because the councils shared and swapped members with confounding regularity; their lines and borders were as broken and ambiguous as the country itself. Most of these local power brokers lived in neo-fiefdoms and, beyond the occasional lip service they paid to democratic ideals, saw no pragmatic reason to change the status quo.

My thoughts, however, were interrupted when one of Modhir's servants brought out the chai and chocolate snacks. I quickly wolfed down my chocolate piece, then sized up the glass in front of me. The chai looked different from what I normally drank, and it tasted different too—more lukewarm and tinged with a spice I couldn't place, which gave it a kick. It gave my stomach a settled, warm feeling, a sensation that quickly spread to my extremities. Ahh, I thought. This must be superchai.

My mind floated away like a piece of driftwood. I daydreamed about women, sports, music, and pretty much anything that wasn't Iraq. By the time my attention ambled back to the present, Sheik Modhir had told Kevin that stealing money served as the sole function of the Iraqi government, which was another reason the Americans were better off paying him directly.

Good Christ, I thought. He's an Iraqi fat cat. No sense of irony and upset that an entity bigger than himself existed to take or tax his money. I had had enough. I reminded myself that I didn't have to be here and stood up, whispering to the battalion XO that I was going outside to check on the men.

"Take me with you," he replied under his breath, grinning slightly.

I walked past the blonde wood and crystal vases and oil paintings and hanging chandeliers and out of the golden house. I found the soldiers posted outside as external security and spent the next forty-five minutes debating the more lasting *GI Joe* villain, Cobra Commander or Destro. When Kevin, his interpreter, and the internal security eventually came out of the meeting house, we loaded everyone back up and drove back to Camp Taji. Our Stryker patrol returned to JSS Istaqlaal at twilight.

THE DESTRUCTORS

"*Gunslinger X-ray,* this is White 6." Lieutenant Mongo's voice punched through Alpha Company's radio room in strained severity. "We've been hit by an EFP. I say again, we've been hit by an EFP. Do you copy?"

"This is Gunslinger X-ray. We copy."

I sat in the company TOC, discussing the cursed history of the Chicago Cubs baseball organization with Lieutenant Rant. Our faces and our conversation froze upon hearing the radio traffic. With Captain Frowny-Face on leave, Captains Pistol Pete and Clay split commander duties for the company; in an instant, Captain Pistol Pete bolted from his seat and seized the hand mic from the radio operator. Lieutenant Mongo and his platoon had only departed JSS Istaqlaal for Hussaniyah twenty minutes earlier to conduct a *Baghdad Now* newspaper distribution for the local populace.

"White 6, this is Gunslinger 5," he barked. "Give me a full SITREP [situation report]."

"We're fine, we're all fine." Lieutenant Mongo's voice contained an odd mixture of anger and disbelief, no doubt due to the fatal nature of EFPs. Surviving one was simply a matter of not being in its trajectory, not a comforting reality for men trained and reared on their own competency and lethality. "We're all fine. It hit my vehicle, in the lead, on Route Ninjas. The Stryker is bent [no longer able to function independently], but we're conducting self-recovery now."

As Lieutenant Mongo and his platoon sergeant, Sergeant First Class B, continued to update our company TOC, I realized that adjusting to the different numbers used in the infantry for radio call signs was now the least of my concerns. Determining who had targeted Coalition forces with the EFP, then successfully carried out the attack, fell squarely on my shoulders as Alpha Company's brand-new lethal targeting officer. Due to my experiences in Saba al-Bor, concern peppered my thoughts, as reliable HUMINT tended to be hit-and-miss in that area unless we incorporated direct money payments for the sheiks. Because of Hussaniyah's size, sprawling urbanization, and homogenous Shia population, I doubted we'd be able to sift through the populace to determine who bore responsibility for the strike. My worries proved illegitimate and unfounded. The next seventy-two hours yielded a surplus of leads and tips for the EFP attack, mainly due to the tireless, thorough work of Staff Sergeant Sitting Bull, Sergeant Secret Agent Man, and Specialist Wildebeest.

First, they met with their historically accurate sources. I'd sit in a back corner of the room, watching, learning, and, most importantly, keeping my mouth shut. The meeting venues varied—sometimes taking place on the JSS, sometimes out in sector—but the tactics didn't. Specialist Wildebeest buddied up to the sources, offering them cigarettes and smiles. Their terp, Eddie, an Iraqi American who lived in Chicago as a construction worker before he came back to Iraq as an interpreter, knew how and when to call the

Iraqis out on their bullshit and when to simply inform us quietly that he thought they had lied. Sergeant Secret Agent Man served as the details man, jotting down notes, backtracking and shifting gears constantly, as a method of pinning down specifics and occasionally catching the sources in lies and exaggerations. Staff Sergeant Sitting Bull brought it all together though, bringing a cold intimidation factor to the meetings that most intelligence soldiers were simply incapable of. Their source meeting with the Iraqi code-named Orlando was just one of a dozen they conducted in the hours following the EFP strike.

"How did you hear about the attack?" Sergeant Secret Agent Man asked Orlando through Eddie. We were all in an old, abandoned trailer that lacked electricity on JSS Istaqlaal. Everyone else huddled around a large black flashlight in the center of the room, while I stood in the far corner, intent on not interrupting or stealing anyone's thunder. I lacked the HUMINT collection team's professional training and simply wanted to understand the process better.

"He says that his friend went to JAM meeting right after crescent bomb explode," Eddie translated. "They talk about how bomb kill whole ghost tank of American soldiers."

Staff Sergeant Sitting Bull laughed. "Those fuckers," he said. "All they did was kill a tire."

"Who was at that meeting?" Sergeant Secret Agent Man pressed.

Orlando took a deep drag from his cigarette and spoke. "Qusay, Jissam, a few other guys he not know," Eddie said. "He want to make sure he get reward this month if he keep talking."

Specialist Wildebeest patted Orlando on the back while Staff Sergeant Sitting Bull spoke. "Ask him when we haven't come through?" he said loudly enough to maintain dominance but not sharply enough to reveal any anger. "He knows if he's right we'll take care of him."

Eddie translated, and Orlando nodded. "He says that Abu Abdullah was in charge of meeting and the bomb. Abu Abdullah say at meeting that he got orders from Ali the Beard in Sadr City to attack."

While Sergeant Secret Agent Man pulled out a link diagram and updated the cell structure of JAM in the area, Specialist Wildebeest talked to Orlando about his family through Eddie. Staff Sergeant Sitting Bull walked over to me.

"Sir, this is the third HUMINT source to claim Abu Abdullah headed this up. The emplacers keep changing but not him."

I nodded. "This is the same guy who has been lying low the past three, four months, right? The one we thought flew the coop to Sadr City early in the summer?" I had spent many hours studying the various JAM players in greater Hussaniyah and often got the details and names mixed up in the process.

"That's the one, sir!" Staff Sergeant Sitting Bull responded with a wide grin on his face. "You're catching on fast."

I shrugged my shoulders. "And you intel gurus always pretend this secret squirrel shit is impossible to understand. Now I know the truth." A few minutes later, I left the team to finish up the source meeting and walked out of the trailer to inform the company and battalion leadership that we had enough independent source verification for an actionable target.

Although everyone's initial reaction in the aftermath of the EFP strike was to do something and do it quickly, cooler heads prevailed, ensuring the proper utilization of the source network. An unfortunate by-product of accuracy was lost time. In the grand scheme of our deployment operations, seventy-two hours was nothing, although it didn't feel that way during that period. While Higher wanted us to move more quickly and applied the pressure accordingly, they deserved credit for listening to me and Staff Sergeant Sitting Bull. Abiding by the principle of precision targeting sometimes meant doing the counterintuitive thing. In this case, waiting rather than acting became just that. Subsequently, three days after the attack on Lieutenant Mongo's Stryker, a cell of five JAM special-groups members had been identified and verified, and bed-down locations for all were confirmed. Captains Pistol Pete and Clay put together a plan for a multiplatoon raid, which battalion leadership tweaked slightly then approved. The plan called for five targets: the cell leader, the financier, the driver of the getaway vehicle, and the two emplacers. The purported cell leader, Abu Abdullah, served as the Wolfhounds' number one target and initial hit for the night.

Although I could have tagged along for the mission, I thought back to my own platoon leader days and remembered how much I detested excess personnel—especially excess officers—who came along on my patrols "just because." So I sent out Staff Sergeant Sitting Bull and Sergeant Secret Agent Man instead, with Lieutenant Mongo's and Lieutenant Dirty Jerz's platoons, respectively, to augment the tactical questioning for the platoon leaders, and I took my place in the company TOC to battle-track. It was a bitter pill, but one that every junior officer must swallow eventually. I reminded myself just how lucky I was not to be back at the FOB serving as Lieutenant Colonel

Larry's lackey. No matter how down I got about my present reality, that thought always brought a smile back to my face.

Perhaps coincidentally, perhaps not, Lieutenant Mongo, SFC B, and their Bad Boys platoon struck first, hitting Abu Abdullah's second cousin's house, where a new source claimed he slept occasionally. Eager to display his loyalties, Daffy Duck marked the house with an infrared Chem-Light dropped on the front stoop, a spontaneous idea Staff Sergeant Sitting Bull contrived. Daffy Duck proved his worth in infrared spades that night, as the platoon's lead fire team woke up a man matching Abu Abdullah's exact description in the front room—a testament to both the silence of our Strykers and the platoon's dismounted movement from them. Abu Abdullah initially played dumb, then attempted to bite one of the detaining soldiers and made a run for it. The fire team leader did not take kindly to these actions and butt-stroked the fat Iraqi across the face with his rifle as he reached the front door, bringing him to the ground. The JAM leader did not resist any more, and the rest of the house was cleared in fluid sequence.

Two more of the cell's targets would be detained that evening: one of the emplacers by Lieutenant Dirty Jerz's platoon and the financier by the mortarmen/tanker combo platoon. The whole mission set lasted less than two hours, and the follow-on effects of our efforts were immediate. Locals came up to our patrols in the following days, expressing concern for the soldiers hit in the blast, and thanking us for detaining the Ali Babas. Three new sources stepped forward during this period and were subsequently vetted and developed by our HUMINT collection teams. All three provided vital intelligence in the coming months, often warning us of potential attacks before they occurred, thereby mitigating the chances of a repeat attack. One of the arguments against waiting to strike back was the possibility that cell members would flee Hussaniyah, as the second emplacer did. He was picked up three months later by another unit in the Baghdad neighborhood of Shu'ula because his name matched a report we input into the massive black-list computer database. Iraqi police detained the driver of the getaway vehicle in the early winter, acting on a tip from a local-national report that he had returned to Hussaniyah from the Diyala Province that very day.

As the mission ended and the three platoons rolled back into JSS Istaqlaal with the detainees bound and blindfolded, I waited outside between the TOC and the motor pool. Lieutenant Mongo and SFC B strolled by first, crowing proudly and grinning widely. Lieutenant Dirty Jerz and his platoon sergeant, Sergeant First Class A, sauntered in behind them, quiet and cool, but ready to call it a night. Then I saw my intel soldiers.

"Fuck yeah," I told Staff Sergeant Sitting Bull and Sergeant Secret Agent Man. "Well done, guys."

Sergeant Secret Agent Man grinned, but Staff Sergeant Sitting Bull simply shook his head in disgust. "Three out of five? Sir, I'm not happy with that. This isn't a damn Meatloaf song."

I tapped him lightly on the head and told him to make the detainee questioning quick. They needed to go to bed. They had earned it.

THE SUN, A SCORPION, AND SECOND CHANCES

I yawned, too tired to bother masking the act with a hand or a sleeve. It didn't matter what country I was in, whether I was at war or at peace, or how much sleep I had gotten the night before. I still fucking hated getting up with the sun. A shiver followed my yawn, a reaction to the recent cold front that had swept through the center of Iraq in mid-October. I zipped up my black polar-fleece top and resumed listening to the conversation between Eddie and the deputy mayor of Boob al-Sham. It was just the latest reminder that I was all bones, and God hadn't seen fit to bless me with any body fat.

"He wants to know if this is like a contract," Eddie asked, stifling a yawn of his own. "He doesn't want to sign contract. He says he only come here because Captain Frowny-Face tell him to come to pick up the freed detainees."

I sat on a torn white couch, marked with cigarette burns and an imprinted rose-petal pattern, in the JSS's designated sheik meeting room. Eddie sat to my immediate left, and across from us were the deputy mayor of Boob al-Sham and a southwestern Hussaniyah mukhtar (a sort of local neighborhood chief). The deputy mayor sported a sharp grey suit, complete with a tie done in a double Windsor knot, while the mukhtar dressed in a simple white dishdasha. Both had arrived with the dawn to go over the specifics of the guarantor release form, which a local authority figure needed to sign before jailed detainees from their particular area could be released. Once the guarantors signed the forms, a grand spectacle of a ceremony occurred over at the Iraqi police compound, where Iraqis and Americans alike clapped for

Lieutenant Rant observes the pragmatic genius of his fly-trap in Alpha Company's tactical operations center, at Joint-Security Station (JSS) Istaqlaal.

released—and usually confused—(former) insurgents. Sometimes the detainees appeared to have reformed or had completed their full sentence and thus paid their debt to society. All too often, though, especially recently, Camp Bucca sent these guys home early because not enough room existed to keep all of them behind bars. I wasn't sure if this was a testament to the efficiency of American combat troops or the flimsiness of the evidence needed for detention in 2007 and early 2008, as compared to the rigid current requirements.

I sighed and smirked at Eddie. He had done this before too. "Tell him it's not a contract. It's a release form. It just says he'll try to help keep the detainee out of trouble from now on and serve as a positive role model."

Eddie translated. The mukhtar nodded knowingly, but the deputy mayor spazzed out again and tugged at his hair. Fucking politicians, I thought. Even the mukhtar looked over at the deputy mayor and made an Arabic facial contortion I interpreted to mean, "What the fuck is wrong with this guy?"

"He wants to know if detainee gets in trouble again, will he go to jail for what the detainee does?" Eddie asked. "I tell him no, but he wants you to say it."

I tugged on my skull cap and bit my lip. "No," I said, "he won't get into trouble. This is an important document, though, not simply an empty formality. He and the detainee need to take it seriously." I silently hoped God understood that lies had a time and a place.

The mukhtar nodded again, picked up a pen, and signed his two guarantor release forms, which corresponded to the two detainees from his neighborhood. The deputy mayor slapped his two hands together, smiled pointedly as if a television camera were recording him signing an international peace treaty, and scrawled his name across his one form. I thanked both of them and stood up.

"I'll go get all of us some coffee," I said. "The ceremony starts in forty-five minutes. We'll just hang here until then."

Forty-five minutes in Iraqi time inevitably turned into two hours in real time, but nonetheless, Eddie and I found ourselves escorting the deputy mayor and the mukhtar over to the Iraqi police station. A squad from Lieutenant Dirty Jerz's platoon joined us at the gate, and to a man, they all looked how I felt.

"Ahh, the joys of counterinsurgency," I said to the squad leader. "Throwing a record-release party for guys who want to kill us."

The staff sergeant grunted and smirked. "Fuck it, sir, we'll just roll him up again," he said. "Anything to make the time go by."

We walked into the compound, escorting the deputy mayor and the mukhtar to their folding chairs, which had been set down in an empty field of dust next to the police headquarters. I found Captain Frowny-Face in the front and handed him the release forms.

"Any problems?" he asked, grinning.

I arched an eyebrow his way. "No more than usual, sir," I replied. "They just wanted to make sure these things wouldn't actually hold them accountable for anything."

My commander gave me a faux look of disapproval. "Remember, Matt, it's an important part of the ceremony. Who knows, it might scare a few of the dumb ones into behaving themselves."

I winked and nodded in agreement, then found a chair in the far back next to Lieutenant Rant, who had coordinated many of these in the preceding months himself. Colonel Najij of the Iraqi National Police and Lieutenant Colonel Muhamed of the Iraqi police sat with Captain Frowny-Face in the front row, along with Sheik Modhir and his son, Hamid. Next to Hamid sat a major from our brigade who I didn't recognize and an American in a suit who I assumed came from some sort of governmental agency. A smattering of NP commandos, regular Iraqi police, a few Iraqi civilians I figured to be the detainees' families, and American soldiers filled out the rest of the rows.

An Iraqi reporter and photographer walked around the scene, with the reporter asking Colonel Najij and Lieutenant Colonel Muhamed questions.

A few minutes later, Lieutenant Mongo and some of his soldiers walked in from the rear, guiding the three detainees by their shoulders, towering over them like skyscrapers. I flashed Lieutenant Mongo an obnoxious thumbs-up as he walked by me, and he did an admirable job of not breaking his stone face of stoicism. They stopped the detainees in front of the audience, spun them around, and walked off. The three "reformed" insurgents stayed. Colonel Najij stood up and gave an impassioned three-minute speech, full of arm swinging, fist pounding, and moustache stroking. As the speech lacked an interpreter, I leaned over to Lieutenant Rant and asked if he knew what was being said, as his rudimentary Arabic was slightly better than mine.

"This happens every time," he whispered back. "There's something about the sun, a scorpion, and second chances. You know how the Iraqis are with their imagery."

As Colonel Najij finished his speech, then was followed in sequence by Lieutenant Colonel Muhamed and Captain Frowny-Face, I wondered about the concept of second chances. I certainly understood it, although I remained firmly in the school of thought that reformed bloggers weren't quite in the same category as reformed terrorists. Nevertheless, after a photograph session with the released detainees, guarantors, and the police colonels, I couldn't help but smile when the three detainees ran into the arms of their families. One elderly lady I determined to be a mother began weeping uncontrollably as she held her son's face for the first time in many, many months. I've always been a sucker for crying women, I thought to myself.

As we sauntered back to the JSS, I reached into the air and slapped Lieutenant Mongo on the back. "Sometimes this job isn't so bad, you know?" I said.

He looked dubiously down at me. "Are you crazy, man?" he said. "Six months from now, this same thing will happen with Abu Abdullah."

I bit my lip. "Good call."

His point was reinforced a week later, when Specialist Haitian Sensation sent me a Facebook message, updating me on the Gravediggers and Saba al-Bor. In his message, he let me know that during a recent detainee release ceremony, Mohammed the Ghost had been cut loose a solid year before his sentence ended. He said the release shocked everyone, including the Iraqi army and Iraqi police leaders.

I stopped thinking about the weeping mother.

THE PORTA-JOHN CHRONICLES

I loved Joe. He wasn't always able to voice his opinions and thoughts directly, due to military customs and courtesies (some of them respected such protocol themselves, some simply feared the retribution of their NCOs, but the end result remained the same: acquiescence), but I always trusted that he would get his point across somehow. One of the time-honored places for such backdoor honesty was the Porta-John, a refuge where men of all ranks, colors, and creeds were both pantless and alone. Shitting was humanity's great equalizer—especially on an army base in a combat zone.

From Kuwait to Camp Taji to Saba al-Bor to Istaqlaal, I always read the walls of the Porta-Johns, especially after the dramatic happenings that polluted day-to-day existence in the army. What better place to learn how the soldiers really felt about things? I wanted more than a "Yes, sir," damn it, I wanted the truth. Sure, the standard artistic renditions of the female anatomy scattered said walls. And you could always count on at least one limerick breaking down the most basic of bodily functions into rhyme. But within this bawdy shell of smut, some real witticisms worthy of commemoration existed. It was like the juicy custard inside a stale donut, but in word form. Admittedly, temptation occasionally struck, imploring me to participate in the Sharpied shenanigans, but officer humor usually lacked the brevity necessary for such contributions. So I continued to simply observe, chuckle, and pull out my notebook to copy the clever ones down for veracity's sake.

—*"Conduct a sniper check in a combat zone. Salute an officer."*

—*"Wash your hands before returning to war! Thanks. —Command Sergeant Major."*

—*"I hate Lieutenant (blank)"* was followed by *"Me too. His blowjobs were less than enthusiastic."*

—A lot of anti-Bush rhetoric generated some pro-Bush rhetoric. Both were equally vitriolic and condemning and probably served as a microcosm of the political consciousness in our nation.

—*"Rangers may lead the way, but that's only because a scout pointed them in the right direction"* was followed by *"Scouts suck! Infantry rulz!"* which was in turn followed by *"Good comeback."* The final response read, *"Thanks, asshole."*

—You could find pretty much every Chuck Norris joke ever. (My personal favorite was, *Chuck Norris once traveled to the Virgin Islands. They are now known as The Islands.*)

—*"I miss my wife"* was followed by *"I miss her too,"* which was in turn followed by *"Don't worry. Jody's treating her real good."*

—*"End the war. There's a secret treaty in the blue water below you"* (an accompanying arrow pointed down into the toilet).

—*A lot of jokes about marines being dumb.*

—*A lot of jokes about sailors being gay.*

—*A lot of jokes about airmen being . . . well, airmen.*

—*"Reenlistment papers found here"* (an accompanying arrow pointed to the toilet paper rolls).

—*"The Sun God is a pussy"* was written after a particularly cold day.

—*"America isn't at war. Soldiers are at war. America is at the mall."*

A NIGHT WITH LIEUTENANT ANWAR

The flame in the distance danced in defiance of the black abyss enveloping it. Its proud orange screams had no base and seemed to hover in mid-air like a torch, unconscious of and unyielding to anything else along the nighttime horizon. I had learned the month before that the flame in the distance was nothing more than a burning oil refinery located miles away from JSS Istaqlaal, but that didn't stop me from staring into it for the occasional lost moment, inevitably thinking about other lost moments in other lost times. I liked to pretend some magic still existed, even in the dark.

I stood on the front porch of our company TOC, pacing back and forth, in a futile effort to keep warm. A bloody half-moon snarled down at us in repugnance. While I normally didn't pay attention to the days of the week—after ten months in Iraq, they all blended together—I knew it was Monday because I awaited the arrival of Lieutenant Anwar, the Iraqi National Police intelligence officer, for our weekly sync meeting. Eddie waited for us inside, but I had found that Lieutenant Anwar liked being greeted outside and escorted into our company area; like most Iraqi officers, he had a flair for pomp and ceremony. I didn't consider either my specialty, but in the name of international partnerships, I acquiesced and did what I could.

Shortly thereafter, a shadow materialized out of the darkness in the shape of Lieutenant Anwar. He was a short, stocky man with dark brown skin and short black hair, and the only thing crisper than his black moustache was

Posing with Lieutenant Anwar of the Iraqi National Police after a meeting.

his police uniform. We certainly made for an odd couple, due to my gangly frame, perma-unkemptness, and wild shock of brown hair that straddled the lines of military regulation. Nevertheless, I always enjoyed our sync meetings, mainly due to Lieutenant Anwar's very real and very fiery passion for his job. Unlike some of his peers, he legitimately wanted to make Hussaniyah a safer place and did not simply go through the motions to placate either his superiors or us. When I first joined the Wolfhounds, one of Captain Frowny-Face's first directives for me had been to temper Lieutenant Anwar's spontaneous, reactive targeting method and develop his analytical approaches. We learned on the job together.

"Salaam aleichem, Cap-e-tan," he said, sticking his hand out of a long pea coat sleeve.

I shook his hand and patted him on the back. "Salaam aleichem to you, Anwar," I replied. "How's life?" We began walking into the building, where the heater greeted us. My body smiled.

"Life . . . good?" he said, chuckling to himself for holding a conversation in English, no matter how basic. "And you?"

"Zien!" I said, using the Arabic word for "good." Anytime an interpreter wasn't around, we tended to keep conversations simple.

As we came into the meeting room, I spotted Eddie's wrinkled skull hunched over in a chair in the center of the room and heard a deep, nasal snore coming from that direction.

"Hey, Eddie," I said, grinning back at Lieutenant Anwar, "you okay, man?"

"Yes, sir!" Eddie said, bolting up. "I . . . uhh . . . just close my eyes for a bit before the meeting, you know?" Eddie worked hard and never stopped being on call for interpreting. He certainly deserved his power naps.

I sat down to Eddie's left, while Lieutenant Anwar sat to his right. I pulled out my notebook and the latest high-value-target list (HVTL) printout from my cargo pocket. The number one name on the list had remained the same since the beginning of the summer. "Have you guys heard anything new regarding Ali the Beard?" I asked Lieutenant Anwar.

"We hear he come up from Sadr City last week for funeral," Lieutenant Anwar responded through Eddie. "But source says he left right after, in convoy of six black trucks. We didn't hear he was here until after he left."

Late or not, this info definitely qualified as news to me. Although not as well organized as Staff Sergeant Sitting Bull's and Staff Sergeant Jorge's source networks, the Iraqis had proven to be very skillful at developing their own independent networks and tended to rely on a larger number of individuals than we did. They relied less on technology and money—our strengths—and more on cultivating personal relationships and developing trust, built-in cultural advantages we simply could not mimic or replicate.

"No," I said levelly, "I had not heard that. Thank you for sharing that. We're still tracking his brother Abbas in Hussaniyah though."

Lieutenant Anwar nodded. "As are we. We get very close many times, but it does not matter until we have him in jail." He slammed his fist on the table for emphasis, then pulled out a packet of cigarettes. Eddie and I both accepted one, and Lieutenant Anwar lit all three. He continued to mumble to himself in Arabic about Abbas.

"He does not like Abbas the Beard," Eddie explained to me between puffs.

I smirked. "I gathered that."

I glanced down at my HVTL for the next name on the list, but Lieutenant Anwar pressed forth.

"What do you know about Qusay al-Juma?"

I bit down on my lip, hoping I hadn't done so too noticeably. While in theory we shared all our information and intelligence with the Iraqi security forces and they did the same for us, in practice neither occurred. I knew Lieutenant Anwar held pieces back from us, and we did the same. Staff Sergeant Sitting Bull, in particular, proceeded very cautiously with what he shared, assuming correctly that the Iraqis' internal units were riddled with leaks and spies for JAM. Further complicating these information exchanges were ambiguous rules about security clearances that read and briefed well but held no place in a fast-paced, ever-evolving counterinsurgency. We waded through them to the best of our abilities. In the meantime, the answer was that we knew a lot about Qusay al-Juma. But the hows and whys of such weren't for Lieutenant Anwar or any other Iraqi right now. I shrugged my shoulders and begrudgingly planted another seed of mistrust in the Mesopotamian soil. "He dropped off our radar last month," I said. "What about you?"

He stared back at me protractedly, and I forced myself to maintain eye contact. "We have tried the past week to gain information on his whereabouts and gathered nothing."

Our conversation continued, with me going down my HVTL and Lieutenant Anwar rattling off names from memory. A slow, methodical, verbal swap meet evolved; when I gave him a tidbit, I got one in return; when I put forth a gem, one was quickly spat back at me. Forty minutes and two cigarettes each later, Lieutenant Anwar leaned back in his chair and said offhandedly, "Did you hear that we detained Hussayn the Star in a raid two nights ago?"

I couldn't help but laugh out loud. I admired his restraint, knowing that I wouldn't have been able to sit on that for an entire meeting. He had probed us and our source network to see if we knew about the detention. While we didn't consider Hussayn the Star to be the high-ranking JAM leader that the Iraqi National Police did, it still served as quite a coup for them, especially from a public relations standpoint. And, in late-2008 Iraq, getting the general populace to trust and believe in their own security forces probably mattered more than taking apart the insurgent cell networks one by one.

"Good for you guys!" I said, standing up to clap him on the back and give him a fist pound for good measure. "We hadn't heard that, but that's awesome. Congratulations!"

He took another drag from his cigarette, clearly satisfied, both for capturing Hussayn the Star and for getting one over on the Americans. I let him bask in his victory for a few more seconds before I walked over to a desk in the rear corner, opened a drawer, and pulled out a box. I had a surprise of my own. I tossed the box over to Lieutenant Anwar.

"Consider that a late Ramadan or early Christmas present," I said.

The box contained a brand-new digital camera I had procured from one of 2–14 Cavalry's supply sergeants back on Camp Taji. It always paid to play nice with the logisticians, and he owed me a favor anyhow. For the past month or so, Lieutenant Anwar had pleaded with us to get him a digital camera, like the ones all American platoons used out in sector. I knew how much practical use the National Police could get out of it and of the slowness of their own bureaucratic supply chain. I also understood how much it meant to Lieutenant Anwar that he'd be able to go back to his commander with this. So, when I had found myself on Camp Taji four days earlier, between a stop at the barber shop and a Taco Bell run, I swung by and picked it up from the supply sergeant.

He smiled, openly and honestly, blinking his eyes in surprise. "Thank you, Cap-e-tan . . . thank you." Eddie added, posttranslation, "This gift means very much to him, sir. You do very good thing for Lieutenant Anwar."

"No worries, man," I said. "Let me show you how it works." As we put in the batteries and Lieutenant Anwar explored the various functions of the camera, he leaned up and put his arm on my shoulder. "Colonel Najij will be very proud of me for this," he stated. "I will return this favor to you, I promise."

I winked at him. "I know you will. I have no doubt."

"Do you have family back home?" he asked suddenly. "Wife?" The questions took me aback at first. Through all our meetings, both official and otherwise, we had never ventured into the realm of personal lives. Figuring this was his attempt to tighten our relationship, in light of the digital camera gift, I answered him.

"I do," I said. "I have my parents, obviously, and a little brother. And a girlfriend."

"Do you have any photographs?" he asked. "I'd like very much to see them."

I pulled my wallet out of my pocket. Behind my debit card and military ID, I found two wallet-sized photographs—one, taken when I was still in college, was of my mother, my little brother, my golden retriever, and myself; the other was of my girlfriend. "That's them," I said, smirking and shrugging my shoulders. "They are all saints for putting up with me and my antics."

"They are very nice-looking people," Lieutenant Anwar said. "I would like very much to meet them someday."

"That'd be cool," I replied, then remembered some sense of decorum.

"What about you, dude? You a family man?"

He quickly pulled out his own wallet. "Yes, I am. I have wife and baby daughter. She is my light." The photo he showed was of himself, dressed in his police uniform, holding a giggling, smiling baby girl, who I figured to be about a year old. In the photo, his daughter reached up and tugged on his nose, while Lieutenant Anwar smiled with a contentment I never saw him flash on the job.

"She is very beautiful," I told him. "You must be very proud."

"I am. She is why I fight for Iraq. So she never sees what I have seen."

Not knowing what else to say, I simply nodded and changed the subject back to the intricacies of the digital camera. Ten minutes later, I walked him back outside, and we parted ways, promising to meet again the next week. Then I stared at the flame in the distance for a while. It still danced.

MASTERS OF WAR

Critics called them war profiteers and vigilantes. Proponents labeled them patriots vital to the Iraq War effort. My interactions with them varied sharply, sometimes evoking my wrath, sometimes invoking my gratitude. Private contractors proliferated in the sands of Iraq throughout the war, and during my time there, they numbered approximately 180,000 in total—about 15,000 more personnel than Coalition forces had serving during the surge's peak. Of that number, only 20,000 or so served as private security guards, but thanks to the company Blackwater's infamous time in theater, they became the public face for contractors in Iraq.

In his presidential farewell address to the nation in 1961, Dwight Eisenhower warned against such privatization and development of the military-industrial complex. Almost fifty years later, half the globe away from America, it appeared that his words were proving both prophetic and fruitless. One couldn't walk a half mile at Camp Taji or any of the combat outposts without seeing a sign of Halliburton's lovechild, KBR—from the trailers we lived in, to the electric outlets we plugged into, to the Porta-Johns we crapped in. In theory, I detested our military's reliance on civilian enterprises and their nine-to-five work mentality. In practice, I happily ate the chocolate ice cream the army would never have provided and basked in air-conditioning the military probably would have fucked up somehow.

Just as with soldiers, there were good civilians and bad civilians. Almost all of both qualified as former or retired military. The good ones understood their job existed to help soldiers, to facilitate whatever facet of the war was tasked to them, and they didn't pretend they still served in the armed forces. The bad ones viewed their job as a perk to retiring from military service, constantly pointed out how much more money they made than the soldiers actually fighting the war, and only cared about their little slice of the Green Machine, big picture be damned.

Bitching about contractors and their exploits in Iraq felt as natural to soldiers as sleeping and smoking. But outside of a few typical and mundane interactions, I never really got too fired up about them; their presence in our brushfire war seemed natural, given our postmodern republic's interpretation of free markets and privatized industry. The military-industrial complex had evolved into a monster with thousands and thousands of money-udders for contractors to suckle off of, and I certainly had no right or reason to call foul. Further, I just didn't see how the daymare of an army of hired guns could ever come to fruition in America—from my perspective, the military presence seemed too strong and influential. One day in the fall of 2008, though, I experienced some of the pitfalls of the growing reliance on the private security firms, albeit on a negligible scale.

At about nine in the morning, when walking back to my room from the showers at JSS Istaqlaal, I spotted something odd: a fleet of up-armored suburbans parked in our motor pool between our Strykers and Humvees. Mildly intrigued, I stopped to watch a group of tall, white, large-chested men walk over to the Iraqi police side of the JSS. Most sported thick, lumberjack beards and baseball caps and wore various mishmashes of military and police gear. I stood a good two hundred meters away from them, but it appeared that they carried a variety of assault rifles as well. One of them looked over at me, so I gave a little wave, while holding my hygiene kit and shower towel and wearing flip-flops. He didn't wave back. Once they disappeared through the IP gate, I continued to my room. When I walked by the motor pool again a few hours later, I noticed the up-armored suburbans were gone. I never did learn exactly why they came to our JSS, although Captain Frowny-Face thought some State Department official had arrived for a meeting that morning. At the time, I assumed they were Blackwater (now known as Xe) personnel, but they could just as likely have been from DynCorp or Triple Canopy, two other private security firms employed by the U.S. State Department.

I didn't give the unknown men with lumberjack beards and safari bush vests another thought until two days later, when Lieutenant Rant walked into the TOC.

"Some Iraqi just came in and said we had destroyed his car," he told me.

"Oh yeah?" I was playing a helicopter video game on my computer, and Lieutenant Rant's story didn't sound like anything out of the ordinary. Iraqis had proven very adept at concocting ways to elicit money from us, and this tale lacked all kinds of creativity points.

"Yeah, but he said it wasn't us, it was Americans in trucks or something, who didn't wear normal uniforms. He said it happened right on Dover too. You hear anything about that?"

I paused my game and looked up. "No," I replied, "but I did see some Blackwater dudes here two days ago. When did this supposedly happen?"

"Two days ago, around noon." Still standing and leaning against a nearby pillar, Lieutenant Rant shook his head. "He said there was a traffic jam ahead, and the trucks were honking and weaving around like mad men and plowed straight into him going pretty fast. He said his wife had to go to the hospital, and his car is completely totaled. He brought in a photo of a busted car, but that could be from anything."

I arched an eyebrow. "That sucks. Think it's true?"

Lieutenant Rant shrugged his shoulders. "Who knows? He wouldn't be the first Iraqi to lie about this, but then again, it wouldn't be the first time those security guys destroyed an Iraqi's personal property. He said they barely stopped, but they told him to come here for reimbursement."

"Hah!" This story became more believable by the minute. "What did you do?"

"The only thing I could do. I listened to him for forty-five minutes because no one else would. Then I gave him a claims card, showed him how to fill it out, and told him to go to Camp Taji with it. Hopefully, they'll pay him there."

"Yeah," I said, "hopefully." I paused and gave a fist pump. "In other news, I'm up to 6,000 points on the helicopter game."

"You bastard!"

While the alleged car wreck paled in comparison to some of the greater private security firm scandals of the Iraq War—like the Blackwater Baghdad shootings in Nisoor Square on September 16, 2007, when seventeen Iraqi civilians lost their lives—it served as a firsthand display for me that contractors played by different rules than those of us on active duty. While the majority of these security contractors doubtlessly executed their duties professionally and honorably, the stark lack of accountability after a crisis continued to plague the firms. Because they were beholden to their respective companies rather than to a nation or a national purpose (like the Iraqi counterinsurgency), private security firms in the Iraq War incarnated President Eisenhower's worst fears. As with any private enterprise, they were motivated to make money and protect their investments, even at the expense of more ambitious and loftier goals. Providing for oneself and one's family definitely qualifies as an honorable intention for an individual, but that can't be said for an organization as a whole. While the military had its own share of scandals over the course of the war, the institution itself held grander ambitions and higher purposes than financial benefit. The same could not be said of the private security firms. It showed.

ALL HALLOWS' EVE

"So, Ali, who do you think is going to win the Super Bowl this year?"

Hooting and hollering from the group of soldiers in Alpha Company's common area drowned out the familiar jingle of the cable television channel ESPN's *Sportscenter*, which played on the television in the front of the room. At a complete loss for words, I did my best to soak up the surrealism of the moment, while standing in the back of the room. Seven of Lieutenant Mongo's soldiers sat on leather couches or stood, holding their M4s, most watching ESPN through the Armed Forces Network on television. Four of them wore skeleton masks on top of their heads, a remnant of the mission they had completed twenty minutes earlier on this Halloween night. One of the others sported a rainbow clown wig and a big red clown nose. Meanwhile, two bound and blindfolded Iraqis sat on the couches between them in grimy brown and grey pajamas, giving the illusion that they were just as entranced by the football highlights on *Sportscenter* as the soldiers. The unintentional comedy of the situation registered off the charts, something not lost on the men assigned to guard the Iraqis.

"Someone needs to record this shit," a junior NCO said as he gave one of the men a bottle of water. "We could be on the next ESPN commercial and get famous."

One of the Iraqis mumbled something in Arabic and held up his hands, likely claiming they were bound too tightly. While a young specialist went over to him to loosen the flex-cuffs, another soldier patted the Iraqi on the back. "I agree, Mohammed. The Patriots suck this year without Tom Brady. Good fucking point. If you ever get out of jail, you should become a broadcaster for ESPN 12: The Hajjis."

The room exploded with laughter, and I chuckled right along. The irony of the moment demanded it.

The backstory for our current set of circumstances wasn't quite as hilarious. Acting on a local-national tip, Lieutenant Mongo's platoon cut short their Halloween party to conduct a raid in Hussaniyah for Abbas the Beard, Ali the Beard's younger half-brother. Both served as high-ranking JAM special-groups leaders. The house reported to us proved to be a dry hole, but in the building next door, the Bad Boys found a man matching Abbas's physical description with two other military-aged males. Captain Frowny-Face gave the go-ahead to bring them in for tactical questioning; according to both American regulations and Iraqi laws, we had twenty-four hours to keep them at the JSS before we needed to free them or officially detain them and transport them to Camp Taji. Once they arrived back at JSS Istaqlaal, though, we realized that the trailer normally used to keep potential detainees had been moved by an engineer unit. Since the HUMINT collection teams preferred to tactically question the men one at a time in the meeting room, we found the next-best option for available waiting space while the three rotated through—the common area.

I left the soldiers and the Iraqis to their football highlights and walked into the sheik meeting room, where Staff Sergeant Sitting Bull and Specialist Wildebeest sat with Eddie, talking to the purported Abbas the Beard. The Iraqi's blindfold had been lifted, and he spoke wildly, tongue wagging like an auctioneer's. Specialist Wildebeest spoke to him, while Staff Sergeant Sitting Bull stared at him protractedly and dismissively.

"How goes it?" I asked.

"Same old story," Staff Sergeant Sitting Bull replied. "He says he isn't Abbas the Beard, but he has heard of him. We have the source Las Cruces coming in to identify him."

"Las Cruces? You seriously couldn't come up with a better nickname than Las Cruces?"

Staff Sergeant Sitting Bull laughed. "Don't hate, sir. It sticks out in your mind, doesn't it?"

I scratched my head. "Yeah, I guess so. Where's Lieutenant Rant?"

"He's inventorying all the stuff they brought back with the three Iraqis in the radio room."

"Cool. Come get me when Las Crucifixion gets here, okay?"

"Will do."

I found Lieutenant Rant in the radio room, just as Staff Sergeant Sitting Bull had stated. He wore a pair of blue latex, antiseptic gloves to keep his fingerprints off the inventory.

"They find anything good?"

Lieutenant Rant shook his head. "Just the one AK every household has. There are a bunch of papers too, but they really aren't worth checking out unless we get confirmation that this is actually Abbas. At first glance, it just looks like typical household stuff, like bills and journals."

A few minutes later, Staff Sergeant Sitting Bull walked into the radio room. "We may have a problem," he told me and Lieutenant Rant.

"What's that?"

"Las Cruces says it's not him. We showed him a digital photo of these guys outside. He says it looks just like him, but it's not the actual Abbas the Beard."

"Fucking fantastic."

"But"—Staff Sergeant Sitting Bull paused, choosing his words carefully—"Las Cruces has mad street cred because he used to be in JAM. He might still be with them. So he might be lying to try to save Abbas for whatever reason."

"Possible," I responded. "Any chance any of the other sources could come in and say definitively?"

He shook his head. "No, sir, not with the time requirements we have. Most of them are too scared to come here, especially at night. They think the IPs and the NPs have rats who'll spot them. Captain Frowny-Face told me to send the photos to brigade, though, for confirmation up there. Sometimes they have more info and better photographs than we do."

I walked back to the common area and joined the soldiers and the Iraqis for more *Sportscenter* highlights. The paradoxical contrast of the situation had faded, and to a man, we all just wanted some clarification so we could go to bed. I fully expected brigade to confirm Las Cruces's assessment, and then we'd free the three Iraqis, apologizing profusely and giving them a free breakfast MRE (Meal, Ready-to-Eat, prepackaged army food) for their trouble. When Lieutenant Rant walked out of the company TOC ten minutes later, blinking in surprise, I asked him what had happened.

"I just talked to some intel major from brigade on the phone. She says it's definitely him."

"Definitely? How definitely?"

"As in 100 percent, no doubt, we're-taking-him-off-the-brigade-HVTL-this-very-moment 100 percent."

"Uhh . . . cool."

Being found with one of the brigade's top targets provided enough to bring in the other two Iraqis as well, so we began drawing up the detention paperwork, and the medics conducted a physical on all three men. About an hour later, as Lieutenant Mongo's platoon prepared to depart the JSS with the detainees in tow, we received another phone call in the company TOC. Captain Frowny-Face answered it, and in the span of thirty seconds, I watched his face turn red, then purple, then finally white. After saying nothing more than "roger" five or six times, he hung up the phone.

"It's not him. They are now 200 percent certain that man is not Abbas the Beard."

A few isolated groans could be heard in the room, but most of us just sat there in resigned silence.

"How . . . do things like this even happen?" Lieutenant Rant asked.

"Have Lieutenant Mongo drive them back home instead of to Taji," Captain Frowny-Face said. "Let's not talk anymore about this until tomorrow."

As I walked out of the TOC and past the common area, intent on screaming away my frustrations in a dark, isolated corner of the JSS, I saw Lieutenant Mongo's soldiers take off the blindfolds and cut the binds of the three almost-detainees. After Lieutenant Rant and Eddie explained the mix-up to the men, they began walking outside to the Strykers, clearly eager to go home. A soldier smiled and sarcastically wished them a happy Halloween. One of the men found with the Abbas look-alike started to hum on his way out the door. It took me a few seconds to recognize the tune he hummed as the *Sportscenter* jingle.

"Good Christ," I said out loud to myself, now standing alone in an empty room. "The world can be a really fucking sick place sometimes."

THE AMERICAN ELECTION

As President-elect Barack Obama strode to the podium in Chicago to give his election day victory speech, four soldiers and I watched on television from JSS Istaqlaal's common area with the light initiates of dawn piercing the glass of the small window in the corner. One of the soldiers, a young black NCO who sat on the couch in front of me, spoke for all of us and to no one in particular at the same time. "Holy shit," he said. "I can't believe this is actually happening."

When the outcome of the election had become clear a few hours earlier, most of the politically inclined on our JSS called it a night, but a few diehards and I stayed up to watch the victory speech in Grant Park. Such a choice had little to do with my own politics and more to do with the knowledge that history had been made, and since I couldn't participate in it, witnessing it would suffice. Further, we all understood the potency of this moment, as it directly related to our professions as military men: The so-called forever wars we fought in would now actually have an ending.

Civilians often asked about the military vote and what the military as a whole sought from American politics. In my experience, soldiers' politics varied almost as much as those of the greater populace. To begin with, even in the best-educated military in the history of the world, a sizable percentage simply didn't give a damn. They came to Iraq to kill people, or for the money, or for the health-care benefits. The political happenstance of their station in life seemed superfluous to the pragmatic needs of the now.

Obviously, the army was no bastion of liberal ideology. A majority of the politically engaged Joes, NCOs, and officers were conservative by nature, if not necessarily Republican in practice—numbers backed up by a *Military Times* poll conducted in the lead-up to the election, which saw 68 percent of those polled voting for Senator John McCain, while 23 percent pledged their support for then-senator Obama. Much of this derived from a variety of socioeconomic reasons, not to mention the military's inherent nature and traditional appeal. However, after five years of war in Iraq and seven years of war in Afghanistan, some soldiers were just as tired of the status quo as the larger population. Such a sentiment, be it spoken or not, was certainly not an indictment of Senator McCain, as he justly received universal respect from the military community for his own service and sacrifices. Beyond that, the military had a long and proud tradition of stoically and silently following and respecting its presidents as the commander in chief, whoever they were and whatever their politics. Such was an absolute necessity in a free society and the bedrock of the American republic. But as private citizens, it seemed, more and more soldiers—particularly junior officers, including myself—yearned for something new and different. The outcome of this election would directly impact our futures, not to mention the future of the nation we all treasured.

And so two soldiers, two NCOs, and one officer watched President-elect Obama's speech in a dusty, dirty room in the center of Iraq at five or so in the morning, putting all the distress and chaos and rage of war on hold, determining that nothing mattered more at this time than what we watched on the screen before us. Some of us were black, some of us were white, and some of us were brown—a fact that, when I realized it, caused me to search for a joke in order to temper the politically correct banality of the situation.

I wanted to somehow include the absurdity of the word "postracial" in the quip but never got around to it. Instead, I got goose bumps when President-elect Obama said, "To those who would tear the world down: We will defeat you. To those who seek peace and security: We support you. And to all those who have wondered if America's beacon still burns as bright: Tonight we proved once more that the true strength of our nation comes not from the might of our arms or the scale of our wealth but from the enduring power of our ideals: democracy, liberty, opportunity, and unyielding hope." I didn't feel like joking around anymore.

Why do I keep fighting it, I wondered. Voting from a combat zone had been one of the proudest moments of my life. Embrace it.

After the speech ended, Specialist Gonzo came up and slapped me on the back. "What did you think, sir? Pretty good, huh?"

I raised my eyebrows and nodded slowly. "Yeah, man. Pretty good."

I sat on the couch for another hour, unable to tear myself away from the election day coverage. Soldiers, NCOs, and officers who had slept the night before cycled in, asking about the results. Some smiled, some cursed, some had no reaction whatsoever. Then I ate breakfast and went to work. My night-time escape as an American citizen ended, while my daily life as a counterinsurgent in Iraq continued. Nothing could've felt more oddly comforting at the time.

FUN AND GAMES

The Stryker hit the ramp of the steel-beam bridge with power, rolling across the platform like an avalanche of metal. I looked over the side from the back hatch where I stood, absorbing the muddy, milky Tigris River in all its twisting glory. We traveled through the Sunni marshlands on winding back roads, waving to the local Iraqis we passed and honking at the donkey carts that got in our way. The urban void of Hussaniyah loomed austerely to our east.

An hour before, back on Camp Taji for my monthly personal refit, I had planned on hitching a ride back to JSS Istaqlaal with the mortarmen/tanker combo platoon. Minutes before our departure though, Captain Frowny-Face informed the platoon sergeants who shared leadership duties for the platoon, Sergeant First Class C and Sergeant First Class W, that he needed them to

Hussaniyah, muddy and desolate, after a heavy rain. A moderately-sized city located north of Sadr City, Hussaniyah was a proving ground for many Jaish al-Mahdi insurgents eager to make a name for themselves.

check out a tip regarding the targeted JAM member Qusay al-Juma immediately. Qusay, who allegedly accidentally blew up an EFP in a trash can the day before at a car garage, had led Lieutenant Dirty Jerz and his platoon on a wild goose chase that night, barely getting away at least three or four times. He knew himself to be a wanted man but was either too stupid or not resourceful enough to get out of town. When SFC W came up to tell me about their frago, he didn't give me much of a choice as to whether I would join them or not.

"Hey, sir," he said, flashing his pearly whites, "get your out-of-the-wire face back on, 'cause we're going on a raid! You can play platoon leader, too, since our lieutenant is back on Istaqlaal."

"Well," I replied, deadpan, "when you sell it like that . . ."

The twists and turns of Route Crush eventually straightened out, and we wove through the maze of wire and Sons of Iraq guarding the front entrance to Sheik Modhir's residence. We turned north on Route Dover, now parallel with the T-wall barriers that lined most of Hussaniyah's perimeter. One of the first techniques in the security step of a counterinsurgency was controlling the entrances and exits of urban centers. A lot of the intricacies of this depended on a city's geographical layout, but in Hussaniyah's case, due to the large canal that sliced across its eastern boundary, doing so proved relatively simple; thus, the city was sealed off on all sides except for three NP-controlled traffic points on the western side. We turned right through one of these points onto Route Texas, NPs waving our Strykers through the Iraqi cars and pedestrians with all the flamboyance of a conductor at an orchestra.

We rolled up to our target grid in the center of Hussaniyah near the main market, finding a small, one-story house whose roof had caved in on one end. We operated in a cramped intersection with only the house in question on one side of the road and a cluster of four red buildings across the street from us, all being two or three stories tall. The market lay on the backside of these buildings. The platoon established a vehicle box cordon around the house, and I joined the dismounts on the ground. As I walked behind the squads, I eyed the tall buildings across from us suspiciously. I found nothing but shadows and black holes through the shattered windowpanes, and nothing moved at all along the rooftops.

"Don't worry about it, sir," SFC C said with a wink and a grin, jogging past me. "If they're gonna get you from there, you won't even feel it."

I pushed away the paranoia and forced myself to focus on the mission at hand. I smirked and stopped thinking. The rest felt easy.

The platoon found nothing but a middle-aged woman and an old woman in the house, both claiming that they had never heard of Qusay al-Juma. I fell into my old role of platoon leader rather naturally, if unfortunately temporarily, and talked with the two women through our interpreter while the men searched the house and the surrounding premises. The women told us that the old woman's son, who was also the middle-aged woman's husband, had bought the house four months before, but he worked in Baghdad and only came up to Hussaniyah on weekends. Their paperwork all checked out, and the husband's name didn't ring any JAM bells for me or for SFC C or SFC W. As I finished up with the Iraqis, thanking them for their patience and understanding, I heard confused shouting outside. I broke away from the conversation and trotted to the front door.

Outside, all of the dismounted soldiers had taken cover behind the Strykers or poles or in a nearby ditch and had oriented their weapons in the direction of the red buildings across the street. The Stryker gunners huddled down in their cupolas, machine guns scanning the rooftops. I huddled in the doorframe and yelled at SFC W, who I spotted behind the nearest Stryker.

"What the fuck is going on?"

"The guys think they saw a weapon over there!" He pointed at the red buildings, although I couldn't discern exactly where I needed to look. "As soon as they pointed it out, it disappeared behind the building!"

"What kind of weapon?" I shouted.

"They think they saw an RPG launcher!"

Well, I thought, this fucking sucks. Things could get messy really fast. If the mystery man with an RPG really did move back to the market area, no limit to potential disaster existed. Hussaniyah's main market functioned as a sort of neo-Stalingrad in terms of urban combat hell. Usually, American troops didn't go in there with anything less than two full combat platoons; the Iraqi police avoided it like the plague, and the National Police only operated there when they got forced to. The reason was simple: Although it was the best place in the area to purchase local fruits and vegetables, the market doubled as a labyrinth of back alleys and alley backs, shops and tight corners and limited fields of view, the ideal setting for booby traps, anti-personnel mines, and close-quarter snipers. No matter how familiar any of us may have been with the market's configuration, we'd never understand it as well as the native Iraqis. In short, if we pursued a fight into the market, we'd be operating on the guerilla's terrain, not ours. I knew things could spiral out of control very soon and very quickly.

A small shape emerged from the side of a building. It looked like a small child.

"Nobody shoot!" I heard SFC C yell loudly somewhere to my front and off to my left. "Nobody shoot! It's a damn kid!"

As the small shape in the distance came into my view, I spotted an object in the child's hand. My own rifle dropped back to the low-ready—I hadn't even noticed raising it—and I saw all of the soldiers in front of me relax their postures as well. When I walked up to the semicircle just behind SFC W and the interpreter, I realized that the object in question was a plastic RPG launcher. Though it was not as large as a real RPG-7, the difference would have been impossible to discern from a distance of any sizable amount.

"Where'd you get this?" SFC W asked the kid, grabbing the plastic toy from him.

The child, a rail-thin skeleton dressed in a white Nike shirt that hung to his knees with burnt red mud smudged all over his face, looked meekly at the ground, clearly upset that his toy had just been taken away from him.

The interpreter yelled at him in Arabic for a few seconds, and finally the boy replied. "Some men handed them out at the market yesterday. All of my friends got one."

SFC C, SFC W, and I all exchanged troubled glances. "Who were the men?"

"I don't know. I'd never seen them before."

"They just started handing these out?"

"Yes. Only to kids."

"Why?"

"They said Americans would want to play with us if we had them."

"How many were handed out?"

"I don't know, ten, maybe fifteen."

After we told the boy that he wasn't in trouble and we wouldn't tell his parents on him, but that we were taking his toy RPG launcher, we instructed him to tell his friends to throw away their toys. He claimed he understood why, but he kept eyeing his old toy greedily.

"I guess the golden groups and special groups of JAM are hoping for a public relations disaster from us," I said as we walked back to our Strykers. "Fucking insane."

SFC W, who held the toy RPG launcher, simply shook his head. "That is some fucked up shit."

I nodded in agreement. "No joke. COIN can be wild. My buddy up north said they sometimes hand out Viagra to old sheiks to gain their allegiance. He says it works, too. I mean, seriously, if an old man hasn't had sex for twenty years, he's going to be beyond loyal to the guys who bring a magic blue pill that makes it happen again."

SFC W laughed. "That's crazy, but a good idea. But this. . . ." He looked down at the plastic toy and started banging it against his chest plate. "They're deliberately putting their own people's children in harm's way, hoping we make a mistake and kill one. What the hell is wrong with them?"

"I don't know," I responded, shrugging my shoulders. I wanted to care more deeply and knew that I should, but I couldn't bring myself to actually do it. I'd been in Iraq for too long to be shocked by much, even this. "I don't know."

It did feel nice being the palpable good guys again after a few months of confusing ambiguity. It made us feel like liberators instead of an occupational force. We drove back to JSS Istaqlaal and threw the plastic RPG launcher away. Two more of the toys were recovered over the course of the next three months, with tragedy somehow avoided each time.

INVASION

The Iraq we knew and understood and fought for and fought against and fought in changed utterly and completely in one week in late November 2008. On a macro level, on November 27 the Iraqi parliament passed the Iraq Status of Forces Agreement (SOFA), which established a timeline for U.S. combat forces to withdraw from the cities and laid out a variety of other technical regulations for our future presence in theater. Only a few days later, our battalion headquarters and staff moved from Camp Taji to JSS Istaqlaal, joining the two line companies already permanently stationed there. This revolutionized our experience on a micro level.

Macro and micro crashed into one another on Thanksgiving Day, the same day the SOFA passed. With battalion putting the finishing touches on their big move, the officers and the NCOs gathered at JSS Istaqlaal for the Wolfhounds' annual Turkey Bowl flag-football game. No doubt inspired by my one reception for six yards—Lieutenant Mongo's dominant performance as quarterback, defensive tackle, and all-around crusher of dreams probably helped as well—the officers won rather handily, much to the chagrin of the battalion sergeant major. As we gathered postgame for an ample meal prepared by the cooks, the discussion at the junior officers' table revolved around how the SOFA impacted us at the ground level.

"I think it's the real reason battalion is moving out here," Lieutenant Rant explained, while we all gorged on sliced turkey, sweet potatoes, and cornbread. "The SOFA calls for all the combat outposts and JSSs to close by next year, right? And all Americans have to be out of the cities at the same time, right?"

"Uh huh," Lieutenant Goo said, drawing out his response.

"Well, technically this place is out of Hussaniyah. That's why they keep expanding it. They are just going to turn this place into a FOB. That way, we won't have to shut it down or turn it over to the Iraqis next year."

"Ooooooohhhh." Lieutenant Goo's reactions rarely failed to entertain.

"That might explain why they are so insistent that battalion move out here now," Captain Pistol Pete said. "I mean, we got three months left. Really, what the hell is the point?"

"This just pisses me off." Unsurprisingly, all of this fired up The Great White Hope. "It's like they're coming out here for a camping trip so they can actually earn their combat patch. We've been making it work out here by ourselves for a year. Why change now?"

"Things are going to change as soon as they get out here," Captain Clay pointed out. "That's for damn sure. It's only a matter of time before we'll be saluting out here and practicing drill and ceremony for parades."

"Could someone explain to me why we're switching brigades too?" The Great White Hope asked. For reasons known only to the strategic-level gods, the Wolfhounds would fall under the operational control of the Fourth Infantry Division's Third Brigade for the duration of the deployment, rather than staying with the Second Brigade of the Twenty-fifth Infantry Division, with whom we'd deployed and under whom we'd spent the first year. While it made sense geographically—we were the only Twenty-fifth unit stationed on the east side of the Tigris and surrounded by units of the Fourth Infantry Division on all sides—we couldn't help but wonder why this move was taking place with about three months left in Iraq. "All of this is really starting to hurt my brain."

I looked around the table and, seeing only dejected and bitter faces, did what I could to inject some levity. "I'm definitely not looking forward to this place turning into *Office Space: Iraq*," I said, referencing the cult film classic. "On the other hand, I heard the Buffalo Bills cheerleaders are coming here in a month or two. That would definitely not happen if it were still just the companies out here."

"Are you serious?" The reaction to my statement was universal—a strained blend of hope, mania, and disbelief. Most of us hadn't seen a real woman (i.e., not a female soldier dressed in camo) for six months or more. The thought of seeing and smelling and hearing a professional cheerleader sent most of our minds into sensory overload.

I nodded my head. "That's what the rumor mill told me. They're called the 'Buffalo Jills.' Get it? 'Cause it rhymes."

A few days later, well past dusk, Captain Clay, Lieutenant Rant, and I stood at the edge of the motor pool, watching battalion soldiers shuffle from the Chinook helicopters that transported them from Camp Taji to their new rooms at JSS Istaqlaal. As part of the logistics of fitting an entire battalion on the JSS, Alpha Company's soldiers, NCOs, and officers moved from the hardstand buildings to trailers next to the motor pool; our new homes soon earned the nickname "Slum City." Shockingly, spirits among our company seemed higher than I thought they would be, given the circumstances. As the platoon sergeants kept reminding them, "Ninety days, men. Ninety days. Suck it up and drive on. And don't do anything fucking stupid."

The three of us had completed our own move to the trailers earlier that day. Our company TOC also moved to that area, and our old TOC would soon be turned into a medical aid station.

"I know it probably makes sense, big picture wise," Lieutenant Rant said. "But this still feels like a big kick to Alpha Company's collective nuts."

"Things roll downhill," Captain Clay said. "That's how the army works. I guess they just wanted to ensure our replacements had to do the same thing with their battalion headquarters, you know?"

Over by the hard stand, an overburdened intelligence soldier holding his rucksack and duffle bag while wearing all of his body armor tipped over, falling to the ground in a heap. Too far away to help him up, we just watched and shook our heads as he collected himself, then his belongings, and kept moving to his new room. I didn't feel like laughing at him since he probably felt the same way about the move that we did.

Housing issues aside, my other concern with being collocated with battalion centered on the concept of decentralized warfare. I had already served in a unit structured on micromanagement and centralization and found it stifling and repressing. Part of the redemption I sought and found with the Wolfhounds had been the ability to seize the initiative for targeting and knowing the freedom existed for me to execute such in practice. While this battalion wouldn't purposefully suppress that, the nature of bureaucracy insisted on stricter control and oversight. More layers and more people meant more paperwork and more red tape and more meetings and more hands in the metaphorical cookie jar of counterinsurgency. I wasn't upset, just resigned to the fact that things wouldn't be the same, and I longed for the lost days of the wild, wild west, be it in Saba al-Bor the previous winter or in Hussaniyah only weeks earlier.

Lieutenant Rant read my mind. "Things will never be the same," he muttered.

"No doubt," Captain Clay replied.

I didn't say anything, just patted them both on the back, then pulled out and lit a cigarette. Between drags, I thought about the Buffalo Jills and how cool it was that they were coming to JSS Istaqlaal. They eventually did come, sometime in February. I proved too intimidated to talk to any of them. I just sat in the back of the cafeteria and stared while they signed autographs and posed for photographs with soldiers. Then I felt like a bit of a creep, so I left and went back to work.

They smelled nice. Like an old world I couldn't remember anymore.

V: STEPSONS OF IRAQ

(OR A SHORT-TIMER'S PROMENADE)

WINTER 2008–2009

The best way out is always through.
—Robert Frost

HOLY, NOW, PENDING

It shot out of the Babylonian dust, shattering the calm harnessed by a sandstone skyline. Surrounded by a haphazard maze of tiny homes and shops lacquered in grime, a sea-green minaret sat on top of the building like a crown. It has overseen easy wars and fragile peaces that leapfrogged for untold life spans, bearing witness to humanity's tragic flaw of eternally repeating itself. The mosque stood as proudly today as on the day it first became a place of worship, many dawns ago. This was just one of those dawns.

The infantry platoon trudged on ahead of and behind me, heads scanning, rifles aching. We were hungry. We were exhausted. We could smell the stench from our own bodies. What we wanted had made that dangerous evolution into what we needed. Despite all of this, the dreamer in me—ignored for many hours and desperate for attention—seized my mind with ironclad resolve, forcing me to stare off to the east, into the sun and toward the mosque. The soldiers continued to walk. So did I, although not consciously but simply out of habit and because I didn't know how not to.

Clouds of red puff danced brilliantly with the violet horizon, casing the Shia mosque as aptly as winter could allow. It was so easy to get caught up in the horrors of the moment, I thought, that the most vivid beauties of existence faded into eternal loops of grey. Time to take a deep breath and capture a mental snapshot. It's what a responsible individual does in times like these.

The now of nowness kicked. It fucking sucked carrying half of my body weight in armor plating, dripping with sweat and anger and impatience, rifle dangling at the low-ready like a forgotten ornament on the backside of a Christmas tree. Why did this country always smell literally like shit? I didn't know. How did I help the counterinsurgency today? God only knew. Those were bitches of the now. They were trivial, fleeting, and banal. And no one cared. Fuck the transient. What really mattered was how this moment survived into something beyond time and beyond me and beyond them and beyond this. Hence the clouds. Hence the puff. Hence the horizon.

Hence the holy.

The sound of a loudspeaker's hollow echo rolled over the shadows of Hussaniyah from the mosque. I recognized the early-morning prayers of the Salah. Back in Saba al-Bor, Suge Knight translated these words for me while we patrolled out in sector and sometimes joined in to pray for us himself; admittedly, all these months later, I still felt threatened by these austere, foreign chants unleashed in Arabic. I justified this primal reaction by comparing the prayers to certain passionate sermons I remembered from the old world, spoken in words I understood but with emotions that I did not. Spiritual cadences from the heart uttered in any language sounded menacing to a stranger. With Suge's help, however, I came to appreciate the tranquility offered by the simple repetitiveness of some Muslim prayers. Peace, love, and happiness were universal goals of all the world's major religions—a truth forever stained with bloody irony. How did we as people foul it all up so blatantly? How did the lives of a well-intentioned majority always seem to be shaped by the actions of zealots in the minority? Why was religion the first tool utilized by the violent rather than violence being the last resort of the religious? Certainly, these complexities were not limited to just Islam. After all, Jesus served as the world's first hippie—he preached the Good Word, traveled the land in sandals, and beat up greedy capitalist pricks—but Christianity still managed somehow to collect its fair share of misbegotten jihads. The history books simply referred to them as crusades—or colonialism.

Sometimes I felt like humanity was the stillborn carcass of what we were supposed to be. Other times I wasn't even sure we had made it to the womb.

I kept walking and gazing at the mosque. Huh, I thought. The only sacred building that had ever captured my attention for this long before was the Sagrada Familia in Barcelona. And I seemed to recall that having more to do with a Spanish señorita standing in front of Gaudi's unfinished masterpiece rather than the church itself. Praise be!

To God.

Right.

I pried my eyes away from the east and focused on the street in front of me. My thoughts, though, refused to transition back to the patrol and instead lingered on the dawn and the mosque. With the minaret crown. With the dancing clouds and the grave chants of the Salah. This was all temporary, I reminded myself, even though it felt oh so normal and everlong and permanent. Whether Stryker wheels rolled over the sands of Hussaniyah for months or years or decades more, that hallowed house would watch over many more easy wars and many more fragile peaces, standing proudly throughout. And some other rambling junior officer with dark bags under his eyes, from my country or another, would peer out at the Iraqi sunrise and wonder.

Like I said. Eternal loops of grey.

My inner reins broke, and I kept walking mentally, joining my physical location a half mile from the mosque. One thought lingered with me, though, all the way through the patrol and back to the JSS: Fuck the transient.

THE OATH

I hadn't always been in Iraq, and Iraq hadn't always been my only history. One time in my own prehistory, the Guinness socks felt as smooth as a hawk's glide as I repeated the words spoken to me:

> *I, Matt Gallagher, having been appointed an officer in the army of the United States, as indicated above in the grade of second lieutenant, do solemnly swear that I will support and defend the Constitution of the United States against all enemies, foreign or domestic; that I will bear true faith and allegiance to the same; that I take this obligation freely, without any mental reservations or purpose of evasion; and that I will well and faithfully discharge the duties of the office upon which I am about to enter. So help me God.*

I let out a deep breath and forced my body to relax. These were serious words, and I knew it, especially since up to that point, I had dedicated my life to keeping my life as unserious as possible. A smile ran across my grandfather's visage, as he stood across from me, having just administered the U.S. military officers' oath of office. His right hand dropped from the air and went to shake mine, and I responded in kind, following that with a hug.

My parents walked up, beaming, and they each pinned a gold lieutenant bar and a set of cavalry sabers onto my jacket. The dress uniform on my body felt alien, from top to bottom; the green jacket and pants felt far too crisp and rigid to be comfortable, and my black tie dug into the bottom of my throat. Even my polished black shoes seemed haughty to a set of eyes used to seeing only basketball sneakers and sandals. Those same shoes, though, hid my one act of quiet rebellion—rather than wearing the issued black dress socks, I sported a pair of black Guinness socks I had purchased in Dublin the fall before. The compulsion I had felt that morning to put them on felt natural, given the circumstances. I needed to remind myself that I could—and would—still be me.

My mom seemed to read my mind as she finished pinning on her gold bar. "We all need our small acts of defiance to get through the day," she whispered. "Just remember to keep them to yourself, okay?"

A loud ruckus sprang forth from the back of the auditorium; it didn't take long for me to recognize my fraternity brothers' hooting and hollering. I smirked. Whereas everyone else in the room wore military dress uniforms, suits and ties, or dresses, they had shown up in pastel Polo shirts and plaid shorts and uncombed hair, still hungover from a beer pong tournament the night before. I'm really going to miss college, I thought.

When I signed my ROTC papers on September 10, 2001, I planned to be an army lawyer. The next day changed a lot of things for a lot of people—including the life trajectory of a cocksure West Coast suburbanite. My dirty little secret from that particular day was a twisted spasm in spirit as I watched the replays of the Twin Towers collapsing into ruins. Something had happened. Something new. Something historic. Something profound. And it hadn't been created in a Hollywood studio, either. America had been attacked, innocent people had died, and there was going to be a reckoning my children and grandchildren would read about someday. I didn't know how, then, but I knew that I would be a part of it. Somehow, someway. I never would've believed in my wildest fantasies back then of becoming a scout platoon leader, but here I was, only a few years later, on the cusp of being all pragmatic and shit. On the way to becoming a genuine combat leader of men. Un-fucking-believable.

It had all seemed so clear back then. And clean. I'm still not sure how or when it changed.

After I swore my oath and our ROTC master sergeant gave me my first salute—gently reminding me that I needed to drop the salute first—I turned to face the audience. An endless barrage of flashing cameras left me feeling like a deer caught in headlights, wordlessly accepting my fate in the final seconds before escaping the bright lights through the oh-so-sweet truck grill of death.

"Well," I started, "first I'd like to thank the army for commissioning me the day before graduation. Considering my philosophy grade still hasn't been posted, big ups to the Green Machine for showing faith in defiance of all things logical."

Laughs. I let out another deep breath. I sought comfort through humor, and once again, I found it. The rest was easy. I thanked my family, my friends, and a litany of ROTC people who had spent hours on end showing me the practical essentials of army life. Then, spurred on by the seriousness of the words I had just sworn to live by and the pure sense of pride I felt for uttering them, I hit the esoteric ramble button of my being.

"You know, I'm here, as a lot of us are"—I pointed to my fellow commissionees—"because of 9/11." Sleeping through it didn't change the fact that it had profoundly affected me. "But that doesn't really matter now. We have a job to do, and we're going to do it. The whys will stay here in academia, as they should, I think. I'm as surprised as a lot of you are that I ended up going the route I've chosen. But I couldn't be more proud or more excited. It's going to be a hell of a ride, that much I know. Catch you on the flip side, and keep it real."

My brother, who sat in the audience next to my girlfriend, later told me I had spent my entire portion of the ceremony looking like I'd been punched in the gut but still managed to smirk during the whole thing. "Quite the feat," he told me. He also said I didn't really smile until I sat back down, when the spotlight shifted to the next new lieutenant. I guess I always hated dog and pony shows, even before I knew what the term meant.

A few years later, when I left for Iraq, I took that same pair of Guinness socks with me. On days I wanted to remember who I had been and who I was and who I still wanted to be, I wore them on patrol, underneath my dirty, dust-covered tan combat boots. They still felt as smooth as a hawk's glide.

HOW TO JOINT-PATROL

"Dude, where'd your moustache go?" Lieutenant Dirty Jerz asked me. "It was finally starting to fill in."

While JSS Istaqlaal still hadn't evolved into a salute zone since our battalion's move there, certain outpost liberties had already been snuffed out. Like moustaches. Originally concocted by the few armor officers on the JSS as a tribute to our cavalry forbearers for morale purposes, the practice of growing a moustache had spread to the other branches and to some of the NCOs and soldiers as a show of company-level solidarity. The field grades frowned upon the so-called Ride of the Moustachioed and thus ordered our

A heavy orange sandstorm did not stop our dismounted patrol through Hussaniyah in the autumn of 2008, nor did it stop these sheep from eating trash.

ringleader, The Hammer, to destroy any and all signs of officer upper-lip hair. Turned out, the only thing infantrymen hated more than hippies and techno music was moustaches. And so, my valiant attempt at a handlebar ended, quite prematurely. Considering that with it I resembled a child molester more than I did one of Teddy Roosevelt's Rough Riders, the order couldn't have come a moment sooner.

"It was my sacrifice to the new gods of Istaqlaal," I said smugly, "last seen at the altar of the porcelain sink."

Lieutenant Dirty Jerz and I walked up the slight, half-mile incline that separated the company TOCs from the new battalion headquarters on JSS Istaqlaal. A chilly, early December wind swirled through the late-morning air, something not lost on the flapping American flag displayed prominently on a pole next to battalion. I needed to drop off some paperwork with the battalion intelligence gurus, while he needed to talk to the Iraqi police dispatcher, whose office was located behind battalion.

"You want to come on patrol with us?" Lieutenant Dirty Jerz asked. "I'm coordinating for some IPs since every patrol has to be 'joint' now. We're checking out that rumored IRAM [improvised rocket-assisted mortar] factory site. You got anything better to do?"

I laughed. "Nope, just a meeting that will take what little is left of my soul. I'm definitely in. What time is your patrol brief?"

"Ten minutes before noon."

"Word."

A wave of IRAM threats had swept the greater Baghdad area in recent weeks, something that instilled legitimate fear in all of us, from the lowest-ranking private to all of the generals at Camp Victory and Camp Liberty. Designed for catastrophic attacks, the IRAM seemed tailor made for assaults on urban combat outposts; in essence, it lobbed multiple bombs, rockets, mortars, or ball bearings over obstacles like fences and T-wall barriers in an arced trajectory. The difficulties of defending against the IRAM compounded its dangers, as an attack could be initiated from the bed of a small truck by remote control. The device sort of reminded me of a Transformer, from the 1980s cartoon show, but I didn't want to sound any more juvenile or irreverent than I already came across, so I kept that thought to myself. While this threat was nothing new to the Iraq War, an IRAM attack on JSS Ur directly to our south in July 2008 had, according to the after-action reports, barely avoided becoming an outright disaster for Coalition forces. While JSS Istaqlaal didn't seem like a prime site for an IRAM attack, as opposed to places like JSS Ur, located in the heart of that city, and Saba al-Bor, a smattering of intelligence reports suggesting that IRAM construction was transpiring in Hussaniyah became a focus of our brigade's leadership. Thus, it became our new daily patrol focus as well.

Although not necessarily stoked to be IRAM hunting, I knew I needed to get back out of the wire, so I felt thankful Lieutenant Dirty Jerz had asked me to come along. With battalion on the JSS, my PowerPoint output had increased exponentially, and a self-respecting man could handle only so much of that. After I dropped off the aforementioned paperwork, I walked back to the Iraqi police dispatch office to thank Lieutenant Dirty Jerz properly for the patrol invitation. I found him talking to the dispatcher through an interpreter.

"I understand this patrol isn't on your schedule," Lieutenant Dirty Jerz said through clenched teeth, "but it's important. We had a new intel report come in, so we have to adjust. We're leaving in an hour. You're telling me you can't get me a few guys in an hour? All I need is two guys."

The Iraqi dispatcher jolted visibly, rattled off a sentence in Arabic into his handheld radio, and waited for the reply. The interpreter heard it and turned to Lieutenant Dirty Jerz.

"His captain say that they have no one available because patrol not on schedule. Sorry, he say, but captain say it should have been on schedule."

Lieutenant Dirty Jerz laughed bitterly. "Of course!" he said. "I'll keep that in mind. Tell the dispatcher it's okay. I don't blame him."

I walked up to him and slapped him on the back. "The IPs being their normal, efficient selves?" I asked.

"Jesus Christ," he said, "same old story, different day. They won't let me out of the gate if I don't have any Iraqis with us, but there's not an IP to be found right now."

"Perception versus reality. It can be a mother fucker. We got to raise that joint-patrol number tally, though. That's what is really important here."

"No shit," he fumed. I doubted I'd ever seen him this aggravated. "I mean, I understand the purpose behind the joint-patrol concept, and when it works the way it's supposed to, it works great—when I can sit down and plan with their lieutenant or squad leader, and we get more than two of them to throw in the back of our Strykers. But it almost never works like that. This is Iraq, not training. It's just turned into another check-the-block exercise."

"Maybe try and get some National Police?" I offered. "They're usually better with adjusting to the mission."

"Yeah, that's my next stop."

At ten minutes to noon, I stood in the motor pool in full battle rattle, next to the platoon's four Strykers, surrounded by forty or so of Lieutenant Dirty Jerz's soldiers and NCOs. Lieutenant Dirty Jerz stood on the back of a lowered Stryker ramp, ready to give his patrol brief—as we all waited for the two junior NCOs who had been sent to retrieve the four Iraqi National Police already coordinated for. We continued to wait for twenty minutes, idle chatter filling the silence. Ten minutes after noon, Captain Frowny-Face's voice came over the radio.

"Blue 6, this is Gunslinger 6. Why haven't you departed yet?"

"Those fucks," Lieutenant Dirty Jerz said to no one in particular. "Major Husayn assured me they'd be ready on time."

SFC A spoke up. "Sir, you better go talk to the commander. I'll go find the bastards and get 'em down here."

While we waited, I sat down next to Barry, the platoon's baby-faced interpreter. "Why are they late, Barry?" I asked kiddingly. It had become a companywide joke to blame FUBAR matters on this young terp, as a sort of hazing ritual. The young Iraqi usually played along, using self-effacing humor as a defense mechanism.

This time, though, Barry did not share in or understand the taunt and instead responded all too literally. "Because they are Iraqi," he said. "We Iraqis do not like schedule. Americans are crazy with schedule. This will never change."

Fair enough, I thought. A more honest answer than I anticipated, but I probably deserved it for attempting to joke with the kid.

Five minutes later, seven bodies crested the top of the motor pool, all running. We could all hear SFC A yelling, "Faster, you bastards. Move faster!" as they moved, causing all of us to break out in hysterics. SFC A, the two junior NCOs, and four very winded Iraqi National Police broke into our circle, ready for the patrol brief.

"Sorry we're late, sir," SFC A said to his platoon leader. "The NPs were giving our guys the runaround up there. They just needed a swift kick in the ass."

"I'm sure you were able to take care of that," Lieutenant Dirty Jerz said, grinning widely. He then gave his patrol brief, while Barry translated the specifics to the four NPs. They said they understood what we sought and what they needed to do when we dismounted.

The IRAM-factory report turned out to be a dry hole; we found nothing but a long-abandoned concrete factory. The National Police performed satisfactorily on the ground with us, as they usually did. And one more joint-patrol got tallied for the great PowerPoint slide in the sky.

MERRY FUCKING FRAGO

"I have celebrated some really bizarre holidays during my time in the army," SFC Hammerhead said from the driver's seat of the Mine Resistant Ambush Protected (MRAP) armored vehicle, which is designed specifically to survive IED attacks. "But this might fucking take the cake."

Exactly one year after I spent Christmas Eve with the Gravediggers in Kuwait, I trolled through the streets of central Baghdad with the Gunslingers Company, hunting for VBIEDs and car bombs. This seemed like normal Iraq counterinsurgency activity until we remembered we were conducting this mission set in the Green Zone, purportedly the safest part of Iraq and home to a multitude of government palaces, villas, headquarters, and international embassies. Iraqi security forces were slated to take control of the Green Zone

Statues of Saddam Hussein, discovered in a parking lot on a large forward operating base in the Baghdad Green Zone.

on January 1, but a rash of car-bomb threats on the area threatened that benchmark date. Thus, in an effort to beef up security until then, division shifted units down to Baghdad a company at a time. Our slot just happened to fall from December 24 to December 26—something relayed to us on the evening of December 23. After all, nothing said Merry Fucking Christmas like a big, whopping plate of frago. Now, having spent over a year in combat, most of us were too tired to care, let alone fight it.

Back in our present, the MRAP's gunner, Sergeant J, yelled from above, "Did SFC Hammerhead say something about cake?" he asked, kicking his legs at the same time. "I want cake! I'm starving!"

I looked over at SFC Hammerhead, who grinned fanatically. "The best part about this," I said, "is all of the air force personnel running around in their PT [physical training] uniforms, looking at us like we're crazy." Apparently, the sight of infantry squads dressed in their full combat kits searching vehicles and clearing buildings was not common within the confines of the Green Zone. "I mean, Green Zone or not, we're still in Iraq, right? Did these chair-force faggots not get the memo?"

As if on cue, Captain Frowny-Face's voice crackled across the radio. "Gunslinger 56, this is Gunslinger 6. We're dismounting ahead and going to check out this building complex on our right, per division's orders."

"Roger that, sir," I replied. "We'll meet you on the ground."

"Have fun!" SFC Hammerhead boomed, as I opened my door, while Sergeant Secret Agent Man, Specialist Gonzo, and two other soldiers dismounted from the back.

"Now I know why you insisted on driving," I muttered back at him. "You're a cagey one."

"Sir," he said, "I've been in the army for ten years. I can smell bullshit a mile away. Let me know if someone starts shooting and you need some firepower. Until then, I'll be right here."

"Check and check!" After flashing him a thumbs-up for good measure, I rounded up my makeshift squad, and we joined Captain Frowny-Face and his men fifty meters to our front, next to a large, lightless compound. The austere, black silhouette of Assassin's Gate, a sandstone arch that marked a prominent entryway into the Green Zone, loomed in the background.

Since arriving in Baghdad in the early afternoon, we had found no signs of—or even any clues about—the reported VBIED. The real highlight of the mission thus far had been the movement south from JSS Istaqlaal along Route Senators, known affectionately as "EFP Alley" throughout Coalition forces stationed in Multinational Division–Baghdad, or MND-B. It had been a few months since I had genuinely feared for my life, but the trip through EFP Alley certainly qualified. Every piece of trash and every shadow we drove by threatened a certain blast that never came. It had taken a few hours for my nerves to steady back out.

As we walked up to our commanding officer's location, we found him already talking to a man of African descent at the front gate. At least it's not humid here, I thought, as I breathed freely in the nighttime air. The drier air was a vast change from Hussaniyah, as were the greenery and tall palm trees that spotted the Green Zone landscape.

"I realize this is a contractor's facility," Captain Frowny-Face said to the man, "but we are still going to check it out. I'm not going to tell you again. Open this gate now."

The African man's English didn't seem to be great, but he understood enough of Captain Frowny-Face's tone to open up the gate.

"Matt," our commander said to me, "take your guys around to the south side. We'll stay over here. Check every fucking thing out, especially all the cars. If it seems stupid, it probably means you're doing the right thing."

"Roger that, sir." There was a time and place for my sarcastic banter, and I knew this was not it.

We moved to the south side of the compound in a diamond formation, with the radio operator, Specialist Gonzo, and me in the center. We came across an empty parking lot and three trailers housing confused Africans in their pajamas. After explaining to one of them why we were there, I learned that they were Ugandans working for the same security contractor that employed their countrymen on Camp Taji.

"But . . . we are in Green Zone," the man sputtered. "Why would car bomb be here?"

"That's a good question," I replied. "And one I don't have an answer for. We're just playing it safe, I guess."

Predictably, we found nothing of interest in the lodging trailers, minus a bottle of lube I made the soldiers put back.

I sent my report via the radio to Captain Frowny-Face, who told us to remount the MRAP and stand by for further guidance. By the time I got settled back into my seat, Lieutenant Mongo was speaking to our commander on the radio, giving him a SITREP from his platoon's end of the Green Zone.

"Roger, Gunslinger 6. We've cleared all the way to the Unknown Soldier monument roundabout. Any word on how long we're going to be out here? In another hour, we're going to be the only ones walking on the streets."

"Negative, White 6, just continue mission." Captain Frowny-Face seemed just as frustrated by the inanity and the repetitiveness of this mission set as we were, but the unwritten rules of command prohibited him from venting out loud. Such was not a burden, however, that anyone on my vehicle carried.

"This is fucking retarded!" Sergeant J crackled from his gunner's hatch. "I mean, I have done some seriously stupid-ass, retarded shit in the army, but this is by far the most fucking retarded. We are searching for a car bomb *in* the goddamn Green Zone. News flash: If a terrorist already got a VBIED in here, it would have fucking exploded already! These fucking colonels and generals need a commonsense sergeant or staff sergeant permanently assigned to them to keep them from doing stupid-ass shit like this."

SFC Hammerhead arched his eyebrows and laughed. "Let it all out, man. Tell us how you really feel!"

About an hour after we cleared the Ugandans' trailers, Captain Frowny-Face again spoke on the company net. "All Gunslingers, the division commander wants to speak to all of us in fifteen minutes. Grid to follow for location. Do not be late. I repeat, the division commander will be speaking to us in fifteen minutes. Do. Not. Be. Late."

Whoa, I thought. The division commander was a two-star general. Maybe this VBIED threat existed after all. At least I'm not in Kuwait this year, I decided. And at least I only have three months left, instead of fifteen. Thank God for small wonders.

We followed the patrol to the linkup location, a small parking lot off the main drag. It nestled up to a small, lush garden that buzzed with evening insect activity, and as soon as I dismounted, a large mosquito made a play for my neck. I smacked and killed it and saw Specialist Gonzo do the same thing on his arm. "Damn mosquitoes are trying to give me Iraqi SARS," he said with a smile.

We stood around for a few minutes, correcting each other's inevitable uniform deficiencies, like loose strands, muddy boots, or unauthorized rifle enhancements. We knew we needed to look as pretty as possible for the general and his entourage. During this time, Lieutenant Mongo's platoon and the mortarmen/tanker combo platoon drove up, parking in Stryker coil formations. Lieutenant Dirty Jerz and his platoon had been left at JSS Istaqlaal for force protection—which none of them seemed to mind—when the frago came down on December 23.

Shortly thereafter, four jet-black suburbans peeled around the far corner, coming to a screeching halt in front of us. The doors opened, and a multitude of sergeant majors, majors, and colonels stepped out, smiling widely, calling over soldiers, and handing out Christmas cookies and hot cocoas. The soldiers reacted tentatively at first, put off by all the rank in front of them, but eventually their stomachs drove them over en masse. The sergeant majors and majors and colonels all smiled widely and proudly.

"I thought this was going to be a speech or something, sir," I said to Captain Frowny-Face.

"So did I," he responded, clearly as shocked as I was. "So did I."

I noticed my bootlace had come undone and bent over to retie it, slinging my rifle in the process. When I stood back up, a stocky man about my father's age faced Captain Frowny-Face and me. He wore two stars on his uniform. "Evening son," he said to me, slapping me heartily on the back. "Thank you for what you're doing here and what you've done for your country. Have some cookies. It looks like you could use them." He held a plate of frosted sugar cookies in his right hand like a waiter.

I did as told and took three cookies for good measure. And so my division commander, a man with a very gruff and very demanding and very hard reputation, fed me cookies on Christmas Eve in Baghdad with a large smile on his face. My eyes felt as big as saucers, and I didn't relax until the general walked off with Captain Frowny-Face to get a company commander's take on the ground situation. Halfway through my second cookie, the division sergeant major shoved a hot cocoa in my hand. "Here you go, Captain," he said with a wink. "General's orders."

I thanked him, walked away, and found Lieutenant Mongo and SFC B standing nearby. "Hold me," I said to Lieutenant Mongo. "I don't know what to think about anything right now."

He laughed and draped his large wing around me. "Neither do I. But I do know these cookies are delicious!"

The general and his entourage left fifteen or so minutes later, and we continued our mission for another two hours before receiving word that we could call it a night. Some of the soldiers slept in their vehicles, but most of us made the short trek to temporary housing. It was worth the walk for a mattress.

I awoke Christmas morning to SFC Hammerhead poking me in the ribs. "Time to wakey-wakey, sir," he said. "More car-bomb fun awaits!"

"Fuck," I said, usually the first word I uttered every morning, whether trapped in Baghdad or not. A few seconds later, when slightly more cognizant, I added, "My mom wrote me a note. She says I don't have to go to war today."

SFC Hammerhead laughed. "Sir, what more do you want? You got a bed, a personal wake-up, and a general delivering goddamn Christmas cookies. I can guaran-dam-tee you that didn't happen the last time I was here."

I sat up and rolled my eyes. "Yeah, yeah, yeah," I muttered. "I know all about the last time everyone was here. No roofs on the outposts and no shitters, either. It was worse than the Marne and Bastogne put together. And half of you guys used slingshots instead of rifles because supply didn't have enough guns. Blah blah blah."

"Cranky this morning?" SFC Hammerhead laughed again. "Man oh man, you are not a morning person."

Thirty minutes and a quick shave later, I sat in our MRAP as we followed Captain Frowny-Face's vehicle to the crossed-sabers landmark, also known as the Hands of Victory, or the Swords of Qadisiyah. Built in 1989 by Saddam Hussein to commemorate Iraq's supposed victory in the Iran-Iraq War, the Hands of Victory had become the war equivalent of a tourist trap for American soldiers in search of a photo opportunity in central Baghdad, something all of the Gunslingers took advantage of, as well, on Christmas day. This former parade ground also served as an excellent command-and-control location for Captain Frowny-Face, as he maneuvered the two line platoons around the Green Zone battle space.

After we took the obligatory aforementioned photographs, and while we waited, most of the soldiers slept. Specialist Gonzo and I, though, had serious, earth-shattering subjects to discuss in the back of the MRAP—for instance, the mid-1990s gangsta' rap rivalry between Tupac Shakur and the Notorious BIG, which ended with both men being killed in drive-by shootings.

"I liked Tupac more," I said. "I mean, 'Hit 'Em Up' has to be the greatest revenge song of all time."

Specialist Gonzo nodded. "Yeah, but Biggie's music was more fun to dance to. Like 'Hypnotize'!"

"True."

"And he has a movie coming out."

"Also true. That is pretty gangsta'."

Specialist Gonzo started chuckling. "How do you know what's gangsta', sir? Aren't you from the suburbs? In Nevada?"

I pursed my lips together in mock annoyance. "Please, I'm the subject-matter expert for all things gangsta' rap," I stated. "I even got a 'Thug Life' tattoo."

"Oh yeah?" I had Specialist Gonzo rolling now. "Where's it at?"

I grinned maniacally. "I Sharpie it onto my knuckles. That way, all the crackers working for the Man can't pin me down, you know what I'm saying? I'm like a guerilla gangsta'."

"Sir," Specialist Gonzo wheezed between giggles, "you're out of control."

"Tell me something I don't know. I used to be normal before Iraq. It's the army's fault."

An hour or so later, a pair of contractors—one middle-aged man and one very attractive blonde woman with silicone-enhanced breasts—drove up in their sedan and distributed Oreo cookies and Gatorades to all of us, wishing us a Merry Christmas.

"Maybe coming down here wasn't so bad," Sergeant J said between cookie bites. "There's no way the cooks up at Istaqlaal would be this friendly, even today."

We spent the rest of the day and part of the night continuing to clear the Green Zone, compound by compound, block by block. We found no sign of a VBIED or even a VBIED in construction. That night, we rotated through the dining hall at Camp Patriot for a very full and fattening Christmas dinner. The next morning we woke up and drove back to JSS Istaqlaal, this time taking Route Tampa north instead of Route Senators. My nerves appreciated this adjustment. When we arrived, I headed to my room, where Lieutenant Rant found me.

"How was it?" he asked.

"You mean other than the giant palaces and the general's Christmas cookies?" I shrugged my shoulders. "It was still Iraq."

KILLING AN ARAB

A couple days after I rang in the New Year with a near-beer in the shower, I stood in the back of a large formation assembled in front of the battalion headquarters on our JSS. I should have been paying attention to the American flag being lowered down the flagpole and the Iraqi flag subsequently being raised in its place, a symbolic gesture resulting from the passage of the SOFA by the Iraqi parliament. But I wasn't. Instead, my mind walked an existential ramble along the cliffs of possibility, daydreaming about lost ideals and what kind of man went to war to observe instead of kill.

Escape.

Forty years from now, on a snowy winter night in front of the fire, with Guinness in hand, neurotic wife somewhere in the near vicinity, and the Little Drummer Boy pahrumpbumpbumpbumping in the background, a young G grandchild bursting with curiosity will climb up on my knee and ask me about my time as a soldier in the far away country known as Iraq. The child's voice will make the word Iraq sound romantic too, not dirty—like it still sounds in my mind.

I will tell said grandchild about said Iraq and the sheiks I met and the terrorists I captured and the soldiers who fought next to me. And said grandchild will be interested and ask questions because it is a G and, thus, naturally bright and inquisitive. The grandchild will ask pointedly, as only a child can, "Grandpa, did you ever kill anyone in the war?"

I will laugh and say no, that I got lucky and was never placed in that situation, in which I'd have served as judge, jury, and executioner for a fellow human being. I was on the front lines, I'll say, as a cavalry scout, proud of my service,

Standing in front of the Hands of Victory, better known as the crossed sabers, in Baghdad on Christmas day, 2008.

and even got a tattoo on my shoulder that wrinkled up over the years, but I never had to kill anyone. It wasn't that kind of war.

I will be a fucking liar when that happens.

Little white lies coming out of the mouth of a little white liar. Who plays the technicalities game with his own grandchild? Yes, technicalities. Because I gave the order to kill someone. Luckily or unluckily, I don't know, but that order never got carried out. Everything changed for me after that. I knew I could and would kill, and everything else was circumstantial. I drank once from the blood-lust fountain and, as a result, would drink from it forever. The opportunity to kill in the name of country, not murder, never came again because lieutenants talked on the radio instead of pulling triggers and because our counterinsurgency became so damn successful that I didn't need to. It wasn't a real war, not by American standards, anyhow. We reacted to explosions in Iraq; we didn't initiate them. That's not how the Red, the White, and the Emo preferred it. I served in a brushfire war, important to be sure, but a footnote in history, not its own chapter. Sometimes I felt ecstatic that General Petraeus and his apostles had proved so good at what they did and so profoundly shifted the war's strategy. I knew that by doing so, they had saved the lives of some of my men—and maybe even my own.

Sometimes I wasn't so ecstatic. I didn't know why. I think it had something to do with the bloodlust fountain.

What about the Iraqis I indirectly killed? By ignoring their pleas, by not caring about their need for secrecy, by walking by them or walking to them or walking with them. I'll never know for sure, and that's the point. That's why the Boss Johnsons and the Sheik Zaydans and the teenage hookers and the widows stuck with me. Because they always knew I'd be fine once I got out of Iraq. I always knew they'd never be fine because they'd never get out. Like Suge. And Haydar. And Lieutenant Anwar. They never left me just as they never left Iraq.

And the kids. And the kids. The ones with eyes like black pools of sorrow. They didn't even know what they didn't have, but they did know they didn't have it.

Like a lizard and its tail. One can either kill the lizard or take the tail, but only the fools and the clowns don't realize the tail will grow back. That's how it was for America and Iraq. We wanted to slice off the chaos tail without smashing in the lizard's head, hoping a democracy tail would grow in the meantime. We learned firsthand that wasn't how lizards or their tails worked.

The grandchild—my grandchild—will giggle and ask if I'm okay, since I stopped speaking a couple minutes earlier. I'll laugh and say, "Yes, I'm fine," put the grandchild back on the ground, and tell it to go play with the dog. Then I'll stare into the embers of the fire, crackling with fleeting possibility, and think of the Arabian sun's glare lost long ago. I will think of faces that no longer have names, names that no longer have faces, and places without events and events without places. I will remember how things were before they changed and how things were after they changed. Then I'll remember why they changed, pretending to myself that I was ever able to forget such in the first place.

I hope that then I won't feel like a stranger to myself.

Escape was never an option.

Returning to January 2009, I snapped to, still standing at attention, and watched the red, white, and black with green script of the new flag of Iraq flapping in the wind, high above JSS Istaqlaal. The Iraqi security forces around me stood proudly and saluted. I carried mixed feelings about the whole affair but couldn't bring myself to really care either way. I just didn't want to crack up in public. Yelling to myself in a Porta-John or an abandoned corner of the JSS would suffice if I could last that long. I would.

Just get back to the old world, I thought to myself. Everything will be fine then. Just get back.

THE DAY OF ASHURA

Staff Sergeant Sitting Bull sat down next to me on the black leather couch in front of the television and frowned. I looked over at him, prying my eyes from the fight taking place on the screen, and ignored the cheers and jeers of the thirty or so other soldiers who watched the fight around us.

"Yo, sir, Las Cruces just called us. He said he knows who planted that IED the Iraqi police found earlier this morning. It's pretty crazy and nothing like we guessed."

I nodded. "Sure. Of course. Las Cruces wants nothing more than to ruin the entire JSS's ability to watch UFC (Ultimate Fighting Championship, a mixed martial arts organization immensely popular with American soldiers). That much I already knew. What more do I need to know?"

Staff Sergeant Sitting Bull laughed. "How about the fact that we got Badr Corps operating in Hussaniyah now?"

My jaw dropped, and I raised my eyebrows protractedly. "Okay, you're right. That is worth knowing. When the fuck did the Badr Corps move this far north?"

"Have fun!" Lieutenant Rant waved from another couch as we stood up. "Today seems to be an insurgent day, not a contractor day. Lucky me!"

Like JAM, the Badr Corps qualified as a Shia extremist group, although that phrase didn't truly encapsulate the organization's history or intent. Originally formed as an anti–Saddam Hussein, pro-Shia paramilitary, the Badr Corps actually fought with Iran against Iraq in the 1980s during the Iran-Iraq War, which ended in a stalemate. The Badr Corps tended to draw from a more educated, wealthier demographic than the upstart Jaish al-Mahdi and had proven far more supportive of Iraqi security forces in the aftermath of the American invasion, as many of their own members joined the Iraqi army and the Iraqi National Police. Nevertheless, elements of the Badr Corps still functioned as a paramilitary on the streets of Iraq, although it was rare for them to operate on this end of Baghdad. Their political capital rested in Karbala, and the organization had played a pivotal role in the Battle of Basra against revolting JAM elements in March 2008.

I walked back to our company TOC to read Sergeant Secret Agent Man's report about Las Cruces's information. The IPs had found three antipersonnel IEDs, filled with steel ball bearings, some four hours before near a populated street corner in the center of Hussaniyah. Although set for remote detonation, the IEDs did not explode, even with the IPs around. All of this struck us as bizarre for three reasons: (1) JAM didn't normally target their own people instead of us, (2) JAM didn't normally use ball-bearing IEDs instead of EFPs, and (3) today was the Day of Ashura, a prominent Shia holiday. JAM seemed as concerned with public relations as we did, so an IED attack on this day failed the basic logic test. And now we knew why. The Badr Corps had planted the IEDs targeting JAM members.

As I scanned his report, Sergeant Secret Agent Man enlightened us with more details. "Basically, sir, the Badr Corps wanted to make a big splash in Hussaniyah to let the populace know they've arrived. Killing JAM leaders in front of everyone on a Shia holiday would definitely do that."

"But aren't they a Shia organization as well?" I asked.

"They are," Sergeant Secret Agent Man replied, tapping his mouth with a pen. "But H-Town is not made up of many of their people, so it seems like a risk they'd be willing to take. Hussaniyah is too poor and too far north to be loyal to the Badr Corps."

"So why didn't they blow it up?"

Sergeant Secret Agent Man tapped his mouth with the pen again. "That's something I've been trying to figure out. I don't know. It was still remote activated; unless the remote was out of range, they should have been able to detonate it at any point. The only thing I can figure is that they didn't want IP blood on their hands. They knew we'd come after them then."

I put the report down. "Okay, that all makes sense. But do we have anyone saying this is the Badr Corps other than Las Cruces? And why is he so sure it was them?"

"He's the only one so far. And he's so sure because he's one of the guys they wanted to kill. An IP who recognized a Badr Corps member driving into Hussaniyah at dawn tipped JAM off, so they avoided all of the Ashura activities and stayed at their safe houses."

I started rubbing my temples and longed for some painkillers. Or a cigarette. Captains Frowny-Face and Clay were all at a battalion meeting right now, so I was the head mother fucker in charge. Hooray. And such.

"What holiday is it again? I get all of these fucking Islamic holidays mixed up, except for Ramadan, because they starve themselves."

Both of the HUMINT collectors laughed. "It's the Day of Ashura, sir," Staff Sergeant Sitting Bull said as he stuck a large wad of dip into his mouth.

"The one where the Shias beat their chests with whips. The actual day changes every year, but it's almost always sometime in January."

"Ah," I said reminiscently, "but of course."

The Day of Ashura commemorated the Muslim martyr Husayn, who died in the Battle of Karbala in approximately A.D. 680. Unlike Sunnis, Shia Muslims considered Husayn the rightful successor to the Prophet Muhammad. Many Shias chose to celebrate Husayn's death by slapping themselves or flailing themselves with chains or maces, symbolically exhibiting that they shared in his pain and sacrifice. A year before—had it really already been a year?—the Gravediggers and I had stumbled upon an evening street festival during Ashura along Route Swords in Saba al-Bor. I danced with Sheik Banana-Hands and his eldest son and ate frosted dates with Boss Johnson, who, despite being a Sunni, had shown up to the event as an act of good faith toward his Shia brethren. The three of us and SFC Big Country then held an impromptu conference on the side of the street, discussing the ills and troubles of the Saba al-Bor area. At the time, I truly believed we had made serious headway in the mending of Shia-Sunni relations in our particular AO. Less than two weeks later, Boss Johnson's car blew up, taking his splatter particles and brain matter with it, less than a mile away from Sheik Banana-Hands's house. And now, one year physically and a decade mentally later, I was dealing with the Badr Corps making a play in the sewer politics of Hussaniyah. Needless to say, frosted dates and chest flailing aside, the Day of Ashura was not my personal favorite of the Muslim holidays.

"Any objections to sharing this with Lieutenant Anwar and his boys?" I asked Staff Sergeant Sitting Bull. "They usually have a quick turnaround with lower- and mid-level guys, and they probably should know that the Badr Corps is making a play."

Staff Sergeant Sitting Bull shook his head. "No, that's a good idea. As long as we don't let them know where we got the info, I don't care."

I walked over to the National Police dispatcher and informed him that I needed to speak with Lieutenant Anwar immediately. Concurrently, the mortarmen/tanker combo platoon went on mission and conducted a follow-up patrol around the Day of Ashura festivities in central Hussaniyah. Under strict orders to stay on the perimeter of the gathering, Iraqi police approached them, informing the platoon leader that another antipersonnel IED rigged with ball bearings had been found. Battalion dispatched EOD, which successfully dismantled it. Meanwhile, Lieutenant Anwar and I met, and I informed him of the Badr Corps intelligence. He thanked me and beat it back to his headquarters only five minutes after our meeting started. I took this as a good sign.

The next day, Lieutenant Anwar claimed they had detained one Badr Corps member responsible for the IEDs, who informed them that they had been dispatched from Karbala to make inroads in Hussaniyah and to attempt to dismantle JAM special groups in our area. He also told the National Police that the other Badr members had fled after the Day of Ashura, and he doubted they'd return anytime soon. We couldn't verify this information, though, because the National Police rejected our request to question their detainee tactically. This spurred Staff Sergeant Sitting Bull to think that they hadn't detained anyone and had instead made up the story to try to impress American forces.

Either way, we never heard of any more Badr Corps activity in the greater Hussaniyah area during our time there.

AIR ASSAULT

Just as our logistical elements began planning for our redeployment back to Hawaii in mid-January, Higher ordered the Wolfhounds to execute a series of air assaults on both sides of Route Dover in an effort to conduct more show-of-force missions. The stated purpose for such missions was "to show the Iraqis what we're still capable of." Both companies were tasked with three air assaults each; for the Gunslingers, the first and second occurred in Tha'alba and Sabah Qasar, small farming and retirement communities south of JSS Istaqlaal, and the third landed in an isolated pocket of northwestern Hussaniyah. I accompanied Lieutenant Mongo's platoon on the second air assault to Sabah Qasar.

Air assaults consisted of the movement of infantry forces by aircraft— almost always helicopters in the modern American military—to pieces of key terrain on the battlefield. Traditionally, air assaults occurred so the infantry units could seize or hold the key terrain, but in the Iraq counterinsurgency, we simply cleared the houses and neighborhoods near our respective landing zones. Sometimes, soldiers rappelled out of the helicopters during an air assault, but nothing that precarious proved necessary for our insertions. We would offload as the Black Hawk helicopters touched down on the ground

An Iraqi National Police commando waits for his Black Hawk helicopter chalk to depart during an air assault mission.

for a few seconds, jumping down into the prone position to secure the landing zone.

When Captain Frowny-Face informed us about the missions and their intent, I expressed some misgivings about conducting show-of-force missions nearly six years into the Iraq War. It seemed like counter-counterinsurgency to me; the Iraqis were all too familiar with our weaponry, and all kinds of historical data proved the success of COIN rested with restraint instead of show of power. Captain Frowny-Face nodded and told me I could e-mail our new brigade commander if I cared that much, as long as I didn't include him in the inevitable mess that would follow. I laughed, said, "Roger," and asked to go on one of the air assaults since I knew, on a visceral level, I'd have a hell of a time.

I awoke with the sun on the day of our air assault into Sabah Qasar. I hurried over to the chow hall for a quick coffee and bowl of cereal, threw on my body armor and helmet, grabbed my rifle, and walked over to the JSS's helipad. I met Lieutenant Mongo en route.

"Your cav buddies are going to forsake you," he told me with a grin. "Doing an air assault is pretty infantry. I thought you all avoided helicopters like the plague?"

"We do," I responded. "But we hate PowerPoint more, so at least this gets me away from a computer for a few hours. Do Black Hawks have barf bags like commercial airplanes do?"

At the helipad, two squads of Iraqi National Police joined Lieutenant Mongo's platoon, in addition to our battalion XO and Captain Frowny-Face. I had been assigned to SFC B's patrol team, and I walked over to him and his guys.

"Don't worry," I told him, "I'm not going to piss in your Kool-Aid. Just let me know if you need me to chat someone up or drink some chai. I know you and your guys know what you're doing."

"Sir," he replied while arching his eyebrows, "we're all just along for the ride on a boondoggle like this. Who knows, though, maybe we'll finally find those weapons of mass destruction."

Ten minutes later, the four Black Hawks arrived, and we began our cold-load training with the grounded helicopters. Every patrol split into two loads for two helicopters, with each load carrying four American soldiers and three Iraqi National Police. It took five minutes for us to learn how to run, jump into, and quickly buckle up inside the Black Hawk. It took another five minutes for us to learn how to jump out and drop immediately into the prone position, rifles in the shooting position. It took us fifteen minutes to get the Iraqis to understand why they needed to point their AK-47 muzzles down in the helicopter instead of up.

For such a violence-centric culture, I thought to myself, they sure aren't big on gun safety.

While we waited for the actual mission to ensue, the bomb-sniffing dogs assigned to one of the other patrols began barking unmercifully at the various Iraqi National Police. The NPs, men who had shown no fear in the face of their own potential deaths on many occasions, shrank away from the German shepherds like turtles retreating into their shells. "Nothing like teaching our canines to be racist!" a junior NCO of Hispanic descent from Lieutenant Mongo's platoon boomed. "They may not be able to see brown, but they sure can fucking smell it!"

Shortly thereafter, we loaded up onto the Black Hawks and took off. My patrol was a part of the first chalk. For most of the NPs, this served as their first experience in a helicopter; as a result, they could not contain their excitement. Even their sergeant beamed like a flashlight. One of the commandos across from me handed me a digital camera, and I snapped a shot of three of them doing their best Arnold Schwarzenegger pose. I, in turn, handed them my digital camera, and they snapped a photograph of an NP commando and me. We both smiled instead of postured.

I garnered a seat on the end of the Black Hawk, and thus had an excellent view of the scenery below us, albeit through a window. Irrigated squares of green and blue intermixed with grainy, desert blobs, with small building blocks suddenly rising up out of the passing dust lands like pop-ups at a target range. Highways became streaking black tears, while roads transformed into isolated angles of dirt specks. A cloudscape of white fluff floated by, seizing us in its wake. Everything about the Iraq I knew so well on the ground changed, except for one thing. The great Tigris River still refused to stir. Even from a bird's eye view in the sky, it still slinked along with all the worry of a worm.

"Two minutes!" the crew chief screamed from the front of the chopper. We all gathered ourselves and prepared for a rapid offload. The earth swirled up at us as we descended, and I verified that my rifle was locked and loaded. "One minute" became "thirty seconds," which became "ten seconds," which became "go go go!" and the large metal door swung across my line of vision. I counted one, two, three, four bodies by me, then leapt out into the sunny unknown, pacing three steps to my right before plunging down to the ground in the prone position, rifle oriented out.

Thank you, Jesus, I whispered, for not letting me fuck that up somehow. The cavalry jokes never would have ended.

As the helicopter took off, its rotary wing beating at the air behind me, I took in our surroundings. We had landed in the middle of a farmer's crop field, and I saw a few locals fleeing from us in every direction. Good Christ, I thought, they think we're reenacting La Drang Valley. Can't say that I blame them, either. Four Black Hawk helicopters landing in a retirement community couldn't be considered normal, even in central Iraq. We stood up and moved to the large security perimeter being established by the soldiers from the other choppers.

It took us about ten minutes to get a proper head count and break into our respective patrol groups. Mine headed southeast to clear a neighborhood of about ten farmhouses and unknown building structures. The locals we encountered seemed, at best, confused as to why we had arrived at their homes in such a fashion; at worst, their faces sealed themselves in absolute panic. No amount of smiling or friendly American bumbling could get them to calm down—given the elderly age of most of the population, I was just glad we didn't stumble upon a dead body, post–heart attack.

At the second farmhouse we approached, we found an old Iraqi man sitting on the front stoop. He spoke in Arabic as soon as we got within earshot of him.

"He say we can take whatever we want," the interpreter told SFC B and me.

"Huh?" SFC B snorted. "What, does he think we're hear to rob him?"

The interpreter spoke to the old man, who grunted back a few phrases, then went back to staring off into the distance.

"He does not care," the terp translated. "He just want quiet."

I shrugged my shoulders. "I guess old people are the same everywhere."

We roamed houses, fields, and shacks, finding absolutely nothing of interest, beyond an old military pistol a retired colonel claimed was a relic of the Iran-Iraq War. I let him keep it, and he kissed me on both cheeks. I silently hoped I hadn't contracted herpes in the process. After three hours of this, we moved back to the landing zone, learning that the villagewide cache sweep had yielded zero people of interest and zero caches. Then the helicopters landed again, picked us up, and whisked us back to JSS Istaqlaal.

Once situated back on the choppers, the NPs celebrated, smiling widely and giving one another high-fives. The American soldiers leaned glumly on their rifle butts, seemingly eager for an early afternoon nap. The Black Hawk pilots interrupted both states of mind by swooping the helicopters on the way back, giving the trip a roller coaster feel.

Once we landed back at the JSS, Lieutenant Rant met us at the helipad. He grinned wickedly at me as I cleared my rifle of ammunition, a golden round twirling to the ground.

"You show those old people what we're capable of?" he asked.

"You know it." I spat for effect. "They're all terrified now."

The seesaw of precision targeting in counterinsurgency certainly teetered one way after our air-assault missions. But as a junior captain who operated only at the tactical level, I guess I didn't really have the right to determine which side this teeter leaned toward.

SETTING SONS

Viva la reconciliation!

"Hello? Is anyone in here?"

I recognized Eddie's voice from the outside door and called him into the company TOC. I sat alone in the TOC, hunched over in my seat, staring intently at my computer screen, clicking the mouse maniacally. Everyone else had left for dinner some minutes before, but due to a game or ten of helicopter, I hadn't joined them yet.

"Sir," Eddie said, "this man, he . . . he is very desperate to talk."

"Oh yeah? What about? FUCK!"

"What's wrong, sir!"

"Nothing. I just crashed." I turned and faced Eddie. "So, what's up with this dude?"

"He say he is new Iraqi police who just reported to the Boob al-Sham station last month. He used to be Sahwa but on the other side of Dover. He say his boss hates him and take away his money, other police beat him, all because he is Sunni."

"Okay," I shrugged. "Same old story, then?" After months and months and months of dealing with Iraqis' complaints and concerns, I'd heard it all. The only request that would surprise me anymore would be for Chemical Ali's vintage pog collection.

"Maybe," Eddie said. "He has big black eye, so maybe not."

The second-worst-kept secret in Iraq in early 2009—behind Iran's various ties with and influences on Jaish al-Mahdi's special groups—was the Iraqi national government's contentious relationship with the Sahwa. Prime Minster Nouri al-Maliki's Shia-heavy government viewed the Sons of Iraq as the American military's personal Sunni militia (Sunni Muslims populated most, though not all, of the Sahwa's ranks) and held them in contempt, often reminding the nationalized Iraqi security forces like the army and the National Police that the Sahwa were not a legitimate military organization but hired mercenaries. In my experience with Sahwa members, I found they reciprocated this distrust. Depending on the Sahwa leader and where his particular anger lay, they accused al-Maliki of being a puppet for either America or Iran.

As our deployment progressed, and 2007 became 2008 and 2008 became 2009, it became increasingly clear that Iraq was not willing to turn the American Sahwa Band-Aid into an Iraqi Sahwa surgery. After months of haggling in the upper echelons of government, they eventually agreed to allow a certain percentage of Sons of Iraq—I heard anywhere from 10 to 25 percent but never read of any conclusive number—the opportunity to transition into official security-force positions, provided they met the prerequisite physical requirements. Further, in the last four months of our deployment, Iraq became responsible for Sahwa payments; as a result, most of the Sahwa leaders trimmed their rosters because the Iraqi government proved far less flexible with payments than the American military had been. Worries that these now former Sons of Iraq would seek employment with the insurgency again spread across Mesopotamia with the subtlety of a drunken weatherman.

At JSS Istaqlaal, we witnessed and dealt with the transition of the Sons of Iraq more and more in the post-SOFA era. When we met with the police commanders, they complained of their new Sahwa recruits, claiming they were lazy, never showed up to work on time, and didn't conduct themselves professionally. And about once a week, a new police recruit would come to the JSS, stating that all of his coworkers doubled as JAM pawns, that they ostracized him without reason or provocation, and that his pay didn't match those of the other police. The Shia-Sunni religious divide rested at the core of this split, running across Iraq like a fault line. Because of all of that, the grievances of this man—Eddie told me his name was Saif as we walked over to the meeting room—with the Iraqi police did not seem out of the ordinary. Unjust, sure, if true, but not unusual.

Still, though, Saif managed to capture my attention when I walked into the sheik room and found the young Iraqi man pacing back and forth, whispering to himself and sporting a large black bruise underneath his right eye.

After forcefully telling him to sit and to calm down, he explained to me what had happened. He began with a huff.

"I was Sahwa for over a year, in Rashadiya, because that is where I live. I do my job good, and I like doing it. It made me feel proud and good to put food on my children's plates. I work with my friends and do many brave things to keep al-Qaeda out of Rashadiya. But then five months ago my sheik tell me and five others we must be policemen because we are younger than other Sahwa."

As he spoke, he flailed his arms to and fro, voice ringing and changing pitches like a Southern preacher's. Ahh, I said to myself. Much respect to the Iraqi's innate feel for the melodramatic. Eddie offered Saif and me a cigarette; I accepted, but Saif continued ranting.

"We go through police training in Baghdad, and all of us complete training, because we know we must succeed for Sunnis and for the people of Rashadiya. I finish near top of my class, so I know I am a good police. Then they tell me I must work in Boob al-Sham, even though I am from Rashadiya. They split all of us up, on purpose, I know."

"Uh huh." I jotted down some notes on my pad and looked over at Eddie, who listened diligently. He has the patience of a saint, I thought to myself. There's no way I could listen to this all day, every day, and not eventually snap and go Columbine on everyone.

"Then I get to Boob al-Sham. They tell me I am not real police. They say I am junior to them just because I used to be Sahwa. I know it is 'cause I am Sunni. Then the police chief dock my pay for no reason, saying that I am late and that I am not wearing right uniform, but those things are not true. And then"—he held his upper cheekbone in his palm, cradling his black eye, and whispered menacingly—"they do this to me."

I leaned across from my chair, patted him on the back, and asked Eddie to have him explain who had done what to him and when.

"I get to work this morning, and they tell me to go to house in Boob al-Sham, to talk to lady who says her neighbor is in Jaish al-Mahdi. I go with one other police who I know hated me before, and then when we get to house, I turn around and he is gone. I walk into house, and ten men in black masks jump on me and beat on me. I fight back good, but I can't fight them all. Then they hold knife to my throat and tell me if I don't quit the Boob al-Sham police and go back to Rashadiya and never come back, they will kill me and kill my entire family." As Saif finished the story, his body shook with rage, and his voice quivered. What he said didn't sound entirely viable, but he certainly seemed to believe it to be so, if nothing else.

I fetched us all a cup of coffee and talked for another thirty or so minutes in an attempt to calm the Iraqi down. I wrote down the names of the men he believed to be involved and assured him that I'd discuss the issue with his police chief. He also claimed that he knew the police chief and most of the men to be JAM members but lacked definitive proof. I asked him to keep his eyes and ears open and to come back to us if he ever learned anything specific. He promised that he would.

"Thank you," I told him, "both for what you're doing for your family and for what you're doing for your country. I know it's not easy, but this is very important, and you're at the forefront of the effort. You should be proud, so keep your head up."

"I will," he stated. "It is my honor."

Three days later, at the weekly joint-security meeting, I approached the Boob al-Sham IP chief and mentioned Saif's name. Before I could go any deeper into my spiel, though, the chief just laughed.

"That guy?" he said. "He quit yesterday after I docked his pay because he showed up to work three hours late. He is all emotion, no brain. We will be better police station without him."

I asked him about Saif's black eye.

"I do not know," the police chief said, eyes blinking repeatedly, now zeroing in on the fact that my questions had been spawned by something other than mere curiosity. "He showed up smelling of whiskey one morning last week with black eye. I just thought it was a drunken fight."

That afternoon, perturbed by what the IP chief had said, I told Eddie to call the cell phone number that Saif had left with us. The number had been disconnected. I asked a few of our contacts within the Boob al-Sham station—all Shia, like everyone there except Saif—about him, and they confirmed the police chief's version of the events. Unsure of what to do at this point, I told The Great White Hope about him since Rashadiya fell in his company's AO; I asked him to keep an eye out and told him that I wanted to talk to Saif.

We never heard from Saif again. One early evening, a few weeks later, I thought I saw him walking on the side of Route Crush at a marketplace as we drove from JSS Istaqlaal to Camp Taji. I shouted out for him from the back hatch of the Stryker, but the person didn't respond and quickly fell out of my vision. The driver asked if I wanted to stop the patrol. I told him no, so we kept driving.

A GENERATIONAL GAP

During the last couple months of our fifteen-month tour in Iraq, a general in our chain of command determined that "a generational gap" existed within the officer corps and, to a lesser extent, within the NCO corps as well. He lambasted the field-grade officers below him, who in turn lambasted us, for our perceived deficiencies. According to the forwarded e-mails that I read on the subject, the general believed junior officers lacked proper discipline and didn't respect authority or military courtesies, and he wanted this rectified. While unconfirmed, a popular rumor spread that the stimulus for all of this occurred when a company commander, of captain rank, responded to a question this general asked with "yeah, sir," rather than "yes, sir."

Many junior officers, myself included, agreed wholeheartedly with the general's premise that a generational gap existed within the officer corps, although our perception of it differed considerably. After spending most of our deployments at combat outposts with our soldiers, we tended to identify and think like our men more than our superiors probably wanted. Such seemed impossible to avoid, though, especially when said superiors showed up in too-clean uniforms, criticized trivial things, like soldiers not shaving enough or not wearing a full uniform while they walked to the shower, and then drove back to the FOB in time for dinner. We fought in a war. All too often, it seemed like they avoided it. The men often feared Higher more than they did hajjis, scattering like cockroaches to their rooms and locking their doors whenever VIPs arrived at the outpost or JSS. Not all of our visitors behaved like that, of course, but enough did to create the stereotype. The good spoke glowingly in public, listened to the soldiers, and if they saw something they wanted corrected, pulled one of the leaders at the outpost aside. The bad criticized in public, talked rather than listened, and never once realized they were treading in someone else's house. Rank required that we respect all of our superiors the same, so we did. It didn't require us to revere or admire them the same.

While the general believed junior officers lacked discipline and openly feared for the future of "his" army and "his" officer corps, we in turn believed that the current institutional establishment lacked the creativity and ingenuity necessary to wage a successful counterinsurgency. The very top of the flagpole implored us to remain flexible and celebrated the innovative, different manner with which we approached problem sets. We were recruited and trained to make quick decisions on the ground, so that's what we did when we arrived to combat. After the first four years of the war, it seemed overwhelmingly clear that approaching Iraq from a conventional mind-set only led to calamity.

Nevertheless, the many layers between the Pentagon's chosen ones and us clouded all of that. At best, our field-grade officers had served on the line in Desert Storm, a seventy-two-hour operation that failed to impress in the fifteen-month deployment era, unless they had fought in one of the great tank battles, like the Battle of 73 Easting. At worst, our field grades had spent their entire line time in garrison. The brutal reality screamed that most of that generation of officers fell into the latter category. Obviously, this wasn't their fault, but many didn't understand, or they chose not to understand, the circumstances of our rearing as junior officers. They thought they imparted lessons about professionalism with rules, threats, and red tape. Instead, they came across as out-of-touch has-beens who never were, with some treasuring simplicity rather than basking in complexity. Even if they had deployed to Iraq before, they had almost always done so as a staff officer—vital to the Green Machine, certainly, but still lacking in credibility for the hypermacho combat-arms world.

I don't want to overstate the generational divide, though. The overwhelming majority of American officers wanted nothing more than to serve their country and their men honorably. Different approaches and techniques existed for such, and sometimes that caused friction among the ranks. Due to the near-automatic promotion rate up to lieutenant colonel, age differences augmented said friction. But this was not a "lions-and-lambs" World War I situation, where the lambs of senior officers sent the lions of junior officers and soldiers off to their deaths by the thousands. But to refer to the Iraq War experience as the "brains and the bureaucrats" certainly wouldn't be unfair.

I never spoke with the general about his generational gap comments, so I didn't know the exact specifics of his argument. But I believed I got a decent read on them, as various field grades regurgitated his talking points to us in the weeks following the initial e-mail chain. They wanted us to enforce the published uniform standards, stop joking around so much with the NCOs and the soldiers, and do a better job of supporting the chain of command. In short, we were told to act more professionally. Irony reared its winking face, as I wore pink boxer shorts emblazoned with pirate skulls and beer mugs underneath my pants at the time. More a passive rebel than an active radical, I just nodded knowingly during the speech, doing my best not to smirk.

An unprecedented number of junior officers were leaving the army, despite all kinds of bonuses and perks being tossed our way, not to mention the tanking economy back home. It had a lot to do with the prospect of multiple deployments, certainly, but at least in my case, that wasn't a deal breaker. The prospect of becoming a field-grade bureaucrat spouting thoughtless drivel to a new generation of junior officers was. I believed that many of the men at the top of the totem pole truly wanted the army to become a learning institution, but in my experience, the giant clog in the middle wouldn't allow for it. An institution as large as the army didn't change overnight, and the "that's the way it was for me, so that's the way it'll be for them" mentality persisted. Honestly, if I could have remained a scout platoon leader for twenty years, I would have stayed in and been a careerist. But the organizational structure didn't allow for such stagnation. Keep moving up the pipeline or jump off of it were the only options.

Even after I submitted my separation paperwork, which would go into effect three months after we returned to Hawaii, I felt a very enticing tug to remain in the military. Every military officer worth a fuck believed the system was better off because he worked in it; looking around at some of my peers who chose to stay in the army and make a career out of it petrified me sometimes, because they would be the men leading my soldiers to combat on the next rotation. If every good officer got out after his initial commitment ended—such wasn't the case, although it sometimes felt that way—the endless carousel of ineptitude would continue to revolve, and those members of our generation who stayed in would chase out the best and the brightest of the next batch. Further, the benefits of a military career were very real and very tempting. They'd pay for graduate school, and all kinds of unconventional opportunities existed, so I didn't have to turn into what I hated, if it came to that. However, I resisted the urge to reup for two reasons: (1) I had life goals and dreams that I simply couldn't accomplish if I made the military a career, and (2) if I stayed in, I'd inevitably have to order men into combat and not go myself. The inherent nature of the profession demanded such. And I knew I'd lose a significant piece of my humanity when I forced myself to issue such an order. I'd been to hell and back with my men, and I would gladly go again since I knew I could get them back. But I also knew I couldn't order others into hell while I didn't go myself, something a senior military commander must do, and do routinely. I knew it to be a character flaw and an emotional weakness, but I understood and accepted both.

I considered it a personal victory but a professional sacrifice. If that meant I was undisciplined, so fucking be it. I knew I had made a difference in Iraq, both for Iraqis and for soldiers. That was all that mattered to me.

THE IRAQI ELECTION

The number of reports we received regarding planned attacks on Iraq's polling sites reached a fever pitch about three days before the

Lieutenant Mongo does not take kindly to a stuffed dancing duck in the Alpha Company tactical operations center and pulls his M9 pistol on it. Luckily, the rest of us were able to intervene before the toy was shot.

January 31 election. It had been a marked date for many months, due to this being the first set of provincial elections in the country since 2005 and the first time most Sunnis planned to participate, both as candidates and as voters. Meanwhile, the Shia voting block did not sound happy about any power sharing whatsoever, while approximately four hundred parties vied for control of the Iraqi parliament. Through all of this, Jaish al-Mahdi loomed insolently in the background, not actively running many candidates through their political wing but clearly interested in the outcome nonetheless. Most American officials believed Sadr's power play would come a few years later, after we left, but no one really knew for certain. JAM's powder keg could explode at any time.

Our role in the elections appeared and felt murky. On one hand, Higher told us that maintaining the peace for the local populace remained our top priority; thus, we would flood the urban areas with presence patrols. On the other hand, the military establishment knew how vital it was for us to stay away from the actual polling sites so as to not project the image that we were interfering with the voting process. Practically speaking, this meant that all able-bodied soldiers rolled out of the wire on election day, parked their

Strykers in an isolated corner far away from the polling sites, and waited for something to go wrong.

To patrol all of the towns and cities in our AO, Captain Frowny-Face sent the mortarmen/tanker combo platoon to Boob al-Sham and Sabah Qasar, while assigning Lieutenant Dirty Jerz's platoon to East Hussaniyah and Lieutenant Mongo's platoon to West Hussaniyah. Meanwhile, our makeshift Headquarters platoon rotated between the three areas, thus maximizing American presence in anticipation of the potential attacks being reported. Iraqi security forces manned the actual polling sites we so desperately avoided, their latest test of self-sufficiency and independent competence. The government had held early voting three days earlier for the Iraqi security forces and our interpreters, for which we helped provide security.

The polls in the Istaqlaal region opened at eight in the morning, so after applying typical army logic and backward planning, we found ourselves out in sector three hours early, at five. I sat in the back of Captain Frowny-Face's Stryker, wedged in tightly between Lieutenant Rant and Specialist Gonzo, avoiding the temptation to lean on the butt of my rifle and sleep. Specialist Wildebeest sat across from us, head cocked back and eyes closed, with a creek of drool rolling down his chin.

"Tired, sir?" Specialist Gonzo asked with a grin, while stifling a yawn of his own. More than any other of my soldiers, he had an uncanny ability to goad hyperbole out of me.

"Yes," I replied. "More tired than any human being ever has been in the history of prematurely ejaculating army missions."

Specialist Gonzo laughed, but I wasn't even sure what my statement meant. I had only slept three hours the night before, so I didn't really care, either.

"That doesn't make any sense," he told me.

I nodded in agreement. "Think about it."

Our bantering stirred Lieutenant Rant out of his daze. "Gonzo," he said, "no one wants to hear about your days as a professional knife fighter in Tijuana."

We all laughed. "I'll remember that one, next time your computer breaks," Specialist Gonzo replied. "Just 'cause I'm Mexican? I mean, I don't make any saltine jokes about you crackers."

Lieutenant Rant and I stared at each other awkwardly, not relaxing until Specialist Gonzo started cackling. "I'm just fucking around with you, sir," he said. "But seriously, I will shiv you and take your hubcaps."

We spent the next seven hours bouncing between Hussaniyah, Boob al-Sham, and Sabah Qasar, checking with the platoon leaders and platoon sergeants on the ground. Concurrently, the battalion TOC radioed polling-site updates every hour that the Iraqi security forces fed them back at the FOB. With nearly twenty polling sites spread across the three urban centers, we skeptically figured something—in this case an IED attack, a drive-by shooting, or an assassination—was bound to happen. But by the time high noon rolled around and the bright ball in the sky blared down on us with maximum attention, we had only heard positive things regarding both the voter turnout and the Iraqis' successfully keeping the peace. Captain Frowny-Face asked the battalion TOC how they knew all of this. They informed him that the reports came from the various brigade and battalion leaders, who were visiting the polling sites, apparently immune to the order put out about the polls.

"I guess I missed that paragraph in the operations order," Lieutenant Rant quipped, "the one that granted field grades exemptions."

I opened my mouth to follow with a wisecrack of my own, but one look from Captain Frowny-Face halted that plan. I shrugged my shoulders instead and opened up an MRE, fishing out the sliced pears and the candy.

After swinging through West Hussaniyah, where we found Lieutenant Mongo and some members of his platoon kicking around a soccer ball with local children, we drove south on Route Dover, linking up with the combo platoon in Boob al-Sham. They had staged their vehicles at the newly constructed burn pit, built in an attempt to bring scheduled garbage collection to the town. We all dismounted and met SFC C outside.

"Anything going on down here?" Captain Frowny-Face asked.

"Sir, we haven't seen or heard shit," SFC C replied while spitting out some dip. "Unless you count kids throwing rocks at a goat."

"That's it?"

"We've seen a fair amount of adults walking toward the school, where the poll site is."

"If you guys get bored, feel free to patrol around. Just stay clear of that school."

"Roger, sir. How long you figure we're going to stay out here?"

Captain Frowny-Face shook his head. "Division wants us out here at least an hour after the polls close, so plan on 1900."

SFC C smiled widely. "Good stuff. It's not like we got anyplace else to go."

I turned to Lieutenant Rant. "See man, false motivation is always better than no motivation at all. SFC C is truly a pioneer in this field."

We continued the mission until 1930, when Captain Frowny-Face gave the word to move back to JSS Istaqlaal. According to the Iraqis, the only significant events occurred in East Hussaniyah, where many local-nationals found themselves omitted from the ballot list. When told he couldn't vote, one of them threatened to blow the school up, resulting in his immediate detention by the Iraqi police. Every one of us felt exhausted by the long, boring day, and I passed out in my bed with my uniform still on, barely getting my boots off.

The Iraqi government released the results of the elections over a week later. A new round of threats resulted, as did another round of those threats proving false. Despite the lack of a major political protest against the elections, only about half of eligible Iraqis voted, causing Lieutenant Rant and me to observe that they had embraced the most democratic and American of options available to them—apathy. Sadrists won a minority share of seats in parliament, including five seats in the Baghdad governorate. Al-Maliki's Islamic Dawa Party, as a part of the Shia United Iraqi Alliance, maintained a plurality of seats, ensuring he'd continue to serve as prime minister. The various Sunni parties did reasonably well, especially in the Anbar Province in the far west.

We didn't care about any of that, though, at the time. The next day, after a joint targeting meeting with the National Police, I played a few games of helicopter and then watched the Super Bowl on the Armed Forces Network. General Odierno, General Petraeus's replacement as commander of Multinational Force–Iraq, or MNF-I, granted us the right to drink two legitimate beers during the Super Bowl. I drank two Guinnesses and passed out in my bed halfway through the second quarter. It had been over seven months since I'd left Europe and drunk real alcohol, so I didn't feel any shame for its quick effects on me. I didn't wake up at all during that night, which proved a most welcome change from the norm.

MASKS

"Telling a terp that his country is safe when he doesn't feel it's safe is as pretentious as it gets," said an army captain in Baghdad who spoke on the condition of anonymity because he was criticizing his superiors. "The terp-mask thing is just the latest disconnect between

what happens on the ground and what people want to be happening on the ground. We're in full-on dress rehearsal now. I think we're in such a hurry to get out of here, we're wanting this place to be safer than it really is."

So read an article that ran in the *Washington Post* on February 13, written by an old acquaintance and new Facebook friend, Ernesto Londoño. The article recapped a series of events that had occurred in Iraq over the previous six months with regard to a ban on interpreters wearing masks to hide their identities while on mission. The ban had technically been initiated in September, although in my experience most junior leaders ignored it openly and allowed their terps full discretion of when and where they wore a mask. Occasionally, field grades would point out the discrepancy, and if anyone of higher rank than that came around, the terps went sans mask, but 90 percent of the time, the ban meant nothing on the execution level. When the *Washington Post* ran an article about the ban in mid-November, citing its impracticality and the dangers posed to interpreters, Congress initiated an inquiry. The outcome led to the Pentagon's delegating authority to battalion commanders—specifically stating that they couldn't delegate it themselves—to lift the ban for specific patrols and in special cases.

While theoretically this sounded like good news for the terps, it carried the adverse effect of focusing concentrated attention on the ban for all patrols, and suddenly the mask ban became a hot-button issue and was to be enforced at all levels. From November to the end of our deployment, allowing a terp to wear a mask without the commander's exemption became the equivalent of shooting a civilian or negligently discharging your weapon, in terms of bureaucratic accountability and the ass chewings levied by Higher. At JSS Istaqlaal, Barry, in particular, openly feared for his life because he couldn't wear a mask in certain areas. After determining that he needed money for his mother's new house, though, he backed off his threats to quit as an interpreter for Coalition forces. Three other terps, one of whom had worked with us for three years, did walk away.

As the anonymous captain quoted in the February article, I provided those words for a few reasons—none of which involved causing a fire for the sake of watching it burn. One, although I hadn't sought out the press, I understood their power in bringing issues to the public. Nothing made large institutions change their decisions more quickly and more emphatically than public pressure. Two, I truly believed what I said—I wanted us out of Iraq too, but not at the expense of the men who had served next to us for so long. It angered the fuck out of me that some public relations fobbits ostentatiously told terps that if they didn't like the ban, they could seek out alternative employment. And three, I couldn't shake Suge's voice at night, as I remembered him imploring me to allow him to keep his mask on.

It had occurred the previous spring, long before my days as a Gunslinger and even before I became an e-swashbuckler through the demise of my blog. While on a Sheik Nour escort mission, we drove along Route Pluto, well into the core of North Baghdad, to an Iraqi police station opening ceremony. While there, some of the Gravediggers and I wandered around, marveling at the new buildings. Obviously, a lot of rank and brass walked around too, but they all ignored us, until a colonel I didn't know pulled me aside.

"Lieutenant, is that big guy your terp?" He pointed at Suge, who unbeknownst to me, had donned his mask.

"Roger, sir, he's mine," I replied.

The colonel spoke quietly and calmly, but with the crispness of a man who didn't enjoy dialogue. "No masks here," he said. "At all. We're professionals, and we're trying to show the IPs that they shouldn't be afraid of their own populace. We can't damn well do that when our own terps are wearing masks, can we?"

"No, sir," I said. "It's my fault: I gave him that discretion. I'll fix it immediately." The colonel nodded and walked away.

I gave Suge authority to wear his mask when he chose to because it was his life, in his country, and he knew better than any of us when and where he felt safe. But I knew he understood the inanity of army rules and orders, so when I told him, rather innocently and ignorantly to "lose the mask," his response shocked me.

"Please, Lieutenant, do not ask that of me!" Suge roared, emotion erupting out of him like lava from a volcano. "I cannot do it!"

Staff Sergeant Boondock and Doc looked over at us quizzically. Suge had never questioned any of us in a serious manner, let alone me, his known sugar daddy.

"What's wrong?" I asked.

"This place," he said, his voice muffled by the cotton, "is very bad, Lieutenant. IPs are work with Jaish al-Mahdi, and they hunt terps. I know this to be true. We are close to my home. I must be careful."

I nodded, understanding Suge's plight, as his fear was justified. A few years back, thirty members of the Mahdi Army armed with AKs had showed up at his construction business and requisitioned all of his assets, financial or otherwise. His smile, and quickness to accede to their demands, had saved his life. Whether I believed Suge was safe or not at the IP station was absolutely irrelevant. While I understood the colonel's points, I felt that we catered to false appearances with that approach. Suge's feeling safe enough to not don a mask at the IP station should have been our goal, not making the IPs think our terps felt safe. It felt like we took off the interpreters' masks to sport one of our own, except ours hid reality instead of a face. Nonetheless, I didn't want to risk running into that colonel again either, so I told Doc to walk Suge back to our Strykers. Staff Sergeant Boondock and I walked around for another hour or so without an interpreter, until Sheik Nour got bored with the ceremony. Then we drove him home and sat in his driveway for ten hours, keeping the hajji bogeyman away.

Many months later, Suge's voice and eyes and desperation and words of lava compelled me—no, forced me—to try to rectify the situation. I couldn't always be his platoon leader; nor would every situation have an easy solution. So, when Londono asked for a quote, I pounced. The article ran. Nothing changed, at least not in our remaining time there.

I got an e-mail a few months later from an old college friend, who was still deployed to a city in Iraq near Hussaniyah as a rifle platoon leader in an infantry company. He told me they still ignored the mask ban too—because it "was fucking stupid as hell."

Indeed.

ACOUSTIC WAR HYMN

I staggered around in the midnight pitch, near the dark, forgotten corners of JSS Istaqlaal, seeking a burning bush but finding only a box full of sharp objects.

It sufficed.

We're almost there, You know. We're almost there.

No. Not home. Not yet. Not never. But to the black hole of what if. Almost, always. There.

A tribute of praise. Monks chanted. Choirs clapped. Ministers preached. The blessed sang.

And baby, sweet baby, in the meantime, the damned stared. Back. With dead-fish eyes.

But still, in the shatter of the still, I must ask, What the fuck.

   . . .

True.

I oriented myself like a bat's squeak and looked into the mud. Sinking, slinking, sinking in my boots made of elastic tears and soulutions and blinking bloodcrust.

My supper is maroon. My star is spoon.

Forever fleeting, looms.

I can think of nothing more sacred than parity, and yet, nothing is less. It's not fair, You know. None of it.

I'd bet the crumbling walls of Little America, Bizarro Iraq, You've heard that one before.

Burning ears are one thing. I's of arrogance are quite another.

The guilt of touching Fortuna's touch is not worthy of guilt at all. Yet. And yet. Yet. Like rain without a rainbow. Like a moonbow without a moon. Like life without the f.

Thank You for guiding me through this. Fuck You for not guiding them through this. Thank You for getting me out of here unscathed. Fuck You for leaving them here or leaving them there, forever scathed.

Fuck You for the will to say Thank You. Thank You for the freedom to say Fuck You.

Freedom wills free will. And.

And.

And breathes reckless mountain air.

If You can splice existence, I can splice phrases.

!

The gobblers wargasmed and the chickenhawks crowed. So we.

Creation sensation seeks a Big Bang penetration operation. Nonsmoker, will make tender hate after the first date.

Happiness Is.

Why?

No.

Why.

KABOOM
No. Never that certain.
kaboom?
Pretty much. This isn't a comic book or a Disney film. Here, the question mark exists, because the question itself persists.
The black hole of what if knows not, but wonders all.
Smooth. Light. This. So much prettier. Than.
Yes.
Life. Liberty. And the pursuit of diggity.
Why burn bridges when You can burn worlds, eh? Thug Life. Like opening up a yogurt top, but splat goes the dreams of why.
The flame in the distance dances in defiance. Until. The song ends with a snuff.
The American clears, holds, builds. Why are we so historically bad at this, again?
Because we are all insurgents at heart. Well. We were.
True.
. . .
The emo fever dream indulges, gesticulating like a lonely igloo:
Hope-dope.
springs eternal
summer smokes
winters blunt
fall is.
. . .
out of order
~
Still.
The gobblers wargasmed and the chickenhawks crowed. So we fought. The rest is.
Another man's morning, and another son's gun.
That's how it goes, You know.
My supper is maroon. My star is spoon.
Forever fleeting, looms.

THE LAST PATROLS

Finally. They finally came. They finally fucking came.

"Who?" SFC Hammerhead asked me in our room.

"Our replacements. The Pennsylvania National Guard. They finally fucking came. All of them. All of them finally fucking came."

Despite it being well past midnight with the lights off in our room, SFC Hammerhead started whooping and hollering and wrapped me up in a big bear hug. We flipped on the lights, waking up Captain Clay and Lieutenant Rant, and gave them the news. Captain Clay joined the celebration, but Lieutenant Rant simply flashed us a thumbs-up and rolled back over in his bed.

Twelve days before our fly-back-to-civilization date, the main body of the Pennsylvania National Guard arrived at JSS Istaqlaal. A Stryker brigade as well, they seemed like the ideal replacements for us, even if some of our soldiers exchanged stereotypical jokes about National Guard soldiers being weekend warriors and civilians playing dress-up. I knew our replacements would be just as confused and overwhelmed as we had been when we first arrived, but that had nothing to do with their training background and everything to do with the Iraq counterinsurgency being as fluid an environment as existed and nigh impossible to grasp unless you were actually there.

Our last two weeks in Iraq, even before the Pennsylvania National Guard arrived, had proven eventful. Depending on whose perspective, either the battalion intelligence elements had ordered the other company to detain four innocent men and then snapped a staged photograph that made them look guilty, or a grand mistake had occurred due to the complexities of the COIN environment. Either way, justice prevailed, and the four men were released after spending a week in the custody of the National Police. Then, after a new round of VBIED-factory reports proved false yet again, our company stumbled upon a house with three EFPs and a mortar round buried in its courtyard. We detained two brothers living there, who eventually revealed that they had just moved to Hussaniyah from Sadr City due to a JAM order put out by Ali the Beard. And then there was the fallout from the awards.

I saw, experienced, and lived through many fucked up things in my time in the army. But nothing, and I mean nothing in a vacuum world where hyperbole doesn't exist, was as much of a clusterfuck as the awards system employed by the military. Broken did not even begin to describe it. Packets were

routinely lost, downgrades occurred without explanation, and award inter-
pretations varied from unit to unit, from year to year, and sometimes from
day to day, depending on who read the packet and that person's mood at the
time. Further, a process that should've lasted a couple weeks often took
nearly a year. So when we submitted the end-of-tour awards in September,
more than six months before we actually left the war, I wasn't surprised. SFC
Big Country and I had recommended nearly all of the Gravediggers for a
medal of some sort, reasoning that they had stayed out of trouble and spent
every day in Iraq on the front. They certainly met the award requirements
laid out by the army. However, when they came back down the pipeline in
late February, most of the platoon's awards had been downgraded to "certifi-
cates of achievement," which PFC Van Wilder and some of the others stuck
on their refrigerators as a joke, like they would spelling bee ribbons. These
downgrades wouldn't have been such an affront to me if I didn't see a multitude of fobbits receive medals—some of which were definitively reserved
as combat awards for combat soldiers—for their service. It always paid to
be close to the flagpole, and nothing, it seemed, would ever change that
about the military. The same series of downgrades occurred with the Gunslingers as well, and it almost always seemed to happen to the Joes, no matter
how meritorious their combat service.

Adding further insult to this travesty was the word that four of the
Gravediggers had been denied their Combat Action Badge (CAB) for the firefight we had engaged in the year before, while intervening between the Iraqi
army and the Saba al-Bor Sahwa augmented by civilians of unknown affili-
ation. Most of the platoon, myself included, had been awarded our CABs in
July, and I had been told the other four were pending due to a clerical error.
Well, after months passed and the awards had been resubmitted three times,
that clerical error turned into a time-consuming albatross no one wanted to
deal with. Yet again, soldiers suffered because leaders proved unwilling
to fight for what their soldiers had so rightfully earned. Considering one of
the missing badges was for PFC Das Boot, who served as one of the point
men for the penetrating dismounts, no question as to their right to the CAB
existed. I did everything in my power, even after we left Iraq, but no one
wanted to untangle a snarl from the year before. I was eventually told "to
stop asking about it, because it's not fucking happening," but I was never
told why I needed to stop asking about it or why it wasn't fucking happening.

The worst award travashamockery happened when PFC Smitty's promised Soldier's Medal returned, downgraded, without explanation. After he

pulled Private Hot Wheels out of the fire, multiple visiting generals heard the story and assured me that they'd fast-track his Soldier's Medal—the highest award given in the American military for a noncombat event. After I heard the words, "Son, consider it done," when I asked about PFC Smitty's Soldier's Medal, I considered it done. It wasn't.

Not all was lost in the award realm. My write-up and recommendation for SFC Big Country's Bronze Star for service got approved, something he had certainly earned and deserved. Captain Ten Bears saw fit to recommend me for a Bronze Star as well, something I knew Lieutenant Colonel Larry would never approve, thanks to my digital rendition of our XO conversation. That proved accurate, and the award was subsequently downgraded. In all honesty, I didn't care; it had been an honor simply to get recommended for a Bronze Star, and I knew exactly what I had accomplished in Iraq. I even learned to take pride in the downgrade, something I picked up from the various Gunslingers who felt scorned and used by the process. This had been happening in the military for years upon years, and not unlike old, crusty World War II or Vietnam veterans, I found that basking in being an army bastard felt nice and strangely fulfilling.

None of that mattered once we started our last patrols with the Pennsylvania National Guard. Initially, only their key leaders went on mission with our platoons, which operated at full strength. Gradually, though, as the number of their soldiers going out of the wire increased, the number of our soldiers doing so decreased. Wars ended every day in this fashion, creating a sort of perma-jubilee in the soldiers' living quarters. At first, the National Guardsmen treaded carefully, their nerves and questions amusing us. In retrospect, I realized that our comfort and ease in the combat environment threw them for a loop, as it would any group of men still holding onto a logical and civilized world. In a way, our insanity prepared them for their new world, and their sanity prepped us for the return to our old world.

I did my best to be available and helpful to our replacements. Their company's lethal targeting officer, a lieutenant recalled to active duty from the irregular reserve but on his first deployment, immediately proved himself a quick study. I felt comfortable leaving the intricacies of the ever-evolving JAM-nation of our AO in his hands. His HUMINT collection teams definitely lacked the experience of mine, but a few weeks dealing with our Hussaniyah sources would change that. Conversely, I did lose my patience a couple times on patrol with the National Guardsmen. One time, I snapped at a staff sergeant who displayed open hostility and impatience with his young platoon leader; I knew firsthand that NCOs could make or break new lieutenants, and I'd been blessed enough to serve with the best instead of this meat rocket. Another time I pulled aside the aforementioned lieutenant and lit into him for forgetting his ammunition on the JSS. Then I gave him some of mine, subtly pointing out that he "wasn't in fucking Kansas."

The afternoon before our last day, while on a patrol in central Hussaniyah, Lieutenant Dirty Jerz and I took a platoon of our replacements to a known Jaish al-Mahdi restaurant and bought falafels. Needling JAM members always proved a good time—I loved complimenting them on their well-trimmed goatees and hair gel abuse, which forced them to pretend to laugh along with me—even if many of them weren't currently detainable. Although initially unnerved by the setting, many of the guardsmen quickly caught on to the game and promised the owner they'd come in at least once a week.

"You guys are going to be fine," I told their lethal targeting officer. "Just keep it fresh and never get too comfortable. Most of your NCOs have been here before; they'll take charge until everyone figures it out. It's a fun job, though—way better than what your artillery officer has to deal with, with all those contracts. That's hell. A sick, sick person invented that job."

As we walked back to their Strykers—ours were now already in Kuwait, ready for shipment back to Hawaii—a series of gunshots resonated in the distance. A few of the Pennsylvanians hit the ground, but most took a knee, looking at Lieutenant Dirty Jerz and me for direction. Another steady purring of shots popped into the air. And then another. We both shrugged our shoulders.

"It's Iraq," I said to everyone and no one in particular. "Gunshots happen."

Lieutenant Mongo, on a patrol with another Pennsylvania National Guard platoon, radioed us two minutes later, telling us that the shots emanated from a National Police memorial service. Apparently, two of their men had been killed a few days earlier in a car accident on Route Dover. Just a twenty-one-gun salute, Iraqi style, spraying AK-47 rounds across the dismal Hussaniyah skyline.

Our last night passed uneventfully. The next morning, the remaining Gunslingers—Captain Frowny-Face, Lieutenants Rant, Mongo, and Dirty Jerz, Staff Sergeant Sitting Bull, Specialist Gonzo, and myself—gathered in the motor pool, saying our goodbyes to a few Iraqi security forces and our interpreters. Lieutenant Anwar swung by and insisted that a photograph of the two of us be taken on his digital camera for his daughter. Eddie wept openly as he said goodbye to Staff Sergeant Sitting Bull, promising to visit us when he returned to the United States. The guardsmen waited around impatiently, as they should have. It was their show now, and they were ready for it—we were now relics of another time and era. They drove us back to Camp Taji, and I was a helicopter ride, a C-130 plane ride, and a charter flight away from somehow surviving this fucking war.

When we turned in our rifles and our ammunition, I felt like I'd lost an appendage.

Two days after we departed JSS Istaqlaal, the camo grapevine informed us that an RPG had been fired at the Pennsylvania National Guard along Route Crush. Rather than reacting to the attack and conducting a movement to contact, the platoon continued moving back to the JSS. Some of our soldiers mocked them when they heard the tale, although I never learned whether the rumor was true or not. Captain Frowny-Face, however, reminded us junior officers that they'd learn, just as we had. The insurgents would test them because they were new, he reasoned, just as they had with us. And then they'd adapt and start figuring out how to crack the COIN walnut.

They were American soldiers. They'd learn, and learn quickly. No other option existed.

On February 23, the day we left Iraq for Kuwait, small-arms fire killed the first Pennsylvania National Guardsman on the west side of the Tigris River, near Camp Taji. I didn't learn about it until three days later, when we landed in Hawaii, and my dad showed me a printout of the article. I nodded my head and hugged my parents. Then I got drunk that night on mai tais at Waikiki Beach with my girlfriend, Captain Demolition, and The Great White Hope. We laughed and toasted each other and got really tired really quickly.

As I drank down my third mai tai that night, starting the inevitable post-war bender, I realized that my relief tasted like guilt. Guilt for being here when others were still there.

I took another gulp.

EXIT STRATEGY

We were wrought up with ideas inexpressible and vaporous, but to be fought for. We lived many lives in those whirling campaigns, never sparing ourselves any good or evil; yet when we achieved and the new world dawned, the old men came out again and took from us our victory, and remade it in the likeness of the former world they knew. Youth could win, but had not learned to keep, and was pitiably weak against age. We stammered that we had worked for a new heaven and a new earth, and they thanked us kindly and made their peace. When we are their age no doubt we shall serve our children so.
—T. E. Lawrence, *Seven Pillars of Wisdom*

As I drove away from Schofield Barracks—and the army and the Green Machine and Uncle Sam and the Gravediggers and the Gunslingers and everything being a soldier and an officer and something bigger than myself encompassed—for the last time, I did my best to make the moment feel surreal. My honorable discharge paperwork sat in my lap, and like most members of my generation, I had watched too many movies and craved clarity in moments of perceived transcendence. Instead, despite my best attempts, I felt only exhaustion as I peeled my car onto the freeway. I wanted to feel like a titan who had just dropped a great boulder of burden. Instead, I felt like a naked man locked outside of a clothing store.

It felt weird. Not surreal. Just weird.

The Hawaiian summer afternoon blared with tropical joy, mocking my detachment. The preceding three months had passed in a blur. Due to a plentitude of stored-up leave and finances, my inevitable postwar bender had spanned the globe, from Hawaii to Australia to Las Vegas to New York City to North Carolina and back again. I had definitely taken years off of the backend of my life, but I didn't give a damn. It was worth it. I found my mental and emotional bearings during the international wanderings, somewhere between Kangaroo Island and Alphabet City, and now knew I could resign myself to a somewhat normal existence.

Somewhat.

Not everyone proved as fortunate as I upon our return to the old world. The standard amount of postdeployment divorces and domestic abuses and DUIs struck our brigade. Hot Wheels, a corporal now due to his taking leadership charge of his fellow soldiers in the hospital, remained in Texas at the Brooke Army Medical Center, still receiving treatment for the burns from his horrific accident. A 2–14 Cavalry soldier I knew got locked away in California for allegedly molesting his younger stepsister. He had seemed a harmless boy. A military intelligence soldier I worked with closely in Saba al-Bor got drunk one night and shot himself dead. He had been a sweet kid. Nothing shocked or surprised anymore. We all had changed in ways that we didn't understand and could never comprehend. Civilization didn't seem to understand or comprehend it, either.

Comparatively, I got lucky. The worst thing that happened to me blew up every Friday night, in and with the weekly fireworks display at the Hilton Hawaiian Village across the street from my apartment. Loud booms and bright lights spawned transient panic, no matter how many times I steeled myself for their inevitability.

Many of us, myself included, found interacting with civilians more complicated upon our return than we remembered. Normal conversation sounded like idle prattling; the chores of daily existence felt like tedious waste. I spaced out during conversations with my peers about politics or pop culture or gossip, nodding and smiling, and realized that I identified now more as a veteran than I did as an American. More often than not, talking to young women only aggravated my impatience with the inane, while talking to young men only exacerbated my disgust for the soft. I still loved my family and my friends, but the truth was, I looked forward to nothing else quite as much as I did nights with other soldiers, when we could swap war stories and relive our respective times in Iraq or Afghanistan.

Even in a spiraling economy, a fair number of my peers joined me on the annual junior-officer exodus out of the military, Captain Demolition and The Great White Hope among them. We all looked forward to an acronymless existence. Captains Virginia Slim, Clay, Pistol Pete, Rant, Mongo, and Dirty Jerz all still owed more time on their initial commitment, so their eventual decisions were pending. The Hammer, now a major, and Captains Whiteback, Ten Bears, and Frowny-Face all remained in the military, and all promised to avoid the purported lobotomy administered at major school for new field-grade officers.

SFC Big Country returned to Iowa to teach ROTC cadets at the university level, something I told him he'd be perfect for, after putting up with my antics for so long. Staff Sergeant Bulldog headed to drill sergeant school, while Staff Sergeants Boondock and Spade remained in Hawaii, preparing soldiers for the brigade's next deployment in 2011. Both moved up to the position of platoon sergeant—Staff Sergeant Spade as the new platoon sergeant for the Gravediggers. Most of the Gravediggers remained in the army in one form or another, with the notable exceptions of Staff Sergeant Axel, Doc, and Specialist Haitian Sensation. All three returned to their respective homes and to civilian life. As for the Gunslingers, SFC Hammerhead moved to Indiana to help train reserve units for combat deployments, while Specialist Gonzo swore up and down he'd finish out his remaining year of commitment before getting out for good. He thought that President Obama's plan to get rid of the stop-loss program would save him from another deployment.

After leaving Iraq, I never heard from Suge, Eddie, or any of the other terps again. I left my e-mail address with Suge, but I somehow doubted he spent much time on the computer. According to the rumor mill, he planned to open a bar and restaurant somewhere in the capital with a few of his interpreter buddies. We all knew who would fill the role of storyteller and spreader of cheer at that bar.

After I got back to Hawaii, I tried to follow the news in Iraq, but it became harder and harder the further removed from that world I became. It reminded me that I had been there, while simultaneously reminding me that

I was no longer there. When American forces pulled back from the cities fully in June 2009, the Iraqis celebrated with fireworks. I found their choice of festivity slightly ironic, yet fitting. A few months certainly hadn't changed their love for all things that blast and go boom.

Some people thought we were tiptoeing our way out of Iraq. Others thought we were doing the only reasonable thing in a world gone mad, walking the thin line between conquering and fleeing. I honestly didn't know. After dedicating myself to the counterinsurgency effort for a full fifteen months, I knew only enough to know that anyone who said he or she definitively knew the answer to the Iraq impasse was full of shit.

A savage war of sticky. I truly hoped peace followed. I waited for Sadr's next move.

I wondered if the GWOT-era leaders and soldiers raised in counterinsurgency actually could change the institution, instead of the institution swallowing them and their experience whole. It'd be too easy for people who hadn't really been there and who hadn't studied the trends of irregular warfare after World War II to write Iraq off as an anomalous brushfire. I walked away from that fight, though. It needed a flag bearer, not a martyr.

The old men would return, as would the old ways. Tradition demanded it.

The unconventional spirit of the young would awaken again when needed once more by their country. Honor demanded it.

I knew I'd miss it. I knew I wouldn't really miss all of it, but memory had a nasty habit of rescuing the worthy fragments from the garbage disposal of the mind. As I neared my apartment building in downtown Waikiki, staring out at the crashing Pacific blue like I had done some two years and a lifetime before, I pinpointed the one thing from my time in the army that I treasured the most.

The answer was easy: Iraq.

Then I pinpointed the one thing from my time in the army that I despised the most.

The answer was just as easy: Iraq.

We lived in a twisted world.

We live in a twisted world.

So much for clarity.

ACKNOWLEDGMENTS

Some might find it odd that I've dedicated a war memoir to my mother. If you fall into such a category, you clearly have never had the pleasure of meeting Deborah Scott Gallagher. Her iron will is matched only by her Southern sense of propriety, and it is she who taught me to love my country, to talk to God openly and honestly, and to trust that buzzing voice in the mind that serves as our conscience. I owe everything to her.

My father, Dennis Gallagher, has been a steadfast rock throughout my life, and only demanded that I seek out the new and explore. He has done his utmost to expose both of his sons to the best of our Irish heritage, while shielding us from the rest. If any of the latter has shown through in this book, I assure you it is through no failure of his, but simply the blood telling.

Luke, my brother and oldest friend, has proven to me time and time again that bravery is not just something we exhibit in moments of passion or adrenaline. Rather, real men wake up with the day and display a humbler sort of courage, intent on getting out of life everything it gets out of us.

Acknowledgments

My grandfathers, war veterans Rear Admiral Jack Scott and Hospital Corpsman Vincent Gallagher, in their own ways, exhibited to me the importance of honor and the significance of being a leader of men. Every time I issued an order to my soldiers, I felt them with me. With them, I must also credit the women that kept them grounded and resolute, my grandmothers, Velma Ramsey Scott and Dee Hastings Gallagher.

Of course, I must mention Anne, who continues to stand beside me, as we figure out the beautiful madness of it all, together.

This book would have never come into being were it not for the men and women of the United States military. Without a doubt, they are our best, our brightest, and our nation's greatest hope in the future. In particular, the cavalry scouts and infantrymen of the Gravediggers made my time in the service worthwhile and memorable. So, to Chris Henning (SFC Big Country), Torri Caldwell (Staff Sergeant Bulldog), Chris Mason (Staff Sergeant Boondock), Chris Ford (Staff Sergeant Spade), Steven Rose (Staff Sergeant Axel), Aaron Cabrera (Sergeant Fuego), Robert Marin (Sergeant Cheech), Nick Richmond (Sergeant Tunnel), Nathaniel Spoltman (Sergeant Spot), Joe Dougherty (Sergeant Prime), Richard McCracken (Sergeant Big Ern), Boyd Samuelson (Sergeant Flashback), Daven Pantohan (Doc), Matt Wheeler (Corporal Hot Wheels), Philippe Dume (Specialist Haitian Sensation), Trey Coleman (Specialist Cold-Cuts), Matt Stover (PFC Stove Top), Kenneth Smith (PFC Smitty), David Ranger (PFC Das Boot), Joel McClure (PFC Van Wilder), Yancarlo Casanova (PFC Romeo), and Suge Knight, I say simply, Scouts Out! I hope you all remember our times and exploits together as fondly as I do. I'll never be able to repay what I learned from serving in Iraq with you, but feel free to try and make me through various bar tabs over the upcoming years.

Of the Gunslingers, Aaron Kletzing (Lieutenant Rant) deserves special mention, for his dedication to duty and for his friendship.

If it weren't for William Clark, my agent, *Kaboom* would still be nothing more than a defunct blog forever lost in the e-seas. The impact of his vision for the project, combined with his calming influence over this impatient young writer, cannot be overstated. And to my publisher John Radziewicz, editor Bob Pigeon, and the entire Da Capo operation, I again thank you for this opportunity. Bob's passion for this book often superseded my own, which was no small wonder.

So to those I mentioned, and to the many others I didn't—Sláinte.

—NEW YORK CITY
OCTOBER 2009

INDEX

A, Sergeant First Class, 212, 248, 249
Abbas the Beard, 228
  questioning, 226–227
  search for, 219, 226
Abu Abdullah, 209, 210, 211, 215
Abu Adnan, 80, 81, 154, 156
Abu Ghraib, 15, 50, 154
Abu Mustafa, 176, 178, 179
Adams, Samuel, 19
Afghan war, politics and, 17, 229
Air assaults, 262–266
AK–47s, 17, 23, 25, 50, 53, 55, 67, 77
  fire from, 14, 136, 188, 264, 286
al-Juma, Qusay, 219, 230–231, 232
al-Maliki, Nouri, 267, 277
al-Qaeda, xii, 268
al-Qaeda in Iraq (AQI), 27, 29, 80, 140, 152, 153, 154, 157
al-Sadr, Muqtadah, 18, 27, 95–101
Alcohol, 14, 98, 173
Ali Babas, 64, 65, 72, 79, 90, 100, 101, 135, 137, 138, 157, 160, 211
Ali the Beard, 209, 219, 225, 226, 283
Ali the Prince, 49

Alpha Company, 198, 200, 201, 202, 207, 208, 236, 237
  TOC of, 213 (photo), 274 (photo)
Anbar, 15, 91, 277
Anwar, Lieutenant, 258, 286
  on Ali the Beard, 219
  meeting with, 261–262
  night with, 217–222
  photo of, 218
AO. See Area of operations
AQI. See al-Qaeda in Iraq
Area of operations (AO), 12, 13, 63, 98, 153, 181
Armed Forces Network, 225, 277
Articles of Confederation, 65
Asaib Ahl Haq, 27
Assassinations, 153–154, 276
Assassin's Gate, 251
Awards, clusterfuck with, 283–285
Axel, Staff Sergeant, xiii, 22, 26, 34–35, 46, 53, 64, 75, 93, 94, 101, 130, 132, 287
  banter by, 8
  Chem-Light and, 98
  detainees and, 36
  at ECP, 45
  Haydar and, 28
  microgrants and, 179

Axel, Staff Sergeant (*continued*)
    photo of, 180, 190
    return of, 291

B, Sergeant First Class, 208, 210,
        254, 264, 266
Bad Boys platoon, 211, 226
Badr Corps, 27, 260, 261
    IEDs and, 262
    JAM and, 259
Baghdad Gates, 14, 184
Baghdad Now, 38, 208
Banana-Hands, Sheik, 49, 67, 79,
        106, 136, 187, 261
    bodyguards of, 68, 107
    chai with, 112, 113
    encounter with, 66, 107
    evenings with, 133–134, 134–135
    on peace, 69
    Sahwa and, 78
    set up by, 49
Barriers, cultural/social/cultural/
        training, 165
Barry, 248, 249, 278
Bassam, 154, 157
Battle of Basra, 259
Battle of Karbala, 261
Battle of 73 Easting, 271
BCGs. *See* Birth control goggles
Beanie Babies, 100, 101, 186
    handing out, 13, 14, 102, 185
Big Army, Middle Army and, 148
Big Country, Sergeant First Class,
        xiii, 28, 30–31, 41, 51, 52, 61,
        62, 64, 69, 70, 72, 75, 92, 96,
        109, 110, 117, 118, 132, 133
    bomb and, 74
    Bronze Star for, 285
    Gravediggers and, 6–7, 10, 11,
        112, 113
    Hot Wheels incident and, 151, 152
    leadership by, 12, 140, 144
    microgrants and, 182
    Mustafa and, 178

night patrol and, 44, 105, 106, 108
    photo of, 35, 113, 180
    recommendation for, 284
    ROTC cadets and, 291
    security scans and, 63
    Shaba and, 47, 50
    Smitty and, 22
    sniper rifle and, 36
    Suge and, 173
    Trash Village and, 184, 185–186
    on Van Wilder, 170
Big Ern, Specialist, 32, 34, 98, 109,
        131
    Das Boot and, 46, 110
    at ECP, 45
    fobbits and, 171
    IP attack and, 162, 165
    photo of, 48
    Van Wilder and, 10
Birth control goggles (BCGs), 8
Bisel, Sergeant First Class, 187, 188
Blackwater, 222, 223, 224
Blog piece, 82, 142–145, 148, 149,
        183, 199
    axing of, 182
    support for, 145, 147
Body armor, 5, 19, 96, 151
Boob al-Sham, 198, 267, 269, 270,
        275, 276
    deputy mayor of, 212, 214
    police, 269
Boom-Booms, 31, 32, 82
Boondock, Staff Sergeant, xi, xii, 34,
        39, 52, 53, 54, 61, 62, 67, 69, 99,
        101, 109, 110, 112, 115, 117,
        132, 158–159, 161, 182, 190
    Banana-Hands and, 133, 134, 135
    bomb and, 72, 73, 74
    borrowing policies of, 32
    call signs and, 97
    city dump and, 184
    counter-IED mission and, 98
    Daraji and, 160
    detainees and, 36

dominoes and, 84, 85, 90
embracing the hate and, 46
Fadl and, 114
future terrorists and, 63
Gravediggers and, 7, 11
in Hawaii, 291
Haydar and, 155, 156
IP attack and, 162, 164
joking by, 181
locals and, 71
mortars and, 75
Mustafa and, 178
New Years and, 12
night patrol and, 42, 103, 104
Nour and, 131
photo of, 48, 62, 93, 141, 180
reassignment for, 188–189
ROE and, 91, 92, 94, 95
ROTC and, 35
snow patrol and, 19, 20
Suge and, 279, 280
Trash Village and, 185
Brady, Tom, 225
Bravo Troop, 16, 22, 36, 40, 92, 118,
157, 189
Shaba and, 47
Bremer, Paul, 65
Brooke Army Medical Center, 152,
290
Buffalo Bills cheerleaders, 236, 237
Bulldog, Staff Sergeant, xi, 18,
22, 33, 56, 61, 62, 63, 66, 69,
96, 99, 101, 118, 132, 133,
158–159, 182
dominoes and, 84, 85
drill sergeant school and, 291
on garbage, 184
Gravediggers and, 9, 11
Haitian Sensation and, 64
Hot Wheels incident and, 151
IP attack and, 161, 163, 164
joking by, 181
Mustafa and, 178, 179
night patrol and, 43, 44, 104, 107

photo of, 71, 167, 180
reverence for, 7–8
rockets and, 109
stealth and, 105
wrath of, 30
Bulldozer (IP), 79, 189
Bush, George W., 3

C, Sergeant First Class, 230, 232
polls and, 276
toy RPG launchers and, 233, 234
Camp Bucca, 50, 80, 95, 157, 160,
213
Camp Liberty, 247
Camp Patriot, 256
Camp Taji, 12, 14, 15, 41, 49, 91,
141, 145, 190, 195, 196, 197,
202, 207, 216, 221, 222, 224,
226, 228, 230, 235, 236, 252
Camp Victory, 247
Car bombs, 84, 184, 249, 250, 251,
252, 253, 254, 256, 283
Care packages, 102
Cavalry, 4, 8, 37, 125, 245, 256, 264
jokes about, 265
Chai, 20, 65, 67, 84, 97, 112, 113,
134
drinking, 13, 168, 182, 205, 207,
264
Chain of command, 272
Checkpoints, 38, 77, 90, 131, 132,
133, 138
in Saba al-Bor, 17, 99
Sahwa, 101, 105, 106, 139, 157
Sons of Iraq, 17, 105, 158
Cheech, Sergeant, 8, 52, 64, 67, 97,
109, 112, 169
fobbits and, 170
IP attack and, 162, 165
locals and, 70
night patrol and, 104
rockets and, 110
Chem-Lights, 94, 98, 187, 211
Chemical Ali, 267

Children, 33, 34, 73, 102, 181, 244
  heat and, 168
  letters from, 103
  lives of, 63, 64, 65
  photo of, 71, 130, 141
  toy RPG launchers and, 233–234
Christmas, 6, 249, 250, 253, 254,
  255, 256
Clay, Captain, 210, 236, 237, 260,
  291
  leadership of, 208
  Rant and, 201
  replacements and, 283
Clusterfucks, 25, 54, 77, 100,
  283–285
Coalition forces, 16, 18, 21, 22, 47,
  134, 155
  counterinsurgency and, 93
  private contractors and, 222
Cold-Cuts, Specialist, xiii, xiv, 100,
  106, 170
  Gravediggers and, 10, 11
  mosque raid and, 118
  night patrol and, 42–43
  redcon-1 and, 129–130
  shootout and, 137
  snow patrol and, 19, 20, 22
Cold Warriors, 40, 146
Combat Action Badge (CAB), 284
Combat outposts, 16, 76, 77, 78, 96,
  109, 112
  explosion at, 150
  photo of, 15
  photo at, 104
Commandos, National Police, 264,
  265
  photo of, 263
Communications, 83, 125, 149
Concertina wire, photo of, 85
Counterinsurgency, 5, 16, 21, 62, 67,
  69, 84, 92, 93, 100, 112, 119,
  133, 147, 175, 189, 198, 219,
  224, 231, 234, 237, 241, 263,
  287

bastardized, 183
counter-, 263
joys of, 214
microgrants and, 180, 183
politics and, 230
precision targeting in, 266
principles of, 38, 119, 175, 202,
  203
success for, 164, 257
tedium of, 70
Curly, Sergeant Major, 38, 68, 188,
  189

D-Wizzle, Sergeant, 14
Daffy Duck, 211
Daraji, Ali, 157, 158
  capture of, 159–160
  questioning, 160–161
Das Boot, Private First Class, 20,
  34–35, 52, 94, 114, 117
  Big Ern and, 46, 110
  CAB for, 284
  call sign of, 97
  children and, 64
  dead dog and, 90
  Doc and, 10
  at ECP, 45
  Estonian soldier and, 46
  night patrol and, 103
  photo of, 61, 93, 180
  water pipe and, 35
Day of Ashura, 259–262
Dear John tales, 82–84
Democracy, 19, 65, 258
Demolition, Captain, 6, 144, 145,
  287
  departure from the military, 291
  EFP and, 126
Deployment, 3, 90, 95, 102
  end of, 278
  surviving, 83, 84
Desert Storm, 271
Detainees, 36, 211, 227
  photo of, 154

Dirty Jerz, Lieutenant, 253, 286, 291
  East Hussaniyah and, 275
  Gunslingers and, 210, 211, 214
  joint-patrol and, 245, 246, 247, 248, 249
  leadership of, 200
  Qusay and, 231
Discipline, lack of, 270–271, 273
Divorces, 82, 290
Diyala Province, 34, 197, 211
Doc, 90, 187, 188, 291
  call sign of, 97
  Das Boot and, 10
  dominoes and, 84, 85
  fobbits and, 171
  garbage and, 184, 186
  Haydar and, 155
  Hot Wheels incident and, 149, 150, 151
  photo of, 180
  Suge and, 279, 280
  Tunnel and, 64
Dominoes, 84–90
Dragunov sniper rifle, 34–37
Dust storms, 47
DynCorp, 223

E-mails, 82, 147, 280
East Hussaniyah, 275, 277
Eastwood, Clint, 68
Economic problems, 272, 291
Eddie, 212, 213, 214, 267, 291
  Abbas and, 226
  Anwar and, 217, 218
  Saif and, 270
  Sitting Bull and, 286–287
  translating by, 208–209, 219, 221, 268–269
EFP Alley, 251
EFPs. *See* Explosively formed penetrators
Eisenhower, Dwight: military-industrial complex and, 222, 224

Elections
  Afghan, 3
  protecting Iraqi, 273–277
  U.S., 228–230
EOD. *See* Explosive Ordinance Disposal
ESPN, 225
Estonians, 16, 46, 157
Executive officers (XO), 140–141, 143, 144, 205, 285
Explosive Ordinance Disposal (EOD), 74, 94, 95, 110, 131, 133, 261
  detonation by, 111–112
Explosively formed penetrators (EFPs), 22, 50, 94, 126, 231, 260, 283
  attack with, 207, 208, 210
  hunting down, 201

Facebook, 4, 215, 278
Fadl, 13, 113, 114, 116, 117
Fasting, 187
Field grade officers, 38, 39–40, 195, 271, 272
  Cold War and, 40
  described, 37
  generational gap and, 270
  terps and, 278
First Amendment, 148
First Cavalry Division, 12
Flashback, Specialist, xiii, 10, 53, 67, 97, 106
  patrol and, 43, 44, 62, 63, 64
  Playboy of, 98
  rockets and, 110, 112
FNGs. *See* Fucking new guys
FOB. *See* Forward operating base
Fobbits, 7, 8, 10, 22, 31, 131, 170, 193–197, 279, 284
Forever wars, 229
Forward operating base (FOB), 7, 12, 14, 38, 41, 132, 143
  photo at, 250
  return to, 168–172

Fourteenth Cavalry Regiment, 12
Fourth Infantry Division, 236
Fragos, 31, 46, 56, 66, 97, 112, 113,
    125, 176
    fragmentary orders and, 13
    merry fucking, 249–256
Friendly fire incidents, 161–166
Frowny-Face, Captain, 199, 200, 212,
    215, 217–218, 230, 248, 252,
    260, 264, 275, 286, 287, 291
    Christmas and, 253, 254
    contractors and, 251
    detainees and, 227
    EFP attack and, 208
    HUMINT and, 201
    parade grounds and, 255
    polls and, 276, 277
    questioning and, 226
    release forms and, 214
    show-of-force mission and, 263
    State Department official and, 223
Fucked up beyond all recognition
    (FUBAR), 182, 248
Fucking new guys (FNGs), 61
Fuego, Sergeant, 12, 20, 76, 159
    Daraji and, 160
    Haydar and, 155
    IP attack and, 163, 164
    joking by, 182
    photo of, 180

Gaul, Sean: death of, 34
General Order No. 1, 14, 18
Generational gap, 270–273
Generator, explosion of, 149–153
Geneva Convention, 29, 162
Ghazi (Haydar's son), 156
Ghost tanks. *See* Strykers
Global war on terrorism (GWOT),
    40, 292
Golden house, 202–207
Gonzo, Specialist, 201, 202, 251,
    252, 253, 275, 286, 291
    Obama speech and, 230
    Tupac/Notorious BIG and, 255

Goo, Lieutenant, 201, 235
Grand Canal, 15, 91, 154, 184
Gravediggers, 6–11, 41, 45, 51, 89,
    95, 109, 110, 132, 145, 155
    bomb and, 74
    briefing, 51 (photo)
    Camp Taji and, 12
    children's letters for, 103
    Christmas and, 249
    counterinsurgency and, 16
    Hot Wheels incident and, 153
    leadership for, 140
    mission of, 97
    night patrol and, 42–43
    operational tempo and, 13
    photo of, 180
    security by, 34, 36, 149, 172
    Shaba and, 47, 50
    snow patrol and, 22, 23
    vehicle-maintenance refit by, 176
Great White Hope, The, 235, 236,
    270, 287
    departure from the military, 291
    high life and, 201
Green Zone, 21, 249–250, 251, 252,
    255
    photo of, 250
Grunberg, Arnon, 145, 146
Guinness socks, 243–244, 245
Gunslingers, 207, 208, 248, 262,
    279, 284, 285, 286, 289, 291
    Christmas and, 255
    patrol with, 249, 250, 252
GWOT. *See* Global war on terrorism

Haitian Sensation, Specialist, 9, 22,
    30, 52, 55, 75, 76, 168, 169,
    190, 215
    Arabic language and, 79
    Bulldog and, 64
    FOB and, 171
    Hot Wheels incident and, 149, 150,
    151, 153
    IP attack and, 162, 165
    mosque raid and, 118

photo of, 35, 180
return of, 291
Smitty and, 10
Hajjis, xi, 8, 31, 43, 95, 160, 280
Halliburton, 222
Halloween, 225–228
Hamid, 206, 214
Hammer, The, Major, 199, 200, 201,
    202, 246, 291
Hammerhead, Sergeant First Class,
    250, 251, 252
    Christmas and, 254
    holidays and, 249
    Rant and, 201
    replacements and, 283, 291
Hands of Victory, 254
    photo of, 257
Hawaii, 4–5, 190, 273, 286, 291–292
    leaving, 8
    return to, 82, 287, 290
Haydar, Sheik, 27, 29, 77–78, 80, 158,
    187, 258
    Bassam meeting and, 154, 155
    military posture/mannerisms of,
    28
    Suge and, 156–157
    water-plant contract and, 155
Heat, dealing with, 166–168
Helicopters, 14, 236, 266, 267
    photo of, 263
    training with, 262–265
High-value target list (HVTL),
    218–219, 220, 227
Holidays
    bizarre, 249–256
    Muslim, 259–262
Hooah, 10–11, 127
Hot Wheels, Private, 61, 90–91, 97,
    98, 109, 135, 285
    Banana-Hands and, 134
    Bon Jovi and, 133
    generator explosion and,
    149–153
    leadership of, 290
    photo of, 150

Hottest Latinas, debate about,
    44, 46
Human intelligence (HUMINT),
    201, 208, 209, 211, 226, 260,
    285
Humanity, losing, 83–84
Husayn, 104–105, 261
Husayn, Major, 248
Hussaniyah, 197, 203, 211, 212, 219,
    230, 235, 237, 242, 247 division
    of, 198
    JAM and, 210, 231
    market, 233
    patrol in, 231–232
    photo of, 231, 246
    raid in, 225–226
    and Saba al-Bor compared, 202
    sewer politics of, 261
    Shias in, 208
Hussayn the Star, 220
Hussein, Saddam, 16, 21, 28, 134,
    164, 197
    Iran-Iraq War and, 254
    statues of, 250 (photo)

IA. *See* Iraqi army
IEDs. *See* Improvised explosive
    devices
Improvised explosive devices (IEDs),
    xii, 18, 21, 22, 26, 31, 47, 61,
    69, 95, 125, 126, 134, 135, 164,
    169, 176, 183
    attacks with, 98, 157, 249
    Bon Jovi, 128–133
    countering, 97, 149, 261
    emplacers, 198
    exploding, 98
    hunting for, 161, 259
    reports of, 184
    ROE and, 93, 94
    See also Vehicle-borne IEDs
Improvised rocket-assisted mortar
    (IRAM), 246, 247, 249
Insurgency, 100, 148, 149, 175, 213,
    292

Internet, 4, 21, 30, 82, 83, 186
Interpreters. *See* Terps
IP. *See* Iraqi police
IRAM. *See* Improvised rocket-
    assisted mortar
Iran-Iraq War, 133, 254, 266
Iraq Status of Forces Agreement
    (SOFA), 235, 256, 268
Iraq War, 80, 222, 247, 263, 272
  departing for, 4–5
  evolution of, 93
  politics and, 229
  success in, 19
Iraqi army (IA), xiii, 16, 28, 48, 49,
    52–53, 54, 55, 98, 101
  Bassam meeting and, 154
  Daraji and, 161
  Shaba and, 47
  Zaydan assassination and,
    153–154
Iraqi National Police (NP), 198, 214,
    217, 220, 227, 248, 249, 266,
    267, 277, 283
  commando, 263 (photo)
  Day of Ashura and, 259, 261, 262
  helicopter training for, 264–265
  Hussaniyah and, 232, 233
  memorial service, 286
  Mongo and, 264
Iraqi parliament, 235, 256, 274
Iraqi police (IP), xiii, 15, 16, 26, 43,
    50, 79, 98, 101, 117–118, 138,
    161–162, 189
  Bassam meeting and, 154
  distrust for, 163
  election problems and, 277
  friendly fire incident and,
    162–164, 165, 166
  Hussaniyah and, 233
  IEDs and, 259, 260
  JAM and, 163
  joking with, 181
  Mojo and, 18
  mosque raid and, 118, 119, 120
  rockets and, 109, 110

sizing up, 120, 163
terps and, 279, 280
Iraqi security forces, 25, 99, 258, 267,
    275, 276
  performance of, 164
  photo of, 154
  Shaba and, 47
  training of, 165
Iraqis, killing, 256–258
Islamic Dawa Party, 277
iWar, 126, 127

J, Sergeant, 250, 252, 255
Jabba the Hut. *See* Nour, Sheik
JAG. *See* Judge Advocate General
Jaish al-Mahdi (JAM) paramilitary, xii,
    18, 47, 49, 112, 133, 140, 152,
    176, 189, 197, 198, 201, 209,
    211, 219, 220
  Badr Corps and, 259
  Hussaniyah and, 210, 231
  IP attack and, 163
  Iran and, 267
  resurgence by, 96
  Sadr and, 95–101
  terps and, 279
  toy RPG launchers and, 234
Jaish al-Rashiden (JAR), 27, 34
JAM. *See* Jaish al-Mahdi paramilitary
Joes, 9, 41, 69, 95, 170, 205, 284
  opinions of, 216, 229
Johnson, Boss, xii–xiii, 45, 258
  death of, 261
  memory of, 125
  remnants of, xiv (photo)
Johnson II, Boss, 78, 79, 90, 154
Joint-security station (JSS), 212, 215,
    227, 236, 243, 245
Jorge, Staff Sergeant, 201, 219
JSS. *See* Joint-security station
JSS Istaqlaal, 198, 199, 200, 201,
    202, 207, 208, 209, 211, 217,
    223, 226, 228, 230, 234, 235,
    237
  Iraqi control of, 258

Pennsylvania National Guard at,
283
photo of, 213
JSS Ur, 247
Judge Advocate General (JAG), 147
Jundis, 49, 50, 157, 159, 164, 187,
188
Junior officers, 40
discipline and, 270–271
exodus of, 272, 291
generational gap and, 271
professionalism and, 272
promotion of, 140
recentralized warfare and, 175
senior officers and, 272

Kevin (State Department rep), 203,
204
Modhir and, 205–206, 207
Kipling, Rudyard, 127
Knight, Suge, 16, 20, 28, 29, 32, 33,
43, 52, 53, 76, 94, 97, 104, 105,
128, 189, 202, 258, 291
Axel and, 75
Banana-Hands and, 134, 136
Big Country and, 173
bomb and, 73, 74
Daraji and, 160
dead dog and, 90
diabetes for, 71
dominoes and, 84, 85
fasting, 187
Haydar and, 156–157
as international man of mystery,
172–174
IP attack and, 162, 163–164
locals and, 70, 72
masks and, 279
microgrants and, 182
Nour and, 132
patrols and, 130
rockets and, 109
safety and, 280
sniper rifle and, 36–37
stereotypes and, 21

Ten Bears and, 172
translating by, 106, 107, 135, 155,
158, 159, 163–164, 173, 242
on tricking heat, 168
women and, 34

Larry, Lieutenant Colonel, 100, 146,
148
blog piece and, 146, 183
Boondock reassignment and,
289
Bronze Star and, 285
congressional inquiries and, 147
leadership of, 40–41, 210–211
Mustafa and, 178
officer trade and, 196
promotions by, 140
standing up to, 41
XO position and, 142
Las Cruces, 226, 227, 259, 260
Laser range-acquisition sight (LRAS),
162
Lawrence, T. E., 14, 91, 289
Leadership, 12, 140, 144, 200, 208,
290
layers of, 39–41
styles of, 7
Little America, 169, 172, 193, 195,
281
Londono, Ernesto, 147, 278, 280
Loyalty, 83, 200, 234

M4 Carbines, 12, 25, 103, 107, 225
Mahdi Army, 27, 43, 68, 97, 101,
113, 116, 176, 280
Mail, 30, 102–103
Marshmallow, Sheik, 24
Masks, terps and, 277–280
McCain, John, 229
Microgrants, 179–183
Middle Army, Big Army and, 148
Military-industrial complex, 222, 223,
224
Military police (MP), 118, 166
Military Times, poll by, 229

Mine Resistant Ambush Protected (MRAPs) armored vehicles, 249, 250, 252, 254, 255
Mission Accomplished, 3, 108, 172
MND-B. *See* Multinational Division-Baghdad
MNF-I. *See* Multinational Force-Iraq
Modhir, Sheik, 202, 203, 214, 231
    Kevin and, 205–206, 207
Moe, Major, 38, 39–40, 142, 177
Mohammed, Colonel, 45, 55, 78, 153, 154
Mohammed the Ghost (Mohammed the Shadow), 47–50, 215, 225
Mojo, 55–56, 79, 80, 81, 82, 189
    General Order No. 1 of, 18
Mongo, Lieutenant, 200, 228, 252, 262, 263, 286, 291
    Christmas and, 253, 254
    detainees and, 227
    flag-football game and, 235
    leadership of, 207, 208
    NP and, 264
    Patrol by, 210, 211, 215
    photo of, 274
    raid by, 225–226
    West Hussaniyah and, 275
Mortars, xii, 69, 74, 75, 126, 283
Mosques, 105, 241, 242, 243
    raids on, 118–124
MP. *See* Military police
MRAPs. *See* Mine Resistant Ambush Protected armored vehicles
Muhamed, Lieutenant Colonel, 214, 215
Muhammad, Prophet, 104, 187, 261
Multinational Division-Baghdad (MND-B), 251
Multinational Force-Iraq (MNF-I), 277
Mussolini, Benito, 41
MySpace, 25, 46, 82

Nahias, 80, 206
Najij, Colonel, 214, 215, 221

National Guard, 283, 285
NCOs. *See* Noncommissioned officers
New Years, 12, 256
Night vision, 103, 125, 137
Nisoor Square, shootings in, 224
Noncommissioned officers (NCOs), 3, 6, 11, 18, 27, 43, 44
    Dear John tales and, 83
    generational gap and, 270, 272
    Hot Wheels incident and, 152, 153
    intervention by, 41
    loyalty of, 200, 245
    photo of, 104
    politics and, 229, 230
    recentralized warfare and, 175
    relations with, 48, 164–165
    worshipping, 9
Norris, Chuck: jokes about, 216
Notorious BIG, Tupac Shakur and, 255
Nour, Sheik, 26, 27, 97, 162, 165, 280
    guarding, 130, 131, 132, 279
    petroleum inheritance of, 28
NP. *See* Iraqi National Police

Oath of office, 243–245
Obama, Barack, 228, 229–230, 291
Observation post (OP), 31, 34, 44, 97, 136
Odierno, General, 277
Office Space: Iraq (hypothetical film), 236
Officers
    careerist, 38, 42
    company-grade, 37
    executive, 140–141, 143, 144, 205, 285
    general, 37
    generational gap among, 195, 270–273
    junior, 40, 140, 175, 270–271, 272, 291
    oath of office for, 243–245

politics and, 229
promoting, 140–141
senior, 272, 273
staff, 193, 272
trading, 196
types of, 37
See also Noncommissioned officers
Oil refinery, burning, 217
1–27 Infantry, 41, 196, 198, 199, 202
101st Airborne, 37
"Only Difference Between
     Martyrdom and Suicide Is Press
     Coverage, The" (blog piece),
     142–149
OP. *See* Observation post
Operation Phantom Phoenix,
     30–34
Operational security (OPSEC), 15,
     146
Orlando, Wildebeest and, 209
Orwell, George, 8
Osama, Bassam meeting and, 154

Palahniuk, Chuck, 143
Patrols, 112, 125, 166, 253, 274, 278
   joint-, 245–249
   last, 283–289
   night, 42–46, 103–108, 129
   photo of, 130
Patton, George, 37
Pennsylvania National Guard, 283,
     285, 286, 287
Pentagon, 148, 271, 278
People other than grunts (POGs), 7
Petraeus, General, 30, 37, 91, 271,
     277
   microgrants and, 183
   strategy and, 257
   website and, 147
Phoenix, 16, 29, 99, 100, 108
   flirting by, 66
   Smitty and, 66, 82
   translating by, 64, 67, 68, 69
Pistol Pete, Captain, 201, 208, 210,
     235, 291

Platoons, function of, 175
POGs. *See* People other than grunts
Politics, 23, 261, 290
   counterinsurgency and, 230
   military and, 229
Polling sites, guarding, 273–277
Pop culture, 126, 290
Porta-John chronicles, reading,
     216–217
Porta-Johns, 125–129, 199, 222, 258
Post exchange (PX), 170, 171, 195
Posttraumatic stress disorder, 21
Poverty, 19, 72, 75
Powell Doctrine, 3
Precision targeting, 100, 266
Press coverage, 140–149
Prime, Specialist, 10, 11, 159
   Chem-Light and, 98
   fobbits and, 171
   photo of, 48, 180
Private contractors, 222–223, 224
Privatization, 222, 223, 224, 225
Professionalism, 44
   junior officers and, 272
Promotions, 140–141, 146, 272
Prostitutes, 174, 258
Public relations, 119, 154, 279
PX. *See* Post exchange

Qadas, 80, 206
Qasim, Nasim Abdul, 187, 188

Rahdi, Mayor, 80, 81, 189
Ramadan, 187–190, 220, 260
Rant, Lieutenant, 214, 223, 224,
     228, 236, 237, 256, 259, 266,
     275, 286, 291
   Abbas and, 226–227
   EFP attack and, 208
   elections and, 277
   Hamid and, 206
   Hussaniyah and, 201
   on motivation, 276
   needling, 201
   photo of, 213

Rant, Lieutenant (*continued*)
  polls and, 276
  replacements and, 283
  Thanksgiving and, 235
Rashadiya, 268, 269, 270
Rassim, 206
Rear-echelon mother fuckers
    (REMFs), 7, 8
Reconciliation, 17, 18, 133–136
REMFs. *See* Rear-echelon mother
    fuckers
Reno-Gazette Journal, 147
Republican Guard, 197, 198
Reserve Officer Training Corps
    (ROTC), 3, 35, 37, 244, 245, 291
Revolutionary Brigade, 27
Rip-Its, 20, 31, 32, 90, 99, 114, 142,
    170
Rocket propelled grenades (RPGs),
    26, 80, 101, 184, 233, 287
Rockets, xii, 108–112, 160
  attacks with, 156, 157
ROE. *See* Rules of engagement
Romeo, Private First Class, 10, 11,
    105
  joking by, 181
  night patrol and, 43, 44
  photo of, 180
Roosevelt, Theodore, 37, 246
ROTC. *See* Reserve Officers'
    Training Corps
Route Crush, 203, 231, 270, 287
Route Dover, 197, 198, 203, 223,
    231, 262, 267, 276, 286
Route Flames, 134
Route Gold, 118, 119
Route Islanders, 91, 92, 97, 136, 158
Route Lincoln, 91, 184
Route Maples, 21–22, 63, 91, 137,
    138, 180, 181, 182
Route New York, 63
Route Ninjas, 209
Route Plato, 279
Route Senators, 251, 256

Route Swords, 50, 51, 67, 106, 189,
    261
Route Tampa, 15, 28, 163, 166, 184,
    186, 256
  IED attacks on, 98
  patrol on, 129, 131, 161, 168, 183
Route Texas, 232
RPG launchers, toy, 233–234
RPGs. *See* Rocket propelled grenades
Rules of engagement (ROE), 51,
    90–95

Saba al-Bor, xii, 20, 21–22, 23, 27, 29
  aid distribution at, 167 (photo)
  aroma of, 170
  combat outpost at, 15 (photo)
  complaints in, 65
  described, 14–19
  Fadl and, 117
  and Hussaniyah compared, 202
  IEDs in, 47
  leaving, 187, 197
  market in, 35 (photo), 91, 137
  microgrant projects in, 180–181
  money in, 17
  patrols in, 42, 45, 100–101
  photo of, 15, 130
  return to, 149
  Route Maples and, 181
  Shias in, 17, 18, 95
  Sons of Iraq in, 76
  Sunnis in, 17, 38
Sabah Qasar, 198, 262, 263, 275, 276
  photo of, 204
Saddam City, 197
Sadr City, 189, 197, 209, 210, 219,
    231, 274, 283, 292
  uprising in, 201
Sadrists, 43, 277
Safety, 142, 152
  terps and, 278, 279, 280
Sahwa, xiii, xiv, 25, 26, 29, 54, 55,
    68, 76, 77, 78–79, 81, 82, 85,
    90, 97

checkpoints, 101, 105, 106, 139, 157
   Iraqi government and, 267
   program, 172
   Sons of Iraq and, 267, 268
Saif, 268–269, 270
Salon (magazine), 145, 146
Sandstorm, photo of, 246
Schwarzenegger, Arnold, 265
Second Brigade (Twenty-fifth Infantry Division), 196, 236
Secret Agent Man, Sergeant, 210, 212, 251, 260
   HUMINT and, 201
   Las Cruces and, 259
   leads/tips from, 208, 209
Sections, function of, 175
Security, xiii, 23, 105, 135, 149, 250
   fliers, 101
   meetings, 270
   peace and, 69
   sweeps, 95
Security firms, 223, 224, 225, 252
September 11th, 3, 244, 245
Shaba, Mohammed, 47–50, 59
Shakespeare, William, 15
Shakur, Tupac: Notorious BIG and, 255
Sheep, photo of, 246
Sheikapalooza, 23–30
   photo of, 24
Sheiks, 17, 18, 34, 81, 82, 121
   Arab culture and, 155
   meeting with, 13, 23–30
Shia United Iraqi Alliance, 277
Shias, xii, xiii, 63, 80, 81, 95, 96, 113, 187, 205, 270
   elections and, 274, 277
   extremist, 27, 47, 259
   holidays of, 260
   Husayn and, 261
   Hussaniyah and, 208
   Sons of Iraq and, 158

Sunnis and, 13, 17, 18, 28, 65, 79, 127, 134, 197, 198, 202, 261, 268
Show-of-force missions, 263
SITREPs. *See* Situation reports
Sitting Bull, Staff Sergeant, 210, 211, 212, 261, 262
   Abbas and, 226, 227
   Ashura and, 259
   Eddie and, 286–287
   HUMINT and, 201
   leads/tips and, 208
   Orlando and, 209
   source network of, 219
Situation reports (SITREPs), 208, 252
Skerk, Lieutenant, 38, 39, 77, 81, 182, 201
   microgrant program and, 181
   stress for, 76
Slum City, 236
Smitty, Private First Class, 22–23, 52, 61, 62, 67, 69, 97, 98, 99, 109, 129, 132, 135, 159, 161, 169, 190
   Banana-Hands and, 134
   children and, 63
   Haitian Sensation and, 10
   Haydar and, 155
   Hot Wheels incident and, 149, 150–151
   IP attack and, 162–163, 165
   mosque raid and, 118
   Phoenix and, 82
   photo of, 180
   rockets and, 111–112
   shootout and, 139, 140
   Soldier's Medal for, 284–285
   Spice Girls and, 130
   stealth and, 105
Sniper rifles, 9, 34–37
Snipers, 66, 120, 233
Snoop Dogg, 16, 76, 77, 78
Snow patrol, 19–23

Soccer field, rockets at, 108–112
SOFA. *See* Iraq Status of Forces
    Agreement
Soldier's Medal, 284–285
Somers, Suzanne, 112, 134
Sons of Iraq, xiii, xiv, 18, 26, 54, 55,
    67, 76, 77, 78, 79, 96–97, 101
    checkpoints of, 17, 105, 158
    rocket men and, 157
    Sahwa and, 267, 268
    sheik council and, 24
    Shias and, 158
    Sunni, 66, 267
    talking to, 106
Sons of Liberty, 19
Spade, Staff Sergeant, 8, 22, 26, 28,
    52, 53, 54, 62, 98, 100, 107,
    117, 119, 187, 288
    Beanie Babies and, 186
    Daraji and, 158
    Gravediggers and, 291
    in Hawaii, 291
    microgrants and, 179
    mosque raid and, 118
    night patrol and, 45
    photo of, 180, 190
    rockets and, 111
    sheikapalooza and, 27
    shootout and, 139, 140
    traits of, 44
Spice Girls, 130, 166
Sportscenter (ESPN), 225, 228
Spot, Corporal, 8–9, 52, 53, 64, 67,
    72, 74, 159, 161, 185
    Daraji and, 160
    photo of, 48, 180
    rockets and, 109, 110
    sniper rifle and, 36
    translation by, 24–25
Stars and Stripes, 147, 148
Steel platoon, 50, 51, 52, 53, 54
Stereotypes, 21, 271, 283
Steve (special ops captain/major),
    118, 120, 121

Sticky bombs, 152, 153
Stop-loss program, 291
Stove Top, Private First Class, 61
    photo of, 180, 190
Strykehorse, 131, 176
Strykers, xiii, xiv, xv, 10, 12, 29, 32, 36
    as ghost tanks, 13, 19, 209
    parking, 253
    patrols in, 98, 169
    photo of, 62, 85, 204
    repairing, 208
    as shields, 53, 111
Stuart, Jeb, 37
Stun grenades, 99, 118
Suicide, 140–149, 290
Sunnis, 38, 44, 65–66, 135, 136,
    157, 187, 203, 230, 269
    elections and, 274, 277
    Iraqi republic and, 18
    mosque raid and, 121
    problems for, 153
    Shias and, xii, xiii, 13, 17, 18, 28,
    65, 79, 127, 134, 197, 198, 202,
    261, 268
    Sons of Iraq and, 267
Super Bowl, 225, 277
Super Mario, 16, 29, 80, 81, 112,
    117, 137, 139, 151, 181
    translating by, 114
Swords of Qadisiyah, 254
Syrians, 85

T–72 tanks, 23, 52, 53, 54, 138
Tactical operations center (TOC), 43,
    46, 50, 61, 69, 75, 93
    photo of, 213, 274
Taji Provincial Community Center, 23
Tamimis, 26–27, 28, 29, 155
Task Force Cobra, mosque raid and,
    118–119, 120
Tattoos, 83, 255, 257
Ten Bears, Captain, 172, 180, 189, 291
    Bassam meeting and, 154
    frago and, 176

Haydar and, 155, 156
recommendation from, 285
rocket attack and, 157
Suge and, 172
Trash Village and, 183
working with, 136
Terps, 29, 33, 36, 66, 80, 85, 105,
107, 109, 110, 115, 132, 158,
172–174, 182, 204, 291
field-grade officers and, 278
masks for, 277–280
safety and, 278, 279, 280
work of, 13, 16, 20, 208–209
Terrorists, xii, 22, 47, 67, 96, 157, 256
Thanksgiving, 235
Third Brigade (Fourth Infantry
Division), 236
TOC. *See* Tactical operations center
Training
barriers to, 15
cold-load, 264–265
Trash Village, 183–186
Triple Canopy, 223
Tunnel, Specialist, 61, 94, 132, 159,
190
Daraji and, 160
Doc and, 64
Haydar and, 155
IP attack and, 165
locals and, 71
mosque raid and, 118
photo of, 180
Turkey Bowl flag-football game, 235
Turner, Tina, 98
Twenty-fifth Infantry Division, 12,
196, 236
2–14 Cavalry, 41, 140, 196, 198, 202,
220, 290
photo of, 180

Ugandans, 195, 252
Uniform Code of Military Justice, 147
U.S. Constitution, 148
U.S. Department of Defense, 147

U.S. Postal Service, 102
U.S. State Department, 26, 202, 203,
204, 223

Van Wilder, Private First Class, 11,
23, 52, 61, 62, 110, 131, 167,
170, 284
Big Ern and, 10
Iraqi women and, 32
night patrol and, 42, 44
photo of, 48, 180
Rip Its and, 32
translation by, 24, 25
yarns by, 10, 181
Vehicle-borne IEDs (VBIEDs), 84,
184, 249, 251, 252, 253, 256, 283
Veterans, 285
Vigilantes, 222–225
VIPs, dealing with, 271
Virginia Slim, Lieutenant, 30, 48,
144, 291
on constitutional rights, 148
Gravediggers and, 50
Vote, 274–275, 276
military, 229, 230

W, Sergeant First Class, 230, 231,
232–233
toy RPG launchers and, 233, 234
War for peace, 166
Warfare
conventional, 175
decentralized, 38, 175, 237
irregular, 292
maneuvers, 5
nonconventional, 183
recentralized, 175–179
Washington Post, 147, 148, 278
West Hussaniyah, 275, 276
Whiteback, Captain, 12, 20, 29, 34,
49, 50, 53, 77, 80, 97, 101, 106,
291
Banana-Hands and, 67–68
Bassam meeting and, 154

Whiteback, Captain (*continued*)
  blog piece and, 142, 145, 146
  finances and, 78
  frago message from, 66
  Haydar and, 156
  mosque raid and, 118, 121
  rockets and, 108
  ROE and, 93
  security meeting by, 81
  security sweeps and, 95
  Shaba and, 47
  sheikapalooza and, 23–24, 25
  shootout and, 137
  XO status and, 140–141, 142, 143
Wild Tigers, 31, 32, 82
Wildebeest, Specialist, 275
  Abbas and, 226
  HUMINT and, 201

  leads/tips from, 208
  Orlando and, 209
Wolfhounds, 236, 262
  Abu Abdullah and, 210
  joining, 197–202, 218
  Turkey Bowl and, 235
Women, 33–34, 70, 173, 174
  dress of, 32
  problems with, 82–84
  soldiers, 8, 46
  talking to, 291

XO. *See* Executive officers

Yusef, 73–74, 75

Zuhayr, Lieutenant: shootout and, 138–140
Zaydan, Sheik, 153–154, 258

Matt Gallagher joined the U.S. Army in 2005 and received a commission in the armoured cavalry. Following a fifteen-month deployment in Iraq, Gallagher left the army in 2009. Originally from Reno, Nevada, he now lives in New York City.